D1602781

THE CHANGING FACE OF
ENGLISH TRADITIONAL MUSIC

ELECTRIC *folk*

BRITTA SWEERS

OXFORD
UNIVERSITY PRESS

2005

OXFORD
UNIVERSITY PRESS

Oxford   New York

Auckland   Bangkok   Buenos Aires   Cape Town   Chennai
Dar es Salaam   Delhi   Hong Kong   Istanbul   Karachi   Kolkata
Kuala Lumpur   Madrid   Melbourne   Mexico City   Mumbai   Nairobi
São Paulo   Shanghai   Taipei   Tokyo   Toronto

Library of Congress Cataloging-in Publication Data
Sweers, Britta, 1969–
Electric folk : the changing face of English traditional music / Britta Sweers.
p. cm.
ISBN 0-19-515878-4; 0-19-517478-X (pbk.)
1. Folk rock music—History and criticism.   I. Title.
ML3534.S914   2004
781.62' 21024—dc22   2003023140

ACKNOWLEDGMENTS

This is not only a book about musical transformations—the book itself has also undergone a transformation from a Ph.D. dissertation to this book version. Particular thanks go to Brigitte Markuse for her excellent editorial work and continuous encouragement in Germany—without which this book version would have never taken shape. I likewise would like to thank Liz Milner and Jennifer Cutting for their expertise and invaluable advises at the final stage of writing.

A number of individual people have accompanied the path of the original research work: First I would like to mention Dr. Albrecht Schneider as the supervisor of the original dissertation, who helped me particularly through the difficult initial stage of the research work. I am especially grateful to Karen Hinson-Rehn for the English revision of the original dissertation. Thanks also go to Professor Austin Caswell and Professor Gary Potter at Indiana University, Bloomington, and Jonathan Stock from Sheffield University for their encouragement. Furthermore, I would like to mention Anja Handrock, Michael Lange, Wolfgang Marx, Hayo Nörenberg, Jörn Paulini, and the other members of the Silen—a former Ph.D. circle of musicology students at Hamburg University. I thank them all for their long-term support, shared insights, and help with the revisions. I am also grateful to opera singer Janina Bächle who pointed out precious aspects about vocal performance styles and to Martina Paulini who had the patience to check and correct my music analyses.

I am extremely grateful to my interviewees for being willing and patient enough to spend so much time, food, and coffee with me: Frankie Armstrong, Joe Boyd, Martin Carthy, Shirley Collins, Jennifer Cutting (also in her function as reference librarian of the Folklore Archive at the Library of Congress, Washington, D.C.), Ashley Hutchings, Rick Kemp, Jacqui McShee, Simon Nicol, Maddy Prior, John Renbourn, Ian Telfer—and journalist John Tobler who shared his expertise with me.

Further thanks go to Malcolm Taylor, librarian at the Ralph Vaughan Williams Memorial Library at Cecil Sharp House, London, for his invaluable help and kind support, pouring out new sources and hinting at new literature whenever I thought I might have grasped an overview. Likewise, to Sam Brylawski (Recorded Sound) at the Library of Congress who pointed out some precious aspects about the background of British-Irish music in the United States. I am also indebted to Maria Jefferies at the Melody Maker for opening up the magazine's archive for me. Extra thanks go to Joe Black (Universal Records), Tim Chacksfield, Mike Heaney (Folk Music Journal),

Phil Smee for helping me with various questions, Neil Wayne (Free Reed Records) for the wonderful photos and posters of Fairport Convention and Steeleye Span, and, once again, Ashley Hutchings and Ian Telfer for helping me with the photographic material.

Special thanks go to the staff at Oxford University Press—in particular to Kim Robinson and Eve Bachrach who have helped the revision process to become as smooth as possible and patiently answered any questions I had.

Finally, I must extend my thanks to my parents for their patience—by no means a matter of course—and consistent support over the years.

CONTENTS

Illustrations follow page 142

ELECTRIC FOLK

INTRODUCTION

A holiday, a holiday, and the first one of the year
Lord Darnell's wife came into the church the gospel for to hear.
And when the meeting it was done she cast her eyes about
And there she saw little Matty Groves walking in the crowd.

FIRST IMPRESSIONS

In the course of the nineteen verses of Child Ballad no. 81, young Matty Groves is se-
duced by a noble lady, yet both, betrayed by a servant, are caught in flagrante delicto by
her cuckolded husband. After killing the inexperienced Matty in a dramatic duel, the
enraged lord also murders his wife, who refuses to renounce her dead lover. The tale
concludes with the memorable lines

"A grave, a grave!" Lord Darnell cried, "to put these lovers in.
But bury my lady at the top, for she was of noble kin."

This dramatic ballad, its first printed version dating back to the early seventeenth
century (Bronson 1959–72: vol. 2, 267), can still occasionally be heard in one of the
loveliest parts of England's Oxfordshire countryside—in the fields of Cropredy near
the old town of Banbury. The performer, however, is not an elderly lady whose fur-
rowed face might only allow a guess of her age, but rather the energetic electric folk
group Fairport Convention, which has been hosting the annual Cropredy Festival
since 1980.

Even though keywords like acculturation,[1] hybridization, or world music have become central issues for modern ethnomusicological scholarship, electric folk music—
whether in England, which is the focus of this book, or elsewhere—has been marginally treated in theoretical writings until recently. This is true not only for
ethnomusicological studies but also for the fields of popular music and music soci-

ology. This book thus tries to close a gap in musicological research by drawing attention to a relatively unknown yet highly influential musical genre. Furthermore, it also addresses central questions related to the current situation of traditional music, such as the nature of the interaction of traditional and popular music, the relationship of revival musicians to traditional material, and the importance of the tradition at present.

BALLADS ABOUT DROWNED sailors and wren hunting set to an electric sound, sword dances performed in vast rock arenas—the genre that has become known as *electric folk* or *English folk rock* first developed in the late 1960s, reaching its musical and commercial peak between 1969 and 1975. These two terms denote a music that emerged in the greater London area from the interaction of traditional English, Scottish, and Irish music (with a strong emphasis on the English side)[2] with contemporary music idioms. The genre comprises, roughly speaking, individual musicians and groups from the whole musical spectrum of rock, jazz, and the singer/songwriter scene who absorbed elements of traditional music and combined them with their own styles.[3] The most eminent exemplars in England have been groups such as Fairport Convention, Steeleye Span, Pentangle, and the Albion Country Band, as well as solo musicians such as Bert Jansch, John Renbourn, Shirley Collins, Richard Thompson, and Maddy Prior.

Electric folk in England is neither simply an "electrification" of traditional songs, ballads, and dances, nor is it an isolated, artificial product that was solely constructed for commercial purposes. Rather, it resulted from a long-term musical interaction process between Great Britain and the United States: initially modeled on the American folk and folk rock scene, the development in England later became a counterreaction to the dominant American musical cultures. Contrary to the general disappearance of vernacular musics, the traditional material in England has become a new means of musical and cultural identity for the performers—who have subsequently revived a general interest in the tradition with their modern interpretations and compositions. Electric folk thereby has not only overcome the romanticized nineteenth-century ideas of traditional music but also the stagnant development of the second English folk revival of the 1950s and 1960s. Moreover, as one of the first—if not the very first—western European examples of a lively interaction between traditional musical structures and modern media, this genre also exerted a strong influence on neighboring cultural areas such as Ireland, Scandinavia, and Germany.[4]

The only comprehensive study of this genre so far is *The Electric Muse*, by Laing, Dallas, Denselow, and Shelton.[5] Published in 1975, it was written when Steeleye Span had just reached its commercial peak with "All around My Hat," while other groups had apparently disappeared or were struggling with a constant change of members. Originally accompanied by a set of three records,[6] the book offered a mixture of critical journalism on American music (Laing, Shelton), elaborate theories about the relationship between folk and rock (Dallas), and a sketchy yet vivid first-hand account of electric folk history (Denselow).

Owing to its rather fragmentary historical account of the English development (Denselow's chapter comprises only forty pages), *The Electric Muse* proved controversial.[7] Moreover, parts of the book were occasionally difficult for lay readers to understand, as the authors assumed familiarity with insider stories, nicknames (e.g., Ashley "Tyger" Hutchings), particular discussion topics, and complex professional histories caused by numerous group splits. This limitation also applies to the carefully researched biographies on groups and performers like Fairport Convention, Richard Thompson, Bert Jansch, and Sandy Denny.[8] As *The Electric Muse* has never been revised or updated to reflect the developments of the next twenty-five years, a restudy of electric folk in England seemed to be more than overdue.

BORN IN THE YEAR when Fairport Convention produced its groundbreaking album *Liege & Lief*—which also included the aforementioned Child ballad "Matty Groves"—I did not experience the emergence of this music firsthand. Instead, like so many listeners and performers of my generation, I found out about electric folk by chance. After a visit to Scotland in 1990 I began leafing through the folk section at Tower Records in London. The "Celtic" sound had just become popular in Germany; Enya had recorded her best-selling second album *Watermark* in 1988,[9] and Clannad's single "In a Lifetime," recorded in 1985, had been on the radio for some time. It was easy to discover more of what I considered then to be "authentic-sounding" (i.e., acoustic) music via Clannad, because each previous recording of the group sounded a bit rougher (i.e., featured fewer electric instruments) to my 1990s ears. It was also easy to learn about Scottish music; although I had come to Glasgow, 1990s "European City of Culture," to play and to listen to classical music, traditional music was always present. One could see bagpipe players at Highland games, and many classically trained musicians from that area could easily lapse into a traditional tune or knew someone from "around the corner" who would know how to play some folk songs.

As a consequence, I soon wanted to see what written material on traditional music was available. I found a considerable number of books on American, Irish, and Scottish music, but to my surprise it proved to be much more difficult to locate sources that treated English folk music—even in England itself. By chance, I came across a copy of *An Introduction to English Folk Song* by Maud Karpeles (1987) that had rested half-forgotten on the shelf of a Cambridge bookshop. It systematically described the features of English folk song, discussed collectors such as Francis Child and Cecil Sharp, and listed some songs that looked familiar, but it did not seem related to anything in the present or to what might have been currently familiar from the radio or other mass media. Although originally published in 1973, the book included no mention of anything called "English folk" or "electric folk." Rather, Karpeles (1987: 103) deplored the misuse of the word 'folk,' which is to be seen in the present habit of attributing the term 'folk song' to any popular, or would-be popular, song that is composed in what is thought to be a folk-style. This is not merely an academic question. It goes to the heart of the matter, for nothing is so likely to debase the currency as the issue of counterfeit coins.

However important as a study of the English folk song tradition, neither Karpeles's text nor the enclosed updated recordings list by Peter Kennedy was helpful in learning about the living or recorded music of my time.[10] None of the recordings listed were currently available in any record shops. Instead, I found many other recordings by Pentangle, Fairport Convention, and Steeleye Span filed under "English folk music," although I did not really connect these groups to anything in the present. I finally decided to buy *No More to the Dance* (1988) by "Silly Sisters" Maddy Prior and June Tabor, probably also because Prior's name was vaguely familiar as the singer on the "Song to Hiawatha" selection from Mike Oldfield's *Incantations* (1978).

By a year later I had almost completed my Clannad collection, had added some June Tabor records, and bought the first Steeleye Span album, *Hark! The Village Wait* (1970), which had just been reissued. It contained a short introduction by music journalist John Tobler that offered my first glimpse into the history of that music. Although rarely ever hearing or reading anything about English folk rock in Germany at that time (again, very much in contrast to Scottish and Irish music), I slowly found an access to this music via the material I had obtained in Britain and the United States.

Yet I still puzzled over the strange position of traditional and folk (revival)[11] music in England, and when I began looking for a dissertation topic—which served as the basis for this book—in the field of systematic musicology at Hamburg University, it seemed almost natural for me to turn to electric folk. Furthermore, on my first research trip to England in May 1995, I encountered a particular situation that corresponded with my first observations.

"Electric folk" or "folk rock" was something many people I met had heard about, but it seemed to be identified with a distant past, and the existence of a coherent current music culture or scene was not easily identifiable for an outsider. "Folk music" was far more accessible, via the folk clubs. Yet when I talked with people outside the clubs it became immediately obvious that "folk music" was seen as a synonym for dilettantism—and a music "one did not listen to." This view seemed to be confirmed during my first visit to a folk club, the Half Moon in Cambridge, and again later at the White Horse in Whitby. The Half Moon had a strongly amateurish character and was predominantly frequented by young performers who introduced themselves shyly and played adaptations primarily from contemporary rock/pop music—almost always on guitar. In contrast, the White Horse clientele consisted only of drunken middle-aged men howling songs and telling dirty jokes.

Similarly, "traditional music" was perceived as "exotic." Some older people still remembered Peter Kennedy's radio show *As I Roved Out*, which had presented traditional recordings during the early to mid-1950s, and the English Folk Dance and Song Society (EFDSS) was a well-known institution, although many regarded it as slightly eccentric and disconnected from reality, which seemed to confirm the impression conveyed by Maud Karpeles's book. I was also surprised to meet only few British scholars during my numerous visits to the EFDSS's Vaughan Williams Memorial Library. It was basically used by American and Canadian academics, British amateur researchers, and numerous folk musicians as a prolific source of new material—but only by a few musicologists.

With the general subject of English folk music being thus marginalized, the reputation of electric folk within academia appeared to be even worse. When I talked with English students from various fields during a stay in Cambridge, my research topic, whether described directly as "electric folk" or as the "interaction of traditional with popular music," was often considered to be rather bizarre or even improper for a scientific work at that time. Moreover, the electric-acoustic fusions of the late 1960s and '70s had been strongly attacked by the acoustic, folk club–based revival scene, and the conflict of electric (i.e., popular) versus acoustic (i.e., folk) music was also a theme of *The Electric Muse*. Likewise, leafing through issues of the British rock music newspaper *Melody Maker*, one could find headlines such as "Hester—Not Ashamed to Do Some Folk Rock" (October 15, 1966)[12] or "Would Tim and Maddy Ever Consider Electric Backing for Singing?" (August 2, 1969). With these first observations in mind, I concluded that the mere documentation of this complex music scene should be only one aspect to be covered. It seemed equally important to investigate the present role of vernacular music, given that electric folk is both a revival music and a cultural expression—a movement that has restored a musical tradition and heritage.

GENERALLY SPEAKING, traditional and revival cultures often represent two completely different structures with different sociomusical environments (see fig. I.1). This is especially the case in England, where the modern revival culture has in fact split into two different directions—the revival scene that emerged in the 1950s and '60s and the subsequent electric folk scene that started in the late 1960s. Tradition and revival are set further apart by another factor: the notated collections predominantly established by the first revivalists of the nineteenth and early twentieth centuries. Strongly influenced by contemporaneous late Victorian ideas ("offensive" and sociocritical material was either ignored or edited), this written form of traditional music was fixed outside its original social context and collected for an educated urban audience that was no longer close to the traditional structures. On a sociocultural level, this additional layer of reinterpretation is embodied in the EFDSS.[13] Despite the coexistence of tradition and revival, the folk and electric folk musicians of the 1960s and '70s obtained their material primarily from these collections, working with the changed material and absorbing, often unconsciously, some of the early ideas and ideals about traditional music. The later Pogues-era folk rock direction, which predominantly works with

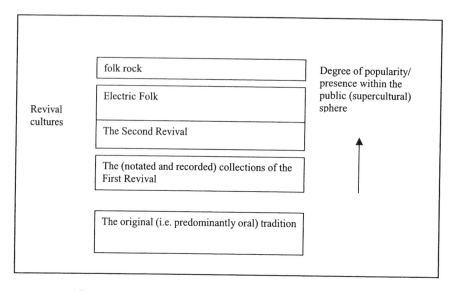

FIGURE I.1. The various English music cultures centered around traditional music and material

idiomatic traditional phrases (e.g., characteristic melodic turns and instrumental sounds), represents another layer, as it is almost completely detached from even the collected source material—and partly from the sociocultural network of the revival and electric folk scenes as well.[14]

ACADEMIC LITERATURE AND ELECTRIC FOLK

Electric folk as a revival culture is inseparably intertwined with the topic of change and transformation. Alan Merriam pointed out in *The Anthropology of Music* that "change is a constant in human experience" (Merriam 1964: 303), for culture is not stable but dynamic, regardless of whether the change is internal (innovation) or external (acculturation). The musical change within musical transformation processes, summarized as a revival, can likewise be understood as a reinterpretation involving alterations of both value and form. As Merriam argued further, despite the element of selectivity (some items are accepted while others are rejected), the extent of change seems to be limited: under normal circumstances, "it is not reasonable to assume that at some point in time West Africans will suddenly begin singing Chinese opera" (ibid.: 305).[15] Similarly, the electrified fusion music of Fairport Convention and Steeleye Span still maintains a distinctly English character with recognizable roots in the tradition.

But how did the change and transformation process of vernacular music in England actually take place? As early as the 1960s, Merriam (ibid.: 319) had asked for more studies dealing with "the dynamics of music change," yet studies that documented actual changes appeared very late—especially with regard to the folk revivals. One significant general contribution regarding the fusion processes in Anglo-American music was Neil Rosenberg's essay collection, *Transforming Tradition* (1993). Focusing on the American revival, it provides a good introduction to the diverse aspects of folk song revivals and the interaction of popular and folk music in the 1950s and 1960s. Although Rosenberg, an expert on the bluegrass revival, proposes no general theory or overall view, his collection offers abundant insight into various central issues such as changing values, as in the case of Riverside recording artist and folklorist Ellen J. Stekert. In her article in the Rosenberg volume, "Cents and Nonsense in the Urban Folksong Movement: 1930–66," Stekert describes how her original enthusiastic and in many ways restricting Marxist ideas of the 1960s increasingly gave way to a self-reflective distance. Another example is Burt Feintuch's essay on "Musical Revival as Musical Transformation." In addition to Merriam, Feintuch has been among the few to point out that "rather than castigate folk music revivalists as if they had somehow corrupted what does not belong to them, as some folklorists tended to do, it seems to me that we should understand folk music revivals as transformations" (Rosenberg 1993: 192)—an idea that became key to this book. To elucidate these different layers of transformation, I have written *Electric Folk* partly in the style of a "thick description"[16] by portraying this complex genre from a variety of angles, including the attempt to depict musical change from an inner perspective.

Moreover, by existing at different sociocultural and musical levels, electric folk can be considered a hybrid genre. This factor not only posed many interesting questions but also made it difficult to decide whether to apply a popular music or an ethnographic perspective. As a consequence, my methodological approach became a mixture of various elements. The focus is nevertheless on ethnomusicology, for I have tried to approach the topic with an emphasis on the traditional material rather than on popular music, which would have required a stronger focus on the elements of rock music and audience behavior codes.

In this context, Edward Macan's study of English progressive rock, *Rocking the Classics* (1997) has been exemplary. The work was valuable to me not only because electric folk and progressive rock share many common features, but also because Macan's eclectic approach focuses on the creation of artistic messages through the specific combination of music, visual images, and verbal expressions. By combining analytical tools from musicology and sociology, Macan provides an effective model for studying the contemporary music scene. Furthermore, he commendably refrains from restrictive metanarratives and focuses on the interaction of musicology and sociology.

Because I decided on a different emphasis (the transformation), however, I had to add a historical description that supplied the framework for my further work. Rather than exhaustively covering all groups and events, my intention was to draw developmental lines between singular but crucial elements and events, including also prelimi-

nary developments such as the First and Second Revivals. Because I wish to emphasize the various layers of the musical adaptation and transformation process, this
book's investigation of the English music scene is also embedded in a description
of the preceding revivals in the United States and an outline of similar developments
in neighboring music cultures such as Scotland and Ireland. The historical focus is
on early electric folk from the beginnings in 1964 until the late 1970s, with a brief
overview of the developments of the last twenty years and the current situation.

Concerning British folk music in general, apart from *The Electric Muse*, only a few
comprehensive studies were available for further background information. For example, Munro (1996) portrayed the folk revival in Scotland with a focus on the relationship to the political climate. Munro also devoted a brief chapter (by Morag McLeod)
to recent developments, including groups such as Capercaillie and the Simple Minds.
There are some investigations of the historical and sociological background of traditional music and the Second Folk Revival, including those by Pegg (1976) and Harker
(1985). These books provide a comprehensive analysis of early collectors' motives and
sociocultural background. However, these works allowed only a limited approach to
contemporary developments, as they were too strongly dominated by neo-Marxist
"metanarratives."[17] One of the more helpful recent approaches has been *The Imagined
Village* by Georgina Boyes (1993), a critical investigation of the ideologies of especially
the first English folk revival. Refraining from overly restrictive metanarratives, she
was, one of the first to point out that the folk clubs were the result of a sociocultural
process. Yet, as with Harker, an empirical investigation is missing here. The small literature list is completed by a number of focused studies, such as an investigation of
the contemporary situation of British folk clubs (MacKinnon 1993) or an analysis of
the American revivals (Filene 1995).

A study by Livingston (1999), which appeared after my original research had been
finished, helped to confirm several observations regarding the electric folk scene.
Feintuch (Rosenberg 1993: 184) earlier pointed out that revival cultures should be understood as separate, complete cultures: "in reality, each revival achieves its own momentum with its own standard repertoire and its own selective view of the past." Livingston, however, became more specific by developing a helpful model for the general
description of revival cultures. She pointed out six essential elements that constitute a
revival music culture: (1) a core group of revivalists, who make use of (2) original informants and historic sources; at the same time evolving an (3) ideology with a distinct discourse around the concept of "authenticity"; completed by (4) a group of followers, with a network of (5) festivals and (6) enterprises such as magazines or
recording companies. These six aspects, although essential to describe a music culture
in general, may not be sufficient to grasp the specific peculiarities of a revival culture,
since they do not occur with the same clarity in the case of electric folk as they do in
the folk club scene. Nevertheless, Livingston seems to be correct in emphasizing that
the discourse around the concept of "authenticity" is a major feature of revival cultures.

The aspect of "having gone electric" has always been a predominant issue in the discussions that emerged concerning the genre of electric folk, which developed partly as a counteraction to the restrictive "authenticity" of the folk club culture.

The major theoretical ethnomusicological approach I decided to use as a tool to describe the complex transformation process, however, is taken from Slobin's *Subcultural Sounds: Micromusics of the West* (1993). Faced with recent developments in sound-producing technology and a global media network, he worked out a flexible scheme to describe modern interaction processes more efficiently.[18] He suggested viewing present societies as an intersection of three types of cultures: *superculture*, *subculture* (or *microculture*), and *interculture*. As Slobin realized, hegemony—here defined as an "overarching, dominating—if not domineering—mainstream that is internalized in the consciousness of governments, industry, subcultures and individuals as ideology" (Slobin 1993: 27)—is neither monolithic nor uniform. Hence, the first type can be described as one (or more) umbrella-like superculture(s) that consist(s) of at least the following elements: (1) a technoscape, mediascape, and finanscape network, such as the music industry, television, or advertising systems; (2) the state and its institutionalized rules and venues such as schools; and (3) the body of culturally shared assumptions, including social stereotypes, standardized styles, and repertoires. The term "superculture" hence also replaces the expression "mainstream," with its negative connotations imposed by earlier metanarratives.

Underneath this so-called superculture exists a large number of subcultures ("micromusical cultures"), each unified, for instance, by a distinct set of rules and musical codes. The term "subculture" is nonnormative within that context, for it is not restricted to the sociological idea of a youth culture. The third type of culture is the so-called "interculture," a crosscutting system or a "kind of large-scale superculture, where whole societies act as the role of subcultures" (Slobin, 1993: 61) that results from the interplay of two partners (e.g., consumer/state in the case of the *industrial interculture*, immigrant culture/mother country in the case of the *diasporic interculture*, and audience/performers in the case of *affinity interculture*).

Of particular interest for this study is Slobin's observation that despite (or maybe because of) the growth of supercultural elements, those microcultures are by no means disappearing, "despite dismal forecasts of earlier commentators. If anything, they are proliferating today as a part of a great resurgence of regional and national feeling and the rapid deterritorialization of large populations" (Slobin 1993: 11). Although he originally developed his "imaginary landscape of musical supercultures, subcultures, and intercultures" (ibid.: 23) on the basis of clearly visible multiethnic societies like the United States and non-Western cultures like Afghanistan, this way of viewing a culture can also be transferred to more homogeneous western European industrialized regions, such as Britain. My investigation of the electric folk scene and the concurrent folk club scene in England confirms Slobin's observations that, despite the dominance of the American popular music culture, general musical diversity is not disappearing. Rather (and somewhat contradictorily), the increasing dominance of the superculture seems to reinforce the development of new musical microcultures and genres, often combined with a revival of older music genres.

OUTLINE OF THE BOOK

These first impressions and a scientific survey led to the three-part conception of this book. Part I frames the historical and theoretical background. Starting with a clarification of the confusing terminology, chapter 1 sketches the developments and underlying sociocultural/political factors of American folk rock and outlines the emergence of electric folk in England. Chapter 2 provides an introduction to the various viewpoints in the theoretical discussion about the relationship between traditional and popular music; this includes the theories of the nineteenth century (with a focus on Cecil Sharp, who strongly influenced the dispute and later criticism regarding electric folk by his strict polarization of traditional, art, and popular music), the American debate on folk rock, and the small number of recent approaches.

Part II portrays the electric folk scene: chapter 3 profiles major groups and individual artists, while chapter 4 analyzes the sociocultural background and hybrid character of a fusion music that exists simultaneously in various performance spaces (e.g., in folk clubs and in progressive venues). Chapters 5 and 6 then focus on musical aspects.

Part III addresses the transformation and adaptation process English traditional music has undergone. Chapter 7 takes up the personal perspectives of various performers, describing their inner adaptation process by analyzing predominantly my own interview material on a comparative level. Finally, chapter 8 considers the revival process within a larger context—first of all, by returning to the United States. Since the 1980s, it can be observed that English music also plays a major role in the search for a new cultural identity within a growing mainstream U.S. superculture. This chapter thus takes a look at the current (English) electric folk scene in the States and its interaction with other immigrant microcultures, especially with the Irish music scene. The chapter also outlines similar developments in related European cultural areas, such as Ireland, Scotland, and Scandinavia.

PRACTICAL NOTES: THE SOURCES AND THE FIELD

Written Sources: Journalistic Magazines

Not having experienced this genre live at its peak in the late 1960s and early 1970s, my first sources about this music were indirect ones such as journalistic articles, especially retrospective ones. My principal literary research took place at the Vaughan Williams Memorial Library at Cecil Sharp House in London, at the British Library, and at the *Melody Maker* archive. Although the EFDSS is said to be extremely conservative, it was, surprisingly enough, the Society's Vaughan Williams Memorial Library that gave me my first access to that music scene, as it holds not only folk song collections and EFDSS-related publications, but also folk magazines, newspaper articles, and studies of modern revivals.

English folk and electric folk, similar to other music revivals, have been the object of numerous journalistic articles and books. Contemporary British music magazines such as *Melody Maker* and *New Musical Express* were the first to provide space for this music from about 1965, when it started to reach a more popular level, until the mid-1970s, when sales deteriorated (except for Steeleye Span's) and the music thus became less interesting for the mainstream-oriented magazines. Although the scene was still developing, the magazines increasingly wrote retrospective and analytical articles from 1974 on, which eventually led to the first major book about the genre, *The Electric Muse* (Laing et al. 1975). I have examined the weekly magazines *Melody Maker* and *New Musical Express* from 1965 to 1975, as these articles reflected what was considered (by the writers) to be important at that time. These sources have long been avoided by musicological researchers, yet it should not be forgotten that journalistic writing and the music industry as well created many terms—such as electric folk, folk rock, and folk baroque—that were later also used in works such as *The Electric Muse* and *The Democratic Muse* (Munro 1996) or scholarly studies such as Macan (1997) and Livingston (1999).

The writing style in *Melody Maker* during the investigated time span differed clearly from the usual writing style for rock music, which was dominated by an interest in nonmusical aspects such as the private life and interests of the stars. In contrast, English folk, starting around 1965, was presented with a much more serious, intellectual touch, often with music analyses and sociocultural interpretations. The electric groups were portrayed in a similar style, although they were simultaneously treated as rock groups—which again illustrates their hybrid character. Pentangle and Fairport Convention frequently appeared in the normal rock sections, and Steeleye Span in particular was often treated like a rock group (e.g., the musicians were asked about their personal interests).

Despite its distinctive headline style, which presented musical events as if they were important political or economic news, *Melody Maker*'s data were highly accurate owing to its weekly publishing frequency. Yet citing these articles as major written sources is not without problems, as some of these writings are strongly opinionated. Many texts focused on selected aspects and stories that were repeated continually. One recurring concern, for instance, was the large number of member changes and the continual "splits," which are normal for jazz groups and likewise occurred frequently in rock groups, but were extremely confusing for the music audience of the 1960s that focused on individual stars as identification figures. Although numerous lineup changes were indeed unusual, they were nevertheless not as important for the performers as

Melody Maker's emphasis suggested. Furthermore, journalistic writing styles for music can tend to be highly individualistic, revealing more about the writer than about the object. This factor is especially of consequence in the case of folk and electric folk, as the majority of the corresponding articles were contributed by a small number of writers, with Karl Dallas being the most prominent and influential. Dallas, who often pointed out his connections to the scene and thus familiarized readers with insider names such as "Tyger" Hutchings, frequently wrote highly complex articles based on his own theories about folk music that have seeped, partly unnoticed, into the national dialogue.

In contrast to *Melody Maker*, *New Musical Express*, which represented a much more popular rock writing style that was less intellectualized and completely focused on performers at a personal level, did not become aware of electric folk until Fairport Convention and particularly Steeleye Span began selling well. Fairport ads appeared in *New Musical Express* only after 1971. Likewise, the revival was not noticed until electric folk had become established as a musical genre, yet performers such as Shirley Collins, the Watersons, and Jeannie Robertson were not presented to the *New Musical Express* audience. Electric folk musicians were treated in a "rock" style in the beginning; Sandy Denny, for example, was presented as a "girl" singer, although the image of folk as synonymous with honesty was also obvious in connection with Fairport.[19] Yet, with such writers as Charles Shaar Murray, the magazine soon started to develop a much more distanced, descriptive style than *Melody Maker*. Often issues such as the discussions concerning electric folk, which were described in *Melody Maker* as being very dramatic, were relatively unimportant for *New Musical Express*, which presented only basic facts.

While in the mid-1960s rock, folk, and jazz were covered almost equally well, after 1971–72 rock had developed such a vast number of styles that groups such as Fairport Convention were given increasingly less space in the popular magazines. This trend is unfortunate in retrospect, as especially in the early '70s a large but noncommercial stylistic variety started to emerge. At one point Ashley Hutchings completely disappeared from these magazines, while earlier stars such as Bert Jansch and Ralph McTell were only present through the listings of their concert dates. Coverage was gradually taken up by specialized folk magazines like *Folk Review* that continued and extended the style of *Melody Maker*, also including writings from several folk rock musicians such as Peter Bellamy, who interviewed Steeleye Span (Bellamy 1973).

My primary sources for retrospective articles and the documentation of present developments were the magazines *fRoots* (Great Britain) and *Dirty Linen* (United States). *fRoots*, the successor of *Southern Rag*, started in 1985 (the magazine changed its name from *Folk Roots* to *fRoots* in 2000) and is currently one of the major resources for folk music worldwide, giving the broadest overview of performers and styles, as well as events, clubs, and festivals. It is edited by the former English folk/blues guitarist Ian A. Anderson, who is relatively close to the English folk / electric folk scene, which has remained one of the magazine's focuses. However, with its distinct terminology like "roots music," the magazine can occasionally be biased against modern developments of the so-called Celtic branch, most prominently represented by Clannad. *Dirty Linen* was founded in 1981 by American fans of British/Irish music. Although more focused on the developments in America (both Canada and the United States), it also extensively covers European musicians, including the Celtic groups. At the time of my research, *Living Tradition* (founded in Scotland in 1993) was regarded by many performers and insiders as the most objective, yet more specialized, magazine dealing predominantly with Irish-British folk music.

The primary magazines of the EFDSS, *Folk Music Journal* and *English Dance and Song*, reacted, generally speaking, indifferently to the emergence of electric folk, although one can detect some differences. *Folk Music Journal*, which focused on English traditional music (especially from a historical viewpoint), showed almost no reaction to the current trends between 1970 and 1974. *English Dance and Song* (1965–75), which aimed at a more popular audience, was more open. Its Winter 1970 issue, for instance, featured Pentangle and the Incredible String Band, and also reviewed recordings by Steeleye Span and Shirley Collins. Yet even at present (2002–3), features on contemporary revival or electric folk—like "Ashley Hutchings on Morris and Dance" (Hemsley 1994)—are rare.

The Musical Sources

Due to the strong influence of cultural anthropology, ethnomusicological studies naturally tend to focus on the conceptualization of music and the analysis of behavior related to music, although Alan Merriam put the same emphasis on the sound of music. Trying to maintain a balance among these three aspects, this book devotes two chapters music analysis. Owing to the lack of previous research on the musical level, I have stayed with the classical analytical approach, focusing on the elements of melody, harmony, and rhythm, while other analytical tools proposed by Tagg (1982) and Moore (1993) are used only as occasional additions. Regarding vocal styles, I have also added some physical descriptions such as the position of the vocal cords. This emic perspective, based on an outside viewpoint, was enhanced further at an etic (internal) level by investigations of performance practice and musical conceptualizations.[20] In general, however, I decided to refrain from any interpretations that would venture beyond the musical texture itself.

Although this book focuses on the description of a single genre, the scale of traditional elements incorporated in contemporary electric folk, as well as the actual musical transformation process (especially regarding vocal styles) could only be assessed by a comparative approach. The source material, which served as the basis for the music analysis, is thus composed of (1) printed material of earlier collectors such as Cecil Sharp; (2) early recordings of English traditional music (with the problems that only a limited number of pre–World War I recordings are available, as earlier collectors preferred written transcriptions to recordings, while later recordings such as Peter Kennedy's recordings and Topic's *The Voice of the People* [1998] are mainly based on post–World War II material); (3) recordings of the Second Revival; (4) recordings of 1960s and '70s electric folk; and (5) recordings of the 1980s and '90s (including folk rock and acoustic works). A list of selected recordings can be found in the appendix. The majority of this material is commercially available, while the traditional and revival recordings can also—sometimes only—be found in British folk archives such as the Vaughan Williams Memorial Library.

This part of my research would have been difficult had it started three or four years earlier, as many recordings had been out of print for twenty years. By chance, the beginning of this research coincided with the reissuing of these recordings on CD. Although generally speaking this was an alleviation, it also caused several problems; many reissues were not identical to the original ones, owing to added or substituted recordings. While extra tracks did not cause a problem, the picture could still become confusing when such changes were not clearly noted in the accompanying booklets. Such was the case when extra tracks were not specifically mentioned or when they were scattered among the original ones in a new order, as on *The Iron Muse* (Topic 1956/1993) and *Blow the Man Down* (Topic 1964/1993). Sometimes the original album was not completely reproduced, as occurred with Shirley Collins's *Amaranth* (1976), which was only partially included in the rerelease of *Anthems in Eden* (EMI/Harvest 1993), or the original versions were replaced by different but not specified song editions, as was the case on *Sandy Denny and the Strawbs* (Hannibal 1973/1991).

Other problems were caused by changed or incompletely reproduced sleeve covers and, quite frequently, original notes omitted from the rereleases. Because album covers played an especially strong role in the late 1960s and early 1970s, the significance of these sleeves and covers is therefore lost for the present-day audience. A good example is the cover of Fairport Convention's *Liege & Lief*. While the outer sleeves of the 1969 original and the first CD reissue from 1986 are identical, the inner one—decorated with numerous pictures from the English tradition (which also gave a good insight into the group's perception of its music)—was missing in Island's CD reissue. Similarly, many arguments in the historical discussion that can only be understood from a historical point of view, such as Fairport's reference to Cecil Sharp on *Liege & Lief*, could thus not be completely validated.

Empirical Research

When I started my research in 1995 it was, especially from my German standpoint, uncertain whether many musicians who had experienced their largest success between 1965 and 1975 were still active and accessible. Obviously, several groups and musicians still went on occasional international concert tours. I was actually able to see many groups for the first time in Germany or in the United States. I also knew that several performers worked as session musicians (such as Fairport drummer Dave Mattacks) or as regular members of other groups (such as Dave Pegg, who was also a bass player for Jethro Tull). Articles in folk magazines like *Folk Roots* and *Dirty Linen* also gave me some indication that there still might be an active electric folk scene in England.

When I finally gained access to the scene, its venues were very much removed from the notice of the general public. The best example probably is Fairport Convention's annual festival in Cropredy. Although never extensively advertised in weekly magazines like *Time Out*, it usually is visited by 16,000–19,000 people, among them a large number of young people who were not born when the group started. Cropredy not only presents the current Fairport lineup and former members like Richard Thompson and Dave Swarbrick as guests, but it also features highly established folk musicians like Beryl Marriott (in 1996) and younger bands like Edward II (1996) and Tempest (1997). Apart from the festival scene with venues at Cambridge, Sidmouth, and South Bank, the musical life is more focused in smaller folk or general music clubs— guitar wizard Bert Jansch, for example, played regularly in the blues/jazz/folk-focused Twelve Bar Club at the time of my research.

Moreover, many groups who had contracts with a major label (like Steeleye Span with Chrysalis or Fairport Convention with Island) were now on independent labels. Consequently, new releases were not always extensively promoted and thus noticed by popular music magazines—as had been the case in the late 1960s and early 1970s. Instead, one had to consult specialized folk magazines like *Folk Roots* or *Dirty Linen* to find out about the newest releases, unless one were included on the bands' direct mailing lists.

It was particularly the written journalistic sources that raised many key questions—not only in terms of gaps in the history and the validity of statements, but particularly with regard to the relationships among the tradition, performance practice, and the current situation. Apart from my own observations during concert visits, personal interviews with leading musicians therefore became an essential empirical part of the research. Despite the former popularity and celebrity status of some performers, the scene in general is quite open, and personal contacts could easily be established at concerts and via journalistic contacts. The atmosphere was always informal; I met the musicians in cafés, pubs, and hotels, via telephone, or by correspondence— but more than once also in their homes, where I enjoyed generous hospitality.

I chose a qualitative, ethnographic approach for these interviews, focused on a highly selective group of informants distinguished by their musical and cultural competence rather than merely being representatives of a larger population. The main focus was on the leading folk / electric folk musicians such as Maddy Prior and Martin Carthy, yet I included also manager Joe Boyd and singer Frankie Armstrong, the latter to check specific questions regarding vocal styles and the impact of Ewan Mac-Coll. The number of interviewees (thirteen) was considered adequate to represent a good cross section of this music scene.

In constructing the interviews, I used a flexible, episodic approach—a mixture of predominantly narrative elements, held together by an identical structure for all inter-viewees that allowed a subsequent comparative evaluation.[21] Except for some general questions about the past (e.g., how the performers started to make music), I asked biographical questions only to fill in some gaps or to verify controversial aspects. With most events already thirty years in the past and an extensive contemporaneous jour-nalistic documentation available, personal recollections often only remained on a com-paratively superficial level. For instance, Shirley Collins's highly detailed account of names and facts in Karl Dallas's "Conversation with the Misses Collins" (Dallas 1978c) had become much less precise in my interview of 1996. Many musicians preferred to talk about present events and current projects anyway, instead of repeating—or "reciting"—stories of the past that had been told a dozen times to numerous journal-ists in previous years.

I therefore decided to set the focus clearly on the subjective level of the performers' perceptions, expressed in their ideas about making music and their awareness of tradi-tional music, thus trying to find a way to understand the music from the inside. The influences of Alan Lomax, A. L. Lloyd, and Ewan MacColl were obvious; Oysterband fiddler Ian Telfer, who had studied English literature, was still familiar with Lomax's systems of Cantometrics and Choreometrics, which were often discussed in Mac-Coll's house where Lomax had visited frequently. As the interviews form a major por-tion of the source material they are, unless otherwise stated, not separately marked in the text. Names and dates are listed in the appendix.

PART I

THE HISTORICAL AND THEORETICAL FRAMEWORK

ONE

APPROACHING ELECTRIC FOLK
A History of Music Revivals, Fusions, and Ideologies

I don't play folk-rock. . . . I like to think of it more in terms of vision music.
BOB DYLAN

Electric folk or folk rock is not just a mere technical combination of acoustic or electric elements—or of folk and rock music. Rather, the musical fusion has also affected the seemingly established sociocultural boundaries of traditional music (ideally noncommercial, orally transmitted, fragile, and working class–related) and rock music (commercial, mass media–related, dominant, and middle class–based). As will be discussed below, these aspects became especially apparent in the heated ideological discussion that evolved with the emergence of folk rock's American predecessor more than thirty-five years ago. Yet the controversy about the relationship between traditional and rock music can be traced even further back, starting with the conception of folk song as defined by Cecil Sharp and further shaped by the ideologies of the subsequent American and English folk revivals and various theoretical approaches (see chapter 2). From the very beginning, expressions like "folk" and "electric folk" were thus highly mutable terms inseparably intertwined with these disputes.

THE PROBLEM OF DEFINING A HYBRID MUSIC STYLE: FOLK ROCK AND ELECTRIC FOLK

The term "folk rock" first emerged in discussions regarding Bob Dylan's appearance with an electric guitar at the Newport Festival in 1965. This nearly legendary incident is one of the most reported and retold performance disasters in rock history: Dylan, at that time one of the central American folk revivalists, was—according to many rock histories and journalistic accounts—booed by his outraged audience for musical and for ideological reasons. As Irvin Silber (1965b: 5) wrote in *Sing Out!'s* "What's Happening" pages:

> The Festival's most controversial scene was played out on the dramatically-lit giant stage halfway through the final night's concert when Bob Dylan emerged from his cult-imposed aura of mystery to demonstrate the new "folk rock." . . . To many, it seemed that it was not very good "rock," while other disappointed legions did not think it was very good Dylan. Most of these erupted into silence at the conclusion of Dylan's songs, while a few booed their once-and-former idol. Others cheered and demanded encores. . . . Shocked and somewhat disoriented by the mixed reaction of the crowd, a tearful Dylan returned to the stage unelectrified and strained to communicate his sense of unexpected displacement through the words and music of a song he made fearfully appropriate, "It's All Over Now, Baby Blue."

Truth or myth? As Bruce Jackson, one of the directors of this Newport Folk Festival, pointed out in an Internet essay, "it wasn't Bob Dylan they were booing." Jackson, whose personal recollections have always deviated from what he could read in rock encyclopedias, finally decided to transcribe the original tapes made from the stage microphones—only to find that the audiences' booing referred to Dylan's *leaving* the stage. In agreement with the festival management, Dylan and his pickup group (members of the Paul Butterfield Blues Band) had only prepared three "electric" songs—after which the audience yelled, according to Jackson's transcriptions, "We want Dylan" when he left the stage. Dylan then returned to perform "It's All Over Now, Baby Blue" acoustically, plus "Mr. Tambourine Man," after which the audience, when the next group was about to appear, in fact yelled "No! Bob!" Dylan was indeed booed for his electric guitar at subsequent concerts, but Jackson (2002) wondered "if those boos were from people who were really outraged and affronted at the electric power or people who read some of the first renderings of the Legend of Newport '65 and thought that was the way to behave to be cool." Yet it is still amazing that even apparent eyewitness accounts, such as Irvin Silber's above, could have misinterpreted the situation (although the stage acoustics seem to have been poor, and, as Jackson also reported, it was announcer Peter Yarrow [not the audience] who first pointed to the significance of the electric guitar—which then could have alerted the journalists who were in the audience).[1]

Nevertheless, the subsequent debate centered on three aspects that would also characterize the discussion evolving around electric folk in England: On an *ideological* level, the use of the electric guitar was subsequently interpreted by some writers and parts of the folk scene as a betrayal of their ideals, the instrument itself being seen as a symbol of commercialized music. At the same time, writers criticized, maybe also due to the image of electric music, the low *sound technical* and *musical* quality. For example, Silber (1965a: 4) complained already about the low quality of the inadequate sound system at the 1965 New York Folk Festival for guesting pop performers such as

Chuck Berry, which "did not allow for a full appreciation of the incredible vitality of . . . his music." Others like contemporary observer Josh Dunson (1966a: 17) remarked that "his side men can keep a beat but there is no soul. When the words come through they don't mean very much," while *Melody Maker* writer Bob Dawbarn (1965c) worried about the hybrid nature of Dylan's new music that broke clearly defined borders: "The trouble comes when he starts mixing the roles. 'Like a Rolling Stone' will offend the folk purists with its strings [*sic*] and electric guitars. It is unlikely to appeal to pop fans because of its length, monotony and uncommercial lyric."

Despite its initial negative connotation, the American expression "folk rock" soon started to encompass two relatively neutral meanings: (a) a style that combined acoustic and electric instruments (but not necessarily for the interpretation of traditional material) and (b) rock music outside (or in opposition to) the commercialized mainstream, and especially played by groups related to the hippie movement. The expressions "British/English folk rock" and "electric folk," in contrast, were much more restricted to the first meaning: Being either borrowed from the American original ("folk rock") or newly invented ("electric folk"), they were used by British journalists, music producers, and record stores as collective labels for a variety of new ("progressive") hybrid forms of contemporary interpretations of traditional English music. In contrast with America, where the discussion about folk rock was always strongly focused on aspects of commercialism, the English debate was much more centered around musical criteria, particularly the unaccompanied singing style of the folk clubs versus the electric versions.

Melody Maker writers like Karl Dallas and Tony Wilson preferred the expression "electric folk" at first.[2] One of the few cases in which "folk rock" was actually used in that early time was *Island*'s advertisement of Fairport Convention's album *Liege & Lief* as "the first (literally) British folk rock LP ever." The *New Musical Express* likewise made little use of this expression. As a technical term, "folk rock" seems not to have really been established until 1973–75. The change became obvious after the publication of *The Electric Muse* (Laing et al. 1975). While Dallas still avoided the expression, Robin Denselow's chapter on "Folk Rock in Britain" made extensive use of this term. After that, "folk rock" started to emerge in many other journalistic and, later, scholarly texts.

From the beginning of this movement, the terminology was used and discussed controversially. English musicians were never happy with the expression "folk rock"; it not only implied a never really intended polarization between folk and rock, but also suggested a clear orientation toward rock, which was not always the case. Many progressive approaches that were also labeled as "folk rock" had little to do with rock music—such as the experiments of Shirley and Dolly Collins or Pentangle's jazzier style. Yet even those playing clearly rock-based music disliked the expression. The former Fairport Convention guitarist Richard Thompson felt the term to be a burden, putting him under an unwanted label. When asked how to define his music, he once replied that the band played "traditional based contemporary British music" (Frey and Siniveer 1987: 250).

Although a terminology like "folk fusions" might therefore have been a much more adequate description of this music, expressions like electric folk and folk rock are historically established and will remain in use. I use "electric folk" in this text not only because it was predominantly used by the earlier British writers, but also because of its predominantly musical connotations. Electric folk is a relatively broad expression encompassing a number of musical fusion styles that are based upon traditional material in various forms. Fusion and change are two further important elements here—a folk musician merely amplifying his acoustic instruments is not playing electric folk. In contrast, the whole complex of synthesizer-based Celtic music as established by the Irish group Clannad is a specific form of electric folk—their sound is very distinct.

The distinction between English electric folk and American folk rock also relates to their different musical sources.[3] Folk rock, as originally coined for Bob Dylan and the Byrds, basically refers to newly composed songs with a form loosely based on traditional ballads and songs. The relationship of folk rock to traditional music is particularly obvious in the use of characteristic instruments like the fiddle or the accordion, although the style otherwise clearly makes use of the rock language.

The folk rock direction in Britain became especially evident with the popularity of the Pogues and the Levellers. Historically speaking, however, this approach already emerged shortly after the first electric folk music had appeared: English bands like Lindisfarne and Irish groups like Horslips had pointed in that direction as early as 1970, followed by groups like the Strawbs and the Home Service. I have nevertheless decided to omit these folk rock groups from this study, since traditional material played only a minor role in their repertoire and their music therefore touches my central research question—the interaction of traditional and popular music—only marginally.

By the expression "electric folk" I thus mean English groups and musicians of the 1960s and 1970s, as well as their successors, who combined traditional music with contemporary music styles. My research focused on English traditional and rock music; despite many musicians actually being Irish or Scottish, this genre nevertheless originated in the London area and developed some distinctively English features. The core materials included, first of all, the Child ballads and songs in the English language that were handed down orally until the nineteenth century. These, in most cases, were mixed with Irish and Scottish material. Many electric folk groups also used material that was predominantly found in England, such as seasonal songs or particular dance forms like the morris dance. Moreover, by incorporating particular instruments (such as the fiddle, accordion, and sometimes brass instruments) or local singing and playing styles, combined with individual arrangement techniques, the English approach became clearly distinguishable from American folk rock, as well as the Celtic (Irish, Scottish, Breton) styles.

It is probably inevitable that some of this terminology will be challenged in the future. However, I propose that a fruitful discussion of this genre should—as will be demonstrated in this book—focus on structural aspects, history, and the prevailing conditions behind the creation of these expressions, rather than on attempting to pinpoint the exact meanings of these once deliberately chosen words.

FROM REVIVAL TO FOLK ROCK: AMERICA

"Folk music" was probably never a purely neutral, descriptive concept, as was evident in the earliest theories regarding traditional music in the late eighteenth and nineteenth centuries. Likewise, in the context of the various twentieth-century folk revivals, the terminology was always combined with political or ideological meanings, in particular with the idea of traditional or folk music as a counterpoint to popular (i.e., commercial) music. Such was the case both in the United States and in Great Britain. At the same time, the story of the folk revivals and electric folk reflects a long-term interaction between the English and the more dominant American music cultures. This process was by no means transparent; the Second Revival in England, for instance, initiated partly by American collector Alan Lomax, was a reaction against both the dominant American music and the isolated First English Revival.

The Folk Revivals in America (1930s–1965)

The beginnings of the American revival of English, Scottish, Irish, and blues music are inseparably linked with the activities of the left-wing organizations that emerged after the social and economic breakdown during the Great Depression. Although left-wing groups had encouraged the use and creation of "proletarian music" from early on, traditional Anglo-American songs had largely been ignored for decades before the mid-1930s (Filene 1995: 97).[4] As Robbie Lieberman (1995: xix) points out in his political analysis of the American folk revival, the transition toward an inclusion of folk song started around 1935, when the Communist Party began to change its cultural focus from mass music to vernacular music. The party adopted the assumption that "folk songs had been created by 'the people,' often in opposition to the dominant culture, and that singing folk songs brought people together to form a community" (ibid.)—an approach that was later adapted by rock theorists.

It was especially the leftist cultural organization People's Songs that in its three years of existence developed the idea of using songs as political weapons, with traditional songs taking a predominant role as means of protest, education, and morale. Founded in 1945, People's Songs not only arranged concerts, meetings, and classes, but also published a vast amount of collected musical material in songbooks, on sheets, and in its central magazine, the *Bulletin*. As social criticism was central for this movement, the focus was less on musical aspects than on textual reconstruction.

At the same time, a new folk-style body of songs, again with a strong emphasis on the textual side, started to emerge—most prominently collected, adapted, or written by Woody Guthrie (1912–1967) and Pete Seeger (b. 1919) who, along with Alan Lomax, also served on People's Songs' board of directors. Music was an integral part of Guthrie's political activities in the strike movement and in the Communist Party. Having left his home in Oklahoma at the age of thirteen and journeying with the Dust Bowl victims to Los Angeles in 1935, Guthrie not only absorbed a vast amount of songs during his tramplike youth but also became a prolific songwriter. He wrote more than one thousand songs—the most famous one being "This Land Is Your Land"—between 1932 and 1952, many of them with a political or socially critical background. In 1939 he went to New York, where he came to know both Lomax, who recorded him for the Library of Congress, and Seeger.

Seeger, the son of musicologist and composer Charles Seeger, had been exposed to traditional American music at home from an early age. He became acquainted first-hand with country ballads and the five-string banjo when accompanying his father on a field trip through rural North Carolina in 1936. Seeger expanded his knowledge further while assisting Lomax on his diverse recording trips for the Library of Congress in 1939 and 1940. These trips enabled Seeger to acquire a vast repertoire of traditional black and white American songs, and he later played a key role in canonizing the material of Leadbelly ("Rock Island Line") and Woody Guthrie. Like Guthrie, he became a prolific songwriter (which included the adaptation of existing tunes and texts).[5] He was also highly active in the union movement and a member of the Communist Party, and his songs showed a strong political and sociocritical edge, most prominently evident with "Where Have All the Flowers Gone?" and "We Shall Overcome." Yet studies of the folk revival such as Cantwell's (1996) have never failed to point out the two men's different social backgrounds; in contrast to Guthrie, Seeger embodied many of the characteristics of the later urban revival that tried to disguise its middle-class background by inventing a new identity.

In 1941 Seeger founded the Almanac Singers, which also included Guthrie. The Almanacs became the most popular music group of the Left and a forerunner of vocal folk groups like the Weavers, the Kingston Trio, and Peter, Paul, and Mary. The group disbanded in 1942 when their members were drafted into the war. The beginning of the Cold War marked a clear change for the left-wing movements, because activists like Seeger and Guthrie were banned from larger public events during the McCarthy era. The Weavers ("Goodnight Irene," "Tzena, Tzena, Tzena"), founded by Seeger in 1949 as the successor to the Almanac Singers, found their commercial career cut short by the McCarthy ban in 1952.[6] Although the group reformed in 1955 and continued to perform until 1963, the First Revival had lost its initial influence and vitality.

Meanwhile, a second, predominantly urban, folk revival started to emerge in the late 1950s. This new music scene first thrived in the intimate atmosphere of the numerous coffeehouses that had sprung up between 1958 and 1960. Besides San Francisco and Los Angeles, the Greenwich Village district of New York—a section of lower Manhattan that was inhabited and frequented by artists, writers, and students and had also hosted the Almanac Singers—especially developed into a central location. Performance venues later expanded to university campuses and to emerging festivals such as the Newport Festival, which started in 1959, first organized, among others, by Pete Seeger.

This Second Revival took off with the Kingston Trio, a vocal group from California, whose smoothed, popularized version of the Appalachian murder ballad "Tom Dooley" sold almost four million copies, offering the first access to an alternative culture in a business that was dominated by the payola scandals of the late 1950s. The revival also found a public platform in the folk music–oriented *Hootenanny* television show that started in 1962. It was named after the hootenanny meetings that had been started by Seeger and the Almanac Singers as an informal way for people interested in folk music to meet with active musicians. ("Hootenanny" was an American slang word similar to "thingumabob"—a thing whose name is unknown or forgotten—that Seeger had picked up on a concert tour.) Although the show was controversial for its popularized aesthetics, it also brought the music of then unknown high-quality performers like bluegrass/country guitarist Doc Watson into millions of households.

The Second Revival, which like its predecessor of the 1930s and '40s was very political, was musically extremely open and fertile. It quickly became a college-based movement, oriented toward an academic, intellectual, and middle-class audience. Although representing a sociocultural group different from the First Revival, it was still closely interwoven with the political and musical activities of its predecessor. For example, Seeger maintained a key position as performer and organizer, while *Sing Out!*, the Second Revival's primary monthly magazine, was the successor of People's Songs' *Bulletin*.

The revival actually comprised a large number of different yet related directions. The most prominent camp was represented by political performers like Seeger and the Weavers, as well as by more commercial groups like the Kingston Trio or the Limelighters, whose repertoire consisted of a mixture of partly popularized traditional and original songs. The other camp was strongly based on the traditional body of Anglo-American music. It was especially in this earlier stage that a large number of female singers such as Joan Baez, Judy Collins, Carolyn Hester, and Buffy Sainte-Marie incorporated many Child ballads into their repertoire. Several of these musicians, notably Baez, later became politically oriented singers; starting to write their own material, these singer/songwriters would later, together with Bob Dylan, Phil Ochs, and Peter de la Farge, form a core group of protest artists. From the middle to the late 1960s on, the Second Revival also witnessed more poetic songwriters like Paul Simon, Richard Fariña, and Joni Mitchell.

Likewise, the revival would offer room and a more popular platform for traditionally grounded performers, such as the Appalachian singer and dulcimer player Jean Ritchie and bluegrass performers (most prominently guitarist Watson) who had pre-

viously been part of a different musical scene and community. It was not solely restricted to white Anglo-American music: although blues elements had already been
inherent in the music of Seeger and Guthrie, it was especially this urban revival that
started to rediscover the country blues. This interest was not only focused on Lomax-
promoted musicians such as Leadbelly and Muddy Waters, but also included performers of the 1930s like Big Bill Broonzy, Brownie McGhee, and Reverend Gary
Davis, as well as songs from the early Lomax recordings.

Modern media played a central role in the development of this revival. An important basis for the rediscoveries of Anglo- and African American music were the field
recordings of the American folk music collectors John Avery Lomax (1875–1948) and
Alan Lomax (1915–2002). Father and son made a famous recording tour for the Library of Congress in 1933, recording ballads, work songs, and field hollers in Mississippi, Louisiana, Kentucky, Tennessee, and the prisons of the South. This material
also became a countervailing influence against the Child canon that, once promoted as
the true folk music of America, was still a prevailing ideal at that time. John Avery
Lomax had already made important progress toward defining a distinctly American
body of folk song with the publication of his book *Cowboy Songs and Other Frontier Ballads* in 1910. But it was especially black musicians like Leadbelly and Muddy Waters,
promoted by the Lomaxes to mainstream popularity in the early 1950s, who demonstrated that the United States had a rich folk song heritage independent of Britain's.

The Lomaxes used a large number of radio shows to promote their material, most
prominently a weekly radio program, *Back Where I Come From*, which Alan Lomax
presented on CBS in 1940 as a mixture of songs and readings addressing specific topics. Furthermore, the Lomaxes' recordings were also made available to the public
through the Library of Congress archival recording series *Folk Music in the United States*.
Created in 1942 as the first documentary anthology of American folk music, featuring
performers such as Muddy Waters, it became highly influential on revival performers,
both in the United States[7] and in Britain.

The Folkways label, which was founded by Moses Asch in 1947, became particularly important for the commercial distribution of original field recordings as well as
contemporary recordings. Folkways was founded by Asch after he had gone bankrupt
with his Asch Recordings, which had featured such artists as Brownie McGhee, Leadbelly, and Sonny Terry. With its central policy of always keeping the records available,
Folkways became essential for the recordings of many folk artists, including Seeger,
Guthrie, and the influential *Anthology of American Folk Music*, compiled by Harry
Smith and first issued in 1952.

After the death of his father, John Avery, Alan Lomax, who had won a Guggen-
heim Fellowship, went to Britain in 1949 to set up the Columbia World Library of
Folk and Primitive Music. Partly assisted by Seamus Ennis and Ewan MacColl on his
trips in Scotland, England, and Ireland in the 1950s, Lomax compiled a still unsur-
passed field recording collection of British folk music. After his return to the United

States, he embarked, accompanied by his assistant, English folksinger Shirley Collins, on his famous "Southern Journey" from 1959 to 1960. In 1960 he received a grant from the American Council of Learned Societies to develop his new classification system for folk music that became known as Cantometrics (and Choreometrics for dance music), a project he directed at the anthropology department of Columbia University until the early 1990s.

The Second Revival already seemed to have started its decline as early as the mid-1960s, when folk music was increasingly integrated into youth activism such as the demonstrations against the Vietnam War. The major portion of Joan Baez's repertoire in 1965, for instance, still consisted of traditional ballads. Soon, however, she became increasingly active in politics and started to use folk songs in demonstrations and marches "as diffusers" against police who wanted to dissolve the assemblies (Hunt 1996a: 27). The revival began mixing with the hippie movement, which diffused the already hybrid scene even further.

The relatively broad term "folk music" was increasingly less related to musical sources and more focused on the idea of a noncommercial performance setting, with Bob Dylan as a major figure. This notion became a major contradiction when the Newport Folk Festival destroyed itself partly through sheer size. Established as an antithesis of the commercial marketing of Anglo-American folk song—as embodied by country music's Grand Ole Opry[8]—in 1959, it quickly became the largest folk festival in the States (hosting 80,000 visitors in 1965). Increasingly mired in financial and organizational problems that were not solved by the appearance of prominent performers of the "rock revolution" such as Janis Joplin in 1968, it was discontinued in 1971 after the Newport Town Council banned the festival in fear of the civil disturbances that had become part of the festival.[9]

American Folk Rock (1965–1970)

Songwriter-poet Bob Dylan (born Robert Allen Zimmermann in 1941) played a key role in the development of what was later to be known as "folk rock." Dylan started to perform in the folk clubs of New York's Greenwich Village in early 1961, mainly with songs by Woody Guthrie whom he also came to know personally at that time. His debut album, *Bob Dylan* (1962), included a large number of traditional songs, yet he soon became famous for his original songwriting, combining traditional structures with contemporary social, political, and poetic messages—such as the immortal "Blowin' in the Wind" (1962) and "The Times They Are A-Changing" (1963). In this early stage, Dylan also borrowed traditional tunes for his songs. For example, "A Hard Rain's A-Gonna Fall" on *The Freewheelin' Bob Dylan* (1963) was based on the tune of the Child ballad "Lord Randall." Having created a Guthrie-like bohemian mystique, Dylan became extremely popular in the States as well as in Europe, epitomizing the anticommercial attitude with which much of the popular music of the early 1960s was identified. This image became so prevalent (even Seeger saw in Dylan's early music the ideal of contemporary folk music) that a conflict with further musical change was almost inevitable.

Bringing It All Back Home (1965) marked Dylan's break with the folk revival style that had been strongly dominant in his songwriting until that point. For Dylan, his growing distance from the folk revival had diverse reasons (Filene 1995: 324). As contemporary accounts indicate, he increasingly seemed to feel restricted by the audience expectations he had created himself with the persona of the rambling singer/songwriter. Moreover, sensing the decline of the folk scene, Dylan, with his highly developed ability to embrace everything as potential influence, seemed to have been looking for a more multifaceted musical language, which he found in contemporary rock music. He had never made a strict separation between folk and pop for himself. As he commented in various interviews (Filene 1995: 322–30), he had also been strongly influenced by country and rock 'n' roll musicians such as Hank Williams, Elvis Presley, and Little Richard—and he made clear references to these influences with *Bringing It All Back Home*. Yet, with the prevailing idea of folk music still representing an ideal of noncommercial music, his use of an electric guitar, additionally backed up by a blues band, at the Newport Festival in 1965 could easily be interpreted as a betrayal of the folk audience—which also seemed to have been put into a different, more distanced role as spectators.

The seeming rejection of Dylan's new music, however, was only brief; the Byrds' electric arrangement of his "Mr. Tambourine Man"—the title cut of what is considered to be the first complete folk rock album, *Mr. Tambourine Man* (released in June 1965)—marked the beginning of the commercially successful American folk rock phase that peaked between 1965 and 1967. The expression "folk rock" was actually a collective term used for a large range of styles, as was evident in *Rolling Stone*'s definition of folk rock as a musical "hybrid with which many young urban folk musicians attempted to fuse revered teachings from the past (Woody Guthrie, Leadbelly, the Carter Family . . .) with an immediate and more personally relevant knowledge of the present (the Beatles)" (De Curtis and Henke 1992: 313).

Musically, the term would soon coalesce into a combination of Dylan's lyrical style with a strongly Beatles-influenced sound that had swept over America with the so-called British invasion of 1964. The folk rock sound was characterized by well-arranged harmonies and a jangling twelve-string guitar sound. This combination became especially evident with the Byrds' version of "Mr. Tambourine Man" and with Peter, Paul, and Mary's interpretation of "Blowin' in the Wind," but was also true for performers like Simon and Garfunkel, Sonny and Cher, and the British singer/songwriter Donovan.

Nevertheless, the expression "folk rock" would later also convey the image of a location (California), as well as referring to a style shared by California-based bands like the Mamas and the Papas or Jefferson Airplane, none of whom had much in common with the folk revival itself. Traditional songs and instruments, for example, played only a marginal role for these new groups—revival and folk rock artists were, apart from the festivals, parts of different scenes. At the same time, for many musicians and journalists the term "folk rock" suggested a rock music that was opposed to the dominating music industry because it focused on self-expression and personal experience rather than profits. The term was occasionally used to describe groups such as the country folk band Crosby, Stills, Nash, and Young, four of the most prominent American songwriters. First and foremost, however, it became a term for the various bands of the hippie culture who experimented with drugs and would go, like Jefferson Airplane, in the psychedelic direction.

American folk rock remained a time-restricted moment. Although The Band would still endure with its highly original fusions, the decline of the hippie culture around the mid-1970s paralleled the decline in American folk rock's commercial success. From that point on, folk rock or electric folk became increasingly associated with a Great Britain that had, starting with the "British invasion," found its own musical language after a long period of imitating American styles. As Happy Traum (1969: 7–8) wrote in *Rolling Stone*: "What American group with ears is not influenced by the Incredible String Band, or Pentangle, or even the Young Tradition, all from England, and all under the spell of trad., in much of the same way that the British bands were influenced by our blues and jug band music?"

THE SECOND BRITISH FOLK REVIVAL AND THE DEVELOPMENT OF ELECTRIC FOLK

Beginnings of the Second Revival (1950s and 1960s)

Although the Second British folk revival that started in the 1950s had a leftist background similar to that of its American counterpart, the development in England went in a completely different direction. The initial situation was also different, as the English Folk Dance and Song Society (EFDSS)—formed in 1932 as a union of the Folk Song Society (founded in 1898) and the Folk Dance Society (1911)—had maintained an influential, almost authoritative, position in terms of scholarship and revival activities. As with the American movement, however, the Second World War became a dividing line for the revival. Traditional music had been disappearing since at least the mid-nineteenth century. Yet its marginal role in English public life became especially apparent in the 1950s, when traditional communities appeared to reject their music even more strongly as unwanted reminders of their class and prewar lifestyles. Despite having been extremely active in collecting the disappearing material and promoting the tradition, the EFDSS found itself in an isolated position that required a change in its politics if it wanted to keep the revival going (Schofield 1994a).[10]

The public rejection of the tradition was only part of the problem, for the Society itself was—and partly still is—closely associated with the upper class, remaining rather secluded and detached not only from those communities it had collected its material from but also from the general public—a contradiction that later became one of the principal accusations of the Second Revival against the EFDSS. While the EFDSS had previously focused on the dance revival—teaching and organizing new morris dance groups, for instance—it now extended its activities to song as well. Additionally, it started to reach out to the public, sponsoring recordings and launching the innovative EFDSS-BBC series *As I Roved Out* by Peter Kennedy (son of EFDSS director Douglas Kennedy) in the early 1950s. This radio show not only presented a large variety of traditional material from England, Scotland, and Ireland but also introduced the singers, who talked about their lives in short interview segments. *As I Roved Out* is still well remembered among the older generation in Britain. Moreover, the EFDSS also established several influential new festivals such as Keele and Sidmouth, the latter one in particular hosting traditional singers.

However, many active impulses for what was later to be known as the (English) Second Revival came from the outside. Alan Lomax, fleeing postwar McCarthyism, had arrived in the British Isles to do fieldwork for Columbia Records. Lomax, who also worked with some of the leading collectors such as Kennedy (England), Hamish Henderson (Scotland), and Seamus Ennis (Ireland), soon began presenting a large quantity of material in various radio series like *Ballads and Blues* (together with A. L. Lloyd and Ewan MacColl) and BBC television shows like *The Ballad Hunter*. Lomax also seems to have been a motivating force behind the early activities of MacColl, who with Lloyd was a central organizational figure of the revival. As MacColl (1990: 271) recalled in his autobiography *Journeyman*, Lomax "had been fascinated by the *waulking* songs he had recorded on the Hebridean island of Barra and argued that they could eventually provide us with a musical form as popular as the blues or the corridas of Mexico. His enthusiasm was infectious."

MacColl (1915–1989), born James Miller, grew up in Lancashire but was born of Scottish working-class parents—his father worked as an iron molder and his mother "went into service when she was fourteen" (Woods 1973a: 4)—a background on which he would always fall back when he became involved in leftist socialist activities.[11] His father had been a militant trade unionist from the 1920s on, and Ewan started to be politically active at the age of fourteen when he began to work, joining the Young Communist League and being frequently involved in strikes. Strongly influenced by Bertolt Brecht, he became a verse editor of the factory papers and started to write songs around 1931. MacColl moved to London in 1945, working as an actor and later becoming known as a playwright before he started to focus on traditional music at the end of the 1940s. He had picked up a vast Gaelic repertoire from his parents, as well as numerous urban songs. Recorded by Lomax as early as 1951, MacColl became one of the first folksingers who could be heard on commercial record in England. In addition to Lloyd, MacColl would also be one of the first collectors to investigate the industrial songs that had been almost completely neglected by the First Revival movement.

Albert Lancaster Lloyd (1908–1982), who grew up in Sussex and London, was similarly involved in socialist/Marxist politics (Arthur CD 1994). His father was a war invalid, and when his mother died in 1924 he was sent through the British Legion to Australia as a migrant worker, employed mainly on farms and at sheep stations. After his return to England in the 1930s, he joined an intellectual left-wing group that included such prominent figures as Dylan Thomas and A. Leslie Morton, who probably facilitated Lloyd's first contact with the Communist Party. The influence of Morton's *A People's History of England* (1938) became especially obvious when Lloyd developed his Marxist theories of folk music in his influential work *The Singing Englishman*, published in 1942. Lloyd was also vice president of the Workers' Music Association, which had been founded in 1936 to promote the musical activities of the working classes and attracted prominent members such as composers Aaron Copland, Benjamin Britten, and Hanns Eisler.

Lloyd was basically self-educated, having participated extensively in self-education programs in Australia. He started to study folk music intensively in the Reading Room of the British Museum in the mid-1930s. He had already acquired a large repertoire of folk songs in Australia and expanded this even further with thematic material such as whaling songs, which he learned when he went to work for half a year on a factory ship in 1937. He subsequently became a highly respected performer, winning the EFDSS Folk Music Festival Competition at Cecil Sharp House in 1948.

Lloyd started to work for the BBC in 1938 with the radio series *The Voice of the Seamen*. About a year later he broadcast one of the first English radio shows to combine recorded traditional folk music with new material he had collected while visiting Leslie Morton in Suffolk. Due to the Cold War, Lloyd found that his Communist background made employment at the BBC and other journalistic work impossible after 1948. He thus decided to work full-time as a folklorist, writing and lecturing about music for left-wing magazines and groups and undertaking extensive folk song research in Eastern Europe, to which he had, owing to his political connections, more access than most Westerners at that time. The National Coal Board hired him to organize a competition to collect mining songs in 1951, which became the basis for his song collection *Come All Ye Bold Miners*. Despite his background and conflicting ideas, Lloyd joined the EFDSS in 1948 and became a member of the editorial board of the Society's *Folk Music Journal* in 1952. In the same year he formed the Ramblers, who were modeled after Pete Seeger's Almanac Singers.

Lloyd met Ewan MacColl in the early 1950s. Both were convinced that British folk music could provide an antidote to the strongly American-dominated popular music of that time. The Second Revival hence became a very conscious attempt to create a genuinely English music. MacColl, for instance, proceeded in three steps, starting with efforts to popularize the English folk music of the nineteenth century, in particular the sea shanties, followed by "classic" traditional ballads and industrial songs, aiming to convince the younger generation that this music was as vital and good as

American popular music. His last step was the *Radio Ballads* documentary series, produced by Charles Parker, Peggy Seeger, and himself. The *Radio Ballads*, which were very popular from 1958 to 1964, constituted a new approach to broadcasting—a collage of music and original sound recordings and interviews on contemporary social issues. They encompassed a broad range of topics: the life of English railway workers as in the first program's ballad, "John Axon," or teenagers in England and Scotland of the 1960s, herring fishing at the Doggerbank, and boxing. Many songs from these shows entered the revival repertoire; in fact, they became so popular that they were thought to be traditional.

The leftist organizations again played a central role in making this material available to the public in the form of recordings. The Topic Records label became a means of distribution for traditional and folk recordings, since the large recording companies like HMV and Decca showed little interest in folk music at that time. Established by the Workers' Music Association as the Topic Record Club before World War II, Topic went commercial in 1957, insofar as it aimed for a market, with Gerry Sharp as business manager and A. L. Lloyd as artistic director. While Topic's early releases had been mostly songs with a left-wing connection, often with a historic flavor, Lloyd started to build a unique catalogue of Anglo-American music that included traditional British-Irish singers like Phoebe Smith (England) and Sarah Makem (Ireland); the ten-volume series *Folk Songs in Britain*; already established revivalists like Louis Killen, Bob Davenport, Shirley Collins, Ian Campbell, and MacColl; the upcoming generation like Martin Carthy and the Watersons; American singers like Hedy West; and Lloyd's field recordings from Bulgaria and Albania. Lloyd also produced groundbreaking recording projects like his anthology of industrial folk songs, *The Iron Muse* (1956) or *The Bird in the Bush* (1966), a collection of erotic folk songs. Topic, as one of the few labels that has managed to combine the recording business with integrity until the present day, exerted a strong influence on the development of the Second Revival and electric folk, as many musicians not only owned these recordings but also copied their styles.[12]

It was nevertheless the folk clubs, as the main venues of the Second Revival, that became key to the development of a coherent scene. MacColl founded one of the first, the Ballads and Blues Club, in 1953—the predecessor of the highly influential Singers' Club, which served as a model for the design of numerous other clubs. Yet the revival did not take off with this "infrastructure" of radio shows, recording labels, and venues alone. These all had been single, more or less disconnected activities—too small to become a whole movement and too narrow socially, attracting mainly a "middle-class" audience, as MacColl (1990: 300) later criticized in his *Journeyman* with the EFDSS in mind.

The Skiffle Craze (1956–1958)

The broad basis for the Second Revival came almost overnight with the sudden emergence of the skiffle craze in the mid-1950s.[13] *Rolling Stone* (De Curtis and Henke

1992: 200) summarized the skiffle as "a tame brand of pop folk music of which Lonnie Donegan's 'Rock Island Line' was the most memorable example—and trad. (trad. jazz), a watered down recreation of New Orleans jazz displayed on such American hits as Mr. Acker Bilk's 'Stranger on the Shore.'"

Despite its simplified, amateurish character and its brief existence, skiffle played a significant role in the further development of British popular music, as well as in the development of the folk revival. Skiffle had evolved in the United States during the late 1930s, comprising a wide repertoire of work songs, gospel hymns, blues songs, and many old English, Welsh, Scottish, and Irish songs and ballads brought to the States by immigrants. Initially a "poor man's jazz," it incorporated every sound-making device available, including homemade kazoos (combs wrapped in wax paper), washboards, harmonicas, bottles, and bowls—and the very name "skiffle," whose original meaning is unknown, remains closely associated with these unusual instruments. No early recordings from before the 1940s have survived.

Skiffle appeared in Britain in the late 1940s in the repertoire of traditional jazz bands as an incidental entertainment, and was especially taken up by Ken Coyler and Chris Barber. Lonnie Donegan (1931–2002), who had originally been a banjoist in Coyler's Jazz Band, became key to skiffle's further development. After the band's breakup, Donegan continued with Chris Barber's Jazz Band, which featured a skiffle segment in its shows from early on—the album *New Orleans Joys*, released in 1954, included two skiffle tracks with the Lonnie Donegan Skiffle Group. Yet the music remained obscure until Donegan's unexpected success with the Leadbelly song "Rock Island Line"[14] in early 1956, appearing at the top of British and American single charts, only shortly after Bill Haley's "Rock around the Clock."

Before skiffle, making music in postwar Britain had been limited to a small group of professionals only. Within an environment that was completely dominated by the tastes of the commercial music industry with its professional songwriters on London's Denmark Street, skiffle offered fans for the first time the opportunity to change from passive listeners to active performers: the instruments were affordable and the uncomplicated style did not require much musical training to perform. As a simplified version of jazz, redefined for a British audience, the melodic line was replaced by a singer, accompanied by one or two guitars with string bass, washboard, and a rather restrained rhythm section, with the harmonies reduced to I–IV–V patterns. Skiffle thus became a homemade music of an amateurish nature, focusing on the element of participation rather than on musical skills. Ewan MacColl, who ran a skiffle group himself, recalled that "in the space of a single year, the sale of guitars rose by several thousand percent, I understand, in the second year of Skiffle—there came a period when you couldn't walk around without seeing somebody with a guitar slung on their back" (Woods 1973a: 4).

With this hybrid of African American blues, Anglo-American folk, and traditional jazz, many British performers and audiences were apparently also exposed to a range of traditional American and British material for the first time. Around 1957 skiffle bands were mushrooming everywhere, even though their music was often disparaged for its amateurish sound. According to Denselow (Laing et al. 1975: 141), the greater London area alone counted more than 600 groups, the most successful ones being the Vipers, Chas McDevitt, and Johnny Duncan.

Skiffle would probably not have flourished so successfully had the 1950s not also witnessed a change in young people's leisure behavior, combined with a location shift. Previously, youth activities had been extremely restricted, as Dave McAleer points out in his vivid portrayal of British musical life prior to rock 'n' roll:

> Before the mid-50s there were few meeting places for teenagers apart from youth clubs, which were often held in draughty old church halls, or in the function room above the local Co-op [Co-operative store]. At these clubs they were supervised by vicars or parents, and in exchange for the membership fee . . . teenagers would get little more than a cup of tea, a biscuit (which was sometimes extra), a game of table tennis and a chance to chat indoors with their mates. (McAleer 1993: 43)

The mid-1950s experienced the spread of coffee bars as new social centers, with the coin-operated American jukeboxes and Italian coffee machines for espresso and cappuccino as focal points of a teenager's leisure time. London's first music-oriented coffee bar, Studio 51, opened in August 1956. As McAleer describes, the coffee bars provided ideal conditions for the new music:

> The most famous of all the thousands of them was undoubtedly the 2 I's at 57 Old Compton Street, Soho, in the heart of London's West End, which was owned by Paul Lincoln. . . . It was in that cellar that many of the top British stars of 1957–61 got their first break, including Tommy Steele, Cliff Richard. . . . At any given time, you would find about 150 teenagers crammed into the basement, rubbing shoulders with record label A & R men who had come looking for likely new talent. (Ibid.)

The collapse of the skiffle movement in 1958 was almost as rapid as its expansion, leaving Donegan as the sole survivor of this music style while everywhere else rock 'n' roll was taking hold. Skiffle nevertheless was the springboard for a broad range of music. Many performers who would be successful in the 1960s started out with skiffle, including the Shadows as well as Beatles John Lennon and Paul McCartney, who had played in the group the Quarrymen. This was not only true for the popular sector, but also for British jazz, folk, and electric folk musicians. Soon after skiffle had faded away numerous jazz bands started to emerge, and their music became the basis for the British blues and folk revival; future electric folk performers like Martin Carthy, John Renbourn, and Rick Kemp all started with this kind of music. Many of these performers were looking for new material and rooms to play in, and they gradually came into contact with the early folk revivalists and their settings—the folk clubs—that did not differ significantly from the coffee bars and early jazz clubs of those years.[15]

From the Folk Clubs to a Musical Dead End (late 1950s–mid-1960s)

Augmented by a broad array of musicians and supporters from the fading skiffle fad, the number of folk clubs in Britain started to explode in the late 1950s, with a peak around the late 1960s. Run by private organizers and often located in the back rooms of pubs where groups would meet once or twice a week, the clubs were of a strong amateurish nature, with a performance pattern consisting of an opening or warm-up performance by resident or visiting "floor singers" followed by the featured guest performers (MacKinnon 1993). Neither the club organizers nor the majority of musicians made a large amount of money from folk music. Full-time professional musicianship was only possible for the few stars at the top like Martin Carthy or Dave Swarbrick—and even for them it was apparently quite difficult to make a decent living. Despite the outstanding musicianship of performers such as the guitarists Davy Graham, Bert Jansch, or John Renbourn, folk music in England remained associated with its amateur origins and an extremely informal code of dress—a negative connotation it has maintained until the present.[16]

In the early 1960s the folk clubs featured a broad range of music, from traditional, unaccompanied singing to singer/songwriter and blues music, with a strong focus on American music.[17] British popular music had been strongly American-oriented as early as the 1920s. Offering an alternative to old-fashioned pre–World War II forms like music hall songs, American jazz, blues, and other popular forms also represented the ideal of a modern life of progress to the strongly class-oriented British society. This became even more obvious after the war, with American music generally preferred to the contrived products of London's Denmark Street. Despite the growing repertoire of the folk revivalists, the clubs of the 1950s and early 1960s were therefore still strongly dominated by American music, and skiffle groups played predominantly American songs as well.

By the mid-1960s, however, the situation had completely changed. As contemporary accounts indicate, so strongly had British-Irish folk music come to dominate the clubs that many musicians started to complain about their narrow-mindedness. The turn to traditional music had apparently been a very conscious process, partly coming from earlier-generation musicians like Cyril Tawney or Louis Killen who had started to explore their heritage. It was especially Ewan MacColl, however, who had a strong influence on the revival's further development. His Singers' Club and the Troubador were the main venues for popular performers such as Lloyd, Killen, Seamus Ennis, Peggy Seeger, and later Martin Carthy, Davy Graham, Bert Jansch, John Renbourn, Peter Bellamy, and Sandy Denny. Although he had played a lot of American and skiffle material in his early career, MacColl changed the politics of his club radically in the late 1950s. Noticing that some performers were singing in dialects or foreign languages they were not comfortable with, he decreed that they could sing only in the language they spoke or had grown up with.[18] MacColl also wanted the musicians to observe a somewhat "authentic" style, singing unaccompanied or using traditional instruments such as fiddle or concertina, with guitars and banjos kept in the background. These ideas were soon taken up by many other clubs, which created a highly restrictive atmosphere; even though MacColl was respected as the central organizational figure of the Second Revival, his dogmatic ways began to alienate many musicians.

The increasing rigidity of the clubs caused many leading performers to reject the clubs. At the end of the 1960s, as Denselow (Laing et al. 1975: 142) described, not only had the clubs started to focus on particular styles (e.g., traditional or blues music) that excluded other approaches, but the so-called traditionalists had increasingly gained the upper hand and created an atmosphere that was governed by the ideal of performing "authentic" music in the form of strictly unaccompanied singing. This exaggerated traditionalism had taken on a very contradictory character, as the revival had developed a stricter performance practice than the tradition itself.

As a result, many skilled performers who had been experimenting with new and more contemporary means of musical expression found themselves trapped in a museum-like culture (which did, in this respect, not differ that much from the EFDSS)—or were even attacked by the hard-core scene. These difficulties were especially the case with Shirley Collins, with Martin Carthy and Dave Swarbrick, and with many of the so-called folk baroque guitar players like Graham, Jansch, and Renbourn. Many other musicians also wanted to make a better living from a music that had existed until then outside the marketplace. Just at that point, while the movement in the clubs stagnated and the dissatisfaction grew, other performers coming from different musical directions like jazz and rock started to discover the traditional material, thereby giving fresh impulses for a further folk revival.

The Electric Folk Years (1967–1975)

There is still no better way to get an impression of the ebb and flow of the numerous popular musical styles in Great Britain between the mid-1960s and early 1970s than by leafing through the pages of *Melody Maker*. Moreover, the early *Melody Maker* provides a revealing glimpse of how the extensively covered American scene was perceived as a model in Britain—and vice versa. One of the major issues of the 1960s was not only which Americans were visiting Britain, but also how British groups were accepted in the States, especially during the "British invasion."

The year 1965 marked the beginning awareness within the mainstream media of the already extant movement that was later called the "Second British Folk Revival." As was the case with popular music before the Beatles, *Melody Maker*'s early coverage of folk music was still clearly focused on American performers like Bob Dylan, Pete Seeger, Judy Collins, and Joan Baez and their visits to Britain. *Melody Maker* title pages featured headlines such as "Suddenly, It's Folk—Folk Boom on the Way: Record companies release more discs in the belief that folk is the new 'in thing'" (February 13, 1965), referring to the American scene and particularly to Dylan. On March 6, 1965, the paper announced the sensational news "Dylan to Tour Britain"—and Dylan's 1966 tour became the fastest sellout Britain had ever experienced. Dylan's folksinger image was prevalent; the Beatles, for instance, showed a clear fascination for his attitude, dress, and "the way he sings discords and plays discords. The way he sends up everything," as George Harrison commented in a *Melody Maker* interview (Coleman 1966: 3). *Melody Maker*, like its American counterparts, was scandalized by Dylan's electrification: on May 14, 1966, Max Jones pleaded, "Will the real BOB DYLAN please stand up!"

Yet the popularity of the American folk revival raised British music journalists' awareness of long existent developments in Britain. Around that time, the English revival began to receive increasingly more space in the magazine, covering performers like A. L. Lloyd, Ewan MacColl, Anne Briggs, and Shirley Collins as a relatively homogenous group. With its growing popularity, this music scene got its own space in *Melody Maker*, first with a short "Focus on Folk" (1965) and then about two years later—while the paper's rock music features described "Freaking Out with the Pink Floyd" (April 1, 1967)—with a "Folk Forum" that comprised one or two full pages. Although the clubs were still mushrooming—evident in the fact that the number of ads for English folk club venues and singers were taking up increasing amounts of magazine space, the musical development within the clubs was, ironically, already dead-ended.

What could be read about the revival in *Melody Maker*, however, remained at the "star" level, concentrating on performers like Shirley Collins, whose experiments would later appear on the progressive Harvest label, and distinctive groups such as the Watersons or the Young Tradition. Yet the increased visibility of folk and electric folk on a more popular level played an important role in reinforcing the awareness and interest in the earlier "authentic" tradition, which is evident in the fact that articles occasionally included the "stars" of traditional music like the English singer Harry Cox, who appeared next to an article on David Bowie, or the Scottish Traveller[19] and singer Jeannie Robertson, who was profiled as "Jeannie—Queen among the Heather" (Dallas 1968c).

At the same time, a broad variety of unusual new styles started to develop. Britain in particular witnessed the emergence of a large number of highly individual musical forms that have become part of popular music history and are still copied or cited as influential. The Beatles and the Rolling Stones headed the "British invasion" in the States in 1964–65, and around 1967 the so-called progressive rock scene started to emerge, with highly popular groups like the Cream, Yes, or Soft Machine now taking up much space in *Melody Maker*. Electric folk, which began at around the same time, occupied, together with the Second Revival, a comparatively small niche in the magazine for a period of roughly ten years.

Although the beginnings of what was later to be known as electric folk were already indicated in January 1965, when *Melody Maker* took note of "that unique duo Shirley Collins and Davy Graham," it was particularly the ad for Pentangle's debut album in 1967, featuring the black silhouettes of five musicians, that revealed much more significantly the development of something new. Placed between the weekly announcements of the folk clubs and booking addresses of individual folk performers, the look of this ad displayed clearly the hybrid character of a musical style that did not seem to fit any of the existing categories. Pentangle, founded by the outstanding folk/blues/jazz guitarists Bert Jansch and John Renbourn, quickly developed a highly complex musical style with extended instrumental passages, frequent time changes, unusual rhythmic patterns, open tunings, stylistic fusions, and unusual instruments like the glockenspiel, sitar, and banjo. Its eclectic repertoire encompassed not only old English ballads but also dance tunes from the Renaissance, blues, jazz classics, and original compositions.

Pentangle was not the first and only folk-based group to experiment so boldly: Davy Graham had experimented with fusion styles as early as 1962–63, later also teaming up with Shirley Collins, who, together with her sister Dolly, had developed a new accompaniment style by using a portable organ and adapting settings and instrumentations from medieval and Renaissance music. Likewise, the Incredible String Band—whose members also started in the folk clubs and later settled between psychedelic/progressive rock and electric folk—created numerous daring instrumental fusions and thus provided the ground for further musical experiments, anticipating much of what would follow with the boom of "world music" in the 1990s.

The year 1969 was not only a high point for American blues/rock singer Janis Joplin, who was "breaking down the walls in Britain" (May 3). It also marked a first peak of the emerging electric folk genre. *Melody Maker* journalists suddenly wrote about "Hung Up on Sackbuts and Crumbhorns" [sic] (Dallas 1969), and it was almost impossible to ignore the large ads for Fairport Convention's album *Liege & Lief*, while the group's former lead singer Sandy Denny covered the front page as "Singer of the Year" on September 19, 1970. Fairport Convention, a band that was just taking its first steps from covering American songs to original songwriting in the developing progressive scene, had been joined by folk club singer Denny in 1968. It subsequently started to incorporate traditional ballads and songs into its repertoire, most clearly displayed on the album *Liege & Lief* (1969), which contained mostly traditional pieces played on contemporary rock instruments and has influenced British musicians for several generations.

Also around that time, many other new bands started to emerge, the most prominent one being Steeleye Span. Founded in 1969 by former Fairport Convention member Ashley Hutchings, this group took the combination of folk and rock to a further extreme: although the material was almost exclusively traditional, the instrumental sound, with its stronger emphasis on bass and later also drums, was much harder-edged.

Hutchings left Steeleye in 1971 to found the Albion Country Band (later the Albion Band). The first lineup of the Albions had assembled to accompany Shirley

Collins, for the recording of *No Roses*. Other musicians and groups tried to continue in a newly composed but folk-related style, like Mr. Fox—a band that was highly promoted in the wake of the popularity of Pentangle, Fairport Convention, and Steeleye Span, but which disbanded in 1971. The former Fairport Convention members Sandy Denny and Richard Thompson would often later incorporate musical and textual elements of traditional music into their songwriting.

Between 1972 and 1975, at a time when Alice Cooper was decorating *Melody Maker's* title pages and Roxy Music was promoting "glam rock," electric folk reached its commercial peak. Steeleye Span dominated the charts with the sixteenth-century Christmas carol "Gaudete" (1972) and the traditional song "All around My Hat" (1975), while Maddy Prior appeared on *Melody Maker's* title page with Jethro Tull's Ian Anderson on November 3, 1973.

Although Lloyd and MacColl had remained stout Marxists and although some of the mid-1960s folk audience had been closely connected with the Campaign for Nuclear Disarmament (CND) demonstrations and the Easter Marches at Trafalgar Square, politics seemed to play only a marginal role for most later musicians of the folk clubs as well as for the electric folk scene. The emergence of the electric hybrid musical form was nevertheless embedded in a heated cultural dispute. In particular, the contemporary folk club scene, as well as the EFDSS (which remained one of the major resources for the musical repertoire), often attacked electric folk performers for their irreverent musical and editorial treatment of the traditional material.

Disappearance of Electric Folk and the Emergence of Folk Rock (late 1970s)

Despite the large variety of approaches and possibilities, the electric folk direction seemed to have come to a dead end by the late 1970s. Pentangle had already disappeared in 1972, and its members were pursuing individual solo projects, often without much public recognition. Fairport Convention, struggling with numerous member changes, announced its breakup in 1979. Likewise, Steeleye Span recorded several albums that were extremely unsuccessful and disbanded at the end of the 1970s. Furthermore, Fairport Convention singer Sandy Denny, who had not found sustained success as a soloist, died tragically in 1978, while guitarist Richard Thompson, who had made a number of highly praised solo recordings, became a member of the Sufi community and did not record between 1975 and 1978. Ashley Hutchings disappeared from the scene between 1980 and 1985, and Fairport's lead singer and fiddle player Dave Swarbrick increasingly suffered from ear problems, finding it impossible to continue with an electric band.

As early as 1975, *Electric Muse* coauthor Robin Denselow had been doubtful about the further development of this style. Fred Woods seemed to confirm this negative view when he wrote cynically that "Steeleye Span collapsed in ruins in 1978; groups such as Horslips, Hedgehog Pie, Lindisfarne and the ICS Band have either died ingloriously or transmuted into something else" (1979: 66).

The explanations for electric folk's commercial failure and disappearance from public notice varied. Echoing the viewpoints of American leftist critics, some British writers such as Woods regarded the commercialization of folk and traditional music as the main cause for its disappearance (ibid.).[20] Others, like journalist John Tobler, saw the problem in the change of popular musical taste during that time:

> Steeleye made this wonderful album called *Sails of Silver*. Produced by Gus Dudgeon who produced all the Elton John hits. But nobody bought it at all. Nobody cared! Because they felt that it was old-fashioned and the musicians were old-looking. There was a lot of snobbishness about that at the time. Musicians had to be young! So the folk people just went underground for a while.

Electric folk had initially developed from the connection of folk music with contemporary popular music styles of the 1960s and 1970s. The styles in popular music continued to change, but not the rock elements that had been integrated into electric folk, despite the abundant musical creativity apparent on the recordings. Consequently, the groups experienced a sinking popularity. Compared to new styles like punk (ca. 1975), disco, new wave (ca. 1976), or funk (ca. 1979), electric folk became anachronistic and disappeared finally from mainstream public notice in the late 1970s.

The emergence of punk seemed to exert an especially strong influence upon that process, leading also in a completely different direction: While the old electric folk groups seemed to have disappeared, one could observe a modified folk rock direction coming into being. Based on an approach that had started not much later than the original electric folk with groups like Lindisfarne or Horslips, it would combine rock music as the basic material with styles and sounds reminiscent of folk music, using instruments such as electric amplified accordions, melodeons, fiddles, and mandolins, and incorporating unspecifiable melodic folk fragments. While, for instance, Steeleye Span singer Maddy Prior had originally tried to perform Scottish songs with a Scottish accent, now Irish, Scottish, and English elements were mixed in an unidentifiable blend. The early electric folk groups had occasionally incorporated traditional elements and also often based their songwriting on traditional topics, but this practice disappeared almost completely with the new groups like the Pogues and the Levellers. Socially critical and political songs were prevalent in the repertoire of these groups, while traditional material played only a marginal role. The Oysterband took a middle position between electric folk and the new folk rock. Originally a céilidh dance band, the group increasingly adapted rock music techniques and socially critical material into its repertoire.

Reemergence (mid-1980s until the present)

Having disappeared from public notice—Mark Slobin's "supercultural network"—did not mean, very much in contrast to what critics had predicted, that electric folk had reached a final end. Many performers started to work (as they had already done before) as studio musicians and to pursue their own projects, independent from popular music styles. Around the middle to late 1980s, with the emergence of new independent recording labels, major groups such as Pentangle, Steeleye Span, and Fairport Convention started to reassemble, although often as part-time bands, and to record again. Now covered by specialist magazines like *fRoots* or *Dirty Linen* rather than popular music publications, the performers reestablished a musical existence very much outside mainstream notice, with a few exceptions such as Richard Thompson, who became an internationally acclaimed guitarist and songwriter.

Most remarkable was the history of Fairport Convention. After their breakup in 1979, the band members met again in the following year to repeat the farewell concert they had given in Cropredy (Oxfordshire)—which in subsequent years turned into one of the largest folk rock festivals in Europe.

The reissue of electric folk recordings on CD beginning the early 1990s has given this genre a new popularity and presented it to a new generation. In contrast to the 1960s and '70s, when A. L. Lloyd and Ewan MacColl were regarded as the authorities on the scene, it is now the Second Revival and electric folk musicians, most prominently Martin Carthy, Dave Swarbrick, and Ashley Hutchings, who are cited and celebrated as pioneers. The electric folk movement of the 1960s and 1970s has now acquired a cult status as a model for other contemporary approaches to folk music. This is the case not only in other European countries but also in the United States, which originally supplied the models for the British revival and electric folk scenes.

TWO

A QUESTION OF DEFINITION
Traditional and Popular Music

> Some people thought we were ruining the songs, but tunes and lyrics have been recycled, stolen and changed forever. That's what makes the tradition a living instead of a dead thing.

STEELEYE SPAN SINGER MADDY PRIOR

A revival genre like electric folk illustrates well the difficulty—and artificiality—of a complete separation of art, folk, and popular music. Classified as a "hybrid" music form, it neither seems to fit any definition of traditional musics nor the concept of rock music as a primarily commercial product. Likewise, it has always been strongly attacked from the outside—by the hard-core folk club scene, with its ideal of an unaccompanied singing style, as well as by various theoretical advocates who have automatically equated electric music with commercialism and thus with mediocrity. As Maddy Prior's remark indicates, however, traditional music has always been mixed with and used by other forms of music as well.

This controversy of electric versus traditional has particularly been influenced by Cecil Sharp. Although his definition of folk music was developed not so much to describe processes but rather to serve a theoretical concept—the romantic idealization of the tradition by its separation from other forms of music—it subsequently became almost accepted as a fact. This chapter will therefore first discuss Sharp's approach before investigating further concepts regarding the relationships of traditional, folk, and popular music.

ELECTRIC FOLK AND TRADITIONAL ENGLISH MUSIC: A DIFFICULT HERITAGE

As Helen Myers (1993) pointed out in her survey of British folk song study, traditional material was published as early as the late fifteenth century—the oldest surviving print at present is a broadside collection of Robin Hood ballads that was published by Wynkyn de Worde around 1495. While these broadsides were single sheets of paper in folio size, printed on one side only, one could observe the emergence of distinct, comprehensive song and tune collections about two hundred years later. Larger compilations like John Playford's *The English Dancing Master* (1651) were an exception in the seventeenth century, but the number of publications increased significantly from the early eighteenth century on, although they lacked a coherent systematic approach. Collections like Thomas D'Urfey's *Wit and Mirth; or, Pills to Purge Melancholy* (1719–20) and Bishop Thomas Percy's *Reliques of Ancient English Poetry* (1765) usually drew from a mixture of sources, mostly printed and heavily edited, but also from personal compositions, and, occasionally, oral material.[1] The predominance of printed sources in folk song collections shifted only slowly to material collected from living singers—as was the case with Joseph Ritson's *The Bishopric Garland* (1784) or the works of the Scottish collectors Robert Burns (with James Johnson, *The Scots Musical Museum*, 1787–1803) and Sir Walter Scott (*Minstrelsy of the Scottish Border*, 1802). The new focus on the living tradition became particularly evident with John Broadwood (*Old English Songs*, 1843) and Rev. Sabine Baring-Gould (*Songs and Ballads of the West: A Collection Made from the Mouths of the People*, 1889–92), who also provided background information about their informants for the first time.

The late nineteenth century marked a change to a more systematic scholarship and institutionalized collecting activities. Scholars and well-to-do individuals began to establish extensive written collections. These collectors included Harvard professor Francis James Child (1825–1896); Frank Kidson (1855–1926) and Lucy Broadwood (1858–1929), both founding members of the Folk Song Society in 1898; English music teacher Cecil J. Sharp (1859–1924) and his assistant Maud Karpeles (1885–1976); composer Ralph Vaughan Williams (1872–1951); and Australian composer and pianist Percy Grainger (1882–1961), who also collected recordings. These nineteenth-century collectors were also figural in developing the first major theories about traditional music.

The Romanticized Nineteenth-Century Picture of Traditional Music: Cecil Sharp

Two collections in particular became well known—*The English and Scottish Popular Ballads* (Boston, 8 parts, 1882–92), by Francis James Child, and *Folk Songs from Somerset* (London, 5 vols., 1904–9) by Cecil J. Sharp and Rev. Charles L. Marson. While Child's eight volumes of textual variants—which were only later completed by Bertrand Harris Bronson's tune collection (Princeton 1959–72)—have shaped the picture of the Anglo-American ballads (known as the "Child ballads") by the material they included, Cecil Sharp was especially influential as a theorist on the further development and present role of folk song in England.

Sharp did not begin collecting folk songs until he was forty-four years old. According to the often-repeated story, he discovered his first folk song during a stay at Rev. Charles Marson's place in Hambridge (Somerset), where he heard the vicarage gardener John England singing "The Seeds of Love," which became the starting point for his extensive occupation with English folk song. Sharp not only began to collect, but also soon started to lecture on this subject, later also joining the already existing Folk Song Society to publish and promote his material.

Sharp and his contemporaries were motivated to collect folk songs by a shared anxiety. Because England was the starting point of the Industrial Revolution, social and structural changes became evident much earlier and were more pronounced than in neighboring countries. As can be inferred from Sharp's writings, his collecting activities were driven by the wish to save the last remnants of the tradition. He pointed out that many of the old singers were already gone or quite advanced in years; the last generation of folk singers (by his estimation) had been born around 1840 (Sharp 1907: 127–28).

At the same time, a clearly nationalistic attitude, characteristic of the late nineteenth century in general, can also be read in Sharp's activities. Music historians can observe the emergence at that time of distinct national styles or schools that drew strongly on indigenous folk music idioms. This movement, which began around 1860, is obvious in Sharp's writings, such as *English Folk-Song: Some Conclusions* (1907), where he argued that England did not have an individual classical musical style. Until then, art music in England had been strongly dominated by foreign composers, predominantly the German Romantics like Mendelssohn and Wagner, who became the main targets of the so-called English Musical Renaissance that emerged in an atmosphere of increasing nationalism around 1880 and 1914 (Hughes and Stradling 2001).

The national school, or "pastoral school," that developed with composers Ralph Vaughan Williams, Gustav Holst, and Edward Elgar, was based on the idea—also shared by Sharp—that the national musical idiom of England was to be found in a particular musical genre, the folk song, which became the basis for various new works at that time. For instance, Vaughan Williams first worked with arrangements of folk songs, later mixing elements like characteristic modal structures, melodic contours, and rhythms with elements of European Romanticism, as represented by Schumann, Brahms, and Wagner. A good example of this style is his romance for violin and orchestra, *The Lark Ascending* (1925). Inspired by George Meredith's poem of the same name, the composition evokes the picture of an idyllic countryside that has become closely associated with romanticized images of England in general (such as the cottages, embedded in soft, green hills, depicted in the paintings of John Constable). While the lark is suggested very directly by the violin through musical imitations such as trills or ascending and descending scales, the rural landscape and tranquil morning atmosphere are expressed through folk song material in an almost abstract way: the orchestral score never directly quotes a complete folk song but rather contains modal structures or melodic phrases the composer had collected from folk material. Other major pastoral compositions included Vaughan Williams's *Five Variants of "Dives and Lazarus"* for string orchestra and harp (1939), Frederick Delius's *Brigg Fair* (1907), and Holst's *A Somerset Rhapsody* (1906–7). Grainger, Vaughan Williams, and Holst also wrote numerous folk song arrangements for various instruments and combinations.

The idea of folk song as the ideal(ized) embodiment of the remote and unspoiled countryside can be found in many theories of the eighteenth and nineteenth century, most clearly elaborated in the case of Sharp, whose principal ideas are expounded in *English Folk-Song: Some Conclusions* and in the introduction to the collection *Folk Songs from Somerset*. Like Vaughan Williams, he clearly had a firm concept of English folk song in mind when he started to collect more than 5,000 tunes. In discussing the term "folk song" and its German origin, in particular Carl Engel's concept of "national music,"[2] Sharp (1907: 3) based his definition on Funk and Wagnall's *Standard Dictionary*, according to which folk song is "a song or ballad originating and current among the common people, and illustrating the common life with its interests and enthusiasms as derived from legend or story; also a lyric poem on a popular theme in the style of such a ballad." Subsequently Sharp (ibid.) defined the term folk song as "the song which has been created by the common people, in contradistinction to the songs, popular or otherwise, which have been composed by the educated."

This basic definition was elaborated further in subsequent chapters of *English Folk-Song*. Folk song is created by the "common people," that is, the noneducated or "unlettered," most clearly embodied in the prototype of the agricultural workers who, in Sharp's idealized view, passed on their songs orally. Sharp hereby clearly followed the earlier concepts of Johann Gottfried Herder, who had coined the term "Volkslied" and pointed out major characteristics of folk song, such as being a part of the illiterate (rural) in a literate (urban) society. Herder and Sharp believed folk song to be communal in two ways: its authors are unknown, and it can be considered to reflect the mind of a community. Here Sharp made an explicit contrast with art music that is, in his definition, the work of an individual, expressing personal ideals only and fixed in an unaltered form on paper. Sharp made an explicit reference to the German brothers Jacob and Wilhelm Grimm, who denied that folk song could have a composer but "makes itself,"—in other words, as Sharp clarified, is the product of continual changes and additions over a long period of time (ibid.: 8).[3]

Regarding the evolution of folk song, Sharp posited a Darwinist system with central aspects of continuity, selection, and evolution. Continuity signified that "insistence of type must be the rule and variation the exception" (ibid.: 16), for Sharp had noticed that many songs had an obvious constancy of text. Often, strikingly similar versions were performed by various people in different regions with an amazing accuracy in reproduction evident when singers were asked to repeat a performance. Variation, in contrast, occurred predominantly on a musical level; according to Sharp, folksingers therefore set more importance on the words than on the tune—which could exist in numerous variants of melodies, modes, and rhythms. Selection occurred in the sense that, as in biology, only those folk tunes survived that served the interests of the community.

Sharp's conception of folk song is characterized throughout by the romanticized Victorian ideal of a pure tradition that exists only in remote rural areas, a notion clearly revealed in the following description:

> Folk-song, unknown in the drawing room, hunted out of the school, chased by the chapel deacons, derided by the middle classes, and despised by those who have been uneducated into the three R's, takes refuge in the fastness of tap-rooms, poor cottages and outlying hamlets. It harbours in the heathen kingdoms and the wilder parts. . . . It comes out very shyly, late at night, and is heard when the gentry have gone home to bed, when the barrack-room has exhausted its Music hall menu. It is to be found when men have well drunk. (Sharp and Marson 1904–9: xi–xii)

Sharp hence depicted English folk song as an unspoiled counterpoint not only to art music, but also to popular music. He must have been well aware of contemporary outside influences on English folk music, such as the Irish immigrant workers and popular music forms such as broadside ballads and music hall songs. Yet he set the traditional material clearly apart from these musical cultures, at the same time also ignoring other strongly present traditional forms like industrial music. Possibly driven by nostalgia as well, Sharp discounted the interaction with contemporaneous commercial music; popular music—predominantly music hall songs at the time—was perceived by him and contemporaneous collectors such as Sir Hubert Parry as "shabby."[4]

Probably due to Sharp's extensive lecture activity, this romanticized view of folk songs as "simple, unaccompanied tunes, with words about country life, seafaring, lore and perhaps the odd one dealing with mills, mines and masters," as Harker (1985: ix) put it cynically, was adopted by the general public and especially by the EFDSS. Even Sharp's critics could not escape his conceptions. As Middleton (1995: 133) points out, A. L. Lloyd added the aspect of the work song, yet he romanticized his workers just as Sharp had romanticized his peasants.

Sharp's concepts have remained highly influential until present. His assistant Maud Karpeles was one of the founding members of the International Folk Music Council (IFMC) in 1947 (from 1981, the International Council for Traditional Music) and subsequently served as its secretary. Many of Sharp's ideas are reflected, partly unchanged, in the "official" definition of folk music that the IFMC drafted in 1954 and published a year later:

> Folk music is the product of a musical tradition that has been evolved through the process of oral transmission. The factors that shape the tradition are: (i) continuity which links the present with the past; (ii) variation which springs from the creative impulse of the individual or the group; (iii) selection by the community, which determines the form or forms in which the music survives.

The term can be applied to music that has been evolved from rudimentary beginnings by a community uninfluenced by popular and art music and it can likewise be applied to music which has originated with an individual composer and has subsequently been absorbed into the unwritten living tradition of a community.

The term does not cover composed popular music that has been taken over ready-made by a community and remains unchanged, for it is the re-fashioning and re-creation of the music by the community that gives it its folk character.

This definition follows Sharp in almost every point, not only concerning the major criteria of continuation, variation, and selection, but even in the absolute separation of traditional and popular music. As Karpeles (1955) emphasized, the major departure from Sharp's definition lies in the omitted specification of the origin of folk music, as the focus in the IFMC definition is clearly on process. Intended as an abstract model that could be applied to any form of traditional music, it is nevertheless based on a concept that did not correspond with reality at all, but was rather the construct of an elite eighteenth- and nineteenth-century worldview.

Deconstructing Sharp: Some Observations Regarding the English Tradition

Despite—or maybe because of—his strong influence, Sharp eventually became the target for substantial criticism. Although critical restudies began to appear in the 1970s, such as Ronald Pearsall's *Victorian Popular Music* (1973), the central debate around Cecil Sharp particularly emerged with Dave Harker's *Fakesong* (1985), a critical analysis of the folk song concept. In many parts provocative in its neo-Marxist arguments, combined with an ironic, occasionally overgeneralized style,[5] Harker's study nevertheless set in motion a healthy debate, especially concerning the role of the EFDSS. In addition to Harker, a number of historical studies and restudies, such as Hughes and Stradling (2001) and Sykes (1993), reviewed not only of Sharp's data but also the sociocultural background of the late nineteenth century, helping to develop a more nuanced picture by casting a different light on the juxtaposition of the electric (commercial) revival and the acoustic tradition. Particular points of criticism included the ideal of a "pure" English folk music that could be clearly differentiated from the neighboring traditions, the strict separation of traditional music from popular/commercial music, the insistence on industrialization as the main cause of the tradition's decline, and the equation of traditional music with oral transmission.

The Ideal of a "Pure" English Folk Music

Within his concept of English folk song, Sharp also clarified its musical characteristics, including modal tonalities, uneven metric structures such as 5/4 (often due to the transcription of the so-called ballad meter, i.e., iambic lines of alternating four- and three-foot lengths), and strophic form (see also Nettl 1990: 58–68). While these features can indeed be confirmed by a musical analysis, it has still been difficult to determine a "true" English folk music that differs from the Gaelic repertoire of neighboring Scotland and Ireland. Except for some distinct forms like mummers' plays and morris dances, and a vocal style that can only be vaguely described, the general body of traditional music performed in England shows many characteristics that are similar to the music from Scotland and Ireland. In addition, as Pearsall (1973) has pointed out, many Scottish and particularly Irish versions permeated the English repertoire at the turn of the nineteenth century.

The Strict Separation of Traditional Music from Popular—or Commercial—Music

The idealized concept of English folk song found its clearest musical expression in what was associated with the term "Child ballad," referring to the ballads published in Francis James Child's five volumes of *The English and Scottish Popular Ballads*. Songs like "The Two Sisters" (Child Ballad no. 2), "Lord Randall" (no. 12), "Edward" (no. 13), and "The House Carpenter" (no. 243) indeed share several common characteristics. All are stories about essential human conflicts—often love stories with tragic ends—that are told in a highly concentrated form by a dispassionate narrator, with various stylistic elements like retrospective dialogue or formularized phrases such as "milk-white steed" or "lily-white hand." Such ballads are not restricted to the British tradition alone, but can be found all over Europe. Yet, as Harker (1985) emphasized, they by no means form the kind of unity that has been ascribed to them since the first edition was published. Rather, Child's collection is a compilation of earlier collections, of which Sir Walter Scott's and Bishop Thomas Percy's songs make up about 25 percent. Child edited much of this material to conform with his moral ideals and theoretical concepts, including the so-called ballad meter, and though he intended to omit commercial material like broadside ballads, several pieces are of that origin (Harker 1985: 113–17).

The repertoire of traditional performers has been much broader than Sharp's and Child's collections lead their readers to believe, and it is also incorrect to speak of a dilution of the tradition through an emerging popular mass music, for traditional music has not existed within a vacuum. On the contrary, it has clearly interacted with contemporaneous forms of popular music, and many traditional singers perceived "the old songs and ballads" as one of many types of music, although they stood out from the other repertoire. Similarly, the Child ballads have played a central role in the repertoire of many performers. Yet one has to wonder if this is because of the influence of Child—or if this was already the case before these ballads became known as the Child ballads.

Scottish Traveller Jeannie Robertson, for instance, "had picked up a few Harry Lauder songs, a half-dozen music-hall pieces, and a handful of cowboy or 'sentimental' ballads of American origin, mainly from gramophone recordings" in her earlier years, as her biographers Porter and Gower (1995: 77) observed. After she became renowned as a traditional singer, however, this part of her repertoire (which was about 10 percent, Porter and Gower estimated) was no longer evident after 1953. Likewise, Sussex singer Shirley Collins pointed out that her grandmother also sang music hall songs at home. Collins herself learned to sing at church but also listened to many other forms of music, such as early baroque music. Folk songs were regarded as rather intimate material that was performed at home instead of onstage—while other, more functional music was performed in public, like the dance music her grandfather played with his little band.

The interaction of these different levels was also evident in the nineteenth century, when many folk song collections were established. The advent of industrialization brought not only the development of new forms of folk songs—such as labor songs— owing to changing working conditions, but also an explosion of urban song and an urban music industry that had a strong impact on the traditional repertoire. This whole complex, however, was completely ignored by Sharp. It was not until Ewan MacColl and A. L. Lloyd that performers, researchers, as well as the general public became aware of the existence of industrial song.

Sharp's strict separation of folk music from popular music, to which he had a strong aversion, can be further explained by taking a look at the changes English musical life had undergone in the nineteenth century. As Middleton (1995: 13–14) has pointed out, the 1890s in particular witnessed the development of new methods of mass production, publishing, and distribution systems in the English music business. It further expanded after the First World War with a centralized publishing system and the growth of the radio and gramophone companies along with the emergence of jazz, Tin Pan Alley songs, and new dance forms.

Yet this was only a second—or even third—step in a long process of development. Music had already been distributed in a precommercial form (if one can speak about such systems at that time) from the sixteenth century on in the form of broadsides. Sold in the nineteenth century for approximately a half-penny, a broadside could contain songs or ballads, as well as contemporary news or literature. Broadsides were a large business; Karpeles (1987: 69) estimated that during the first half of the nineteenth century around fifty broadside printers existed in London alone, and Pearsall (1973: 211–12) concluded that a ballad about the murder of Maria Martin, which had taken place in 1827, sold 1,650,000 copies. Broadsides were often composed by a single author and either set to a popular tune or a partly reworked traditional tune. Companies would often send paid men into rural areas to collect tunes solely for these commercial purposes. As many of these tunes were often well known, they were in most cases not printed on the sheets, but instead indicated by the remark "To the tune of" (Pearsall 1973: 212).[6]

Broadsides remained popular until the Victorian age and were often used by traditional singers who merged this material with the other repertoire. Popular folk songs of the Second Revival like "The Foggy Dew," "The False Bride" (published between 1685–88 as "The Forlorn Lover"), the transportation ballad "Van Diemen's Land," and

"All around My Hat," which was also a well-known street song in the 1830s, first appeared as broadside ballads. In many cases, however, popular ballads from the oral tradition were also printed as broadsides so that both forms existed simultaneously, making it difficult to establish which form may have influenced the other. The Child
ballad "Tam Lin," for instance, was printed on a broadside in 1558—but it also seems
to have been around before that. Likewise, "The Seeds of Love" and "The Spotted
Cow" existed in both forms (Kennedy 1984).

Nineteenth-century England offered a huge market for music publishing, with do-
mestic music making ("piano in the parlour") flourishing as one of the major leisure
occupations of middle-class and upper-working-class households (Sykes 1993: 404).[7]
Furthermore, public life at that time witnessed the emergence of various kinds of public house entertainment, as well as brass bands and the increasingly popular choral
trend. However, as Russell emphasized in his extensive study, *Popular Music in England*,
the most striking feature of nineteenth-century music history was probably the emergence of the music hall industry in the middle of the century. It is difficult to establish
an exact date, as the early predecessors—something between a singing saloon and a
music hall—were already present before the term was first used. Usually Charles
Morton is attributed as the founder of the "first" music hall in 1849. After 1860, however, the term was regularly used to refer to a "place of elevating entertainment for the
people" (Russell 1987: 75).[8]

The music hall business emerged gradually. Music halls became extremely popular
in the 1860s, when the business began to crystallize and the "music hall 'star,' an individual performer with a defined stage persona, was beginning to emerge" (Russell 1987:
77). In the 1880s, short-lived locations were increasingly replaced by more permanent
sites, while in the 1890s, the drink trande—that had been a major component of the
business—became less important financially and the entertainment itself became the
main product. By around 1914, the business, now more centralized, had become a
fairly respectable mass entertainment industry, which was also reflected in the audience structure. In the early stages, many singers and most of the audience had come
from a working-class background, but increasingly the halls were frequented by the
middle class as well.

The entertainment in music halls did not consist exclusively of music, but also included acrobatics, juggling, dogs, birds, sketches (from the 1890s), as well as segments
from opera and ballet. Many new songs with a wide range of subjects emerged within
the music hall environment. Often funny or sentimental, the songs addressed the conditions of daily life very directly. The majority of the writers and composers, apart
from singer-writers like Charles Coburn, remained faceless. The music hall repertoire
was, like the broadside, absorbed into the traditional repertoire, yet these songs rarely
ever appeared in early collections—although Sharp must have known them well, as
well as industrial songs like "The Factory Girl" and "The Forlorn Weaver."

Sharp's apparently deliberate decision to ignore music hall material has to be understood within the context of the utilitarian and empirical thinking of Victorian England, which generally had a (partly contradictory) poor opinion of music, as the studies of Hughes and Stradling (2001) and Pearsall (1973) demonstrate. Although the educational value of classical music was accepted, music halls were rejected because they had always been associated with images of drunkenness and depravity. Sharp's idealized concept of folk song can hence be seen as a clear countermovement against this spirit of his time.

The Disappearance of the Tradition

Sharp and his successors blamed industrialization for the marginalization and increasing disappearance of traditional music. Although it cannot be denied that industrialization was the primary cause of the structural changes that would affect traditional lifestyles (e.g., by the emigration to the cities), it was not, however, the only one. Chris Bartram (1996), for instance, has argued convincingly that the disappearance of fiddle music in southern England was a by-product of structural changes within the Anglican church that led to the demise of the old church bands and introduced choirs and church organs. This development was furthered by the introduction of new instruments that led to the evolution of the village brass and silver bands and the popularity of modern dances like the foxtrot. The old bands (composed of wind instruments, boxwood clarinet, fiddle, bass viol, serpent, and cornet), which had played not only at church services but also at local dance events, gradually became superfluous: "Deprived of their vital place in society the old bands stopped practicing, and eventually died out" (Bartram 1996: 2).

The Exclusiveness of Oral Transmission

Although orality is a key feature in the transmission of traditional music, it is not as exclusive as may seem. Sharp's characterization of the archetypal folksinger as an illiterate agricultural laborer bound to oral transmission seems to have been an idealized notion. As Sykes has demonstrated, the majority of the English working classes (between two-thirds and three-quarters) appear to have been literate around 1840, and those in the countryside were evidently even more literate than those in the city. Also, transmission was not exclusively oral, but singers would often keep tunebooks where they took down texts and tunes. Sykes (1993: 460) thus comes to the conclusion that "the songs being collected were the result of a web of transmission, oral and written, and extremely difficult to disentangle."

In the twentieth century, it seems that modern—aural—mass media became involved in the transmission process as soon as they emerged. As already noted, traditional musicians have always used mass media like sheet music as sources for their repertoire. This was also true for the new forms of media. Irish Traveller Margaret Barry, for instance, always tried to learn songs from the most popular recordings to respond to the demands of her audience, also picking up song texts that were printed in

newspapers. She is also said to have acquired the semitraditional "My Lagan Love" au-
rally after hearing it coming from the doorway of a record shop, staying outside and
listening until she had learned it.[9] Moreover, traditional singers were not solely mediators of the songs; they sometimes also composed new songs. Porter and Gower
(1995: 137) report that Jeannie Robertson had, for instance, "the marvellous trick of
singing us a song she thought we might not have heard—and afterwards admitting
that she had composed it the day before while doing the washing-up."

Reevaluation of the Musical Material Presented in Nineteenth-Century Collections

Not only do the aspects discussed above make an adequate investigation of traditional music difficult, but the notated sources themselves can be problematic. With
only a limited number of original recordings available, the early written collections of
Sharp and his predecessors were of critical importance for the revivalists and electric
folk performers. Yet the reliability of these collections is questionable. A closer investigation of the material casts doubt upon the "authenticity" promoted in the clubs (including the attempt to stay as close to the sources as possible). It is instead more essential to ask *how* the sources should be interpreted, involving musical style as well as
editorial practice.

Unaccompanied Singing

Sharp's emphasis on unaccompanied singing created a musical ideal of performance that cannot be completely confirmed and was not always recognized by the
singers themselves. It is clearly evident that Sharp disliked accompanied folk song, a
bias that was adopted by both English revivals and, as Dallas (Laing 1975: 109) correctly remarked, has probably destroyed much of what could have helped us in understanding the instrumental tradition. Furthermore, in his theoretical writings Sharp
(1907: 57) pointed out that "with the folk-singers of to-day the sense of harmony is
very rudimentary. It was only few of them, for instance, who were able to recognize
their own songs when I played harmonized versions of them on the piano; and still
fewer who could sing them to the simplest instrumental accompaniment."

For Sharp, this "vagueness of hearing" was also evident in the singing tradition's
flattened sevenths. Yet traditional singers were frequently members of church choirs
and thus well familiar with that tradition, often transferring it to their singing. Another counterexample exists in the harmony singing of the Copper Family, which has
been transmitted for more than two hundred years. Yet Sharp also took the predominance of unharmonized folk songs as a further corroboration of his theory. Although
many songs were indeed often sung unaccompanied, this was again not an exclusive
feature but was often a matter of prevailing circumstances. As can be heard on the
recordings of Peter Kennedy, songs were often accompanied by the instruments that
were at hand. Moreover, many so-called traditional instruments were actually fairly

recent additions—the melodeon, for instance, was incorporated into the tradition only around 1820.

Editorial Changes

Sharp changed the material he collected in various ways. Although the prime objective of the EFDSS, as stated in the first volume of the *Folk Song Journal* (1899: iv), was "the collection and preservation of Folk-Songs, Ballads, and Tunes and the publication of such of these as may be deemed advisable," the early collectors were quite free in their editing practices. As Sharp stressed in the preface to *One Hundred English Folksongs* (1916: xvi):

> Logically, the words should be accorded the same treatment [as the tunes]. But this, unhappily, is not always possible to do. Indeed, it has reluctantly to be confessed that owing to various causes—the doggerel broadside-versions of the songs that have been disseminated throughout the country for the past several centuries; lapse of memory; corruptions arising from the inability of the singer to understand words and phrases which have come to him from other parts of the country. . . , the free and unconventional treatment of some of the themes, etc.—the words of many of the songs are often very corrupt and sometimes unintelligible. It has therefore been necessary to make alterations in the words of many of the songs.

In order not to offend his readers, Sharp (ibid.: 123) generally also ignored topics such as seduction, pregnancy, and material with obvious sexual allusions. Tunes were approached with a similarly deliberate attitude and sometimes even recomposed: "If they are intrinsically beautiful, what matter if they be corrupt or not?" (see also Pegg 1976: 77).

Notational Aspects

Sharp and contemporaries tried, consciously or unconsciously, to fit traditional music within the forms of regularly structured music, hence homogenizing many of the details of the irregular parlando style that is inherent in the music. Unlike their American counterparts who started early to record American Indians, the English revivalists only slowly discovered the technical possibilities offered by sound recording. Percy Grainger, strongly influenced by Bartók in method and objectives, started to use the recording machine in 1906, but he remained an outsider in England with this approach. Although Sharp used the machine in 1907 and Vaughan Williams in 1909, recording technology was rejected by many early revivalists. The collector Anne Gilchrist told Grainger that she did not consider the machine an adequate substitute for the human ear because it reproduced dynamic differences too inadequately (Yates 1982: 266–67).[10] Likewise, Kidson disliked the phonograph because it presented "excessively elaborate rhythms" (Harker 1985: 207); he sought an abstract original version of songs he could only discover by not listening accurately. Sharp rejected the phonograph for more practical reasons, as it often made the singers nervous.

Grainger learned by using the phonograph that "irregulations" were an integral part of traditional music. He observed, for instance, that George Wray, who did not sing in a strict metrical framework, joined in with his music with the same irregularities when a recording was played back to him. Grainger (1908: 155) thus concluded: "This frequent uniform repetition of irregularities, goes, to my mind, to prove that very many of them are not mere careless or momentary deviations from a normal, regular form, but radical points of enrichment, inventiveness, and individualization."

In 1908 Grainger recorded nine songs for the Gramophone Company by the traditional singer Joseph Taylor, which became the first commercial British recordings of folk song. Yet his recorded work evidently had little impact; except for those of the American collector James M. Carpenter, comparatively few field recordings were made in the 1920s and 1930s. The major collecting trips did not take place until the late 1940s, when many traditional singers had already died, and consequently many questions about performance style were left unanswered.

An understanding of Victorian and Edwardian conceptions of music and an awareness of the collectors' editorial techniques is thus required for a sophisticated appraisal of these collections. Moreover, it was inevitable that subsequent revivals of English traditional music would involve further changes, because of the biases and limitations inherent in the collectors' methodologies. Nevertheless, a complete repudiation of Sharp would not be justified. A. L. Lloyd called for a reevaluation of Sharp that would examine him within the context of his time. Rather than depicting him as a romantic dreamer, Lloyd emphasized the political side of the collector who, as a socialist, had strong opinions about social conditions, also "taking a courageously oppositional view of the Boer War, for instance, at a time when idiot patriotism was raging" (1965: 97). Lloyd also defended Sharp's editorial practice, arguing that he at least made the material available—and always also indicated the changes, hence never deceiving his readers.

At the same time, it is now evident that the interaction of traditional with popular music in the 1960s and '70s was not so unique as it then seemed. Some theorists like Harker have even denied the existence of "authentic" traditional music, pointing to the mass media and related business interests that were involved even in the pre-Sharp and pre-Child collections. Similar arguments were, ironically, used to demonstrate the corruption of the idealized tradition by electric folk music.

TRADITIONAL, FOLK, AND POPULAR MUSIC IN THE MODERN LITERATURE

Recent discussions about the possibility of transcending the presumed gap between traditional and revival cultures, as well as the role of the media in that process, have evolved between two extreme viewpoints. One position, which is especially represented by the British neo-Marxist school, denied the possibility of closing the gap between traditional and popular music, identifying commercial production as the major problem. The other extreme, which was especially supported by revivalist collectors and later by popular music theorists, regarded the modern aural forms of musical transmission within rock music as an almost direct continuation of the oral tradition (or at least on a similar level), albeit for very different reasons.

Traditional Music—A Commercial Product Only: Dave Harker

It is characteristic of much of the literature dealing with British and American folk revivals that the descriptions of these and especially the electric folk cultures are shaped by negative connotations. Similarly, many major studies of popular musics and of modern mass media have taken a negative viewpoint. As Charles Hamm pointed out, two "metanarratives" (broad, all-encompassing theoretic models that are unproved but accepted as truth) are still dominant: Earlier writers (of the 1930s) started the "myth that commercial production separates superior from inferior music, and that music consumed by a mass audience must, by this fact alone, be inferior to the music of a more selected group" (Hamm 1995: 11). This idea also had a strong impact on folk music studies; the interactions of music hall and traditional music, as well as the fact that a large portion of the oral material stems from commercially produced sheet music, have long been ignored by researchers. This bias has also been true for many studies of modern developments such as electric folk.

The other primary metanarrative, heavily influenced by neo-Marxist approaches, particularly influenced European popular music studies from the 1960s until the 1980s:

> Underlying much of this literature is the assumption that capitalist production negates "authentic" expression by certain groups, here defined . . . by class. Even though popular music has the potential to create or intensify class consciousness and solidarity among the working classes, this rarely happens in practice because the means of production and dissemination are in the hands of the dominant classes. (Hamm 1995: 25)

This idea resurfaced in many theories which argued that the point at which a "folk culture" becomes a mass culture is marked by the moment when it is recorded and is thus subjected to the processes of the mass media. A good example is Harker's *Fakesong* (1985). Although this study of England's first folk revival generation was crucial to the investigation of sources and motives behind the folk song collectors, Harker reduced it mainly to the contrast of bourgeoisie and working class, understanding folk song as an invention of the bourgeoisie, who took and changed the songs of the working class to fit their own purposes.

Harker denied the possibility of a modern continuation of the tradition, as documented in the collections, by arguing that the form and process of mediation had been strongly influenced by subjective interests. The majority of collections such as Playford's *English Dancing Master* and D'Urfey's *Wit and Mirth* did not include any material from personal fieldwork, but instead relied on other collections or even added new words to fit ancient tunes. Later mediators and publishers such as William Chappell (*The Ballad Literature and Popular Music of the Old Time*, 1855–59) were also strongly influenced by market considerations in their choice of songs; Chappell's main criterion seems to have been singability, and many of the earlier collectors did not bother to provide any sources or names, so that "anon." does not necessarily indicate a tune of unknown authorship.

"Classic" collections like the Child ballads that became the basis for modern folk song and ballad scholarship were partly based upon these earlier collections, as Child only used notated manuscript sources from Britain. Consequently, he inadvertently included a substantial number of broadsides and music hall songs—material that was actually viewed as being inferior. Similarly questionable to Harker was the material Sharp collected, which again comprised a considerable number of commercially oriented songs that had emerged with the evolving music hall business around 1840. In order to obtain the most "authentic" material, Sharp preferred older singers (aged 60–70 years) as the sources for his songs; however, as Harker (1985: 189–95) argued, even their repertoire was mainly obtained in cotton factories or comprised commercial songs from about 1850 on.

Harker thus argued correctly that British folk music was not the idealized object that Sharp described. *Fakesong* also identified several important gaps within folk music research, which had, until then, basically been focused on material studies (music or text), but had rarely taken sociocultural aspects into consideration—or rarely evaluated its own position. This dilemma also applied to the International Folk Music Council's definition of folk music, which was not based on an analysis but a prescription. Moreover, Harker exposed the inherent contradiction that the "purely" traditional early collections actually contained much popular/commercial music, which also belied Child's and Sharp's definitions of Englishness.

Yet the problem of *Fakesong* is that Harker ends up with a metanarrative as restrictive as the concepts of Sharp and contemporaries that he criticizes. Harker negated the existence of "true" folk song, arguing that the early collections that were the primary sources for Child's famous collection were published for commercial purposes only (i.e., always with market considerations in mind). He excluded the whole transformation process, as well as the musical styles that are also connected to the conception of folk song. Although this critical school (Lloyd, Harker), with its strictly Marxist and sociological orientation, has to be regarded as a healthy reaction to the extremely conservative initial dogma of the EFDSS, it is of limited help for further research into fusions of traditional music with rock and other genres.[11]

Folk and Electric Folk as a Corruption of the Tradition: Pegg, Woods, Watson

In considering folk and electric folk, most theorists—with a few exceptions like the much earlier Dallas in *The Electric Muse* (Laing et al. 1975)—started from metanarratives similar to Harker's by regarding mass media as a bourgeois means that is used to separate the working class from its identity. Almost ten years before Harker, Pegg, for instance, came to similar conclusions in *Folk: A Portrait of English Traditional Music, Musicians, and Customs* (1976). Arguing that nineteenth- and twentieth-century collections were based on individually chosen and changed material, he concluded that folk music was only an idealized construct and was, in reality, probably nonexistent. By equating the use of the media with the intention of making money, Pegg perceived the folk revival and electric folk as part of a capitalist marketing strategy in the same category as broadsides (or broadsheets), eighteenth-century ballad operas, or Percy Grainger's arrangements of morris dance tunes: "In the early 1960s folk was used as a commercial label, in the hope that it would help to sell gramophone records. . . . The more recent development of electric folk-rock bands is only one of a series of attempts which have been going for several centuries to make money out of the old tunes" (Pegg 1976: 119).

Although Pegg's arguments have again to be understood as a provocative reaction against Sharp and contemporaries, the validity of his statements is questionable, as they are not verified by fieldwork observations but are solely based on abstract theorizing. As with many studies, Pegg mentions electric folk only briefly at the end of his book, and then only the most popular and commercially successful groups.

The criticisms aimed at electric folk have often been directed at Steeleye Span. In his general overview, *Folk Revival: The Rediscovery of a National Music*, Woods (1979: 98) harshly attacked Steeleye Span, who, around 1974, "also began to take liberties with traditional texts, [with] a lack of respect they would have never shown in their earlier days." Behind Woods's criticism of Steeleye Span for corrupting traditional music, one can clearly read the fear that commercial success always results in musical clichés. Steeleye Span indeed picked out recognizable elements from the tradition like pagan songs referring to wren-hunting traditions ("The King") or mummers' plays and ancient costumes for their stage shows. Yet retrospectively, this form of electric reinterpretation has had as much or as little influence on the original material as the acoustic interpretations. It is more likely that Steeleye Span have given their audiences a new access to the music, building a bridge to present-day interpretations and interest in the tradition.

Similarly, Watson (1983) accused Steeleye Span of "cultural exploitation" through marketing a song like "The Blackleg Miner" (from their first album, *Hark! The Village Wait*, in 1970) to an audience that had no relationship to the tradition of old labor songs. By arguing that the middle-class rock musicians have misused the songs by playing them for a middle-class audience instead for a working-class one, Watson conforms with Hamm's second metanarrative. His analysis of "The Blackleg Miner" starts from a clear concept of how the song should be correctly interpreted: that is, with a direct singing style that does not distract from the text, and with a subordinated instrumental accompaniment. Consequently, he judges Steeleye Span's first two verses, which are sung a cappella in two-part harmony, as follows: "Sung slowly, they combine a courtly prettiness with a dirge-like atmosphere and both elements appear immediately foreign to the content of the song" (ibid.: 145). By increasing the focus on the musical side (e.g., by adding interludes, electric instruments, and the repetition of the first verse at the end), Steeleye's musical interpretation is seen, as are Lucy Broadwood's and Benjamin Britten's, as unsuitable, for "it has been plucked from its original social-aesthetic function and used as a vehicle for a sound and a rhythm" (ibid.).

Woods's attitude is characteristic of many other theoretical works. Although Harker regretted that early folk studies had rarely taken sociocultural circumstances into account, the same limitation was characteristic of studies of the Second Revival or electric folk. For example, Woods (1979: 95) understood the revival and electric folk not as a part of a transformation process but as a deliberate, partly naive action: "The Folk Revival itself has also seen attempts to dress up for presentation to a wider and different audience. . . . The two main avenues of experimentation have been a retrogression into a medievalism not always perfectly understood by its practitioners, and a movement towards certain elements of rock music." Woods attacked Shirley Collins in particular for having invented these trends with her album *Anthems in Eden* and judged its long-term effect as being regressive rather than progressive: "Once the novelty of the sound is over, therefore, there remain few areas for a continuance of development, and the music quickly becomes sterile because it lacks the essential core of rightness; it is neither creatively progressive nor constructively recreative" (ibid.: 96).

One of the few positive attempts was, according to Woods, Peter Bellamy's ballad opera *The Transports*. The problem with Woods's criticism is, again, that he did not take contemporaneous circumstances into account. Collins's experiments were parallel with the general development of the early music movement, which at that time experimented with these sounds. While the efforts of David Munrow's Early Music Consort could indeed sound shallow and unprofessional to a much more experienced and knowledgeable present-day listener, they nevertheless were part of a larger development and the basis for current knowledge and practice, and Collins's fusion experiments also should be seen from that angle.

It is remarkable that A. L. Lloyd, whose writing was strongly Marxist-influenced, never criticized the electric folk movement. Lloyd had developed a highly individual interpretation of folk song, understanding English it as "something that came out of social upheaval" (Lloyd 1967: 4). This perspective sometimes resulted in interpretations such as explaining the anonymity of folk songs by the poverty of the authors and relating obviously pagan topics, such as the hunting of the wren, to peasant revolts. However, Lloyd never blamed the modern media for the decline of folk song, which, as he judged realistically, had been connected with the print media since the sixteenth century: "folk-music was already on the way out before the appearance of the gramophone about 1900 or the radio about 1920" (ibid.: 52–53). Rather, he saw the problem in the change of living conditions; for example, with the disappearance of spinning mills, spinning songs were no longer called for, but were also not replaced by anything else.

The Close Relationship between the Modern Mass Media and Oral Forms of Transmission: The Lomaxes and Karl Dallas

In contrast with the positions of Pegg, Woods, and Watson, other theorists instead emphasized the (at least at first sight) striking resemblances between the oral tradition and modern aural forms. Rejecting Child's manuscript-based collecting, American folk music collectors John A. and Alan Lomax regarded the archival recording machine as the only means of adequately capturing the subtleties of performance. With the possibility of enhancing the sound in recordings and the commercial availability of records, they believed that a more direct contact between the rural ("traditional") and urban ("revival") culture could be established, the latter being able to continue the former. This assumption did not prove to be true in the case of American folk music. As Rosenberg (1993: 12–13) has stated, the texts were easily adapted, but not the performance style, even when "authentic" recordings were used as sources.[12] Early critics of this idea, like Charles Seeger (1948 and 1949), cited the large social differences between the traditional and urban/revival cultures as a primary factor. The recordings, although able to capture stylistic subtleties exactly, carried the material out of its original social context into revival cultures that embodied a completely different social group with values and codes differing from those of the original performers.

This phenomenon could also be observed with English folk and electric folk: The music was revived in a different sociocultural environment with a different performance practice, behavior, and codes—for example, in folk clubs with their paradigm of unaccompanied singing, or on festival stages with a comparatively distanced and passive performer-audience relationship, the audience often having little or no relationship to the music. Moreover, the traditional material was carried into a star-oriented culture. As Oysterband fiddler Ian Telfer pointed out in Alun Howkins's BBC documentary *The Other Muse* (1981), the revival performers grew up in a culture in which people want to be stars, an attitude that has infected the folk scene, too. This was particularly made evident when Scottish Traveller and singer Jeannie Robertson was "discovered" by *Melody Maker* as the "undisputed Queen of folksong" (Dallas 1968c).

The relationship between orality, as the main characteristic of traditional music, and the modern (electric) mass media was extensively discussed by Richard Middleton (1995: 68–83), who criticized the treatment of modern media as a homogeneous unity, despite the existence of alternatives like the pirate stations in the 1960s. Middleton's attention was particularly focused on 1960s and '70s media/technology analyst Marshall MacLuhan[13] and his followers, who worked out the essential elements of oral and literary culture. Emphasizing that communication technology and culture are related as cause and effect, MacLuhan came to the conclusion that the electronic media were restoring many of the characteristics of speech and thus of oral transmission.

The assumption that the balance and interplay of the senses was destroyed by literacy has particularly permeated popular music culture. Middleton cites the particular example of Dallas, whom he accuses of having adopted MacLuhan's ideology without really thinking it through. Dallas suggested that rock could be understood as a kind of folk music, not through the perception of rock as a music for the masses but owing to the parallels between electric (i.e., popular) and traditional music: traditional music has always been closely connected to the various forms of mass media—be it earlier collectors, broadsides, and MacColl's and Lloyd's use of modern media for their purposes. "At every stage of this development, for good and ill, commercial pressures were at work" (Laing et al. 1975: 121). Dallas argued that it was not the broadcast media of the twentieth century that eroded folk music, but rather the print media, in particular the broadside printers of the nineteenth century. The Second Revival and the electric folk movement, in contrast, had taken traditional music back from a fixed, notated version into a living context—the stage. Thus, both positive and negative aspects of the mass media should be taken into account when investigating the evolution of traditional music. It seems questionable to go as far as Dallas in condemning the activities of the earlier revivalists. Although one might call the material they collected "fossilized remains of an ancient culture in a state of increasing degeneracy" (ibid.: 108), where would we be without it?

From Dallas's viewpoint, electric folk was a new form of traditional music, as it fulfilled the various criteria of the International Folk Music Council's official definition of folk music, much in contrast to the notated versions of earlier collectors:

(1) Composition and transmission processes were oral; rock musicians, particularly in the 1970s, rarely worked with notated music, especially if they picked up a new song from fellow musicians. This oral—or rather aural—element was intensified by the existence of modern media (radio and recordings) that had become transmission mediators, as much new music was learned from recordings.

(2) The three essential ("evolutionary") elements of continuity, variation, and selection were also inherent in rock and electric music of that time. *Continuity:* An active, not antiquarian, re-creation process characterized individual performers or bands as well as the whole music scene. The emerging large variety of interpretations of one song, here called "cover versions," made the original authorship increasingly difficult to establish. The connection between past and present was especially evident with electric folk: traditional elements were contained in the material, embellishments, and instruments, while at the same time modern instruments, techniques, and media were involved, as well as new songwriting based on the old style, as can be observed with Richard Thompson, Sandy Denny, and others. *Variation:* Unlike the first two revivals, but similar to the rock scene, electric folk did not keep strictly to the "originals," and thus allowed the development of a large number of variations of the same version. *Se-*

lection: The performers selected the material. They were well aware that not all traditional material was of the same quality (see Maddy Prior's comment in this chapter's opening epigraph).

(3) On a musical level, the electric instruments, with their capability of sustaining notes, showed clear parallels to the drones produced by traditional instruments.

But is aural really the same as oral? Dallas pointed at the limits of his approach himself, realizing clearly that electric music was significantly different from the old tradition. On the one hand, the new instruments and technology allowed new possibilities of expression; on the other hand, the technology was expensive—and the costs "[tied] the rock musician to the money structure of the music business more securely than any of his predecessors" (ibid.: 131). And with electrification, the distance between performer and audience expands, making interaction difficult, if not impossible.

Middleton (1995: 82) argued against Dallas that electricity allows no return to oral techniques. Instead, its productive forms mix oral and literary effects; for example, the product of a recording studio is much more precise than a simple oral rendition. A recording is a finished product, fixing one version of many, while the oral tradition never is fixed. (The latter, however, is the case with performances of the electric folk bands, as can be heard in Fairport Convention's various interpretations of "Matty Groves.") Recordings thus present a high form of abstraction. Rock music theorist Simon Frith (1984: 5) also emphasized that transmission via modern media is not identical with the processes that take place in traditional music structures: "Between the original music and the eventual listener are the technological processes of transforming sound to tape and disc and the economic processes of packaging and marketing the final product."

Middleton preferred Shepherd's approach, which is based on MacLuhan's, by arguing that "consciousness, hence cultural forms, are largely conditioned by the media through which reality is perceived and organized" (1995: 75). Shepherd (1982) indeed worked out distinct characteristics for the oral culture (i.e., improvised, spontaneous) and the electric/industrial culture (consciously manipulated musical structures, "idealization" of sound). He subsequently investigated how these oral and electric elements were used by a music genre to express a worldview. Yet this theory does not answer the question about the relationship between oral transmission and the electric mass media satisfactorily, and Middleton likewise remains vague on this point.

Folk and Folk Rock as an Opposition to Commercially Oriented Popular Music: Simon Frith

If revived folk music could not transcend the social and structural gap, it could at least transcend the gap ideologically, as could rock music (of the 1960s) with a certain "folk ideology"—so rock music theorists like Simon Frith argued. As Frith (1984) pointed out, "folk authenticity" was judged in America on two aspects: its political correctness and its popular origin. Theorists especially relied on the latter aspect to demonstrate the resemblance between folk and rock—but from the audience's viewpoint. Although folk music has also always had a commercial side, if set against mass-produced popular music and thus judged in relative terms, folk and rock music seem to stand apart from popular music.

These theories clearly fell back on two aspects of Sharp's overall definition: (1) folk song reflects the lived experience of the community, and (2) folk song is a communal experience. These notions were expressed by, among others, *Rolling Stone* writer Jon Landau: "[Rock 'n' roll] was unmistakably a folk-music form. Within the confines of the media, these musicians articulated attitudes, styles and feelings that were genuine reflections of their own experience and of the social situations which had helped to produce that experience."[14]

By understanding rock music as an authentic "reflection of experience," it can therefore be clearly differentiated from popular music and its mass production, which embodies values different from the folk ideal. Likewise, the audience is "believed to be relatively autonomous—their tastes are 'genuine.' The music business can serve these tastes but it can't manipulate them" (Frith 1984: 6), a feature that is also characteristic of the relatively small classical and folk audiences. According to Frith, the myth of community remained a part of rock music—and, accordingly, American folk rockers offered an experience of community.

However, this broad approach does not illuminate the ideological discussion that emerged when Bob Dylan picked up an electric guitar and played rock (not popular) music. Moreover, this relatively common viewpoint also does not help us to understand the actual musical transformation process. It is also doubtful that "the folk" can be equated with the audience for anonymous mass music, as has been done in many popular music studies. The persistent difficulties of sustaining an accurate critical discussion are partly due to the vast range of meanings encompassed by the expression "folk music" (here, identical with "traditional music"), especially in sociological, popular, or rock music literature, which is often disconnected from the "official" definition.

GETTING AWAY FROM STATIC CONCEPTS

To summarize, the use of the term "folk music" is a history of categorizations rather than a description of music in its own terms. Especially when researching traditional music or electric folk, the matter of definition becomes extremely difficult. Returning to Charles Hamm, it seems that only by eschewing restrictive metanarratives might one be able to understand popular music and its electric components adequately; a provisional definition of electric folk, as outlined in chapter 1, can only serve as a preliminary tool with which to investigate the underlying process of the development.

Dallas argued that the oral and aural traditions show an obvious resemblance. However, the involvement of electric forms of media always implies a change as soon as the music, whether acoustic or electric, is presented on a stage. Following the suggestions of Shepherd (1982) and Middleton (1995), I instead propose that one should distinguish between the different oral, aural, and written spheres (which is the case in the tradition as well as in rock music), yet refrain from any judgmental interpretations. With this goal in mind, understanding the modern transformation is by no means a simple process; instead, it becomes even more complicated as a new (aural) layer is added that follows different rules. The various elements—oral transmission, continuity, variation, and selection—mentioned in the IFMC definition are indeed essential to the nature of this music. Yet the absolute way in which such definitions are often articulated and perceived clearly leads the discussion about the nature of traditional music in an unproductive direction.[15]

Furthermore, to grasp the true nature of the folk revivals an adequate scientific analysis has to go beyond mere static description and should explore the process behind the revivals to a much greater extent than has been done so far. Electric folk is the result of a complex internal (endogenous) and external (exogenous) adaptation and transformation process. Consequently, an open concept like the one Mark Slobin has developed in his *Subcultural Sounds: Micromusics of the West* (1993) will be much more useful here. Before coming to this point, however, this study will take a look at the multifaceted music, history, and sociology of electric folk.

PART II

ELECTRIC FOLK AS
A MICROCULTURE

THREE

THE PERFORMERS AND GROUPS
Individual Biographies

Who knows where the time goes?   SANDY DENNY

As is probably the case with any music genre, the history of electric folk in England is less a strictly chronological sequence than a patchwork of individual biographies. Most particularly, however, it is the story of three major groups: Pentangle, Fairport Convention, and Steeleye Span. I thus will take up the historical perspective once more, since many performers are now only known by name—if at all. Because the electric folk scene is difficult to separate from the overall folk scene and as several of these performers became figural in later fusion projects, I have also included musicians such as Shirley and Dolly Collins and Davy Graham who represent the interaction of traditional and contemporary music on an acoustic level. Sandy Denny and Richard Thompson serve as examples for the continuation of traditional elements within modern rock songwriting.

The Oysterband represents a modern folk rock style, but remains related to the electric folk scene through its background as a former dance band and through its collaboration with folksinger June Tabor. As this is not the case with folk rock bands like the Levellers and, to some extent, the Pogues, they have been omitted here. For the same reason I have also left out early folk rock bands like Lindisfarne and Horslips, short-lived groups like Mr. Fox, and, despite their huge influence on the possibilities of fusing instruments and styles, the Incredible String Band.

To help clarify the confusion caused by the high number of member changes within the bands, the appendix provides a list of the groups' lineups. Following a loosely chronological order, I will start with Shirley and Dolly Collins, two tradition-based acoustic performers.

SHIRLEY AND DOLLY COLLINS

Although today not widely known, Shirley and Dolly Collins can be regarded as innovative central figures of the English scene.[1] In spite of their traditional background, the sisters were always keen to experiment acoustically and electrically to discover new arrangement possibilities. Shirley, with her soft, clear voice, was respected during the Second Revival as a highly individual singer of traditional songs; she made recordings with the experimental guitarist Davy Graham as well as with the various bands of electric folk bassist and organizer Ashley Hutchings. A composer of sensitive, deceptively simple arrangements, Dolly, who often accompanied her sister on a portative organ, would later also write the instrumental arrangements for Peter Bellamy's ballad opera *The Transports*. Dolly also appeared on albums of the Incredible String Band, Iain Matthews, Mark Ellington, Chris Darrow, and Tony Rose.

Shirley (b. 1935) and Dolly (Dorothy Ann) Collins (1933–95) grew up in the Hastings area of East Sussex in a family of partly Irish descent that still fostered traditional music. The sisters picked up many songs from their grandfather and their aunt. When Peter Kennedy's radio series *As I Roved Out* began in 1954, the sisters saw a chance to get on the air and wrote to the BBC. Bob Copper, himself a well-known traditional singer from Rottingdean (near Brighton), was commissioned to visit the Collins family home, yet he ended up recording mainly the mother instead of the sisters. The first contacts were established, however, and Shirley would later cite Bob Copper as an important source of her traditional repertoire.

A keen piano player, Dolly became a music teacher. Having also written some minor pieces, she was introduced by her uncle, writer Fred Ball, to composer Alan Dudley Bush, who accepted her as a student. Bush had taught composition at the Royal Academy of Music from 1925 on. A member of the Communist Party, he was supervisor of the Labour Choral Union from 1929 to 1940 and cofounded the Workers' Music Association in 1936. Although Dolly's studies had been made possible through the association's workshops and summer schools in Hastings, she had so little money at the time that Bush had to halve his fee, and Dolly could only attend classes every three weeks. These lessons nevertheless significantly shaped her future work; after 1945 Bush had changed his avant-garde style into a consciously simple compositional approach, which became characteristic of Dolly's folk song arrangements as well.

Shirley's social life was strongly dominated by the workers' movement and the activities of the Labour Party. Although she took evening classes in folk music at Hendon Tech in her late teens, her musical focus was much more on American music, as she recalled in an interview with Karl Dallas (1978c: 13): "I became much influenced by Jean Ritchie and loved American music at that time as well, partly because one did hear American music on the radio. I mean, it was accessible, whereas English music really was not, you know, it was hardly ever played."

After an office job at the trade union office in Hastings, Shirley went to college in London, discovered the Cecil Sharp House, where she would go to evening classes and singarounds, and also met Peter Kennedy, son of the director of the English Folk Dance and Song Society (EFDSS) and organizer/producer of the radio series *As I Roved Out*. Through him, she made her first recording on *Folksong Today* (1957/58), appearing side by side with traditional singers Harry Cox and Bob Copper. Shirley also worked as an editorial assistant for Alan Lomax's anthology, *The Folk Songs of North America*, and helped with a series of field recordings, *The Folk Songs of Britain*.[2] In 1959 she accompanied Lomax on an extensive field collecting trip through the States, which left a strong impact on her later musical style: "I came back from America cured of my illusions and then started to listen to English, Irish and Scottish music. After that, it just turned, and it's stayed with me that it's English music that holds me" (Dallas 1978c: 13).

Returning to England in 1960, Shirley became a member of Ewan MacColl's folk/skiffle band, the Ramblers, for a short time. Although she had been involved in the activities of the workers' movement, politics would never affect her—or Dolly's— music making in the way it did MacColl's, which caused some later tension between the performers. Solo again, Shirley recorded the EP (extended play) disc *Heroes of Love* in 1963. Although she developed a distinctly English style, the strong American influence remained obvious in her use of accompaniment instruments like autoharp, five-string banjo, and dulcimer, which stood in clear contrast to the ideal of unaccompanied singing that had been increasingly adopted by a number of British folk clubs.

Her next project, the recording of *Folk Roots, New Routes* with guitarist Davy Graham in 1964, was even more radical, causing several aggressive reactions from the hard-core folk scene around MacColl. Collins had already met Graham at the London-based coffee house and music club the Troubadour, but it was her husband, recording producer Austin John Marshall, who brought them together to make *Folk Roots, New Routes*.[3] This pioneering album, a unique fusion of diverse musical styles, anticipated much of what would later be called "electric folk" or "folk rock," although it received little outside attention at the time because it did not fit into any existing categories. The partnership of these extremely different musicians was both unusual and difficult, as Collins recalled:

> He was sort of involved in drugs. And I never was. I mean I was so *pure*. So I didn't drink, I didn't smoke, I didn't do drugs, I didn't want to! I had young children. I think I was really quite unsophisticated, then. So—I didn't approve of Davy's lifestyle. But we were good friends. He was a really nice man and a wonderful musician. And somehow, some of the songs really *jelled*, they really worked.

Collins and Graham also played various gigs together before they went different ways again. Shirley made her next innovative recording, *The Sweet Primeroses* [sic], with her sister in 1967. It contained some of her favorite traditional songs like "All Things

Are Quite Silent," "A Blacksmith Courted Me," and "The False Bride"—classic English folk songs she had acquired via direct contact as well as via indirect sources like recordings and the radio. This album also presented Dolly's distinct and simple arrangement style and her portative organ for the first time. The arrangements became further elaborated on subsequent recordings like the bleak *Love, Death, and the Maiden* (1970), which also featured Pentangle drummer Terry Cox guesting on percussion.

Shirley Collins's next LP, *The Power of the True Love Knot*, was released in 1968 and produced by Joe Boyd, who was working with Fairport Convention and the Incredible String Band at that time. Group members Robin Williamson and Mike Heron joined Shirley on several tracks, with Williamson on Japanese sticks, tin whistle, and shahanhai, and Heron on finger cymbals and African drum—which gave the album a rather exotic touch. Dolly Collins, who had met the band at a concert, appeared, in return, with her portative organ on the Incredible String Band's *Hangman's Beautiful Daughter* (also released in 1968).

Apart from these musical excursions, however, the sisters were still looking for a more distinct sound that would fit the traditional material. It was the embryonic early music scene, whose members were at that stage still experimenting with the sound colors of then unfamiliar instruments like the sackbut or crumhorn, that offered them a solution. Shirley Collins recalled:

> In the mid-1960s I sort of started listening to a lot of early music, going along to the Musica Reservata rehearsals, and met David Munrow there. And it just happened, really, that we got hold of Dolly and said, "Come up and listen, if you can." See, she just started writing arrangements to the songs. I gave her the songs that I wanted her to arrange and all fell into place after that.

Anthems in Eden was the first outcome of this collaboration with David Munrow's ensemble—which later became known as the Early Music Consort. Perceived as fairly exotic, the album was issued in 1969 on EMI's progressive Harvest label, which was less oriented toward buyers with a background in early music or folk music than toward progressive rock audiences who listened to Pink Floyd. *Anthems in Eden* was presented on the BBC radio as well, thus enabling the sisters, who were well respected in the folk circuit despite their adventurous experiments, to reach a wider audience.

At that time, Shirley and Dolly also worked with the Young Tradition. A vocal ensemble formed by Peter Bellamy (1944–91), Royston Wood (1935–90), and Heather Wood (b. 1945) in the mid-1960s, the Young Tradition was one of the most distinctive groups on the folk circuit. With a focus on unaccompanied singing, they managed to create a striking sound by mixing the harmony singing style of the Copper Family with their own interests, ranging from classical music to the Everly Brothers. Shortly before the Young Tradition disbanded, they made a final recording with Shirley and Dolly of traditional Christmas songs (*The Holly Bears the Crown*) that was not released until 1995.[4] The group left a clear stylistic mark on the scene before it disbanded after three albums and numerous tours in 1969. Peter Bellamy committed himself completely to folk music; one major outcome was his ballad opera *The Transports* (1977), which was arranged by Dolly Collins. Though Bellamy's artistic achievements were acknowledged by various journalistic writers after his suicide in 1991, his uncompromising manner apparently alienated him from many people within the scene, and he also seems to have scraped only a meager living as a folk performer. Royston Wood's career as an arts journalist was cut shout when he died in a car accident in 1990. Heather Wood moved to the United States, where she is still active as a performer and organizer.

Over the next decade Shirley Collins became well known for her collaborations with Fairport Convention founder Ashley Hutchings, whom she had met in 1970. Their marriage in 1971 marked the beginning of a series of highly original recordings. The electric folk LP *No Roses* (1971) featured the first of many lineups of the various Albion (Country) Bands, at that time formed loosely of a number of eminent folk and electric folk musicians who accompanied Shirley's singing of favorites from her vast repertoire. She also appeared on Hutchings's pioneering *Morris On* and *Son of Morris On* and toured extensively with him. After *No Roses*, both briefly went on tour with Richard Thompson, John Kirkpatrick, and Young Tradition singer Royston Wood in Devon. In 1974 Collins and Hutchings started to tour with the Etchingham Steam Band, a purely acoustic group that did not survive for long owing to financial reasons. Shirley also worked in various theater projects of the Albion Band at the National Theatre until the late 1970s, when she divorced Hutchings. Her final album, *For As Many As Will* (1978), saw her again teaming up with her sister, followed by an Australian tour in 1980.

Shirley stopped singing in public shortly after that but is still a well-respected authority in the present folk scene, giving talks and—at the time of this writing—working on a book about her field trips with Alan Lomax. Dolly increasingly suffered from health problems and concentrated on compositional and arrangement work, writing advertising jingles as well as song cycles. She died in 1995.

MARTIN CARTHY AND DAVE SWARBRICK

Martin Carthy has been regarded as one of the most influential British singers and guitarists since the mid-1960s.[5] Born in Hatfield, Hertfordshire, in 1940, he grew up in Hampstead, London. After working about eighteen months in the theater, he started to sing and play guitar in coffee bars, gradually moving from skiffle and American repertoire to the English material he encountered in the folk clubs.

Carthy became a resident singer at the Troubadour in the late 1950s and a member of Redd Sullivan's Thameside Four (with Marian Gray and Pete Maynard) in 1961. With this group, he was exposed to a large variety of material, imitating blues and jazz as well as gospel. After three years, during which he also started to build up a large repertoire of traditional music, Carthy decided to work primarily as a solo performer, with short appearances with such groups and performers as Rory McEwen, Lisa Turner, and 3 City 4. In contrast to many American folksingers who used traditional songs only as a starting point, Carthy stayed with the traditional material. In 1965, when he was looking for an accompanist for his first solo album, *Martin Carthy*, he met fiddle player Dave Swarbrick:

> I started working with Dave Swarbrick because I couldn't have done the albums all with guitar. I had to get someone else in. I first of all thought that I'd get someone to play the banjo. Then I went up to Dave at the Campbell's club (the Jug O' Punch club in Birmingham), we were discussing a couple of songs, one of them was "Sovay," which I was just learning, he liked it. The other was "The Two Magicians," which he also liked. So he came down and stayed overnight, did the session the next day. (Dallas 1977: 9)

Dave Cyril Eric Swarbrick was born in London in 1941 and grew up in Birmingham. Originally intending to become a painter, he attended the Birmingham College of Art in the late 1950s. Around that time he began to play guitar in Beryl Marriott's Ceilidh Band in Birmingham. Marriott encouraged Swarbrick to take up the fiddle he had played during his childhood. He joined the Ian Campbell Folk Group in 1960. With the Aberdeen singer Ian Campbell and his sister Lorna at its core, the Birmingham-based group was one of the first revival bands to have a fiddle player and to develop a predominantly British repertoire, building on the large Aberdonian family repertoire of the Campbells.[6]

Swarbrick quickly gained a considerable reputation as a highly skilled and imaginative fiddle player. Accompanying A. L. Lloyd on various solo recordings and projects, he acquired a large repertoire of traditional songs—another reason for his outstanding position within the folk circuit. By the end of the 1960s Swarbrick had nevertheless become frustrated by the limited possibilities for experimentation within the restrictive English folk scene. He was more than ready to leave the scene when Joe Boyd asked him to guest with his instrument on Fairport Convention's *Unhalfbricking* in 1968.

Meanwhile, Carthy had teamed up with Swarbrick as a duo in 1966. Their collaboration—which lasted until 1969—is documented by five LPs and one EP, which all proved groundbreaking in the development of the British folk revival in terms of both material and singing and playing styles. For example, *Byker Hill* (1967), featuring innovative arrangements and a carefully selected repertoire, has long been regarded as one of the decades' most influential folk albums and is still outstanding among Carthy's and Swarbrick's many recordings. As Carthy pointed out to music journalist Ken Hunt (CD 1991):

> It was the first real "decision album" I was involved in. Before that I got a lot of songs and just did them. It was a "decision album" in the sense of making decisions about doing stuff

in funny time signatures and actually working on it and making it work, deciding that we really wanted to do things a particular way. . . . We hadn't thought in 1962 that we'd ever be able to do those songs like that.

Carthy was already regarded as an authority in the folk circuit, exerting a substantial influence on his fellow musicians. Conducting careful research on his material in the archives, he not only built up a broad musical repertoire but also became highly knowledgeable about traditional music's repertoire, history, and style. At the same time, he remained extremely open-minded about musical innovation—very much in contrast with the traditionally oriented venues of the 1960s and '70s revival scene in which he was performing. Having developed an elaborate, yet transparent, ornamented accompaniment style that left the tune in the center, he became one of the leading guitarists of the so-called folk baroque style. This term was apparently coined by Karl Dallas and other contemporary writers to describe a British guitar style that mixed elements of the American blues guitar with a classic, contrapuntal, and ornamented language, often to accompany traditional Anglo-Irish material. Always willing to pass on his vast repertoire, Carthy often encouraged fellow musicians to experiment and also influenced some visiting Americans such as Paul Simon, who learned "Scarborough Fair" from him (Dallas 1977).[7]

The partnership between Carthy and Swarbrick ended when Swarbrick joined Fairport Convention as a permanent member in August 1969, which made booking plans for the duo almost impossible. Carthy himself, always open to new musical possibilities, joined Steeleye Span in 1970, staying for eighteen months and making two recordings with the group. Returning to solo work after his departure from Steeleye, he also joined Ashley Hutchings's Albion Country Band in 1973 for a brief period. Around 1972 he also became a member of the eminent Yorkshire vocal group, the Watersons, following his marriage to Norma Waterson.

The Watersons originally consisted of the sisters Norma (b. 1939) and Lal (1943–98), brother Mike Waterson (b. 1941), and their cousin John Harrison. The Watersons' performances were partly based on the tradition of English family singing, and with their striking a cappella sound the group soon became one of the focal points of the folk scene in the mid-1960s, receiving top billing at clubs and festivals and also appearing on television. The group disbanded in 1968 but reformed in 1972, with Carthy replacing Harrison, and made several influential recordings including *For Pence and Spicy Ale* (1975). Around that time, Carthy became an internationally known performer. While continuing his solo work, he went briefly back to Steeleye between 1977 and 1978, until the group dissolved.

After his time with the Albion Country Band, Carthy had worked on several projects with the melodeon player John Kirkpatrick. Kirkpatrick could also look back on a broad career as a soloist as well as a highly sought-after session musician, member of the Albion Country Band, and accompanist to Fairport Convention's former lead guitarist, Richard Thompson. In 1976 Carthy played guitar on Kirkpatrick's recording of Cotswold morris tunes,[8] *Plain Capers*, while Kirkpatrick became a member of Steeleye Span through Carthy, and in 1978 both worked in the National Theatre production of Flora Thompson's *Lark Rise to Candleford* with the Albion Band, which had become the theater's semiresident house band. Carthy and Kirkpatrick started to play as a trio with the trumpeter Howard Evans, and this trio became the core of Brass Monkey, a brass-dominated five-piece folk band. Due to the complicated concert schedules of its members, Brass Monkey could only appear sporadically between 1983 and 1987, but it made two recordings that offered an interesting alternative to the prevailing electric interpretations.[9]

The early 1990s saw Carthy teaming up with Swarbrick again, but also touring with his wife Norma Waterson and daughter, the fiddle player Eliza Carthy, as Waterson:Carthy. Recent projects have included the ensemble Wood, Wilson, Carthy (1998) as well as a revived Brass Monkey and a new solo recording, *Signs of Life* (1998).

Swarbrick's musical biography remained inseparably intertwined for many years with the history of Fairport Convention. Partly due to hearing problems, he withdrew from the electric scene in the 1980s, but he has continued as a solo musician, as a partner of Carthy, and with his acoustic band Whippersnapper. Despite poor health, he still appears frequently at the annual Cropredy Festival.

DAVY GRAHAM

Although little known outside the folk scene, Davy Graham is, in addition to Bert Jansch, John Renbourn, and Carthy, still regarded as one of the most influential and adventurous guitarists of the so-called folk baroque movement.[10] Using nonstandard tunings like DADGAD, Graham has influenced many guitarists both with his technical style and with his fusions of folk, blues, jazz, classical, and ethnic music that were way ahead of their time. Likewise, his original composition "Angi" seems to have inspired many guitarists to start playing English-style music. Denselow (Laing et al. 1975: 144) wrote that Graham's recordings "were rather like delayed time bombs; their initial impact was not enormous but the long-term effect was devastating."

Graham was born in Leicester in 1940. His father came from the Isle of Skye, while his mother was from Georgetown, Guyana. He grew up in London's colorful Notting Hill area and became serious about music after he was given his first guitar at the age of sixteen. His early repertoire consisted of contemporary hits by Lonnie Donegan as well as blues and jazz pieces. After an interlude in Paris in 1958–59, Graham established himself in London's club scene as the most musically and technically innovative folk/blues guitarist at that time. His finger picking became further exposed to a broad audience by an appearance in Ken Russell's BBC documentary *Hound Dogs and Bach Addicts: The Guitar Craze* (1959).

The experimental EP *3/4 A.D.* (1961), also featuring British blues revival pioneer

Alexis Korner (1928–84),[11] was little noticed by the general public, but it had a huge long-term influence on the folk scene as it featured his famous composition "Anji." Later spelled "Angi," it blended classical, blues, and jazz techniques and became a challenge for any aspiring guitarist. The origin of the piece was rather incidental, as Dallas (CD 1996) pointed out: "According to Davey, he was working on the Am–G–F–E^7 chord sequence of Jack Elliott's 'Cocaine Bill' when he hit the wrong strings and 'Angi' came out." "Angi" was popularized by Simon and Garfunkel and by Bert Jansch, who still plays the piece frequently.

Graham's first album, *The Guitar Player* (1963), was released on the Pye's Golden Guinea label and reflected his preoccupation with jazz. His subsequent six albums were released on Decca, and both *Folk Blues and Beyond* (1964) and *Folk Roots, New Routes* (1965) became touchstones for future generations. On *Folk, Blues and Beyond* Graham added jazz, blues, and Indian ragas to folk tunes, backed only by bass and drums. The album contained a variety of material that was typical for Graham but was far beyond anything else in that was currently being played in the folk clubs. It included pieces such as "Cocaine," which Graham had learned from Ramblin' Jack Elliot during his visit to Britain, Charles Mingus's "Better Git It in Your Soul," and "Maajun (A Taste of Tangier)," which is based on a melody Graham heard during his stay in Morocco in 1962. The album also contains a traditional English song, "Seven Gypsies," which Denselow (Laing et al. 1975: 145) cites as the beginning of the folk baroque style. *Folk Roots, New Routes* with Shirley Collins broke even more ground. These albums were followed by *Midnight Man* (1966), on which he combined blues with rock, and *Large as Life and Twice as Natural* (1968), on which he again mixed folk, blues, jazz, and elements of Indian ragas.

After revolutionizing the folk club scene, Graham suddenly disappeared from public view for several years, probably owing to health problems caused by heroin addiction. Little is known about this period. He switched to classical guitar in 1973, considered giving up performing, and then got a contract with Stefan Grossman's label Kicking Mule. His first recording with Kicking Mule was *The Complete Guitarist* (1979), again with an unusual repertoire that ranged from the German Lutheran hymn "Ein feste Burg" to Vaughan Williams's "Down Ampney" and "Lord Mayo," followed by *Dance for Two People* (also 1979). Graham also increasingly started playing instruments other than guitar, such as bouzouki, oud, and sarod. He still performs occasionally.

BERT JANSCH AND JOHN RENBOURN: THE YEARS BEFORE PENTANGLE

Bert Jansch and John Renbourn were members of the internationally successful electric folk group Pentangle, and also central figures of the British guitar school that later became known as folk baroque.

Bert Jansch

Enigmatic, charismatic, yet also extremely private, Bert Jansch has garnered a reputation complicated by a number of contradictions, anecdotes, and myths.[12] He was born in Glasgow in 1943 and grew up in Scottish working-class surroundings. With almost no money at hand, his mother could finance piano lessons for him and his older sister Mary for only about three months. Although Jansch evinced little interest in these classical piano lessons, this brief period nevertheless gave him an idea of keys and scales. His genuine interest in music blossomed when he first saw a guitar at a school music class and decided to become a guitarist. Until he owned his first guitar at sixteen, he tried to build the instruments on his own. Around 1960 he started to turn up at the Howff, a prominent folk club run by Archie Fisher in Edinburgh, where he also received his first proper guitar lessons from coorganizer Jill Doyle, Davy Graham's sister.

Quickly exhausting Doyle's knowledge, he turned to Archie Fisher, who had been the first guitarist to introduce the banjo-derived clawhammer technique to Scotland. Fisher became a major influence on Jansch, who, in the second half of 1960, moved into the Howff, observing visiting musicians and practicing for hours. It must have been around that time that he picked up Davy Graham's piece "Angi," which became central in his repertoire and was popularized by him, first in Scotland and later in England. When Fisher and Doyle moved to Glasgow, Jansch remained at the Howff to teach and play. He met Robin Williamson, future founder of the Incredible String Band, in 1961. Sharing a flat with him, and later with another creative future Incredible String Band member, Clive Palmer, he was exposed to a vast range of music. When Williamson was offered a gig at the Troubadour, run at the time by Anthea Joseph (later a driving force in Joe Boyd's Witchseason office), in January 1963, Jansch followed him to London to perform there as well.

After an interlude of extensive traveling in France and Morocco, Jansch decided to settle in London, moving in and out of numerous friends' flats. He made a second appearance at the Troubadour in March 1964. It was in London that he got to hear musicians like Charles Lloyd, Charles Mingus, and John Coltrane for the first time, although Jansch denies any direct American influence on his playing:

> The clawhammer techniques I learned, I learned in Scotland, and I learned them from Scotsmen who had already gone through all that. The American players I heard were Brownie McGhee, Big Bill Broonzy, Leadbelly, and Woody Guthrie. They were the mainstay for me at that time. All the others came later. (Grossman 1990: 48)

Jansch quickly established himself as an outstanding musician. He became a resident at the Scot's Hoose for a year and also at Les Cousins, which guaranteed him a regular, albeit small, income. He recorded his first solo album, *Bert Jansch*, for Transatlantic in 1965, evidently having been introduced to label owner Nat Joseph by a close friend, folksinger Anne Briggs.

Born in Toton, Nottinghamshire, in 1944, Anne Patricia Briggs has influenced many performers of the British folk world with her singing style and repertoire. Discovered in the early 1960s by Ewan MacColl and A. L. Lloyd at one of the Centre 42 festivals[13] in her hometown of Nottingham, she was mentored by Lloyd. Through him, she took part in a number of pioneering revival recordings, including *The Iron Muse* (1963) and *The Bird in the Bush* (1966). Her singing and ornamentation style became a model for many later folksingers such as June Tabor and Christy Moore. She also popularized much of the material she had originally learned from Lloyd, like "Willie o' Winsbury" and "Reynardine," as well as her own songs, which were included on her first solo LP *Anne Briggs* (1966).[14] Later managed by Jo Lustig, whose work was shaped by a highly commercial attitude, she felt herself increasingly in conflict with her own convictions and the music business. After another solo album, *The Time Has Come* (1971), she withdrew from the scene, leaving a third album unfinished.

Briggs became a major influence, especially in terms of folk song repertoire, for Jansch. She taught him traditional songs like "Blackwaterside," "Jack Orion," and "Rosemary Lane"—pieces she had learnt from Lloyd during her performances with the Centre 42 Festival and that would become central to Pentangle's repertoire as well. While Denselow found the beginning of folk baroque on Graham's *Folk, Blues and Beyond* album, John Renbourn (Grossman 1990: 86) discovered this style in the partnership of Anne Briggs and Bert Jansch: "I think Bert learned a number of good tunes from her which he then found that the ornaments could be played on the guitar. That became labelled the 'folk baroque.'"[15]

"Blackwaterside" remains one of Jansch's central pieces, which he still performs almost every night he is on stage, always giving a clear acknowledgment to Briggs. Jansch and Briggs also played various gigs together, although unfortunately they were never recorded. Jansch, in return, taught Briggs to play guitar in DADGAD tuning. Her song "Go Your Way My Love" was the first piece that resulted from that collaboration and was later included on Jansch's album *Nicola*.

Bert Jansch was followed by *It Don't Bother Me* (1965), *Jack Orion* (1966), and *Bert and John* (1966), his first recording with his new musical partner John Renbourn, with whom he shared a flat near London Zoo around late 1964. Jansch not only left his mark with his guitar style, but also became well known as a songwriter; "Needle of Death," for instance, is still regarded as one of the best British songs addressing drug problems. He gained the attention of the music media from early on: *Melody Maker* wrote in a 1965 review that "he already shows the kind of international charm that could appeal to a wide audience. And his guitar playing can be very decorative."[16]

Jansch became one of the few commercially successful British guitarists and songwriters of that time: *Jack Orion* and *Bert and John* (1966) both sold well, and he started to play in such major venues as the Royal Albert Hall and Carnegie Hall, as well as with the Jimi Hendrix Experience in the Royal Festival Hall in 1967. His subsequent LP, *Nicola* (1967), was recorded in the pop style and arranged with an orchestra.

Jansch's biographer Colin Harper (CD 1993: 3) describes *Nicola* as an attempt to break out of the folk circuit. Yet *Nicola* failed in that respect, as did later solo recordings. Although always highly acclaimed inside and outside Great Britain, Jansch's recordings would never sell in the large numbers *Melody Maker* had expected. His individualistic lifestyle, increasingly dominated by his alcohol problems, was too unpredictable to allow him to become a star mass audiences could identify with.

John Renbourn

Although John Renbourn still cites Jansch and Graham as two major influences, he is a central figure of the British guitar style himself—not only as a performer and cofounder of the electric folk group Pentangle, but also through numerous video/tape/book publications. Always keen to explore, he not only became well known for his guitar technique, but also for his experimentations with medieval and renaissance material.

Born in London in 1944, Renbourn started to play guitar in the 1950s when he was still at school. As he recalled in an interview with the American guitarist Stefan Grossman (1990: 83), his early playing style was, like that of many others, clearly influenced by the then-popular skiffle craze as well as by visiting Americans like Chas McDevitt, Dickie Bishop, Johnny Duncan, and Jack Elliott in particular: "After [his visit], a lot of people were playing fingerpicking or flatpicking and fingerpicking of a simple nature, based mainly on Jack Elliot's style. . . . And then, of course, after that there were a lot of people playing mixtures of black American music."[17]

Renbourn had already played in the clubs while a student at Kingston Art School—early *Melody Maker* reviews date back to 1963—and became a professional guitarist in the blues and folk club scene afterward. He started to record through working with the African American singer Dorris Henderson, who had come to England in 1965 and needed an accompanist for her first album *There You Go* (1965). Henderson also had a regular spot on a television program called *Gadzooks! It's All Happening*, where Renbourn met future Pentangle members bassist Danny Thompson (b. 1939) and drummer Terry Cox, who were playing in the house band with Alexis Korner. In 1965 he made his first solo album, *John Renbourn*, for Transatlantic. He subsequently teamed up with Jansch and with singer Jacqui McShee, who had been involved in the folk and blues scene since 1960. With her sister Pam, McShee ran a club called the Red Lion in Sutton, where she had booked the two guitarists with whom she subsequently became friends. Nevertheless, as she recalled, the actual musical partnership was initiated by the guitarist Chris Ayliffe:

> He played twelve-string and I used to sing with him. We did mainly American blues and jug band type of things. He worked in a music shop, and he knew John Renbourn and Bert Jansch. They used to come in. And he introduced me to John and Bert. He consciously pushed me to towards John and Bert. And I did start working with John Renbourn in 1966.

His playing was far more delicate than the sort of guitar players I had been playing with. I still had a job then. I mean, it was still a hobby to me. But it became more serious when I was with John—because we traveled further.

The collaboration of Renbourn with McShee and Jansch finally led to the formation of Pentangle, with which their further biographies are inseparably intertwined.

PENTANGLE

Celebrated as the "first folk supergroup" (Dallas 1970g), Pentangle was one of the most innovative and internationally successful folk-based groups of the late 1960s. Yet it was less accessible than Fairport Convention or Steeleye Span; after the original group had disbanded in 1972, Karl Dallas wrote in *Melody Maker* that

> When I was talking to Ashley Hutchings the other day he told me he didn't have a Pentangle album in his collection, and I suppose most of our electric folkies would say the same. But where would they have got without the trail-blazing of Pentangle and Bert Jansch in particular whose superb *Jack Orion* solo album itself anticipated so much that was to come later? (Dallas 1973a)

When Pentangle's first recording was advertised in *Melody Maker* on May 18, 1968, the group had already existed for eighteen months, although this was almost the first time it had been announced as "the Pentangle." The band came into being at a time when Renbourn and Jansch were at the peak of their solo careers. The idea of founding the group had come from Renbourn, as McShee recalled:

> Pentangle started at the end of 1966. John and Bert used to share a flat together, and I was always up there rehearsing with John. And John said to me, "We are gonna have a group, you are going to be the singer." And it was as simple as that! I mean, I stayed with it because I did love the music. I didn't actually think I'd be earning a living. And when the band started, a lot of people seem to think it was an overnight success. It wasn't! We were going for about a year before.

The early Pentangle was still a more experimental band than anything fixed, as Renbourn pointed out: "Pentangle came together as a loose jammy band at late night gigs in London—places like the Cousins in Soho and later at the Horseshoe Bar." McShee added:

> We started off with a drummer and a bass player—just to try out. None of us can remember what their names were, who they were. But they didn't last very long. It was very strange! We had a few rehearsals but I think John was doing a weekly TV show, and he was backing Julie Felix. And Danny Thompson was on the same TV show. And he asked Danny if he'd be interested in coming along to have a play. It wasn't like an audition, it was

just—come along and see what you think. And he said, "Oh, I know this drummer," that he worked with Alexis Korner. It was Terry Cox. And they came along.

In contrast with other electric folk groups, the band's configuration was very stable, having only one lineup—McShee, Renbourn, Jansch, Danny Thompson, and Terry Cox—until its dissolution in 1972. The group's name came from Renbourn's interest in medieval music and culture. In one of his books, the pentangle had been described

> as being the sign that was on the inside of King Arthur's shield, so we decided it would be a good name, because it was valuable to protect us from evil as much as anything else! And it seemed like an innocuous enough name and we chose it. Of course, when we went to play in America in the '60s we hit up against the California culture which was very much into Tarot cards and the occult and all things esoteric, and almost by coincidence our stuff sort of slotted right in with that. (Harper CD 1992)

At the end of 1967 the early Pentangle—still without a name—started to play on a regular weekly basis at the Horseshoe Bar and at Les Cousins in Soho. During the week the band members were separately on tour or working. The group had a broad repertoire to start with, which became the basis for their later eclectic selection of recorded material, including old English ballads, American folk songs, blues material, jazz classics, dance tunes of the renaissance, and original compositions. Renbourn added:

> The common ground was blues/jazz and some folk. I guess that the jazz/blues side of Pentangle came from getting together with Danny and Terry. At least it gave the "band" a real groove. But the "folk" side probably came mainly from Jacqui, Bert, and myself. Danny and Terry had worked recording sessions with Julie Felix, Redd Sullivan, and so on. But most of the folk songs came from us three.

Pentangle later incorporated medieval and renaissance material stemming from Renbourn's increasing explorations in these musical periods. His solo recordings from that time, such as *Sir John Alot of Merrie Englande's Musyk Thynge and ye Grene Knyghte* (1968) and *The Lady and the Unicorn* (1970), contain a large selection of this music. But Pentangle's style and concert sets were not fixed in the beginning. Grounded in high musical and technical standards, the group developed a complex musical style with extended improvisational passages (their early gigs at the 400-seat Horseshoe resembled rehearsals), constant rhythm changes, open tunings, stylistic fusions, and unusual instruments such as glockenspiel, sitar, and banjo. With a "modish Eastern drone" and the "slight touch of tabla feel," as *Melody Maker* writer Tony Wilson (1968a) put it, Pentangle was thus meeting a prevalent interest of that time. The group initially worked acoustically; the instruments themselves were not amplified but were played directly into the microphone. Renbourn picked up the electric guitar only at a later stage and then only temporarily.

Pentangle's subsequent international success was not only the result of their high musical quality, but also of the skilled management behind the group, for they had acquired Jo Lustig as manager in early 1968. McShee mused in an interview with Maggie Holland (1993: 29) that probably Thompson or Renbourn brought in the New York manager, since they knew Julie Felix, who was managed by Lustig at that time. Although McShee, like many other performers of the folk scene, did not like Lustig's management style, she acknowledged his skills: "I think he was very, very good at public relations and promotions, I think that was his forte." The best example is still the first album cover, which had only silhouettes—and no photographs of the members—that were soon expanded to posters. As McShee pointed out further:

> He said he kept us a secret. That was his ploy. He decided that that was the best thing. Because John and Bert were known anyway. They were getting a really good reputation as solo artists. And the record company, Transatlantic, didn't actually want to have the band. They wanted John and Bert to stay as solo artists. Nat Joseph at Transatlantic didn't like the idea of having the band. He made it very clear. I mean, it was in quite early days.

Lustig moved the group quickly out of the folk scene by making them stop doing their regular Sunday gigs. With Jansch and Renbourn already being extremely popular, Pentangle received a great deal of attention from the beginning. Jansch remembered the group's first larger gig:

> We spent a whole year doing that club and then the Pentangle was formed, and the first gig we did after that was the Festival Hall [on June 29, 1968], which was sold out—no publicity, nothing, just virtually taking all the people that had come to the club and putting them into the Festival Hall. (Grossman 1990: 51)

Lustig not only took the group out of the club scene and got them on radio sessions for the BBC, but he also organized extensive tours and acquired the best technicians and producers. For *The Pentangle* (1968) the group went into the recording studio with Shel Talmy, one of the top producers at that time. However, according to McShee, Lustig seems to have had no influence on the choice of recorded material.

Pentangle's quick success was also evident on a financial level: Jansch and Renbourn had been two of the leading acts in the folk clubs and belonged to the top earners. McShee remembered that, with £5 per gig, Jansch and Renbourn were getting the highest fees possible in that scene. Yet it had still been difficult to make a living. Pentangle thus suddenly offered the performers a new financial dimension, as McShee recalled: "We were getting gigs through Transatlantic, and Danny, Terry and I were paid £22.50, which was a lot of money" (Tobler 1995: 33).[18]

Pentangle thus became one of the major acts of Transatlantic, the original label of Jansch and Renbourn, and its the first two albums (*The Pentangle* and *Sweet Child*), released in 1968, were widely acclaimed. In addition to performing at the Royal Festival Hall, the musicians also completed their first of five United States tours in that year.

In 1969 the group reached its commercial peak with *Basket of Light*, which charted for six months. Pentangle released two singles from that album, "Sally Go Round the Roses" and "Light Flight," the latter of which became the theme song for the hugely popular BBC series *Take Three Girls* and charted in the Top of the Pops rankings.

The international concert tours (five to the States, eight British tours, and three Scandinavian tours, plus trips to Australia and continental Europe) as well as performances at international festivals (Newport and Isle of Wight in 1969) were highly celebrated. Yet, like many performers of the folk/electric folk scene, the band members lacked the typical celebrity behavior of successful rock or pop groups. Their stage presentation was unusual for the popular music sphere of that time: the group would often split, with Jansch and Renbourn playing a duo, then adding McShee—who would sit rather than stand. As she has explained in various interviews, this choice was because of the almost traumatic experience of her first gig, during which her knees had been shaking so much that she barely felt able to control them. Despite her focal position as singer, she never presented nor felt herself to be a real front person. The instrumentalists, well-known solo performers in their own right, were also musically as important as the vocalist within this jazz-related style.

Cruel Sister, released in 1970, was the group's first all-traditional recording. By this time internal tensions were taking their toll. Danny Thompson was not happy with the material, and manager Lustig was dissatisfied with the sales. *Reflection* (1971) again brought disappointing sales again, but critics considered it a "masterpiece," recorded in a sixteen-track studio for the first time. After the expiration of the Transatlantic contract, Lustig negotiated a new deal with Warner—the group's American label—in 1972, but, despite their success and lineup constancy, the group disbanded the same year, after having released *Solomon's Seal*. On March 31, 1973, Karl Dallas could only write in *Melody Maker* that "Pentangle dies . . . with a whimper."

One of the major problems was the extremely long tours. Recording sessions that were crammed in between tours added to the strain. Renbourn remarked in an interview with Grossman (1990: 88–89):

> There were a lot of pressures on us that had nothing to do with the actual creation of the music and very little to do with putting the music across. We were eventually playing stadiums with people like the Grateful Dead, Canned Heat, and big American rock bands, all kinds of stuff and it was no fun whatsoever. . . . It just became more a way of going out and not really playing and coming back again. So the music itself stopped, I think, quite some time before the group actually no longer existed.

Moreover, the musicians had always simultaneously pursued their solo careers and individual studio projects. Terry Cox, who had worked with Alexis Korner and Roy Orbison, also played sessions for David Bowie and Elton John in the early days and was still doing many sessions for other people during the existence of the group. Between Pentangle dates, Jansch had, like Renbourn, recorded solo albums like *Birthday*

Blues (1969) and *Rosemary Lane* (1971). The latter was one of his most highly acclaimed albums, yet his solo career seemed about to slip.

First Cox left, then Thompson, both going back to their individual projects. Cox, a sought-after session musician, indulged his second love by opening a restaurant in Minorca. Thompson also became a highly successful session musician (with the likes of Kate Bush, Eric Clapton, and Hannes Wader), occasionally teaming up to perform as a duo with the songwriter/guitarist John Martyn, and has toured and recorded with Richard Thompson (no relation) as a duo and as a member of the Richard Thompson band. Jansch continued as a solo performer, playing as well with various ensembles such as the Bert Jansch Conundrum with Martin Jenkins and Nigel Portman-Smith.

Pentangle's dissolution before its contract ended created licensing problems with Warner. This meant that all the band members had to pay off some debts until the 1980s, and that Renbourn had to wait several years to record again, his first new solo album being *The Hermit* (1976). He continued to work with McShee as a duo, and both later became the core of the John Renbourn Group with Keshav Sathe on tablas, the American fiddle player Sue Draheim, and Tony Roberts (their recordings included *A Maid in Bedlam* in 1977 and *The Enchanted Garden* in 1980). This group lasted for about six years and toured extensively, finding a large audience internationally in connection with the emerging Celtic movement.

Pentangle was reassembled in 1982. As McShee recalled in her interview with Maggie Holland (1993: 29), Claudio Trotta, who had promoted the John Renbourn Group in Italy, was a Pentangle fan. He asked the musicians to re-form Pentangle and tour Italy which, with its newly developed interest in acoustic music, provided a good audience. The band completed the Italian tour and also (with new management) one in Australia. They appeared at the Cambridge Folk Festival as a four-piece band after Terry Cox dropped out due to an accident. This lineup did not last long, however, because Renbourn, stimulated by his interest in early music, decided to enter Dartington College and obtain a music degree. He taught there as well and continued his career as a solo guitarist, also touring extensively with Stefan Grossman and writing guitar books.

The group was reconstituted again in 1984, when a new album (*Open the Door*) was released with Mike Piggott (guitar, fiddle) replacing Renbourn. From then on, the new Pentangle has witnessed several changes: Thompson left again and was replaced by Nigel Portman-Smith for *In the Round* (1986). Cox was replaced by the ex-Fotheringay drummer Gerry Conway for *So Early in the Spring* (1989), while Rod Clements (guitar, fiddle, formerly Lindisfarne) replaced Piggott. This lineup lasted until 1994. In 1995 Jansch finally decided to drop out, too, and has continued to perform as a soloist. Although the new Pentangle has existed much longer than the original one, it is still the old lineup that is commonly associated with the group. Nigel Portman-Smith complained in 1992 that people still thought of him as being Danny Thompson, while Gerry Conway often got called John Renbourn (Harper CD 1992).

Jacqui McShee, who released her first solo album, *About Thyme*, in 1995, is the only original member left. She carries on with the group as "Jacqui McShee's Pentangle," which has released two albums, *Passe Avante* (1998) and *At the Little Theatre* (2000), at the time of this writing.

FAIRPORT CONVENTION

Fairport Convention has held a key position in the electric folk scene up to the present day. It was Fairport that achieved the first genuine musical and technical fusion of folk and rock, most obviously on its groundbreaking recording *Liege & Lief* (1969).[19] With that album, traditional material was consciously revived for a broader, rock-oriented contemporary audience. The band's frequent changes in lineup proved the source of both its greatest weakness and greatest strength. Fairport's many members have influenced a host of bands, including Steeleye Span and the various Albion Bands, plus individual performers such as Richard Thompson, Sandy Denny, Dave Mattacks, and Dave Pegg, who either became known as individual singer/songwriters or made guest appearances as session musicians on countless recordings in the folk, electric folk, and rock scenes.

The beginnings of Fairport Convention can be traced back to the years 1966–67. While still at school, bassist Ashley Hutchings (b. 1945) had already founded and led a number of amateur bands in the north London area of Muswell Hill. Fairport Convention grew out of one of these projects, the Ethnic Shuffle Orchestra (1966), with Ashley Hutchings (vocals, upright bass), Simon Nicol (b. 1950) (acoustic guitar), and Shaun Frater (drums). The Fairport band took shape between April and June 1967, when Richard Thompson (b. 1949) came in and Frater was replaced by Martin Lamble after the first gig. In July the group was completed by two singers, Judy Dyble and Ian (later Iain) Matthews. The name "Fairport Convention" refers to the house of Nicol's father, which was called "Fairport." Nicol's father had died in 1964, and the family had to rent Fairport out—one of the rooms was taken by Hutchings and another was used as a rehearsal space.

With this lineup Fairport started to gig in London's "underground" circuit, including the UFO Club at Tottenham Court Road. The UFO Club, which had been established by John Hopkins and Joe Boyd in 1966, was the central meeting place for London's progressive rock scene—bands like Pink Floyd regularly played the club at that time. The name of Joe Boyd is inseparably intertwined with the musical events of the late 1960s. Production manager at the 1965 Newport Festival, he ran the Elektra Records offices in London for a year afterward and was also cofounder of venues such as the UFO Club. He produced Pink Floyd's first single, "Arnold Layne," and became manager and producer of groups and performers such as the Incredible String Band, Fairport Convention, Nick Drake, and Billy Bragg. Though these musicians all had different styles, Boyd saw them all as sharing a common ground:

What always interests me is originality and genius, some kind of unique quality, and it doesn't really matter what kind of music it is. And for me there wasn't a big difference between what Syd Barrett was doing and what Mike Heron from the Incredible String Band was doing. Or what Richard Thompson was doing—or Sandy Denny. They were all really great musicians with a lot of originality in their compositions and quite intelligent people who were good to work with. And they were doing music which I personally found exciting, and for me there wasn't a conflict between the different types of music. I found the Incredible String Band in the folk clubs, but I pushed them very hard into the psychedelic scene because I thought that was where their real audience was.

Boyd negotiated Fairport Convention's first contract with Track Records for a single ("If I Had a Ribbon Bow") and an LP with Track's mother company Polydor in November 1967. The major part of Fairport's repertoire was still American material, yet the influences of the underground/progressive scene can be clearly heard on the LP *Fairport Convention*. Fairport was also one of the first British bands to interpret (besides the always favored Bob Dylan) the songs of Joni Mitchell, who was at that time unknown. The Fairporters became acquainted with Mitchell's music via Boyd. Despite his obvious influence, Boyd retrospectively described his impact on Fairport Convention, as with the Incredible String Band, as supportive rather than domineering, which was also confirmed by Simon Nicol:

If you look at his influence I think it is probably not too great in terms of the overall career, but getting it started, if you look at the material that was on the early records. I think he had an influence on that, although Ashley and Richard were quite—not forceful, but very clear people. I mean, they would never argue at anything but they would be stubborn once an idea had formed in their heads, and everybody looked up slightly to Ashley because he was older and everybody looked up to Richard because he was so talented—and Joe managed to keep the whole process moving forward without really pushing too hard. He was a good producer for a young band.

Fairport's singer Judy Dyble, whose voice was not considered strong enough to front a band, was asked to leave after the first recording. But because Fairport Convention was seen by many as the English answer to the American folk rock band Jefferson Airplane, they had to acquire a new female singer. The band held auditions in the spring of 1968, and asked Sandy Denny (b. 1947), folksinger and short-term member of the Strawbs, to come in. Although Denny already had a good reputation as a singer, Boyd was reluctant at first to hire her, "because she was a much stronger personality than the other people in the group—but she had so much respect for Richard that she really deferred to his judgment."

The fusion of folk and rock was a gradual development that took place on several levels, although the central folk rock period was restricted to the years between 1969 and 1972. Around May 1968 Fairport Convention was gigging extensively at BBC radio sessions, still with covers of American material, although their repertoire was gradually broadening.[20] Fairport's first deep musical contact with traditional English music can be traced back to Sandy Denny, who had to learn the band's repertoire. In return, she familiarized the group with her own material, stemming from her own songwriting and—predominantly—the traditional repertoire she had acquired by singing in the folk clubs. The impact she was going to make is clearly anticipated in an interview Thompson gave with *Beat International* in 1968: "We think ourselves as a folk-based band. This is even more pronounced now that Sandy Denny is with us. . . . She really knows what the folk tradition is all about, and the group as a whole are drawing from the English roots. The fact that we're electric doesn't make any difference" (Humphries 1997: 18).

Fairport subsequently started to adapt the traditional material into their own musical style, which was rock. Their first two recorded attempts to combine traditional songs with elements of rock music, "Nottamun Town" and "She Moves Through the Fair," can be found on the group's second album, *What We Did on Our Holidays* (1969)—although these tracks are usually considered immature compared to the folk-rock fusions of *Liege & Lief*. Feeling uncomfortable with the band's traditional side, singer Ian Matthews left after *What We Did on Our Holidays* to found his later highly successful band Southern Comfort. Fairport Convention, at that time, was slowly expanding from underground circuits to universities and club places. It was at one of those gigs that the innovative interpretation of "A Sailor's Life" came into being, as Hutchings (Humphries 1997: 28–29) recalled:

> We were in a dressing room at Southampton University waiting to go on stage, and Sandy was playing around in the dressing room, and picked up the guitar and played and sang "Sailor's Life." We loved it, and said, "Let's do that." We picked up our instruments and joined in—we had a little tuner amplifier in the dressing room, and we busked along. Then the time came to go on stage. We made an instant decision, I mean we were all buzzing with that because we enjoyed doing it so much . . . "Let's get out there and at it!"

Yet Simon Nicol relativized the importance of the song retrospectively in 1996:

> Everybody says, "Well, it's the track of 'Sailor's Life' which really marked a change—that was when the sun came up, you know, for folk rock." But that was done in a very free-handed way. It wasn't structured, it wasn't a decision that we would learn exactly the way she would have sung it solo. And—we had no idea. We just like started improvising and playing around with the spirit of the story of the song. And it came together very quickly and it led on, it became a talisman, really, for what that form of music could develop into. Everybody was impressed with it, but Ashley saw with his vision that this was something that could be picked up and run with.

Fairport's musical approach met with general approval among many of the dissatisfied musicians of the folk club scene. The fiddle player Dave Swarbrick—guesting on the recording of "A Sailor's Life"—saw a chance to interpret the old songs and ballads with more contemporary and also more extreme musical means. Yet *Unhalfbricking*, recorded in the winter and spring of 1969, still showed—like *What We Did on Our Holidays*—that the band could have gone in a variety of stylistic directions. Besides the interpretations of traditional songs, these albums also include cover versions of Bob Dylan and Joni Mitchell material, as well as songs written by Thompson and Denny.

It seemed that Fairport Convention was about to go straight for commercial success: The band appeared at the Royal Festival Hall with the American singer/songwriters Jackson C. Frank and Joni Mitchell in September 1968, *Unhalfbricking* was selling well in the States, and Boyd was about to organize Fairport's Newport debut. Then a tragic accident occurred in May 1969. While driving back from a gig, the group's van veered off the highway. Drummer Martin Lamble and Thompson's girlfriend, clothes designer Jeannie Franklin, were both killed and several band members were injured. Although *Unhalfbricking* made it onto the British Top 20 and several benefit concerts were held for the band, it was not certain whether Fairport Convention would carry on. When the group members finally decided to re-form they also decided—as a means to overcome the shock—to take off in a new direction. Nicol surmised that the accident probably drew much more attention to *Liege & Lief* than it would have received under normal circumstances:

> I think that was probably enhanced by the fact that the band had had this tragedy and . . . we came back. It was like a *comeback* for us. And everybody was very kind about that, they were very encouraging that we should not suffer too much of what we'd been through but the new lineup would be a success and that everybody would fit in very well. There was a great deal of enthusiasm for what the band was doing, and it was a good thing that we had such a strong product at that time. I mean it was one of those accidents of time that came together—and if we hadn't had the crash we'd probably still have made *Liege & Lief*, but there would have been less of a fuss about it.

Supported by manager Boyd and inspired by The Band's rediscovery of its musical roots, especially blues, on *Music from Big Pink*, Fairport Convention tried to develop a definite English rock idiom as a clear counterpoint to the then-dominant American music. A selection of this new direction can be heard on the album *Liege & Lief*. Released in 1969, it consisted mostly of traditional material and represented the true beginning of what was later to be called "electric folk" or "folk rock" by contemporary journalists, for the group not only electrified the old tunes but created a completely new style out of traditional and rock elements.

For *Liege & Lief*, two new band members, fiddler Dave Swarbrick and drummer Dave Mattacks, made a strong impact. With his complex and virtuoso fiddle playing, Swarbrick added a new tone color to Fairport Convention, whose instrumental lineup otherwise did not differ from that of a contemporary rock band. In contrast with Pentangle, Fairport amplified all their acoustic instruments directly via electronic pickup, so the fiddle was neither covered by drums and guitar nor overamplified. Although Denny knew a large number of traditional songs, it was especially Swarbrick who gave the group a legacy in terms of traditional music. He added songs, jigs, and reels of the British-Irish dance tradition and incorporated, like guitarist Thompson, elements of the old style in his original songwriting; he even composed a folk opera (*Babbacombe Lee*, 1971). Dave Mattacks (b. 1948) could already look back on a substantial professional career as drummer. As an extremely reliable and distinctive musician, yet without any experience in folk music, he had to develop a completely new drumming style, which became so uniquely his own that younger groups like the Oysterband who did not want to sound like mere Fairport imitators had to seek for an alternative approach.

Liege & Lief was a clearly planned project. Already in July 1969, before drummer Mattacks was recruited, the journalist Tony Wilson wrote an article in *Melody Maker* titled "Fairport Convention Present the New Electric Sound," with Simon Nicol pointing out that it was going to be a "conscious project." Joe Boyd had rented the band an enormous Queen Anne mansion named Farley House eleven miles outside Winchester in Hampshire; the parallels to The Band's having lived in a house called the Big Pink were clear. Here the group fully integrated Swarbrick and Mattacks, rehearsed the material of *Liege & Lief* for about three months, and then went in the summer and early autumn of 1969 into the studio (Sound Techniques) to record the album. As Hutchings recalled:

> We all lived in the house and worked on the material that went on *Liege & Lief*. So that was a very focused way of working. So *that's* why I think the album came out so complete, so much of a whole. Whereas before the other albums, they were very diverse: Sandy would write a song and say, "I've written this song!" Richard would come in, "Well, I have written this song." And this time we were all together in a room, all coming up with material, "Oh yeah, I like that, let's change that." You know, "Oh, I've got a tune, how about this." It was very exciting!

Nicol also saw a contrast to the previous working style:

> The band didn't do any gigs for—well, it must have been four months. It was between the accident and the comeback at the Festival Hall—March to August, something like that, quite a long time. I mean, that was a tremendous luxury for us at that time because up to that point we were working pretty well, every other day we'd be up doing a gig and then you'd be going into the studio, and you might have like, you know, six hours in the studio and then you might not be back in the studio again for another week. This was like all concentrated rehearsal time, and when we went into the studio it was unbroken time.

Fairport Convention played several gigs with their new material before the album was released. Journalist Robin Denselow (Laing et al. 1975: 161) portrayed the main gig at the Royal Festival Hall on September 24, 1969, as follows:

The Fairports played very loud and with extraordinary intensity that night. I particularly remember guitarist Simon Nicol launching into the robust tune of "The Deserter," drums, fiddle and bass crackling out through the amplifiers, and over the top of all, Sandy's clear voice re-telling the old story of the young man walking through Stepney, who has too many drinks with the recruiting party, finds he's enlisted, deserts, and is recaptured.

Whether or not this was really *the* gig that split the folk world in two, as Fairport biographer Patrick Humphries (1997: 55) suggests, it indeed raised a considerable public awareness for this new approach. *Liege & Lief* was also the result of the productive collaboration of Swarbrick and Thompson, Swarbrick being able to recall a large number of songs and Thompson working creatively with the material, adding new tunes or texts. Gaps in the texts were filled in by Hutchings, who developed an enthusiastic fascination with this music:

> Dave Swarbrick brought a knowledge in his head of tunes. I was the academic, I was the one who would go to Cecil Sharp House. And libraries. I was the one who'd say, "All right, I'll look that up," and say, "Oh, let's take that ballad." And Swarbrick would say, "Well, I can remember the first verse." And Sandy would say, "Oh, I can remember two or three verses." And then maybe we'd ring Martin Carthy or Ian Campbell and say, "Have you got any verses of that song?" But then I would be the one who'd tend to go off, go to London, maybe, and find texts or find a tune if we weren't happy with [the material], because apart from what went on *Liege & Lief* we had more material, of course. If you saw us in concert at that time we did, I don't know, two hours. So *Liege & Lief* was just a part of what we did at that time. And things didn't get recorded, a lot of traditional songs that we were working on.

Liege & Lief, which became a mixture of various approaches, included a selection of electric (i.e., rock) interpretations of classic Child ballads ("Tam Lin" and, most famously, "Matty Groves," the piece that has been played subsequently on almost every Fairport gig ever since), rewritten songs with a new text to a traditional tune ("Farewell, Farewell"), new songs in the old style ("Crazy Man Michael"), and, for the first time, jigs and reels played on electric rock instruments. The result was something new rather than mere "electrifications" of the tradition, as Joe Boyd pointed out: "They started with the repertoire for *Liege & Lief* from a completely different perspective. Instead of taking their style, the Fairport style, and fitting songs into it, they were taking the music as a starting point, the pure traditional form, and trying to play with the rhythmic feel of pure traditional music, but using electric instruments."

The album was released in December 1969. It sold, from a folk music perspective, in large numbers and became Fairport's best-selling album.[21] Yet when *Liege & Lief* was advertised several weeks before its appearance, its lineup, which is still regarded as the ultimate Fairport Convention formation, did not exist any more. As *Melody Maker* reported on November 22, 1969, "Now . . . Fairport Hit by Split," for Ashley Hutchings and Sandy Denny had departed. Hutchings had become increasingly more inter-

ested in the traditional material and wished to pursue that direction even more intensively. He left to found other groundbreaking electric folk groups, first Steeleye Span
and then the various Albion Country Bands. Denny, by contrast, had—like Dave
Swarbrick—seen Fairport as a move out of the restrictive folk clubs. Since her intention had been to broaden her repertoire, she naturally felt shut in again by having to
sing exclusively folk music. Denny founded her own band, Fotheringay, and after its
dissolution a year later started a solo career.

The remaining Fairport members were now joined by bassist Dave Pegg. After
playing guitar and bass in various Birmingham bands, Pegg had become, like Swarbrick, a member of the Ian Campbell Folk Group. Playing upright bass and also learning to play the mandolin, he thus had become acquainted with a large range of traditional material. Changing Hutchings's relatively basic style to extremely elaborate
lines, his bass playing had a strong impact on Fairport's sound, as Nicol recalled: "We
were happy with Peggy coming into the band and the way that sort of energized the
whole musicality of it. Because Ashley wouldn't ever claim to be a bass player, a musician, first. He's a ringmaster first, I think—who plays the bass perfectly."

Fairport made its United States debut in April 1970, going on tour with Jethro
Tull. They were highly acclaimed by music magazines like *Melody Maker* and appeared
at the Bath Festival in front of 300,000 listeners in June 1970. On their second U.S.
tour later that year, they also gigged at the Troubadour in Los Angeles, playing with
American singer Linda Ronstadt and with members of the rock group Led Zeppelin,
with whom Pegg was acquainted from his time in Birmingham (Humphries 1997: 72).

The next album titles *Full House* (1970) and *Angel Delight* (1971) referred to the place
the group had moved to: a former pub, the Angel, in Little Hadham near Bishop's
Stratford. Nicol remembered about the time of *Full House*:

> It was a huge difference because Ashley had gone and taken his vision with him and that
> we'd lost Sandy who was visually a centerpiece and an inspirational singer. So we were
> stuck, really. I remember feeling a little bit rootless, I mean sort of unguided, that we'd gone
> off and had to make another record and we had to keep doing the gigs and keep the diary,
> keep the people at the office interested—that sort of thing. So we just had to find out what
> we could do, making the best of the five of us. But it took a while to settle down. And then
> Richard upped and left, which was a bigger blow than we realized.

Full House, considered by many to be one of Fairport's strongest recordings, benefits
especially from the fruitful Swarbrick/Thompson collaboration, as is evident with
"Walk Awhile" and "Doctor of Physick." It was the group's final recording with
Thompson as a band member; he left in January 1971 to continue his solo career, becoming a highly acclaimed guitarist and songwriter and occasionally guesting on various folk and electric folk projects. Thompson was not replaced. Swarbrick, who had
started to dominate the group anyway, became the central figure and, although not a
singer, found himself in the role of lead vocalist.

Manager Joe Boyd also departed that year to work for Warner Brothers in the States. He had been fighting various problems with the other bands he managed: the Incredible String Band had converted to the Church of Scientology, and Sandy Denny and her band Fotheringay were often difficult to work with, as were Richard Thompson and Nick Drake.

The following period from 1971 to 1975 became, due to the constant change of members, extremely confusing, even for the pop/rock media that were oriented to personal stories and the lineup changes of groups. Although *Angel Delight* appeared in *Melody Maker*'s charts, Fairport's problems became more obvious with the folk opera *Babbacombe Lee*, written by Swarbrick and released on the Island label in the summer of 1971. Swarbrick's writing lacked the colorful diversity that had been evident in his musical collaborations with Thompson, and the band's backing was criticized as being monotonous—the absence of a strong vocalist became especially evident here. Thus, although Island had invested considerable publicity work and the album was received positively by critics, *Babbacombe Lee* did not sell well.

Extremely dissatisfied with the sales of the album and with his role as guitarist, Simon Nicol, the last original member who had remained in the band, left after *Babbacombe Lee* and became a full-time member of Hutchings's Albion Country Band. Nicol's departure seemed to indicate a clear ending for the band, which was struggling not only with its lineup changes but also with its general musical direction. *Rosie* (1973) was almost impossible to finish until the guitarist Trevor Lucas (from Eclection and subsequently Denny's band Fotheringay) came in. Lucas took Nicol's place as lead guitarist, supported by Jerry Donahue (also formerly of Fotheringay). Dave Mattacks, likewise unhappy about Fairport's direction, left soon after Nicol to play with the Albion Country Band and to pursue various other musical projects, but returned after only a brief while. Fairport's music at the time was a mixture of traditional—which was becoming less dominant—and, increasingly, newly written material. However, the band was, to the occasional frustration of its members, still identified with the *Liege & Lief* period.

Denny, now married to Trevor Lucas, joined the group again for an ambitious but financially disastrous tour, after which Mattacks left again and was replaced by Bruce Rowland. This lineup recorded a new album, *Rising for the Moon* (1975). Although it is today regarded as one of Fairport's finest albums, with many songs written by Denny but without any traditional material, its lack of commercial success (and persistent personality conflicts) caused the band split up yet again, with Denny, Lucas, and Donahue leaving.

Despite its many internal problems, Fairport Convention remained highly popular abroad. Dave Pegg (Humphries 1997: 124) recalled a tour to Germany in 1976 when, owing to current the popularity of Irish bands like Clannad, Fairport's concerts were sold out. Ironically, although Fairport was still associated with folk music, its material at that time was almost exclusively rock-oriented.

The next several years marked Fairport's low point. *Gottle O'Geer* (1976), originally meant as a solo album for Swarbrick, was used by the band to break free from their Island contract. Philippa Clare, the group's current manager, negotiated a deal with Vertigo (a division of Phonogram) for six albums, the first one being *Bonny Bunch of Roses* (1977), with Simon Nicol returning. Although the album was well received, the band was unable to recapture the musical and commercial success of its *Liege & Lief* period. Fairport's last album for the company was *Tipplers Tales* (1978). As Nicol recalled, the group still owed Vertigo four recordings, but because of the disappointing sales the company, Nicol said,

> actually paid us off—which tells you what the record industry thought of us in 1978. We knew that we could sell a few thousand copies of this *Farewell, Farewell* and I think we *wanted* it because we thought at that point that was the end of that band. We found a little company, called Simon's Record, who did put it out. They were very small, independent, they were obviously not part of the mainstream big business.

The reasons for Fairport's declining popularity and final breakup were not only to be found in the group's stylistic and musical problems in the mid-1970s, but also in a change of musical taste. Nicol continued:

> We did feel a little bit like a dinosaur at that time. Let me say punk started in 1976/77 abouts, and we finished in '79. You know, you do a festival in France and with quite good money, but you get there and everybody else would have funny-colored spiky hair and safety pins everywhere, and the noise would be appalling. And the audience would be just bottling the stage. I know the punk was a necessary evil in the plan, it was good for a lot of things that happened with the independence or the destruction of the autonomy of the large companies—and the Yeses and the Led Zeppelins of the time. It was a natural thing to happen. But we were caught in the middle. We weren't part of the big band massive thing and we weren't part of the punk thing.

The band members went off in different directions. Dave Pegg became a member of Jethro Tull in 1980 (where he remained until 1995); Nicol played again in Hutchings's various Albion Bands and guested on numerous folk and electric folk projects; Swarbrick, who was suffering from hearing problems, went back into the clubs, playing acoustic music again; and Mattacks extended his session work, playing for well-known names like George Harrison, Paul McCartney, Jimmy Page, Cat Stevens, and Elton John.

The group's actual dissolution, however, only lasted for a brief time. Despite having played an official "farewell" gig in the small Oxfordshire town of Cropredy (near Banbury) in 1979, Fairport played its next gig the following day. The band regrouped for a reunion concert at the same location in 1980, which proved so successful that Fairport decided to repeat it the following year. As biographer Humphries (1997: 151) pointed out, the story of Fairport from the mid-1980s onward has remained connected with the annual Cropredy Festival.[22] The group's reunion meetings, always held on the second weekend in August, developed into a large three-day outdoor festival at Cropredy—often with 16,000–19,000 visitors. The festival presents many contemporary electric folk bands as well as old colleagues like Richard Thompson or Ashley Hutchings's various Albion Bands. Fairport usually plays the whole Saturday night—the concert often being like a trip through the group's history with many former members guesting.

Simon Nicol, Dave Pegg, and Dave Mattacks regrouped as a trio in the mid-1980s, with Nicol assuming the role of lead singer. For this lineup's first new album *Gladys' Leap*, released in 1985, Ric Sanders (from the jazz group Soft Machine) was asked to play fiddle on three tracks as Swarbrick was not available, and Thompson also performed on one track. *Gladys' Leap* not only contained the song "Hiring Fair" (written by Ralph McTell), which became a modern counterpart to the ever-popular classic "Matty Groves," but the album also received extremely enthusiastic reviews—which had not happened for a long time. Sanders became a full member, and after adding guitarist and multi-instrumentalist Maartin Allcock to the lineup, the band went on tour again.

Since 1985 a number of Fairport Convention albums have been released, presenting the performers as mature interpreters of high-quality songs, with Nicol emerging as a strong singer. Traditional songs still play a central role in the band's repertoire, yet the group has found it increasingly difficult to discover good material not yet interpreted by others. The major portion of the songs is thus newly written material. Having learned from its most unstable period in the mid-1970s, Fairport, lacking a good songwriter until recently, has sought its material from other writers, often predominantly British songwriters like Huw Williams, Ralph McTell, Steve Tilston, and Jez Lowe. Sanders and Allcock, younger and thus representing a different musical generation, also brought a new sound color to the band by adding synthesizers to the classic guitar-fiddle blend.

This lineup remained the most constant one in the group's history until 1997, when Mattacks and Allcock left. Mattacks was replaced by former Fotheringay/Pentangle drummer Gerry Conway, who has given the group a less heavily rock-oriented percussion sound. Allcock's successor, fiddler Chris Leslie, not only added a stronger folk sound but also emerged as a skilled songwriter on *The Wood and the Wire*, which was released in 2000. Today Fairport Convention remains a part-time band, gigging for half a year, recording albums, and playing Cropredy, with the members pursuing other musical projects and jobs during the rest of the year. The business side is handled by Dave Pegg's own recording label Woodworm, which grew out of the *Farewell, Farewell* album that had been dropped by the original label and was bought by Pegg. Woodworm, run by Pegg and his wife Chris, gives the band an independent presence outside the larger rock music business.

INDIVIDUAL CAREERS OUT OF FAIRPORT CONVENTION: SANDY DENNY, RICHARD THOMPSON, AND ASHLEY HUTCHINGS

Sandy Denny

Although somewhat underrated during her lifetime, Sandy Denny is today acknowledged as one of England's finest female singer/songwriters.[23] Alexandra Elene MacLean Denny was born of Scottish parents in Wimbledon in 1947. Uncomfortable with the strictness of classical music lessons—she studied piano for a brief time—she nevertheless showed an excellent musical ear from early on, and her singing talent also seems to have surfaced before secondary school. Leaving school before her A-levels, she started nurses' training at Brompton Chest Hospital before enrolling at the Kingston School of Art in 1965. Although she studied art and sculpture, she became primarily involved in the folk scene on campus that also attracted fellow students John Renbourn and Eric Clapton.

Denny slowly established herself as a singer on the folk club circuit. Her early repertoire was, other than a few British/Irish folk songs, heavily dominated by American singer/songwriters like Tom Paxton and Jackson C. Frank, with whom she socialized around 1966.[24] She first discovered folk songs through the recordings of Bob Dylan and Joan Baez, although she showed little interest in the material's history. She also became a competent guitar player, probably having learned some finger picking from Frank. Yet it was her voice that captured her audiences from early on. Karl Dallas wrote in a 1966 *Melody Maker* article that "Sandy Denny has the sort of rich soaring voice that could make her a British Baez, though the comparison does her an injustice." One year later he wrote that "she has a sense of timing many would-be jazz singers would envy, which makes even the most tired old overdone folk lyric sound fresh and new" (Dallas 1966e and 1967).

In 1967 Denny joined the Strawbs, with whom she made one album, *Sandy Denny and the Strawbs*. Recorded in Denmark, the LP contains one of Denny's earliest and still best-known original songs, "Who Knows Where the Time Goes?" This lineup separated after half a year. The Strawbs—from 1970 to 1971 with future Yes keyboardist Rick Wakeman as a full-time member—continued with a highly successful career in rock, while Denny went back briefly to the folk clubs. However, feeling restricted with the limited artistic possibilities of the clubs, she joined Fairport Convention in 1968. As Tony Wilson (1968b) remarked in *Melody Maker*:

> As a solo folksinger, Sandy had become frustrated. A good singer and a fair guitar player, Sandy worked the usual rounds of clubs and concerts but the big break seemed constantly to elude her. "I wanted to do something more with my voice," says Sandy explaining her move. "Although I can play guitar adequately I was feeling limited by it, it was a kind of stagnation. I was developing but the guitar was restricting."

Many later writers regard the period that comprises the albums *What We Did on Our Holidays, Unhalfbricking,* and *Liege & Lief* as Denny's and Fairport's artistic peak.[25] Contributing not only traditional material but also several of her own songs like "Fotheringay," Denny made a strong impact on the band's sound. Yet she left Fairport Convention in the autumn of 1969, even before the release of *Liege & Lief.* Joe Boyd recalled in a BBC interview that instead of enjoying her success, she instead became increasingly depressed.[26] As he pointed out, Denny had never been comfortable with the "being on the road" that was an essential part of performing this kind of music; she found the constant travel exhausting. These problems were intensified by her fear of flying: she preferred traveling by road with her later band, Fotheringay, and resisted doing a U.S. tour as long as possible. However, the basic musical reason for her departure from Fairport was her unhappiness with the folk direction Fairport Convention was then following. Having initially wanted to break out of the folk repertoire when she joined the band, she found herself being pushed back into it while making *Liege & Lief.*

Fotheringay, named after the introductory song on *What We Did on Our Holidays,* was founded in 1969 (with Trevor Lucas, Jerry Donahue, Pat Donaldson, and Gerry Conway) and highlighted Denny's performing and songwriting. Her songs are characterized by a melancholic, almost dark atmosphere, combined with an emotional intensity that was also evident in her singing. Even though writing would always be a tedious process for her, she nevertheless assembled a number of songs that would make up most of the group's album, *Fotheringay.* Yet despite being hailed by *Melody Maker* as one of the "new hopes of folk-rock," Sandy Denny broke up the group after only one year, giving a farewell concert at London's Queen Elizabeth Hall on January 30, 1971.

The reasons offered for Fotheringay's dissolution vary. Joe Boyd saw the band's democratic organization as a significant cause of its split, apart from financial difficulties.[27] (Karl Dallas had welcomed this step toward an antistar, egalitarian group, but with Denny's boyfriend Trevor Lucas as a member, this strategy might also have been necessary for personal reasons.) In Boyd's eyes, the emphasis on consensus made studio work extremely tedious, and he found the band's first album rather disappointing. With the second (never completed) Fotheringay album, the situation was, according to Boyd, even worse. Others, however, blame Boyd's insufficiently supportive management for the split as well. Fotheringay had been formed against the suggestions of Boyd, who had wanted Denny to pursue a solo career at that point.

After Fotheringay Denny did choose to continue solo, with many of her Fairport Convention and Fotheringay colleagues guesting as band musicians for her recordings and tours. Albums like *The North Star Grassman and the Ravens* (1971), which contains some of the material intended for the unfinished second Fotheringay recording, and *Sandy* (1972) were highly acclaimed by the critics. She also guested on Led Zeppelin's fourth album, duetting with Robert Plant on "The Battle of Evermore," and appeared on Lou Reizner's version of the Who's rock opera *Tommy.*

Although Sandy Denny was voted female singer of the year by *Melody Maker* readers in both 1970 and 1971 and was extensively covered by writer Dallas, who had been a great admirer of her music from her early folk club performances in the mid-1960s, she did not have the expected breakthrough into a more popular segment of the industry with her solo work. Some assumed that her lack of success was partly caused by the focus on American singers Linda Ronstadt and Joni Mitchell, who were dominating the scene at that time.[28] It could also have been that Denny's often moody and melancholy songs were simply not appealing to a larger audience—and that she had been too strongly associated with traditional music, although it played only a marginal role in her later repertoire. *The North Star Grassman and the Ravens* and *Sandy* contain only one traditional song each; the rest are cover versions and her own songs, although all were strongly influenced by her familiarity with traditional music. Trying to rid herself of the traditional tag, she would later even refuse to sing this part of the repertoire at live gigs, to the regret of many listeners (Murray Winters CD 1998).

Nevertheless, behind the scenes, there were personal and managerial difficulties. Prone to insecurity and depression, Denny had a drinking problem that made her performances extremely variable and increasingly affected her voice. Yet precisely when everything started to work more smoothly, around late 1973, her recording label started to withdraw its support. Denny married Trevor Lucas that year and joined Fairport again for a world tour in 1974 and *Rising for the Moon* (1975). The tour was strenuous and financially disastrous, and Denny and Lucas left Fairport the same year. During her two years of absence from the music scene, her daughter, Georgia, was born. Denny then returned to the scene, apparently with a clear direction in mind. She recorded a new album, *Rendezvous*, in 1977, and completed a solo concert tour with a last performance at the Royal Theatre on November 27, 1977. Her private life, however, deteriorated during these years, as Heylin's biography reveals. The drinking problem was further aggravated by drugs, and her marriage was at an end as well. She died on April 21, 1978, after lying in a coma for five days following a cerebral brain hemorrhage caused by a fall.

Richard Thompson

After leaving Fairport Convention in 1970, guitarist and singer Richard Thompson became a highly acclaimed solo artist and an eminent songwriter, often incorporating elements of British traditional music into his compositions.[29] Thompson, whose songs have been covered by a large variety of artists, also remains a leading figure among British guitarists. As Joe Boyd recalled, it was Thompson's guitar playing that first called his attention to Fairport Convention when they were playing in the underground scene at the UFO Club: "What made them interesting at first, they were very much like an American West Coast band, and really what I was interested in with them was Richard Thompson. Because I thought he was a great guitar player—and they were playing music that was quite familiar to me but also quite different, because it was English."

Richard John Thompson, born in 1949, first started to play the acoustic guitar in his early teens. After close to two years of classical guitar lessons, he picked up the electric guitar. His early repertoire consisted of material from Buddy Holly and the Everly Brothers; as Berman (CD 1993: 25) pointed out in the liner notes for *Watching the Dark*: "He progressed rapidly, practicing the chords he'd picked up from watching his father . . . and his older sister's boyfriends, who offered impromptu lessons." Thompson played with his various groups in pubs and social halls, but occasionally also in folk clubs, rehearsing the folk/pop songs of Richard Fariña, Bob Dylan, and Phil Ochs. Although slightly familiar with Scottish music, owing to his father's Scottish background, he considered the folk music he encountered in the clubs at that time to be dull (Humphries 1996: 30), an attitude he shared with many of his contemporaries and which was completely changed when he recorded *Liege & Lief* with Fairport Convention.

Thompson showed a strong love for poetry in his schooldays and might have studied English literature after his A-levels if he had not had a music career in mind. When he left school in 1967, he apprenticed with a stained-glass maker for about half a year, which allowed him enough time for music in the evenings. His talent as a songwriter was soon evident with Fairport Convention, of which he was a founding member, with reflective songs like "Meet on the Ledge" or "Genesis Hall." Some of the now-classic Fairport songs like "Crazy Man Michael" were products of his collaboration with fiddler Dave Swarbrick. Thompson left Fairport in 1971 after *Full House* and an American tour.

Henry the Human Fly!, his first solo work, appeared in 1972, featuring many of his former Fairport colleagues. It was an attempt to create an English form of rock 'n' roll by blending elements of English traditional music with American rock. Thompson soon became involved in numerous other electric folk projects, including Shirley Collins's *No Roses* and Ashley Hutchings's *Morris On*, in addition to many guest appearances with Sandy Denny. It was Denny who introduced him to her friend, folksinger and backup vocalist Linda Peters, whom he later married. Richard and Linda Thompson soon became known as a duo, their first recording being *I Want to See the Bright Lights Tonight* (1974).

Around 1973 Thompson became interested in the Islamic Sufi religion. He and Linda converted that year and joined a Sufi community. Although the Thompsons were still recording and performing in public, this period clearly shows the marks of a constant tension between their Muslim beliefs and their artistic concerns. Thompson incorporated elements of Sufi mysticism in his songwriting, and his lyrics often carried a double meaning. Yet he performed increasingly less, reaching a point around 1976 when he was not sure whether he would ever play the electric guitar again. Between 1975 and 1978 the Thompsons were largely absent from the scene. Slowly returning to view, first with some guest recorded appearances, as on Denny's *Rendezvous* (1977), Thompson left the Sufi community around 1978. Jo Lustig—who remained his manager even during that time—arranged a new contract with Chrysalis, with *First Light* (1978) becoming the first release after his absence.

Thompson had already attained a cult status as guitarist and songwriter before his Sufi period. Yet, although his songs were increasingly covered by more musicians, he had never had a hit single, which would have brought him greater commercial success. With *Shoot Out the Lights* (1982), a collection of high-quality songs such as "Wall of Death," he became established in the States, where he moved in the late 1980s with his second wife, Nancy Convey. His success increased after signing a contract with Polydor. In 1988 he moved to Capitol, who promoted him to a larger audience, and his albums, such as *Amnesia* (1988) and *Rumor and Sigh* (1991), started to sell respectably (*Rumor and Sigh* also contains one of Thompson's most popular songs in performance, "1952 Vincent Black Lightning." Written in traditional English ballad style, the unusual story of love and tragic death centers around a motorcycle, the Vincent Black Lightning). The sales numbers have still been moderate, however, compared to those of other rock musicians.

Although Thompson left the electric folk scene long ago and "pure" traditional songs are rare in his concert repertoire, his exposure to traditional music still shows in the incorporation of Scottish/Irish elements, like the imitation of bagpipes, in his music, as Joe Boyd emphasized:

> He had been exposed when he was young to Scottish music through his father—but really, he was a rock 'n' roller when I met him. It was a slow process of becoming more and more interested in the melodies and possibilities. If you listen to his guitar playing now, you can hear so much influence from bagpipes of all kinds. I think so much of the way he shapes his solos, in the way he tries to get his guitar to sound, is very strongly influenced by the traditional sound of pipes. So no matter if he is playing some rock songs that have nothing to do with folk music, it's always that influence which is one of the things that makes him a unique guitar player. And the first things he sang were quite traditional in their atmosphere—so I think his style of singing has been shaped that way, which is one of the things that maybe limits his popularity because a lot of people resist that kind of singing. Because it's too much like folk music.

Thompson's relationship to traditional music extends far beyond a fostering of his Scottish roots. For example, he has always been interested in American Cajun music, which inspired his songs "Cajun Woman" (on Fairport Convention's *Unhalfbricking*) and "Tear-Stained Letter" (on his solo album *Hand of Kindness*). In 1991 he also made a guest appearance on Beausoleil's album *Cajun Conja*.

He still frequently appears with Fairport Convention at the annual Cropredy Festival, guesting also on numerous recordings of the English music scene. In 2002 his acoustic narrative "1952 Vincent Black Lightning" won the Bluegrass Song of Year award for the version recorded by the Del McCoury Band.

Ashley Hutchings

Bandleader, arranger, and bassist Ashley "Tyger" Hutchings needs to be mentioned separately, having contributed substantially to the folk and electric folk movements as founder or founding member of Fairport Convention, Steeleye Span, and the various Albion Bands. Many journalists have acknowledged his organizational skills, drawing together the best musicians for highly original projects, as Joe Boyd pointed out:

> I think in a way the most interesting career is Ashley's—in regard to all of this, because he stuck to what he believes in and has had a big influence on English theater music and all sorts of things. And he in a way is the one person who has stayed inside folk music and taken the ideas from *Liege & Lief* and kept it fresh, things that are really keeping within the spirit of the music.

Although he occasionally visited folk clubs in the mid-1960s, Hutchings did not really learn English traditional music until Fairport Convention started to work on *Liege & Lief*. Strongly influenced by Dave Swarbrick, he soon became almost obsessed with traditional material and has become known, because of his archival and comparative research, as the "academic" of the scene (see Humphries 1997: 65).

Hutchings grew up in the Muswell Hill area of North London. As he explained to journalist John Tobler (LP 1991), his nickname "Tyger" referred to his behavior on the football field: "I spelt it with a 'y' because I thought it was more arty." Following his father, who had been a pianist with his own dance band, Leonard Hutchings and His Embassy Five, Hutchings started performing in the early 1960s, leading a number of short-lived groups like Dr. K's Blues Band and the Ethnic Shuffle Orchestra, which became the core of Fairport Convention, with Hutchings on stand-up bass and Simon Nicol on guitar. After leaving school he worked briefly as a journalist with magazines like *Furnishing World* and *Advertisers Weekly* and was also assistant to the managing director of Haymarket Press, until he realized that he could make a living from making music.

Hutchings formed Fairport Convention in 1967 and stayed with the band for two years. Only a few weeks after leaving Fairport, he assembled the core band that was ultimately to be Steeleye Span, with whom he made three albums until he left the in 1971—before the group reached its commercial peak. In the same year he founded the Albion Country Band, originally a loosely formed group of musicians to accompany his wife at the time, Shirley Collins, on *No Roses* (1971). It was also Collins who gave the band its name: "We realized that with all those musicians it would probably be a good idea to give the collective a name and that was the one we came up with."[30]

No Roses was especially remarkable because it was one of the largest folk rock recording projects made at that time, as Fairport member Simon Nicol pointed out:

"Because everything else was quite with small forces involved, I mean, there were only five people on *Morris On*. But then suddenly there was this big project and every track was going to have a different arrangement, different feel, different combinations of music suggesting the periods of the time." This embryonic Albion Country Band finally encompassed about twenty-six musicians, including names such as Richard Thompson, Simon Nicol, Dave Mattacks, and the Watersons. Collins recalled amusedly that "it got very complicated, because Ashley kept inviting other people to come in and join in. I really had a ball, and it's been really some time, but it's still bringing me some money."

This Albion Country Band became the forerunner of the various Albion Dance Bands—or (from 1977 on) Albion Bands—being, like many jazz bands, a flexible organization of rotating musicians. With Hutchings as organizational leader, it has united eminent musicians from the folk and electric folk scene such as John Tams (melodeon); John Kirkpatrick (melodeon); Martin Carthy (guitar); various Fairport Convention members; and early music specialist Phil Pickett (recorders)[31] for numerous musical projects. The focus has always been on playing English traditional, material as well as rock pieces and songwriting, on electric and acoustic instruments "centered around Hutchings's conviction that the culture and traditional folk music of the British Isles could form the basis of an interesting and commercial strain of contemporary rock music" (Suff and Tobler CD 1993: 1) Hutchings later said about the reasons for this focus that "it's just that I don't feel British, I feel English. It's rather false, this lumping together of the countries—I feel that Scotland and Ireland and England are very different countries, as different as France and England, say" (Anderson and Heath 1982: 10).

The first Albion Band albums, like *Battle of the Field*, were almost exclusively based on English traditional material—very much in contrast to Steeleye Span, which also used Irish material. The strict focus on English material was later relaxed and expanded to include a broad range of English country dances, 1950s rock 'n' roll, medieval music, blues, rock, ballads, and original songs.

Most notable has been Hutchings's impact on the revival of morris dance and English country dance music—which is probably the only case in which the revival and electric folk movements have had an influence on the existing tradition. The interest in English dance music, which has remained a specialty of the Albion Band, started when Hutchings was gathering the material for the morris dance record *Morris On* (1972). "It was hearing William Kimber on record for the first time—the record that the EFDSS put out of Kimber playing and talking," as Hutchings recalled (Anderson and Heath 1982: 10),[32] that sparked his interest. He subsequently produced and played on a series of related albums, including the *Compleat Dancing Master* (1974), *Rattlebone & Ploughjack* (1976), and *Son of Morris On* (1976).

Hutchings also had a short interlude with the Etchingham Steam Band. The band, whose core consisted of Hutchings and Shirley Collins, focused on Collins's repertoire of Sussex material. The band was formed at the time of short working weeks and power cuts in 1974; as its name indicated, the band did not need any electricity, and some of the early gigs were even played by candlelight. Hutchings played acoustic bass guitar, while the percussion was provided by children's hobby horses with morris bells. Although the band received standing ovations at the Royal Albert Hall, Collins and Hutchings had to abandon the band when they could not make enough money with it.

Hutchings had developed an interest in theater with Steeleye Span. He also used theatrical elements in the Albion Band shows, as well as participating in various stage and television projects such as for the Christmas program *Here We Come A-Wassailing*. The Albion Band provided the music for Keith Dewhurst's adaptations of Flora Thompson's *Lark Rise to Candleford* in 1978–79 and was also associated with Bill Bryden's Cottesloe Theatre Company at the National Theatre in London's South Bank Centre. After a long period with the National Theatre, some of the musicians (John Tams and Graeme Taylor) left to found the Home Service, which pursued a more direct folk rock direction. Hutchings also made various concept recordings like *By Gloucester Docks I Sat Down and Wept* and *An Evening with Cecil Sharp*.

Despite the constant lineup changes, Hutchings's bands have kept some constant elements like Albion Day, a festival day of the band, that was first staged at Cheltenham in 1989. Since 1990, the bands' sound has been hard to distinguish from that of a good rock band, always easily switching between acoustic and electric formations—long before MTV promoted the unplugged trend. The 1994 release *Acousticity* offers a good example of this versatility. Yet, as Hutchings emphasizes, he is still most at home with the electric sound.[33]

STEELEYE SPAN

Steeleye Span brought the combination of folk and rock to a much stronger musical extreme than did Fairport Convention. Although Steeleye's early material was almost exclusively traditional, the musical sound was much harder-edged, due to the stronger emphasis on the rhythmic elements, the clearer predomination of the electric instruments (especially electric guitar and bass), and additional sound effects.[34]

The group's core musicians, Maddy Prior and Tim Hart, were not rock musicians, but they adapted the strategies of rock performances, including incorporating traditionally based theatrical elements such as mummers' plays. Steeleye Span worked at a highly professional level, both in regard to its music and its management, which was run by Jo Lustig during the group's heyday. It became, as Denselow pointed out (Laing et al. 1975: 163), "the most successful folk-rock band of all, one that was to bring a highly amplified version of British traditional material into the vast rock shows in the American stadiums and into concert halls across the world."

Steeleye Span was formed by Ashley Hutchings in late 1969. In an interview with John Tobler (LP 1991), Hutchings explained that, following his departure from Fairport Convention, "I felt we needed to throw ourselves into traditional music—it was far too soon to abandon it, and I was very excited by this direction. After we started performing the *Liege & Lief* material, I got to know a number of folk musicians, and that gave me the confidence to form Steeleye Span."

Hutchings had rehearsed with Irish musicians Andy Irvine, Johnny Moynihan, and Terry Woods (who were members of Sweeney's Men), as well as with Bob and Carole Pegg (from Mr. Fox), but without any lasting result, because Sweeney's Men dissolved when Irvine and Moynihan decided to go solo.[35] He finally came up with the lineup of Gay Woods (vocals, concertina), Terry Woods (vocals, guitar), Maddy Prior (vocals), Tim Hart (vocals, guitar), and himself (bass).

Until they were asked by Hutchings to join Steeleye Span's first lineup, Maddy Prior (b. 1947) and Tim Hart (b. 1948) had been working as a relatively successful folk duo in the clubs for about four years. Living in St. Albans, Hart started to play guitar at the age of thirteen, also picking up the banjo and singing. After a short interlude of playing rock music in France for three months in 1966, he formed a folk duo with Prior later that year. The daughter of a writer, Prior had spent her early childhood in Blackpool and started singing in the clubs by imitating American singers like Joan Baez, before rediscovering her own tradition.

The duo had already recorded two albums (vols. 1 and 2 of *Folk Songs of Olde England*) before they met Hutchings. Both had been looking for new musical possibilities, as Maddy Prior recalled:

> Steeleye was different because it was using a different medium. Which was essentially louder—and with more people. Which were two things both Tim and I were deeply interested in. We wanted to work with other musicians—rather than just the two of us, because I didn't play an instrument. And Tim was playing all these various things, that was kind of silly, really! And we wanted to do something a bit wider and a bit more adventurous and there was only so much we could do with the two of us. It had been talked about going electric for a while—but we didn't really think it would involve us, to be honest.

According to Prior, the first lineup of Steeleye Span happened more or less by chance:

> Ashley lived around the corner in Muswell Hill. And we were in Archway. And Terry and Gay were staying in the house at the time when Ashley was trying to get it together. He was trying to get the band together with Sweeney's Men, but Sweeney's Men were at that point splitting up and he asked Terry and Gay to be involved and then, because we were in the house, they asked us. So we went and "got it together" in the country. Steeleye was out of nowhere, really, at that point. And because we didn't know Terry or Gay—or Ashley—we were all looking around to see what everybody else was doing and if it worked. It didn't relate very much to anything else we'd done. I think that was good. It gave us a lot more freedom to try different things.

The group's name was suggested to Hart by Martin Carthy. It refers to a Lincolnshire folk song entitled "Horkstow Grange" in which an old wagoner, Jon Span—nicknamed Steeleye Span—is defeated by the tyrannical farm foreman John Bowlin in an obscure, violent quarrel. This first Steeleye formation never performed live; it recorded one album in 1970, *Hark! The Village Wait*, after which it disbanded. A major problem was the extremely different characters and musical ideas of the two folk duos and Hutchings. As Prior reflected in 1996, "It split up for a million reasons, one of them being 'getting it together' in the country, which was a disastrous idea, nobody should ever do it! Because you don't know these people. And suddenly being thrown together for three months—in the middle of nowhere. It's a really stupid idea. How could we expect it to survive?"

Terry and Gay Woods left after the recording and continued as a highly successful duo.[36] With the Woods' departure, the group was in need of additional instrumentalists. Carthy—who had been eager to join in, as gigs with Swarbrick had become impossible owing to the fiddler's overlapping schedules with Fairport—was suggested by Tim Hart. "Maddy and I knew Martin, and I got the feeling that he might be interested in joining Steeleye—I knew he was interested in what we were doing . . . so then the four of us had got together" (Tobler CD 1991a). Carthy had a major impact on the group. He was not only a prolific source of material, but he also gave the group more security in handling the material. With the leading position he held in the folk scene, he gave the group authenticity.

The group was still in need of another instrumentalist, as it remained heavily dominated by voices and guitars. With Peter Knight (fiddle, mandolin, vocals), another skilled musician was added. Hart remembered that "Peter was ideal, because he . . . was a trained musician, and Martin and I knew quite a bit about music and wanted someone who was a bit more than an ear-playing fiddle player, . . . someone who could read music and understood arrangement" (ibid.).

This lineup, still without drums, made two albums in 1971, *Please to See the King*, which charted in April in the Top 50 of the U.K. album charts, and *Ten Man Mop or Mr. Reservoir Butler Rides Again*. The group members also worked as musicians and actors in the London Royal Court Theatre, first in *Pirates*, then in Keith Dewhurst's *Corunna*. In August 1972 the group provided music for a modern stage version of R. L. Stevenson's *Kidnapped* at the Lyceum in Edinburgh.

Hutchings left Steeleye Span at the end of 1971. The band members disagree about why he left. Hart remarked that

I seem to remember it came from when we were doing a stage play, "Corunna," plus America came up and Ashley basically didn't want to do what Martin [Carthy] and Maddy and I wanted to do. . . . Ashley had a very precious attitude towards traditional music at that time, and regarded it as a quaint art form, whereas we'd been working with it for years. We found his attitude very curious—this rocker who thought it was a very fragile thing. We had already discovered it's a fairly robust sort of music, and it's lasted for hundreds of years—it doesn't matter what you do with it, because it's going to outlast you anyway. (Tobler CD 1992)

Hutchings himself explained that he had wanted to explore a different terrain and founded the first of the many Albion (Country) Bands, which have remained his principal experimental field ever since. Carthy also left. According to Hart, the reason was a disagreement between him and Carthy about another musician joining: "Martin and I fell out over the fact that he wanted John Kirkpatrick to join, and I wanted Rick Kemp, and eventually Maddy and I formed a band" (Tobler 1991: 27). Carthy went back to his solo work and later joined the Watersons. Hutchings was replaced by bassist Rick Kemp, a studio musician and member of Michael Chapman's band. Kemp had a significant impact on the group's sound, as he—like Fairport Convention's Dave Pegg—added a new, more complex bass style. Guitarist Bob Johnson replaced Carthy.

The first rehearsals of the new formation—Prior, Hart, Knight, Johnson, and Kemp—took place in the Irish Club in London's Deaton Square. The change Steeleye had undergone became obvious after the first U.S. tour in 1972. Before, the band had been a loud electric folk band; afterwards, Steeleye turned increasingly into a modern rock band, using a similar musical language but with a stronger emphasis on the vocals, which had always been a strength of the group, and colorful stage presentations. The band also started to experiment with new elements, as was reported in a *Melody Maker* interview: "Maddy has been talking about incorporating Morris and mumming plays in some way for months. So we thought we'd try out this little bit in the States and see what happens" (Dallas 1973c). During their U.S. tour the musicians had a chance, while playing in auditoriums of 20,000 people, to observe the other bands they were touring with. The band tried to adapt to the taste of this broader audience, for example, by excluding the slower songs and leaving out the spoken introductions, while simultaneously starting to incorporate show elements derived from the tradition. Denselow (Laing et al. 1975: 166–67) wrote:

> They caused considerable amazement in the vast auditoriums of the American West in the summer of 1973; thousands of kids were waiting to see Jethro Tull when on came a support band bathed in blue light and dressed in mummers' costumes that covered them in ribbons from head to feet. When they started singing, it was the eerie, haunting chant "The Lyke Wake Dirge," an unaccompanied tale of the soul's journey from the corpse to purgatory. . . . For their 1974 world tour, they took it a stage further. Their concerts included a ten-minute mummers' play in which the band wore costumes and masks, and acted out Tim Hart's re-write of a medieval story. It involved authentic characters like Little Devil Doubt and the King of Egypt's Daughter, and was an amusing electronic knock-about (voices prerecorded, booming out through the speakers).

Most essential, however, was a conscious change in management, as Hart pointed out retrospectively (Tobler 1991: 29):

We'd also done a lot of American touring by that point, and we knew what we wanted and it wasn't folk club gigs, we wanted to go out there with the Jethro Tulls and the Sha Na Nas and the Beach Boys and all the other people we were gigging with and actually be on a par with those bands. We didn't want to be in this strange folk/rock category that seemed to have a ceiling to it, which I never recognized—when Maddy and I started off, everyone said we couldn't make a living doing folk music.

The former manager Sandy Roberton was replaced by Jo Lustig, and the Steeleye members, who were openly interested in commercial success, remember him more positively than anyone else from the folk scene. Lustig soon negotiated a new recording deal for the group—which had previously recorded for smaller companies—with the progressive Chrysalis label.

By moving assertively into the realm of rock music, Steeleye Span experienced its largest commercial success and became one of the best-selling electric folk bands in Britain. *Below the Salt*, which was briefly in the U.K. charts soon after its release in the autumn of 1972, was their first real commercial success. *Parcel of Rogues*, released in early 1973, became another hit album. The popularity was not only restricted to rock versions of traditional songs like "All around of My Hat" (1975), but happened also with unusual pieces such as the a cappella Christmas carol "Gaudete" (1972), which reached the Top 20 of the British single charts. In 1973 the group finally decided to add a drummer and brought in Nigel Pegrum. A series of successful albums followed that could be, in contrast with most of the other folk and electric folk groups, measured in chart positions. With *Now We Are Six* (1974) the group produced its first Top 20 album, including a hit single, "Thomas the Rhymer." The follow-up, *Commoner's Crown* (1975), charted only briefly, but *All around My Hat* (late 1975), produced by Mike Bratt, became the group's most successful record. It was on the charts for five months, peaking in the Top 10, with the title track even becoming a Top 5 hit.

The next year proved a turning point for Steeleye Span, which had separated from Lustig. *Rocket Cottage*, again produced by Batt, did not even dent the Top 40. Steeleye Span commentator Tobler (CD 1992) saw a reason in the impending punk rock revolution, for "Steeleye could hardly compete with Sid Vicious and Co." In 1977 Knight and Johnson left, while Carthy and accordion player John Kirkpatrick came in, which moved Steeleye back closer to the folk scene. *Storm Force Ten*, released that year, did not bring the group back to the charts. After recording one more album, *Live at Last*, in 1978, the group disbanded early that year. For *Sails of Silver* (1980), produced by Gus Dudgeon, Steeleye was briefly re-formed with the classic lineup of Hart, Prior, Kemp, Pegrum, Knight, and Johnson. Nevertheless, the album again did not sell well, and Chrysalis did not want to renew the group's contract. Hart left in 1983, and

Steeleye Span's last gig was at the Theatre Royal in Norwich. Hart recalled these final days:

> I felt Steeleye had run its course—the band looked bored, the audience looked bored, it was no longer exciting, and the proportion of spectacles in the audience, which is one of the things you notice from the stage, had become deafening—the audience glinted back at me, which meant they were getting older. They used to be at the front of the stage waving, and then they were staying in their seats and glinting. (Tobler 1991: 29).

In contrast to Hart, Pete Frame (1994: 15) contends that the heterogeneity of the group had split the audience into "purists horrified by Carthy's move to commercial folk-rock; M.O.R. audiences appalled by Steeleye's decision to pack up." The band members pursued different directions. Hart moved to the Canary Islands, where he still lives. Prior performed on recordings with Jethro Tull (*Too Old to Rock 'n' Roll, Too Young to Die!*, 1976), Mike Oldfield (*Incantations*, 1978), and Status Quo (*Don't Stop*, 1996). She also made several recordings with the Carnival Band that was formed in 1984 to perform popular medieval, renaissance, and traditional music—like *A Tapestry of Carols* (1987), *Sing Lustily & with Good Courage* (1991), and most recently *In Concert* (1998), discovering and reviving material (carols, hymns) that had long been neglected by the folk scene. She made solo recordings as well, including *Year* (1993), *Flesh and Blood* (1998), and *Ravenchild* (1999). Prior, who is now married to Rick Kemp, lives near Carlisle.

Prior's two *Silly Sisters* projects (1976 and 1988) with June Tabor are still regarded as classic modern folk recordings. Born in 1947 near Stratford-upon-Avon, Tabor studied French and Latin at Oxford and became a librarian. Citing Anne Briggs, Belle Stewart, and Jeannie Robertson as major influences, she became famous for her highly ornamented, unaccompanied singing style. Occasionally criticized for her mannered approach, she has always been receptive to new musical projects like the *Silly Sisters* or *Freedom and Rain*, a 1990 recording with the electric folk group the Oyster Band. Most recently she has ventured into jazz; her album *Aleyn* has thus brought her attention from outside the folk and electric folk worlds.

After several compilations were released in the 1980s—often without the band's approval or knowledge—Steeleye Span was re-formed in 1986 but, like Fairport, recorded for smaller labels. *Back in Line* (1986) was released by the group's own label, followed, after a three-year break, by *Tempted and Tried*, which was released by the Chrysalis-related label Dover. Rick Kemp, who was suffering from physical problems in his left shoulder, was replaced by bassist Tim Harries. Kemp still works as a session musician, as well as recording solo albums. A major change occurred when the group recorded the album *Time* in 1995, joined by founding member Gay Woods, who took over as female lead vocalist after Prior left in 1998 to focus on her solo career. At the end of 2000 Woods again left the band, which struggled without female lead singer until 2002, when Prior returned for a Steeleye Span reunion tour and album, *The Very Best of Steeleye Span—Present*.

THE OYSTERBAND

The Oysterband stands between the early electric folk style of groups like Fairport Convention and Steeleye Span and the later folk rock direction that is most prominently represented by the Pogues. It started in the late 1970s as the Oyster Ceilidh Band, formed at Canterbury University as an informal and flexible dance band that played primarily traditional English dance music. From the original semiacoustic lineup, which played on the group's first album *Jack's Alive* (1980), John Jones (melodeon, piano, vocals), Alan Prosser (guitar, fiddle), and Ian Telfer (fiddle, viola, concertina) have remained at the core of the subsequent formations. At this early stage, these performers also played with the acoustic Fiddler's Dram (of which Cathy Lesurf [vocals] and Chris Wood [bass, percussion] were likewise members of the Ceilidh Band), which specialized in English country music and music hall songs. When Fiddler's Dram disbanded, the Ceilidh Band also started to incorporate song material into its repertoire, with the Oyster Ceilidh Band changing into the Oyster Band (since 1992: Oysterband). Furthermore, the band added electric instruments, and the lineup of Jones, Prosser, and Telfer was completed by bassist Ian Keary. Yet until 1984 the Oyster Band still recorded traditional dance music—in its broadest sense—including on *English Rock 'n' Roll: The Early Years, 1800–1850* (1982) or on *Lie Back and Think of England* (1984).

Tired of playing exclusively traditional music and wanting to reach a larger audience, the Oyster Band changed its direction around 1985. Traditional material started to play an increasingly smaller role, while original songwriting became more important. As with the Pogues and Billy Bragg, the band members wanted to make room for their political convictions, writing, for instance, songs opposed to Margaret Thatcher's government. Fiddler Telfer emerged as a skilled lyricist, while Prosser and Jones wrote the music.

The band also started to develop a new, more rhythm-oriented musical style, as singer and melodeon player Jones emphasized in a *Folk Roots* interview (Coxson 1990: 50):"We used to play some good music—it had layers of harmony and was really nice but what it didn't have was that drive that I think is inherent in the music. Irish music changes for me when you add the bodhran. When percussion of any kind joins in and underpins something, it whacks it home."

However, the performers found it difficult to play its music without imitating Fairport or Steeleye:"Drummers, even drummers outside the folk world, who've liked our music have said they can't actually work out how to play to our music without going into the, shall we say, Fairport/Steeleye sort of thing" (Jones in Anderson 1986: 30). The group therefore started to employ a sound with a more constant pulse on all four beats, rather than the backbeat sound, which emphasized beats two and four. With a stronger emphasis on the rock side, especially by playing a lot of material at a higher speed, the group left behind much of its originally differentiated musical language focused on the careful elaboration of the single song phrases.

With this new sound, the Oyster Band increasingly distanced itself from the folk and electric folk styles. *Step Outside*, recorded on the new label Cooking Vinyl in 1986 indicated this new direction. Subsequent albums like *Wide Blue Yonder* (1988), produced by Clive Gregson, ventured even further into the rock domain. Bassist Keary, dissatisfied with the approach, left and was replaced by Chopper, while drummer Russell Lax (who had come in for *Step Outside*) was replaced by Lee Partis. Characterized as "folk rock," the band is now musically closer to bands like the Pogues and the Levellers than to Fairport Convention and Steeleye Span, yet it can still be differentiated from other rock groups by its use of acoustic instruments associated with folk music like the fiddle.

The new direction also opened wider financial possibilities for the band and new rooms to play in, as the band gradually left the electric folk circuit. This affected the band's audience as well. As Jones pointed out in an interview with the German folk magazine *Folk Michel* (Hanneken 1991: 9), the band had indeed lost a lot of the old audience, yet was replacing it with a much larger and younger one. The musical transformation was reflected in a change of the band's outfits from plain folk-style clothing to black leather, sunglasses, and short hair—a conscious move, as Jones explained:

> I can't quite tolerate the dressing for art's sake but not only were we going into the big wide world where people were going to make criticisms of us, we wanted our music to have a wider currency and to have a wider accessibility to a large range of people. There is something about you that ought to look as if you mean business. I think that's particularly true with the fiddle player and the melodeon player. The fiddle being played by someone with extremely short hair and a leather jacket is a very strong image. (Coxson 1990: 52)

As with the changes of Fairport Convention in the late 1960s, the Oysterband's transformation from folk through electric folk to folk rock has been made into a central issue for the magazine *Folk Roots*, most prominently by journalist Colin Irwin, who wrote at one time for *Melody Maker*. Yet despite its radical change, once in a while the band still ventures into the traditional area, as it did with *Freedom and Rain* (1990) with guest singer June Tabor, or for a céilidh evening in Camden in 1996, when the band played exclusively traditional dance music to a large audience. Moreover, the group still sees a connection to the tradition, although its attitude has changed, as Jones pointed out:

> When we play a set of tunes next to something that is more of a rock song, is more contemporary, we don't play them as a nostalgic set of jigs and reels so everybody does a parody of a dance. The polkas or reels that we play are just as hard—not light relief. The tension is still in there. If it takes a shift in your dress, attitude, in order to convey that then it's a shift that I've been very happy to make. (Ibid.: 53)

These inner musical tensions between modern rock and a still influential folk background might also be one reason for the Oysterband's high-quality live performances—something that has been characteristic of many of the electric folk musicians discussed in this chapter.

FOUR

THE ELECTRIC FOLK SCENE
A Sociocultural Portrayal

I lived in London, which was very lucky for me, because it meant I could see all kinds of music. So I would be out most of the nights of the week, going to blues clubs, rock venues, folk clubs, jazz. And if you listen to the Fairport early on, you hear all the kinds of influences, like the jazz, folk, blues, everything before we settled on folk rock. And I remember very clearly seeing a lot of traditional singers.   ASHLEY HUTCHINGS

A microculture like the electric folk or folk rock scene can be regarded as a unified yet heterogeneous entity with several recognizable musical and structural features that set it apart from other music genres and scenes. From a sociocultural standpoint, it is, to return to Livingston's (1999) points mentioned in the introduction, a coherent network consisting of the following elements: (a) a core group of performers (Fairport Convention, Steeleye Span, Pentangle), with internal member interchanges among the groups and clear "authority figures" such as Martin Carthy;[1] (b) distinctly traditional source material that is used as a basis for musical performances; (c) a group of followers (audience) with a specific unifying body of knowledge, for instance of the complicated group lineups and lengthy songs/ballads; and (d) a network of festivals (most prominently Cropredy), specialized magazines, (mostly independent) record companies, and (increasingly since the mid-1990s) fan Web sites. Although this core structure of the electric folk microculture is clearly recognizable, the relationships of its outer boundaries to other genres such as progressive rock are extremely blurred from both a musical and sociocultural perspective. Nevertheless, to fully understand the character of this genre, we have to return to the London of the 1960s.

ELECTRIC FOLK AND THE DEVELOPMENTS OF THE LATE 1960s

As capital city of the United Kingdom and the Commonwealth, seaport, trade center, and a major industrial site, London—the socioeconomic center and wealthiest region of Britain—has always buzzed with a vast range of local and ethnic microcultures. From early on, it has been a natural focal point of Slobin's (1993) supercultural network, including the entertainment industry and the BBC. The greater London area was thus able to provide the necessary infrastructure and audiences to become the starting point for various emerging musical styles and trends, including skiffle, the underground culture, and the revival and electric folk genres.

London has always been the base of the English Folk Dance and Song Society (EFDSS), and folk revivalists Ewan MacColl and A. L. Lloyd moved to this city because it offered them vast working possibilities and connections. Here MacColl found the platform for his work as an actor and playwright, while Lloyd, who had started to work at Foyle's bookstore after his return from Australia in the early 1930s, established his first and most important connections to left-wing groups. It was therefore only natural that the folk revival began in London, and it was only much later that folk clubs spread all over Britain or that dramatist Arnold Wesker's Centre 42 tried to decentralize art from London. Moreover, many of the early revival musicians and electric folk performers like Ashley Hutchings were either born in the region (London and southern England) or moved there, because the city offered better possibilities for young musicians than any other place in Britain. Hence, before taking a closer look at the outer and inner factors that characterize what is summarized as the electric folk scene, I will take a deeper look at the various venues and ideological backgrounds that would provide the fertile ground for its development.

The Folk Club Scene

Electric folk implied a change, for many of its performers initially came from the revival scene. The revival's major performance venues were the numerous folk clubs, apart from the seasonal outdoor festivals like Cambridge and Sidmouth. "Venue" can actually be misleading, for the clubs were more like events—weekly meetings that were located in one of the small back rooms of a pub, easily missed by outsiders. Guaranteeing a small, intimate, and communal atmosphere, the folk clubs allowed a close interaction between performer and audience.

With its strict performance ideals, the core of the revival seems to have been relatively isolated, yet the folk scene was nevertheless closely connected to the general sociocultural developments at that time. Due to the impact of an improving socioeconomic situation on the level of education and employment in postwar Britain, an explosion occurred of youth subcultures, styles, and movements from the 1950s onwards, and the folk scene came to be rather closely associated with the middle-class–based youth counterculture.[2] Although popular images of the youth opposition emerged as early as the mid-1950s, most clearly embodied in John Osborne's play *Look Back in Anger* (1956) and its main protagonist, the university dropout Jimmy Porter, the predominantly middle-class university culture was still conformist at that time. It was not until the late 1950s that real changes took place—most obviously with the

Campaign for Nuclear Disarmament (CND) and the annual CND Aldermaston March at Easter that started during this period, attracting large crowds and considerable media attention. Like its earlier American counterpart, the civil rights movement, which was connected with the American folk revival, the British CND movement was also closely intertwined with contemporary music scenes, especially the "trad." jazz movement and the folk revival scene.

The revival scene thus started to expand quickly in the 1960s, and the ads in *Melody Maker* from the mid-1960s on provide a good account of the large number of venues and variety of performers that emerged at that time. The charge of dilettantism was often brought against the revivalists, and it is true that the small group of talented performers like Martin Carthy or Davy Graham was far exceeded by the vast number of amateurs. As MacKinnon (1993: 85) observed, "folk audiences do appreciate quality and talent, but they do not seem to demand nor even expect it." Trained musicians have been rare in this basically informal scene, which has always been open to performers with little formal background. Accordingly, journalist Karl Dallas (1965) observed that "too few people still have much idea what the sound of British traditional music really is. It does not consist of merely leaving your guitar at home, nor singing as uncouthly as you can." Mick Jagger's harsh criticism of the scene was likewise directed at the amateurish side of this music: "The Dylan and Donovan thing is very refreshing, but I shudder to think of the tenth-rate beat groups playing rotten folk music just because it's the 'in' thing of the moment. . . . I hope the folk thing doesn't get too big—really—it sort of tends to attract anybody who thinks he can play guitar and sing."[3]

Another point of criticism was aimed at the revival's connection to the "beatnik" or British Trad/CDN subculture, as Davis (1990: 181) labeled it. Representing the oppositional middle-class youth, it conveyed an overall image of stylized shabbiness. Music journalist Eric Winter (1965), for example, asked in a characteristic *Melody Maker* headline "Is Folk a Dirty Word?" and elaborated that "Some are confusing mild eccentricity with scruffiness. For instance, Bob Davenport wears his hair thick and bushy. And clean! And Alex Campbell always wears jeans. Clean." Although this particular youth culture has long since disappeared, the negative image is still prevalent, as was confirmed in his interview for this book by producer Joe Boyd, who described folk-based music as being "considered unsexy and therefore square, un-hip, anti-, against the trends."

Playing folk music outside the folk clubs was difficult, for alternate locations were rare. For a short time, the Centre 42 Festival, a project of leftist political organizers in the early 1960s, also offered a stage for folk musicians such as Anne Briggs, who had been discovered when the festival came to her hometown of Nottingham in 1962. Centre 42 was born out of the Trade Union Congress's Resolution 42, which announced the intent to become more involved in cultural activities. With playwright Arnold Wesker as the main organizer, the festival aimed to provide a leftist alternative to the predominantly London-based high art events, but it failed due to financial problems. The Trade Union Congress nevertheless became, rather involuntarily, connected with the emerging progressive rock movement after it acquired the Roundhouse, a former steam engine hall and empty gin storage place in London's Chalk Farm. While waiting for funding for its renovation, Wesker lent the Roundhouse to photographer/editor John Hopkins, who turned it into a major venue for the emerging underground scene in 1966 (see Schaffner 1991).

A Place for Electric Experiments: Progressive Rock

The electrification of traditional repertoire seems to have partly been a natural process, as traditional musicians have always picked up the instruments that were at hand, whether fiddles or electric guitars. And indeed, groups like Fairport Convention, Steeleye Span, and Pentangle were not the first to combine traditional and electric instruments. Especially in Scotland, some amateur electric bands were playing traditional music at village dance halls in the early 1960s. However, the emergence of the electric folk genre in the late 1960s was no coincidence. It was the result of political and social upheavals and a reorientation of the younger generation, creating an audience that was willing to accept this hybrid music form.

Such acceptance had not previously been the case, as Alan Currie Thompson (1977) has written. The aforementioned Scottish bands were in a difficult position at that time. One example discussed by Thompson was a band named the Echoes that emerged around 1961. With a lineup of electric guitar, bass, drums, and accordion, this group anticipated much that would follow about ten years later, although, in contrast with the electric folk movement's focus on songs, the Scottish electric bands were exclusively dance bands.[4] Despite being received warmly at an old people's home, the band was rejected by teen audiences "because the dancers wanted modern music, not our amalgam of traditional tunes with a rock base," as former band member Thompson (1977: 4) recalled. Rejection also came from traditional musicians, who regarded the electric instruments as inappropriate, and finally the band disbanded: "The last straw came when my father, a fiddle player and a purist, shook his head sadly after hearing us rehearse and said: 'Boy, will you never learn? Jimmy Shand's tunes were never meant to be played on electric guitars'" (ibid.). Another contemporary band, the Cherokees, in contrast, was much more successful with this fusion because they played the traditional material only in small doses.

It was the London of the late 1960s that would provide fertile ground for the development of electric folk. And electric folk would have its first successes through the vocal tradition. The primary fusion of traditional material with contemporary (predominantly electric) styles occurred outside the folk clubs, which were dominated by the ideal of unaccompanied music.

The development of electric folk was closely linked with many other contemporary developments, especially with the counterculture that took root in 1967, along with changes in art, culture, morality, and politics. Sociocultural changes had already become obvious by the mid-1960s, reflected in the new image of "swinging London" as a vibrant, cosmopolitan city with a rich musical and social nightlife.[5] By then, a vast number of young, creative people were attending the various art schools, a new government-subsidized form of vocational training that provided educational opportunities for recent graduates with limited financial means. The schools produced a large number of trendsetting photographers, designers, dramatists, and rock musicians (including Ray Davies, Pete Townshend, John Lennon, and Keith Richards) and soon became centers for the counterculture, for the CND, for experimentation with newly developed drugs like LSD, for Beat literature, and for rock music. Britain was at that time still strongly influenced by the American superculture and sociocultural developments such as the anti-Vietnam demonstrations and the hippie culture of San Francisco. Since direct contact with the U.S. counterculture was limited because international travel was still expensive, Britain's counterculture soon developed a completely individual style, covering all areas from art and fashion to music and "happenings."

London became the center for the underground (or progressive) culture of the late 1960s, providing the necessary infrastructure for rock music experiments. One example was the vast number of music venues—such as the Middle Earth, the Electric Garden, or the Marquee Club in Soho—that emerged, becoming the starting point for groups like the Rolling Stones, the Yardbirds, and the Who and also offering the room for "happenings," which were a mixture of jam sessions, film events, and costume parties. The economic prerequisite for this development—and a further reason why the emergence of new electric music forms like progressive rock and electric folk could not have happened before 1970—was that recording technology and equipment had become affordable for both performers and audiences.[6]

A number of creative people like economics/sociology lecturer Peter Jenner, photographer John Hopkins, and music producer Joe Boyd—who had already been active with launching short-lived underground magazines and the London Free School at Powis Gardens in Notting Hill—were essential to these developments. They became the organizers for some of the major happenings of the underground, such as the presentation of the new underground newspaper *IT* in the Roundhouse on October 15, 1966, with leading London designers, artists, and pop musicians present.[7] *IT*, cofounded by John Hopkins, soon suffered financial losses, and Hopkins and Boyd, who needed to focus on a different source of income, began looking for a place that offered more space for sound-and-light workshops. At the end of 1966 they moved to a former Irish dance hall in the cellar of 31 Tottenham Court Road in London's West End. The UFO Club, as this venue was called, quickly became a cult location for the underground circuit in London, with permanent "house bands" such as the Soft Machine and Pink Floyd. A house style developed characterized by lavish light shows and acoustic effects. Boyd, the musical director of the UFO, also brought other innovative groups into the club, including the Incredible String Band and Fairport Convention. Although Fairport was the only electric folk band that came directly out of the underground or progressive circuit, the underground scene's general influence should not be underestimated, as several other electric folk groups were affected by it. Fairport was soon joined at underground venues by acoustic folk musicians as well, which enhanced the hybrid character of this music further, combining elements of the electric, progressive, and traditional styles.

FINDING A NICHE FOR A HYBRID MUSIC STYLE

Electric folk or folk rock thus came into existence at the borderlines of several different subcultures, particularly the progressive scene and the folk revival scene. Apart from the various stylistic influences, the infrastructural aspect (i.e., the network of performance spaces) of the progressive scene was critical to the further development of electric folk. Yet the combination of these different sounds and styles created various practical and ideological difficulties.

Performance Spaces between Progressive Venues and Folk Clubs

In addition to combining different instruments or fusing various styles, electric folk also involved a change of the physical spaces in which the music was presented. Fairport Convention, for instance, started as a rock band and played in underground venues like the UFO Club as well as in town halls and at universities, which had become the primary venues for the progressive bands. When Fairport picked up traditional material, it thus brought the group into a completely different arena, physically and socially. Steeleye Span, whose founding members came from the folk clubs, faced even more daunting physical changes. A first step for the acoustic duo Maddy Prior and Tim Hart, for instance, was playing at a Women's Institute evening and at a blues club—two places that not only paid better but also appeared to be more open and receptive to innovation than the folk clubs (Tobler 1991: 30). When the Steeleye musicians later picked up electric instruments, the technical sound requirements obliged them to adopt the locations that were used by the progressive bands, in particular the university halls and auditoriums.

The other principal performance space for electric folk groups was provided by the annual seasonal folk and progressive music festivals. Most of the early British folk festivals were organized by the EFDSS, often with a focus on dance. For example, the Sidmouth Festival, founded in 1955, was originally a dance festival, although it increasingly featured several revival musicians.[8] The other well-known festival founded by the EFDSS was the mid-July Keele Festival. Started in 1965, it was almost the only festival with a clear emphasis on traditional music. Guests at the first festival included singers such as Margaret Barry and Flora McNeil, in addition to revival performers like Anne Briggs and Martin Carthy, while the first workshops were run by Ewan

MacColl, Peggy Seeger, A. L. Lloyd, and Peter Kennedy. The Keele Festival was canceled in 1981 due to declining ticket sales and the diminishing role of the EFDSS, but it was revived three years later and continues today as the National Folk Festival. The EFDSS has long lost its key position as the original motivator behind these festivals. In the case of Sidmouth, it gave up its coordinating role in 1986.

Several other British folk festivals, such as Cambridge, Crawley, Mull of Kintyre, Warwick, and the Hebridean Celtic Festival, also were started in the mid-1960s. The famous Newport Folk Festival in the United States, which encompassed a broad range of music from traditional to contemporary and commercial, was founded in 1959 and had no counterpart in Britain until the Cambridge Festival started in 1965. It took a long time before the electric folk bands became frequent guests at these festivals. As Humphries has pointed out (1996: 163–64), the appearance of Richard and Linda Thompson in Cambridge in 1975 was still perceived as unusual. Moreover, the major electric folk bands preferred to appear with rock groups at progressive events, as Pentangle did at the 1970 Isle of Wight Festival. Today this differentiation between electric and acoustic has become marginal for many festivals. The performer list for recent Cambridge Festivals, for instance, has featured both, although electric folk has found its own niche with the Cropredy Festival that grew out of the Fairport Convention reunions beginning in 1980.

Electric folk thus became a music scene that existed in various locations. The performers often moved between electric and acoustic styles and venues. The musicians would play large halls (in the case of Pentangle, in venues like Royal Albert Hall in London or Carnegie Hall in New York) and also the small folk clubs, despite their internal ideological struggles. This ambivalence was well illustrated in the career of Sandy Denny. Having felt too restricted by the folk clubs, she began performing with the Strawbs and then with Fairport Convention, which offered her not only better payment but also new places to play and a different audience. Yet Denny would still occasionally return to the clubs, as she pointed out in a *Melody Maker* interview: "People are much quieter [there], unlike non-folk clubs. I seem to sink into an air of nonchalance that you don't get in a non-folk club." For musical reasons, however, she would never go back to the clubs completely: "Once you know what can be done with six people and like the result, the simplicity and naiveness of one voice and a guitar is rather insipid" (Wilson 1968b).

The change in venues was often accompanied by changes in presentation, which was especially evident in the case of Steeleye Span. Going on tour with larger, commercially successful progressive bands, the group was suddenly playing in front of more than 20,000 listeners. Observing bands like Jethro Tull, Steeleye started to include theatrical elements derived from the English tradition and gave up the lengthy spoken introductions that had been so much a part of folk club performances. As Steeleye guitarist Bob Johnson remarked in a *Melody Maker* interview from July 1973:

If you're playing in a very, very big auditorium any word you speak into the mike is absolutely lost and therefore there is no point at all in introducing the songs. Since many of them can't even see the stage any gap is one of boredom once again. So you've got to have things flowing at what seems like a demoniacal rate on stage but in certain circumstances is not at all. (Dallas 1973c)

As Tim Hart added in another *Melody Maker* article, Steeleye Span would also adapt, not always approvingly, its choice of repertoire to the new performing situation, reducing the number of slow songs (Dallas 1973d). Rick Kemp saw a further reason for Steeleye's success in the States: "In America they very quickly let you know, they would applaud if they could see the effort and if they could see the spirit in the thing being correct, but if they didn't see that—then they didn't applaud."

As Maddy Prior emphasized, the differences in audience reaction also had to do with Americans' unbiased openness toward the music and its presentation. Leaving the critical voices of the English revival scene behind, Steeleye Span quickly started to develop a unique performing approach:

We lost the influence of the folk revival. Suddenly this little judgmental voice was gone. And the American audience was so much more enthusiastic than the English audiences anyway. They just responded better. We had started to bring in theatrics, pretty much about the same time that we went to America. It started to be a rock band rather than a traditional band that was loud. Which of what it had been before. I remember at one point I was changing the costume seven times through a gig! We had lights, dry ice, and really kind of rock equip. And we had mummers' outfits, I was throwing myself around the stage like a lunatic! And it was great fun! I thoroughly enjoyed it. America just released that kind of drama sense—because I found the whole thing is very colorful and I think the problem with the revival had always been how colorless it was, it was drab and puritanical.

When the folk musicians changed their sound from acoustic to electric, their original audience from the clubs did not automatically change their musical taste. Ian Telfer recalled that after the Oysterband switched to a more rock-oriented style, it began playing at different venues and also to different audiences:

Certainly in Britain, people are very loyal to venues. I'm not sure that everybody realizes that. There are people who would only go to dark rock clubs because that's the place they like feel comfortable in, and there are people who will only go to elegant theaters and concert halls because that's the kind of place they want to identify with. So it's not so much changing the music, it's changing the kind of venue. When we began to play rock clubs, people who are happiest at folk clubs didn't want to follow. It's not that they didn't like the music necessarily—that is not an automatic consequence—they may still like the music, yet somehow not like to go to rock clubs.

The Radio

Outside the live venues, radio was a natural place to hear changing music styles at a time when records were still expensive for most young people. Radio was used extensively by A. L. Lloyd, Ewan MacColl, and Alan Lomax to promote traditional music in the 1950s and early '60s, with Peter Kennedy's *As I Roved Out* being a particularly popular program, still remembered by many older people four decades later.

Traditional English music, however, has always had trouble obtaining acceptance and airplay on the BBC's monopolistic public radio channels, even with such popular shows as *Folk on Friday* (which changed later to *Folk on 2* and *Folk on Sunday*). Progressive rock faced a similar problem. As Frith (1984: 117) pointed out, radio was still the major means of record promotion in the 1950s and '60s. Yet until the late 1960s it was almost impossible to hear rock music on the BBC.[9] Progressive rock and related styles would probably not have reached their degree of popularity had it not been for the private—or pirate—radio stations. Springing up around 1967, these illegal stations were modeled on the American style of radio presentation and filled the musical gap by playing both popular rock music, and unknown, experimental material. Programs such as *The Perfumed Garden*, hosted by John Peel of Radio London, were indispensable to the distribution of experimental and progressive music to a wider audience. The pirate stations were finally closed down by Postmaster General Tony Benn in August 1967.[10] After massive protests, the BBC finally launched Radio 1 a month later in September, and Peel started to present new music in a nightly radio show called *Top Gear*, about which music journalist John Tobler recalled: "He played this kind of stuff because it was very obscure at the time. So if you were trying to find out about somebody new, you'd listen to John Peel." Tony Wilson's *Melody Maker* article "A Day in the Life of John Peel" gives a good impression of the variety of material that Peel presented:

> Last Sunday, for instance, a relatively new trio, Andromeda, made their radio debut, and the list of first timers is quite impressive—the Cream, Jimi Hendrix, Bonzo Dog Doo Dah Band, the Nice, Procol Harum, Pentangle, Fairport Convention, Tim Rose, Traffic, Fleetwood Mac, Jethro Tull, Ten Years After, Tyrannosaurus Rex . . . (Wilson 1968c)

Peel thus played an important role in making electric folk popular by supporting many groups such as Pentangle and especially Fairport Convention in his radio shows. As manager Joe Boyd explained, the immense importance of this station for publicity became particularly clear with the Incredible String Band:

> I had the idea to put them from folk clubs pretty much straight into the Festival Hall, and everyone thought I was a bit crazy. But we filled the Hall! Because at that time, there was a pirate radio—and John Peel was playing, he had a show at night called *The Perfumed Garden*, and I knew he was playing the Incredible String Band all the time and so it was a

demonstration of the power of that kind of radio and the power of really breaking down those kinds of categories.

With progressive rock, record albums became much more important than singles as a sales entity, which resulted in the unprecedented situation that "rock album sales had overtaken pop single sales for the first time in 1969 and the industry reacted accordingly" (Stump 1997: 73). Peel's private and public radio shows focused on playing lengthy album tracks instead of the short singles, which was unusual for that time. Folk and electric folk groups both profited from this situation; although Fairport Convention and Steeleye Span released a number of singles, of which Steeleye's "All around My Hat" (1975) became the most successful, electric interpretations of traditional pieces were usually not released as singles because of their length. Thus they could not have reached such a large audience outside the folk clubs had they not been played on these specialized radio shows.

Radio sessions in which relatively unknown new groups like Fairport Convention had the opportunity to perform live became an essential part of Peel's radio show *Top Gear*. As Humphries (1996: 55) wrote, "these radio sessions were an important opportunity to gain access to a wider audience than could ever be reached by their endless travels up and down the M1."[11] Peel's role as an eminent authority is also corroborated by a statement from a music coordinator at London's Brunel University in a *Melody Maker* article from 1969: "We book anyone John Peel likes."[12] It was Peel's opinion that counted, and his interest in electric folk apparently helped the music gain acceptance from a larger audience.

Independent Recording Companies

With the boom in American folk music, recording companies suddenly started to realize the emergence of a new market, as *Melody Maker* (Coleman 1965) observed: "Record companies release more discs in the belief that folk is the new 'in thing.'" The British market, however, was strongly dominated by the major companies like Decca, EMI, Philips, and Pye. Traditional music, as well as most folk music, appeared primarily on the originally noncommercial independent label Topic (which was especially focused on traditional performers and some of the stars of the folk scene) and other small labels that quickly sprang up after 1965.

While the work of Lloyd and MacColl for Topic was carefully thought out and well rehearsed, many of the British folk recordings of the 1960s were, due to limited financial resources, quite rudimentary in terms of both recording techniques and musical quality. A simple, cheap recording process with only a small number of available copies was common, and the accounts of Maddy Prior and Tim Hart of the recording of their first LP, *Folk Songs of Olde England, Vol. 1*, for the label Teepee illustrate this production style:

We went into the studio at 2 o'clock and came out at 5 o'clock, and we'd made our first album. . . . We got to make this album through Theo Johnson. . . . He sort of discovered us—it was at the Mother Hubbard folk club in Lughton, some time in '67, I think. He had actually come to see someone who was doing a floor spot and Maddy and I were doing the gig, and he said 'Do you want to make a record?,' and we said 'Yes, all right, sounds like a good idea,' and we went into this studio at 37, Dryburgh Road, Putney, and for an afternoon, made an LP. The photo session took longer than the album! . . . and there's a couple of word mistakes, when Maddy & I got our words tangled, and Tony Pyke said 'Doesn't matter, doesn't matter, what's the next track?,' so we carried on. (Tobler CD 1991b)[13]

The album was still in mono, for "Tony Pyke . . . was convinced stereo wasn't going to catch on because nobody was going to buy two speakers" (Tobler 1991: 25). (Stereo would, of course, predominate from 1969 on, enhanced by the popularity of progressive rock and its sound experiments.) As Tobler comments further, the album did not sell well, but it earned Prior and Hart a good review from Maurice Rosenbaum in the *Daily Telegraph* and increased the payment for their gigs from ten to fifteen pounds.

The small size of the independent recording companies also created enduring royalty problems. Many of the labels could not survive for long and were sold to other enterprises, with the result that the performers often did not receive any royalties, especially after the reissue of the albums on CD. Sometimes they did not even know that an album had been reissued. Tobler, who started his own recording label that includes many reissues, remarked about this situation:

One thing you'll find, and this is why I started the record label, is that many of these musicians have been ripped off! That they've made a record for somebody in the past and the company has gone bust—but the record has not been returned to the artist, it has been returned to whoever has bought it. What happens usually is: the album is owned by the person who paid to record it. And the deal was that that person would pay royalties to the artists. Having paid in advance originally. But what often happens is that the record company goes out of business and somebody buys the stuff.

Many performers—revival as well as electric folk—were already cheated out of their finances with the first releases, even if they had recorded for larger companies. As Martin Carthy recalled:

I've no idea how many any of my records have sold, except once Max Hole told me that *Crown of Horn* had gone over 10,000. I can remember getting a statement from Fontana saying that I'd sold 500 copies, and that was when I'd seen more than 500! After that I decided not to bother to look at statements any more. As far as I was concerned, the folk side of Fontana was a tax write-off, to help Dusty Springfield make her records, or Kiki Dee. (Anderson and Holland 1985: 9)

With the development of fusion styles, not only the recording process but also the labels changed, as several of the electric folk bands moved to larger—predominantly independent—labels. Bands such as Fairport Convention and Steeleye Span, as well as early music experimenters Gryphon, found places with the top progressive labels. As with folk music, the early recordings of progressive rock had only been possible due to the existence of alternatives like Island Records, John Peel's Dandelion Records, and Chrysalis. John Renbourn and Bert Jansch started recording for Transatlantic and continued there with Pentangle. (It was ironic that the group disbanded shortly after manager Jo Lustig negotiated a contract with Warner Brothers.) Fairport Convention started on Joe Boyd's Witchseason label and then moved to Chris Blackwell's leading independent label Island, while Steeleye Span, whose first three albums had been issued on small folk labels like Mooncrest, negotiated a contract with Chrysalis via Lustig. Founded in 1968, Chrysalis had progressive bands like Jethro Tull and Procul Harum under contract—later also popular bands like Spandau Ballet and Sinead O'Connor or, in the United States, performers like Pat Benatar, Billy Idol, and Blondie.

The major labels, which had been unwilling to record this music in the beginning, were relatively slow to catch up. Yet in 1969 Malcolm Jones from EMI founded the progressive EMI label, Harvest Records, which later became the primary label for Pink Floyd and also featured Shirley and Dolly Collins's folk and early music fusion *Anthems in Eden*, Ashley Hutchings's revived morris dance *Son of Morris On*, and the Albion Band's *Rise Up Like the Sun*.

With the comparatively larger independent rock labels, recording conditions for electric folk groups improved, since these companies had more financial resources to devote to professional production and engineering, and they could give the bands more time in the studio. As Macan (1997: 190) has observed, the vast range of musical styles in the late 1960s not only made commercial predictions difficult, it also caused the recording labels to be more open to new approaches, encouraging the musicians to experiment and giving them "a control of the recorded product in terms of production, graphics and album cover art, packaging, etc., that earlier popular musicians could have only dreamt about." Many of the musicians interviewed for this book agreed that they had been given completely free rein in the studio, including approval of the record cover design.

The impact of working with more sophisticated recording companies was especially apparent in the sound of Pentangle and Steeleye Span, who, although they did not use synthesizers, started to experiment with various sound effects. As bassist Rick Kemp recalled, when Steeleye began to become commercially successful, Chrysalis obtained the best producer possible in Mike Batt for *All around My Hat* and gave the band enough time in the studio for experiments and a well-rehearsed production. Making connections with the more commercial side of the industry also proved advantageous for later ambitious folk projects like Maddy Prior's and June Tabor's two

Silly Sisters records. As Prior recalled, her Chrysalis connection was a key factor in achieving the high quality of these albums:

> I had the resources, with Chrysalis's backup, to make an album with musicians, with all the musicians we liked. And so it was the first album that was a folk album in that general way that had a bit of money—so we could actually make a decent sound. And actually use the musicians we wanted to.

The Business Side: Management and Finances

Folk music has always been viewed as noncommercial on both the performance and financial levels. In 1965 Karl Dallas wondered, for instance, if folksingers were overpaid—not meaning to attack the stars of the scene, but rather the idea that even those without talent could make money. As he concluded in *Melody Maker*: "It's become very commercial, to be uncommercial" (Dallas 1965). Hence one problematic result of the musical fusions after 1967 was that electric folk groups presented their music within a commercial context—something that had previously been rejected by the revival scene. As Prior explained, this was partly perceived as an almost personal insult:

> When people find something that they really love, they don't want it to be commercialized as they see it, especially by somebody else. I didn't mind, because I was doing it. And for me it wasn't wrong because I was enthusiastic about what I was doing, whereas for other people it was probably ruining their music that they loved dearly and bowdlerizing it and putting rock beats to it and flattening it out.

Moving to the electric sphere also had economic consequences for the bands that previously had performed mostly in the folk clubs. As MacKinnon (1993) emphasized, the revival scene was amateurish as a business enterprise. Recordings normally sold only in small numbers, and most gigs were not well paid. The folk clubs were run by amateurs, and the entrance fees were low. Gigging trips were often made in privately owned cars (sometimes in a small tour bus, as in the case of the Watersons),[14] or by train, both modes being extremely exhausting. The musicians often stayed with friends to save expenses for hotels and food.

Many performers were not professional musicians when they started. Jacqui McShee still had a job when she began performing with John Renbourn in 1966, although that would change when they started to perform outside London. Similarly, Shirley Collins was still working in the 1950s, while her sister worked as a music teacher. Collins admitted that her income from folksinging was relatively moderate: "No, I didn't make a lot of money at it, I made enough to live on—all the time I was performing."

The situation of the electric groups was different because they were more closely associated with rock music and the music industry. The musicians of Fairport Convention turned professional quite early—the underground circuits and university sites offered larger payments than the folk clubs ever could.[15] This might also have been a motivation for fiddle player Dave Swarbrick's joining Fairport Convention, and his former musical partner singer/guitarist Martin Carthy's subsequent decision to become a member of Steeleye Span. Tobler suggested that "when Swarbrick joined Fairport it meant that all Martin Carthy's gigs had to be canceled. It was as simple as that. It was simply a question that he wasn't making any money."

Yet compared to other popular groups, the commercial success of electric folk remained moderate, even during the peak years when Pentangle and Steeleye Span enjoyed high record sales and played in large venues. For example, although extremely successful from the perspective of the electric folk scene, Steeleye Span was not listed among Chrysalis's forty all-time best-selling albums in 1998.[16]

With the changes of musical style and recording companies, the management of electric folk groups often also changed to a much more professional level. While acoustic performers announced their gigs in small weekly ads next to *Melody Maker's* folk page, the recordings and engagements of Pentangle or Fairport Convention were much more professionally promoted, as is evident from the one-page ad for Fairport's *Liege & Lief* or Pentangle's announcement of its first album. These groups were thereby able to reach a much larger audience than had ever been possible for any folk performer. Although bassist Rick Kemp clearly attributes Steeleye Span's success to various musical qualities (in particular to the group's strong vocals), he believes it was also the result of the work of the producers and managers:

> If you find people that can sing together and that are used to singing together, it's a big help and you're on the road to making a good record. And I think we very quickly wanted more popularity than we had. And I'm not quite sure any more to what degree it came from us! Really, I think it was more from management and from producers. But we were quite willing to do so.

With Joe Boyd (who worked with Fairport Convention, the Incredible String Band, and Sandy Denny) and Jo Lustig (who was mainly responsible for the success of Pentangle, Steeleye Span, Richard Thompson, and Anne Briggs, as well as the Chieftains and, briefly, Fairport), the folk and electric folk performers were now in professional hands. Yet the transition to a more professional level was problematic for the performers, especially for those being managed by Jo Lustig. While Boyd seems to have been a relatively sensitive, Lustig's style was much more aggressive. As he explained to Colin Harper (CD 1992), "my philosophy is very simple: if you can apply commercial techniques to crap, it can happen. Why can't you apply it to fine music?"

Although almost all musicians acknowledged Lustig's skill and his part in their success, they often had personal problems with him that caused tension within the groups. Jacqui McShee described his way of working with the expression "divide and rule":

He would say something to John, something slightly different to Bert. So they'd be saying "What's going on here?" Then he'd say something different to me. In that way he sort of kept control of all of us until we all got together and said, "Hang on a minute, what's going on?" He did actually cause a few arguments until we discovered what was going on.

Pentangle was, according to the musicians, partly killed by its success—the result of Lustig's ruthless management style. The tours became so stressful that they had neither time nor energy left for new musical work. Moreover, as McShee recalled further, Lustig would use any opportunity to promote the group, even if the circumstances did not fit:

> I am not saying it was because of Jo that the band split up in the end, but it didn't help. He would ring me up and say, "Can you go and do this interview, they've asked for you." And I'd look at the magazine and I'd think "They don't want to speak to me. This is a guitar magazine. They want to speak to John or Bert." And I'd find out later on that Bert had turned it down and that John had turned it down. They didn't want to do the interview, so he was sending me along to do it, but . . . really the chap didn't want to talk to me, he wanted to talk about guitars. And there were all things like that that were silly.

The dilemma became even more painful for folksinger Anne Briggs, whose ideas and ideals of an uncommercial folk music suddenly collided with the demands of a larger music business. As she regretted in an interview with music journalist Ken Hunt (1989: 14), "I should never, ever, ever, have gone in for that flirtation with the pop side of folk. I should have stuck within the traditional thing that I did best and should have explored it more thoroughly. With hindsight, I . . . should have had the capability of becoming a fairly reasonably knowledgeable musicologist." Although her reputation as a singer grew constantly, Briggs started to feel uncomfortable about the way Lustig pushed her to produce songs one after another and to become a focus of media attention. Briggs had always embodied the figure of the rambling, unpredictable folksinger, and when the conflict between her musicianship and the business side became insoluble, she left the scene completely in 1973. It would do Lustig injustice, however, to put the blame completely on him. The members of Steeleye Span, for instance, who were openly interested in a commercial career, remember Lustig more positively than anyone else from the scene.

Yet, even in the case of Steeleye Span, which was probably the group that came closest to professional rock music in terms of presentation and career, management issues were problematic—owing to the group's own attitudes. According to Maddy Prior, one of the problems was the performers' unwillingness to accept that their niche was mid-position rather than top-market:

> Jo was from that lineage where anything went. If it's old—great! So he would look at us and thought there was a strong possibility for us in that nice middle market. It is a big market. But that wasn't where we saw ourselves at all. So we were always working against each

other a little bit. He was always getting us things to do we didn't wanna do. And we were not adamant enough to say no. Because we wanted to be—"accepted." We're not working-class enough to go "bullshit" and not do it. So we were nice to people and polite.

Thus, as Tim Hart pointed out to Tobler, the Steeleye musicians partly lived beyond their means:

Jo did his best and never ripped us off, but we made some bad business decisions in under-writing our American tours—I think he warned us, but we didn't listen. He said we spent too much money and we couldn't afford limousines, but we told him to get them. Then we got presented with loads of silver discs and a royalty cheque for £38 in the same week, and when we asked what had happened, he said we'd paid back £40,000 of American touring debt, and we said "What £40,000 of American touring debt?" (Tobler 1991: 27)[17]

In general, many electric folk performers and groups were relatively unstable (some musicians developed severe alcohol problems), which probably also prevented a larger success. Such was the case with Bert Jansch as well as with Fairport Convention, whose constant lineup changes made consistent management and musical development very difficult.

Royalties were also limited, because the income from the arrangement of already existing songs was much smaller than from original compositions. Although popular music performers could live entirely from making recordings, this was difficult for performers of traditional material, as Martin Carthy explained:

I never stopped, I have to gig, I keep doing gigs—I couldn't, you know, I have bills to pay. You don't make that sort of money from making folk records, because you don't have the writer's royalty, because I'm not the writer, I can't do that. It's traditional—and you cannot, you must not copyright it to yourself. And I accepted that. And have, instead, accepted the royalty from an arrangement.

Nevertheless, traditional tunes have often been used as musical (and thus financial) "gold-mines" (Schneider 1991: 307). While British folk groups and performers were always careful to treat their sources correctly, always giving the reference "trad./arr." (a practice they adopted under the influence of Lloyd and MacColl) and claiming only the copyright for an arrangement, this was not always the case with performers from the popular sector. One example is the song "Scarborough Fair," which was popularized by Simon and Garfunkel on *Parsley, Sage, Rosemary, and Thyme* (1966). Simon learned the song from Martin Carthy, who recalled: "He came round to see me, I wrote the song down for him, and he went out the next day and, as it seemed, copyrighted it. So when I got a copy of his single—then it was 'Scarborough Fair,' written by Paul Simon."

The single and all subsequent albums state Simon as the author, which seemed to have earned him and his partner Art Garfunkel a fortune, while Carthy was not even mentioned as the source of the song. Carthy sued, yet his revival ethics obviously collided with those of the music business: His publisher wanted him to claim the song as his own, and that would even have been possible, as Carthy's recording from 1965 predates that of Simon and Garfunkel, which strikingly resembles his. Carthy, however, refused to do so:

> What my publisher wanted me to say all the time was that my version was the original version. If he could demonstrate in court that this version that I sang was the original version, then he could have Paul Simon paying millions. And I didn't understand that, and I kept presenting him with other versions. What happened was that my publisher took Paul Simon to court, and Paul Simon paid him off basically—on the condition that I had 50 percent of the payoff. And because I had a deal with the publisher, that meant that he took 50 percent of my earnings—what I got was 50 percent of 50 percent!

Cases like this one occur relatively frequently in the rock/pop music business, where every major company has an entire law department. Dannen (1991), for instance, offers insight into the business practices of major U.S. companies like CBS, where even a star like Simon did not always maintain full control of the public presentation of his works. And although copyright infringements and overdue royalties are considered rather harmless from an American corporate perspective, the impact of these cases on the electric folk and folk scenes—which have not usually been protected by readily available lawyers—has been much more serious, given the fragility of the traditional music culture and the performers' relationship to the material.

Labeling a Hybrid Music Form

From the viewpoint of a marketing system that has to work with clear classifications, a hybrid style defying any categorizations can occasionally be advantageous, but it might also cause many problems. As pointed out in chapter 1, the music industry and journalists have always struggled to find an appropriate label for electric folk—an effort obvious from the beginning, when the first experimental performers appeared in *Melody Maker*. Being either labeled as electric folk or later as folk rock, they were partly covered on the folk pages and partly on the rock pages, while Pentangle was sometimes even tagged as avant-garde jazz. The problem of labeling has been especially evident in the record and CD stores, where this music is commonly either shelved under "World Music/Folk" or, as often happens with Fairport Convention, under "Rock," while Sandy Denny can be found under "Folk." Likewise, folk rock groups like Lindisfarne are usually shelved under "Rock," while the Oysterband is filed under "World Music/Folk," making it difficult for potential buyers to find the music, especially if the stores are as large as HMV or Tower Records in London. Maddy Prior even wondered if the commonly used term "folk rock" might actually only be valid for one group—Fairport Convention:

They called us [Steeleye Span] "folk rock," but it isn't really. We find that a very odd term, because it's only used for us and Fairport. And we're as different as chalk and cheese. It's a group of one. But being English, we wouldn't like to be in a category. We've never been a part of a scene. That's always been one of the things that's made the folk scene find us quite difficult to deal with. Because we've never been attached to any of it. And you couldn't guess where we were gonna go, mainly because we didn't know. And there's never been an ideology behind it. So you can't pin it down to being a particular way or align to anything—except traditional music. And I think that's been its strength and weakness. From a commercial point of view it's a weakness. It's too eccentric.

"Folk rock" or "electric folk" was—more or less—accepted as a convenient label by the musicians, similar to the "progressive" movement that was by no means a well-defined entity, despite the unifying label. Today, although the Oysterband has now changed its repertoire to contemporary material, it is still treated as a folk group and, like Richard Thompson, is still covered by the eminent British folk magazine *Folk Roots*. As Ian Telfer remarked: "To British people, I think, we are still a folk band, and we would be even if we didn't use a violin and didn't make any reference to traditional music. It's a label. The music press can only operate through labels, and the digital storage of information positively demands them."

The labels have changed over the years as well. Ashley Hutchings pointed out:

They never really knew where to put us. In the '60s, with Fairport, we were kind of tacked on to the hippie psychedelic scene. And in the '70s we were tacked on to the kind of left field of the rock scene, or what was called "progressive music." And rock music that was like *thoughtful* was called "progressive." Then we were kind of tacked on to the left side of that. But in the '80s and in the '90s, the generation of the interest in folk rock, we've tended to be—unfortunately—tacked on or allied to "easy listening" kind of M.O.R., that they put on Radio 2, which is the radio channel in Great Britain, which has Frank Sinatra. Weird, isn't it? And so they have never really known where to put our music—and they still don't know!

Labeling confusion is thus another reason why this music has been, except during its commercial peak between 1969 and 1975, difficult for outsiders to notice.

INTERNAL CHARACTERISTICS OF A MUSICAL MICROCULTURE

Despite the hybrid character of electric folk, and although some performers like Maddy Prior deliberately deny ever having been part of any scene, it is still reasonable to speak of a coherent musical microculture. "One of the small units within big music cultures," as defined by Slobin (1993: 11), it is, like other microcultures, unified by common categories or variables like persons (here especially the performers), music, space, behavior/attitudes, and an internal network. In some respects Prior is correct: the microculture (or "scene"—which is used synonymously here) of electric folk is relatively heterogeneous, comprised of clearly distinct and homogenous units like the folk clubs, as well as more open venues like the (progressive) university scene. Electric folk therefore shares several common characteristics with the genres of progressive rock and folk.

The Performer Network

A look at the musicians' backgrounds reveals that, while sharing several common aspects such as performance venues and musical features, electric folk and progressive rock clearly differed on both social and educational levels. Progressive rock was, as Macan (1997: 144) pointed out, "never a working class style"; rather, it was the "vital expression of a bohemian, middle-class intelligentsia," basically located in the "white-collar" region of southern England. Several performers had a postsecondary (college/university) education (not always completed); for instance, Tony Kaye, Rick Wakeman (Yes), Karl Jenkins (Soft Machine) had all been music students, while the members of Pink Floyd had studied architecture.

The electric folk and revival performers were different. Although a few of them were middle-class (Simon Nicol's father, for instance, was a doctor), a working-class background seems to have been more prevalent. Even though Sandy Denny's father worked in the civil service (and later the army), or Richard Thompson was the son of a policeman, their families were still grounded in working-class culture. Most of the electric folk performers who started in the late 1960s were less highly educated than progressive musicians. At best, a few (like John Renbourn and Denny) had attended art schools.

Moreover, working-class experience was not only much more present in the background of performers like Martin Carthy, Jacqui McShee, or Shirley Collins, but also in the early institutions of the folk revival. Centre 42 and Topic Records, for instance, were offsprings of the Workers' Music Association, and the central figures of the Second Revival, Ewan MacColl and A. L. Lloyd, both had working-class backgrounds and were outspoken Communists (which would cost Lloyd several jobs during the 1950s). This was also reflected in their work—in writings like Lloyd's *Singing Englishman* (1944) and in his recording project, *The Iron Muse* (1956), which focused on industrial music. The early Topic stars like Jeannie Robertson, Margaret Barry, and the Stewarts of Blair (who all came from families of Travellers), as well as the Sussex-based Copper Family, clearly represented the lower levels of a highly class-conscious society. However, except for Shirley and Dolly Collins, whose mother was recorded for the BBC by Bob Copper, the majority of these traditional singers were not actively involved in the Second Revival, although they performed at festivals and acted as musical role models.

Both the revival and the electric folk scenes have been distinguished by a relatively close network among the performers, not least because of the informal performance atmosphere and close performer-audience relationship in the folk clubs. Due to the small size of the local scenes it was relatively easy to get to know the various performers, especially for club organizers such as Jacqui McShee:

> The evening would start with a few floor singers or usually with the person that was actually running the club, because I ran a club myself with friends in South London. And we would get up to do a few numbers and anyone else that was local that wanted to, and then you'd have the main act. John Renbourn used to come and play there. And Bert Jansch, and lots of other people around at the time. So I met quite a few people through that as well. That would have been in about 1964–65. It was quite a small scene, but I think there were probably small scenes all over the country. And people gradually traveled, I mean, you traveled quite a long way to do a gig. And you didn't get much money. So it had to be worth it, I mean, I was working at the time. I worked in an architect's office. So I had a regular income, but for somebody like John who didn't or Bert who didn't, it would have to be worth the while to travel, so it gradually grew and grew.

A characteristic of electric folk bands has been the large number of member changes. While Pentangle's lineup remained relatively stable during the band's early period (1968–73), Steeleye Span and especially Fairport Convention went through an extreme number of personnel changes. This was problematic from the rock/popular music market at which the groups aimed, for both fans and journalists clearly focused on individual personalities. While Maddy Prior and Tim Hart became focal points for Steeleye Span, the situation with Fairport Convention was much more chaotic. The band made its groundbreaking albums with the lineup of Denny, Swarbrick, Thompson, Nicol, Hutchings, and Mattacks. Sandy Denny was clearly one focal point,[18] and the other was Richard Thompson. Both, however, dropped out, as did leader and bassist Ashley Hutchings. Although Dave Swarbrick was and is a strong personality and performer, the sound that had been associated with these musicians was missing and could not be replaced due to the constant lineup changes. Moreover, the musical quality seemed to suffer as the new performers had to learn the material from scratch, while the others grew tired of teaching it.

Performer interchange among the groups was a further characteristic of this genre. As in the progressive scene (Macan 1997: 146), many electric folk musicians played in two or more groups. Simon Nicol, for instance, has played with Fairport Convention, but he was also a guitarist in Ashley Hutchings's Albion (Country) Band and guested on recordings by Richard Thompson, who himself guested on Sandy Denny's albums and sometimes accompanied her on concert tours. In some cases, the musicians have not been identified with specific groups so much as with their individual instruments. If, for instance, a high-quality accordion player is needed, John Kirkpatrick will be asked to be guest or a member.

The reasons for the frequency of member changes are difficult to clearly pin down. The organization of some groups was similar to that of jazz bands that are centered around a permanent leader, with the other members changing. Many electric folk bands—particularly Hutchings's Albion (Country) Bands—had more of a project character, meeting primarily for specific recordings like *No Roses*. Similarly, the early Pentangle was also seen by the musicians as a temporary experiment: Bert Jansch and John Renbourn still continued with their solo activities, while Terry Cox and Danny Thompson also played jazz sessions. This became a problem, however, when Pentangle became highly successful and concert trips began to demand more of their time—one reason why the group finally split. Another reason for the frequent member changes, especially of Fairport Convention, was suggested by John Tobler: "I think there were a lot of power struggles: 'I want to be in charge of this band and if you don't let me, I'm gonna go and start my own band.' I mean, that's largely why Ashley left Fairport and why he left Steeleye."

The electric folk groups often lived in a kind of symbiosis with progressive bands, going on tour with them and frequently joining these groups as band members. At one point, Fairport Convention and Jethro Tull shared two members (Dave Pegg and Ric Sanders), and also went on tour together. Electric folk can therefore also be characterized as a scene that is relatively open, as Tobler pointed out: "It's very difficult to tell where the boundaries of folk rock are. . . . For example, Jimmy Page and Robert Plant can be playing at Cropredy, which is a folk rock event, and they definitely aren't folkies, although Sandy Denny did one of Led Zeppelin's albums."

Since the 1990s the situation has become much more stable, although many groups exist as part-time bands whose musicians also work with other groups, projects, and recordings. The Albion Bands have been particularly accepted by the folk scene as project bands that are centered around Hutchings. Pentangle, which in its second stage also underwent frequent member fluctuations, changed its name to "Jacqui Mc-Shee's Pentangle," because McShee has remained the only permanent member. Steeleye Span's lineup stayed relatively constant after its re-formation—until 1998, when Maddy Prior left and was replaced by founding member Gay Woods.[19]

Fairport Convention was amazingly stable for more than twelve years (1985 to 1997), with Dave Mattacks occasionally dropping in and out because of independent projects and the other members taking the opportunity to follow the trend to play "unplugged," which they had occasionally done before. A distinct change occurred in 1997, when Maartin Allcock left and was replaced by Chris Leslie. Yet because Simon Nicol has become a strong front singer, the impact of these changes has apparently not been as significant, particularly since many "new" musicians are often familiar faces from the scene. When Mattacks dropped out of Fairport in 1998, for instance, he was replaced by Gerry Conway, who was already well known as the drummer with Fotheringay and Pentangle. Similarly, Chris Leslie had performed before with Richard Thompson, Dave Swarbrick's Whippersnapper, and the Albion Band. Like the progressive rock performers who, as Macan (1997: 146) put it, "almost seem to have formed a guild among themselves," these musicians also seem to have developed something like a "sonic code" (ibid.) with recognizable style elements (see chapters 5 and 6, this volume), which makes these kinds of transitions possible.

Authorities

Despite the extensive use of archives, the relationship of electric folk—and partly also of the folk scene—to institutions like the EFDSS has remained quite reserved, with academic scholarship playing only a marginal role. Until recently English folk music has seldom been the focus of academic musicological research; instead, most of the academic research has been done in fields like the social sciences or history. Peter Kennedy, for instance, one of the eminent authorities on the field of English folk music, has worked as a collector, performer, and broadcaster, but not as a representative of a university department. Hence, it seems almost to be natural that nonacademic or private organizations like the EFDSS have assumed some of the role of academia.[20]

Within the electric folk scene, however, not the EFDSS (which is seen as a microculture in itself, partly detached from the tradition), but rather MacColl and Lloyd—who initially did not have academic training by modern standards—became scholar-like authorities for musicians and journalists. Sometimes the musicians have mentioned feelings of anger at not being told the whole truth about MacColl's and Lloyd's various activities (see chapter 7, this volume). This frustration has been especially evident regarding Lloyd's vagueness about the sources of his repertoire. Something similar could be observed with journalism. While some music writers were regarded as valid authorities by their readers, among the musicians acceptance of some journalists was occasionally not based on respect, but on fear, since these journalists had the power to promote or destroy a performer's reputation. Martin Carthy, for instance, partly blamed Karl Dallas's extremely negative reviews for the breakup of an early Albion Country Band lineup.

After the deaths of MacColl and Lloyd, the subsequent authorities were again not academics but revival musicians—those particularly like Carthy and Dave Swarbrick who had been in direct contact with Lloyd. As MacKinnon (1993) has observed, high status in the folk scene is defined by knowledge of British music traditions, vast repertoire, and originality of style; Carthy has also been respected for his technical sophistication. His musical style became a model and was copied frequently, which enhanced his position even further. As became evident during the interviews with various performers, here with Maddy Prior, his position is also grounded on his vast knowledge of the tradition:

> He is now the sort of premier of the tradition, really. He knows the tradition better than anybody now that Bert and Ewan have gone. That is a practitioner. There are probably other people who know more about folklore, but Martin knows the actual practical tradi-

tion probably better than anyone else in the country now. He's got a great memory for tunes and words. And he remembers songs very well.

As Prior pointed out in the previous chapter, working with Carthy meant a change in status for the early Steeleye Span, earning the group acceptance within the revival scene. In contrast, Ashley Hutchings felt that with the death of MacColl and Lloyd, the "father figures" of the revival were irreplaceably gone.

Making Music as a Woman

It is not without reason that this book cites female performers like Maddy Prior, Jacqui McShee, or folksinger Frankie Armstrong as the main sources of information. While many emerging genres of the late 1960s like progressive rock were by and large male affairs, restricting women mainly to passive roles as wives, girlfriends, groupies, or behind-the-scenes assistants, from the beginning the British electric folk scene made more room for female performers. As Macan (1997: 135) observed, "female singers featured much more prominently in the folk music revival of the early 1960s than in any other genre of contemporaneous rock."[21] This was apparent in the States with singers like Joan Baez, Judy Collins, Carolyn Hester, and Mary Travers of Peter, Paul, and Mary, as well as in England. A *Melody Maker* article entitled "Fine Feathered Folk" (Dallas 1966e) listed a number of highly talented singers such as Sandy Denny, Frankie Armstrong, Shirley Collins, Isla Cameron, and Jacquie and Bridie (Jacqueline McDonald and Bridie O'Donnell). The subsequent electric folk genre featured a number of singers like Jacqui McShee, Sandy Denny, and Maddy Prior who were not only front persons but who also played strong roles within the groups. Denny wrote the songs for a major portion of Fairport's nontraditional repertoire (75 percent of *Rising for the Moon* [1975] consisted of her material), and Prior was, besides Tim Hart, the main spokesperson for Steeleye Span. A large number of female solo performers like June Tabor also emerged in the electric folk scene.

The stronger presence of female performers was almost a natural result of the revival's predominant focus on the vocal repertoire. While on the instrumental side, morris and sword dances performed by male performers were predominant, the vocal side of the tradition has always featured many female singers who were especially well received by the public. Jeannie Robertson, Margaret Barry, the Stewarts of Blair, and Phoebe Smith are only some of the traditional singers who experienced something like star status.[22] Although singers like Harry Cox, Joseph Taylor, and Walter Pardon were also highly respected, they never acquired the popular recognition that Robertson did. Female instrumentalists were rarer, but they existed; examples included pianist/organ player, composer, and arranger Dolly Collins, or fiddler and singer Carole Pegg, who formed half of the highly experimental electric folk group Mr. Fox and later became a musicologist, now teaching at Cambridge University. That Sandy Denny was also a skilled guitar player was long overlooked, perhaps owing to the persistent folk club bias in favor of unaccompanied music.

The present electric folk scene is currently witnessing the emergence of a number of skilled and commercially successful female solo instrumentalists like Kathryn Tickell on Northumbrian bagpipes and fiddler and singer Eliza Carthy, both of whom have also fronted various groups. Other examples include the harp duo Sileas, the all-female electric folk quartet, the Poozies,[23] and in the States, the accordion player, keyboardist, and composer Jennifer Cutting, who led the electric folk band the New St. George.

Despite their prominence, female performers in the British electric folk scene obviously encountered problems similar to those of female musicians in the rock scene, especially when changing from the clubs and the acoustic side to a modern electric lineup with a band. For example, a *Melody Maker* interview, quoting former Fairport singer Judy Dyble, was entitled "Pop Is So Male-Oriented. They Don't Think a Lady Can Tell Them Anything" (Dallas 1970f). Discussing the problems of a female instrumentalist in the pop business, this article hints at an assumption that was often mentioned in the music press at that time—that a "girl singer" had to be tough to survive in the business.

This attitude was also obvious in Boyd's description of Sandy Denny's management of her band Fotheringay. As he pointed out in the 1988 BBC radio tribute to Denny, he had observed a tendency toward a "democratic" band structure with successful female performers, especially when their partner was a member of the group as well. Denny's boyfriend, Trevor Lucas, played guitar in Fotheringay, and this partnership was apparently one reason for her reluctance to start a solo career. Furthermore, Denny always tried to avoid the exhausting life "on the road," and her alcohol problem was partly a way to cope with the stresses of travel and her leadership role. The same syndrome occurred with the male performers of Fairport Convention and Pentangle during their strenuous tours, yet the effect on Denny was much more devastating.

Nevertheless, female performers' experiences and opinions are extremely varied. Steeleye Span singer Maddy Prior seems never to have encountered any gender-related problems:

> I've always worked with men, and I've never had a problem with being a woman. It's never held me back. It's never bothered me. And I've never felt that it bothered them. I have a bit of a problem with a lot of feminists' stances because it's not my experience. My experience with blokes is that they have exactly the same problems as us, in some ways worse because they try to keep some front up.

Folksinger Frankie Armstrong, on the other hand, clearly disagreed with Prior. Armstrong, who became known for her feminist approach, described the folk scene as being almost naturally male-dominated in its ideology:

I think it helped to be a strong woman. By 74/75 I was very consciously singing songs about and by women, both traditional and contemporary. Some men and even some women would really criticize me for it, and I'd say, "But you will have had men singing and they may well have sung songs by and about men all evening, and I doubt you'd even think of criticizing them for it." Say Johnny Collins would spend half the evening singing sea shanties and maybe some rural and lyrical songs, but mostly from the man's perspective—which is fair enough—I mean he sings good songs well, but the fact that I got criticized for singing about women was very interesting. And, of course, in the women's movement I got criticized for singing traditional songs about women in relation to men.

Armstrong developed a consciously feminist approach toward the songs' contents:

It was a baptism of fire, it really made me very strong! I had to learn to say, "This is what moves me. These are the songs that are important to me. They tell me about my ancestry, about my women's resilience in the past." Masses of the ballads were about women defying conventions in whatever form. They might well finish up dead as a result, so you can't be more defiant than that! There were songs about women's lustfulness. There are some very funny, wonderful songs—like the "Buxom Lass"—they're often very humorous and tender and respectful of women. They're not pornographic in the slightest, and the women are often the initiators of the sexual encounter. There are a great variety of women's songs—work, trade union, love, and lust.

The electric folk scene clearly developed a different, much more condensed internal network than other contemporary popular music cultures. At a time that still celebrated sexual freedom, the scene witnessed almost any possible (often short-lived) partnership combinations among the performers. Yet marriages among the performers occurred frequently: Shirley Collins was married to Ashley Hutchings (both would found the Albion Country Band), while Maddy Prior later married Rick Kemp. Likewise, one could observe several duos such as Bob and Carole Pegg (Mr. Fox), Terry and Gay Woods (Steeleye Span and the Woods Band), and Richard and Linda Thompson. Sandy Denny was married to Trevor Lucas and previously had been close to Jackson C. Frank, whose songs she promoted as part of her repertoire. In the case of Martin Carthy and Norma Waterson one can even observe the beginning of a family tradition. Together with their daughter Eliza Carthy, they have formed the successful group Waterson:Carthy, while several other family members have also participated in recordings and concert performances.

The Audience

The electric folk fan/audience structure is difficult to analyze, due to the many changes this scene has undergone over the last thirty years. So far, in the field of folk music, only one statistical investigation has been conducted by MacKinnon (1993). Yet even in this case, the author could only investigate the audience of the 1980s, which was characterized, for instance, by a basically middle-aged dominance with 59 percent being male, 41 percent being female, and the majority of listeners (who tended to attend regularly) being between thirty and thirty-nine years old.

Although actual numbers for the electric folk scene are missing, one can still point out some general aspects. For example, MacKinnon (1993: chap. 4) observed that active participation instead of passive listening was essential to the folk audience; the major portion of the folk club goers would also join in the performances in one way or another, rather than only allowing professionals to be onstage. This characteristic can partly be transferred to the electric folk sphere. Despite the emergence of "star musicians," the performer-audience relationship is still relatively close. The atmosphere at the Cropredy Festival, for example, is low-key and congenial: fans and performers meet at the same beer stand, chat with each other, and ask for autographs, without the star hysteria that accompanies rock groups. Instead, one can discover Jacqui McShee—who had been cheered half an hour ago onstage—standing in the same crowd, watching the next performer without being bothered much.

When the first electric groups performed at universities or on gigs with other progressive groups, it is most likely that their audiences were at least similar. However, as Macan (1997: 151) remarked in his investigation of the progressive scene, it is extremely difficult to do a "statistically accurate demographic study" from our present-day viewpoint. The audiences today for electric folk are highly mixed. Visiting Cropredy, one can observe many veteran fans from the late 1960s, as well as an even larger number of young people who have never heard anything of Sandy Denny but instead became interested in Fairport Convention through their newer recordings. Steeleye Span bassist Rick Kemp also confirmed this observation:

> A Steeleye fan seems to be a fan for life. And that's commendable, it's nice to have an audience that doesn't let you down. And I think, maybe I'm wrong, but all the people that came at the height of those three or four years when we had the hit records—there were very few of those. I think there is a greater awareness, now, in England, coming from world music and the popularity of WOMAD and that sort of thing. And from where it descended in country. And bands like Clannad have helped enormously, have caused to raise the awareness. And the Oysterband. And there are bands on the fringe of it, like Edward II.

The extremely varied performance venues have to be taken into consideration. At venues like the Fabrik in Hamburg one encounters more middle-aged audiences (as at a concert of Fairport Convention) than, for example, at university sites (e.g., Bloomington, Indiana, where June Tabor and Maddy Prior, who visited separately in 1993, attracted audiences in their mid-twenties).

Intellectually, the fan network is held together by a shared knowledge of a core repertoire that includes certain cornerstone pieces such as, in the case of Fairport Convention, "Matty Groves," "Who Knows Where the Time Goes," and "Meet on the

Ledge." Although these songs are almost thirty years old, knowledge of their lengthy texts is essential to gain inside access to the scene, as they have assumed a codelike function. For instance, Fairport often plays with the melody of "Matty Groves" during its concerts, inserting it suddenly during a completely different song, and a complete understanding of this "game" and its hidden implications is only possible when a listener is thoroughly familiar with the piece's content and tune.

Fans also display familiarity with the often complex histories of lineups, with nicknames like "Swarb" (Dave Swarbrick), "Peggy" (Dave Pegg), or "Tyger" (Ashley Hutchings), and with certain insider stories, such as Sandy Denny's early death, which are often referenced with only a few words in various fanzines like *Porthole*. Likewise, the critical discourse about the music is shaped by a distinct terminology that magazines like *Folk Roots* and authors/biographers like Humphries (1997) have often derived from song titles or recording phrases (e.g., "trad./arr.").

There are still many open questions to be answered about electric folk's audience. What made the music appealing to the audience? Apart from the music itself, was it also an implicit nationalism, as Macan (1997: 154) observed for the progressive groups? Perhaps, although the bands also have a large (in the 1970s even larger) following abroad, especially in Germany. These are just some of the aspects that still need to be investigated but have remained outside the scope of this book, which focuses on the performers.

THE ELECTRIC FOLK SCENE IN THE 1990s

While the bands and performers have disappeared from broad public view, a scene that could almost be called "independent" still exists and is much more homogeneous than in the 1970s, maybe because it has existed for such a long time. Having developed the instruments for survival as a niche market, it is today distinguished by the following characteristics:

1. *A vast network of performance venues*, from town halls (e.g., Steeleye Span has appeared at the Cambridge Corn Market Exchange) to smaller clubs like the Twelve Bar Club in London, where Bert Jansch played regularly while the research for this book was under way.

2. *Seasonal folk festivals as the principal festival venues*, with Cropredy as the major event. In contrast to outdoor rock festivals, these events are covered only marginally by such mainstream media as the music pages of London's weekly magazine *Time Out*. Cropredy is mainly publicized in genre magazines such as *Folk Roots* and via an internal mailing list.

3. *The emergence of specialized folk magazines after 1974*, when electric folk increasingly disappeared from popular music magazines. Today, rock magazines like *The Rolling Stone* occasionally review some electric folk recordings, but for inter-

views, tour dates, and other basic coverage, specialized magazines like *Folk Roots* and its American counterpart *Dirty Linen* have become essential for the scene. From the mid-1990s on, Web sites such as www.greenmanreview.com have become of increasing importance. Much cheaper, more easily accessible, and—above all—more flexible than print magazines, they represent an important new layer of communication between fans, journalists, and artists.

4. *An independent, low-key business and marketing strategy:* Almost all groups and performers appear on relatively small, independent labels partly owned by the bands (e.g., Woodworm, owned by Dave Pegg) or, in the case of folk music, on Topic, which has become the primary label for contemporary folk and for musicians like June Tabor, Martin Carthy, and Waterson:Carthy. Even though these labels offer the performers an alternative to the mass-market-oriented popular music business, marketing problems remain. The financial resources for extensive promotion are missing, as label owner John Tobler pointed out: "Running a record company, you just discover how different it is having a great record and being able to sell a great record. Because it's getting things like radio play and getting good reviews—that's the hardest part. There are a lot of wonderful records about that nobody has ever heard because there is no promotion."

Today electric folk performers, like progressive rock groups, often release their albums after time gaps of several years. This extended pacing is possible only because the musicians have a long-established fan base; it would have meant an end to their careers in the 1960s or 1970s. Many recording sales are made via an internal network. Most of the groups have their own fan mailing lists, for instance, and many CDs are also sold at concerts and especially at festivals. The specialized magazines like *Folk Roots* and *Dirty Linen* provide reviews and some affordable space for advertisements.

There are signs that the younger generation may be able to rebuild a wider audience for electric folk. Eliza Carthy was highly promoted by Topic, and her album *Red Rice* (1998), which pictured her in a punk outfit, sold extremely well. In 2000 she became the first folk musician in more than twenty years to sign a contract with a major label, Warner, which released her album *Angels & Cigarettes*. The album seemed to indicate a shift from traditional material toward original songwriting, but it did not sell well and Carthy returned to Topic, apparently for several reasons. As she remarked in an interview with Joe Lust (2002: 44), while the cooperation with Warner's U.S. division (which had signed her) went well, the British division "never seemed to understand that I already had a career that they could build on."

While John Peel could still be heard on the BBC in 2003, broadcasting has remained problematic, with little air time available in England for either electric or acoustic tradition-based material. While in the 1950s and 1960s radio was essential for raising awareness of traditional music in England, folk and electric folk now often get only a small niche, if anything at all, within the BBC. Even then, it is presented as a minority program, often scheduled for late at night when the audience is very small (a current [2003] exception is Mike Harding's show on BBC Radio 2 at 8 p.m. on Wednesdays, featuring performers like Maddy Prior or the Oysterband and special events from Scotland).[24]

In contrast with other contemporary musicians of short-lived music trends, traditional performers have always had a performance platform they could (and would) return to: the folk clubs. Although the clubs still exist and play a major role for the acoustic performers, one can also observe some changes here. For example, more popular folksingers like June Tabor have moved to larger venues like art centers. Tabor reported that she rarely ever works in folk clubs now because

> what I do require is a lot of concentration and I feel people should be given the opportunity to concentrate and sit comfortably, so I tend to work in a theatre style setting really. You still get a considerable degree of intimacy, but you don't get the attendant problems of pub rooms, karaokes downstairs, juke boxes and bar staff who didn't want to be on duty. I've heard the most aggressive glass-washing imaginable during my sets. (Irwin 1993a: 65)

Yet Tabor's move out of the folk clubs toward the art centers is viewed somewhat critically by representatives of the older performer generation like Martin Carthy, who has emphasized the clubs' ability to provide performance spaces independent from the competitive demands of the mainstream music business. Although the clubs are amateurish and inefficient as business ventures, they still offer an interaction between performers and listeners, musical beginners and professionals, not possible elsewhere. Carthy values the mutual musical exchange:

> In art centers I walk in, I get up at eight o'clock and I start singing and I have an interval at ten to nine and I get back on the stage at quarter past nine and I get off stage at half past ten and I leave. And have I heard any other music? Naw! All I've heard is me—and I've heard all that. One of the reasons why it is nice to go to folk clubs is that you get to hear the residents, you hear the floor singers. And occasionally you'll hear one of your mates will turn up, and he'll do a couple of songs from the floor. The whole ethic is something really rather praiseworthy. And generally speaking, exciting as well. Because we've all shared in this thing, it was ours, and the whole concert ethic is not an "our"-thing but a "me"-thing. I'm a person who actually believes in "us"—I'm a socialist! I don't like the lauding of the individual. I was never a CP member, but I do not like personality cults.

Although a part of the original audience of the 1960s has stayed with the older British folk and electric folk performers, the major portion of listeners today are from a younger generation that in some cases was not even born when these groups were at their peak. Cropredy, for example, is visited by many young families. Rick Kemp mentioned a similar change with Steeleye Span:

One thing that I've observed through the popularity of Steeleye in the sort of mid-'70s to the '80s, for instance, was that we got a completely different audience. I don't think the other one went away entirely; we always knew people that came to see us, you know. They are a much more settled middle-class audience than the audience of the early days, which was just pretty left-wing tendencies. It was just there was a shift of audience attitude after popularity, after a lot of radio shows, after a lot of television exposure, after big record sales.

With the changed audience, electric folk has also lost its original controversial side. Electric instruments in folk music are accepted as normal now, as Ashley Hutchings pointed out:

I think our music has become acceptable, it's no longer confrontational. It was confrontational in the late '60s, really '70s. People went "Wow," you know, they got angry at that music, disgusted. Not only folk fans—rock side as well: "We don't want all this folderol stuff or this diddle-dee, diddle-dee, diddle-dee stuff in the rock arena." And the folkies were saying: "We don't want all these loud instruments in our music."

Some pioneering performers are not even generally known to the younger audience anymore. Davy Graham is a prime example. As he recalled in an interview with Stefan Grossman (1990: 18): "Ten years ago . . . they all knew who I was. . . . When I went to Toulouse, the guys who were organizing had pictures of John Renbourn all over the place, all his records and stuff."

The 1990s witnessed the emergence of many younger British bands and musicians—acoustic as well as electric. Young performers from a variety of British regions have shown a clear interest in the acoustic tradition, including fiddler Catriona Mac-Donald from Shetland, who has teamed up with accordion player Ian Lowthian; Jennifer and Hazel Wrigley (fiddle and guitar) from the Orkneys; singer Kate Rusby from Yorkshire; and fiddler Eliza Carthy. Although these performers have often listened to the music of the earlier folk and electric folk groups, they have developed a relatively down-to-earth attitude toward the electric sound. Eliza Carthy, for instance, although backed by the electric Kings of Calicutt in 1996, has clearly stated that she prefers playing an acoustic instrument and rather dislikes the electric fiddle, comparing its sound with that of an "angry wasp" (Anderson 1996: 45).

At the same time, these musicians have introduced new instrumental sounds to the old material. One band that has developed a particularly distinctive sound is the Poozies, whose electric sound is produced by Patsy Seddon's and Mary MacMaster's amplified harps, which have also taken over the bass function. Most exceptional is probably the Northumbrian bagpipe player Kathryn Tickell, who in 2000 assembled a new group, Ensemble Mystical, that includes a carynx, an approximately 2,000-year-old Celtic boar-headed horn. The Kings of Calicutt have incorporated the hammered dulcimer, which, especially on the Waterson:Carthy recording, *common tongue* (1998), is well integrated with Martin Carthy's percussive guitar sound. The fusion element is sometimes even stronger here than in the previous generation's music; Eliza's interpretation of "Billy Boy" on *Red Rice*, for example, incorporates African and reggae elements.

Many of these musicians play at a highly advanced technical level that only few of the earlier folk and electric folk generations reached (fiddler Catriona MacDonald and singers Kate Rusby and Kathryn Roberts have won the BBC Radio 2 Young Tradition award). One can also observe some other differences: the singing style, although clearly English due to the use of a rather soft voice, lacks the variety and individuality one could hear thirty years earlier.

The strong promotion these musicians have received from early in their careers (e.g., in form of comprehensive articles in *Folk Roots* from the mid-1990s on) may not always have been helpful, since many of them, like Eliza Carthy, were still in the process of developing an individual style. Nevertheless, Carthy indeed has turned out to be probably the most successful performer of the new generation. In her case, a strong connection to the old tradition was maintained while she played for a local North Yorkshire sword dance team (she was their first new fiddler since 1956).

The development of folk and electric folk in Britain thus remains an unfinished story. Not all musicians of the older generation, however, are positive about the future. Shirley Collins's criticism is typical of some other veteran performers: "They've got talent, they've got ability, they've got facility with the voices they've got, they've got facility with their instruments. But I don't think they have a profound understanding of the music they play. They want to make it sound attractive—and instantly attractive. But they don't seem to know how to get to the heart of it."

Despite bringing in fresh impulses by incorporating influences from contemporary styles, several of these younger musicians often do not seem to go back to the original sources. Instead—and this is especially the case in the folk clubs—the revival or folk rock performers are taken as models. Martin Carthy, for instance, feels quite uncomfortable with being constantly copied:

> You've then recorded it and you've become part of that body of information, so you expect that you're going to be used. That's O.K. But I wish that the people who do that would actually go back a bit further. Instead of saying "Oh great, another Martin Carthy record," they'd look at other ones, say Sam Larner or Walter Pardon, Joseph Taylor, any kind of traditional music. (Anderson and Heath 1982: 11)

This was why Carthy did not include too many original transcriptions in his songbook (Kennedy 1987). The development has interesting parallels with the early music movement of the 1960s and '70s, when numerous musicians like recorder player Frans Brüggen and harpsichordist Gustav Leonhardt went back to primary sources to find new and more intense means of expression. A large portion of the subsequent musical generation, however, either reduced the expressive means to the unusual sound of the instruments alone, or started to copy these musicians without reviewing the original sources, and thus lost considerable expressive ground.

One obstacle for young folk and electric folk performers has been the difficulty in gaining access to original material. Although the archives indeed hold a large quantity of material, the strict British copyright law restricts possession of private copies of archived material, which in turn makes a thorough study of original styles quite difficult.[25] It will thus be interesting to observe the impact of the recent twenty-volume British-Irish recorded anthology, *The Voice of the People*, which was released by Topic in 1998. Through this collection a wide span of traditional material will be available commercially for the first time in decades.

Cecil Sharp and Edwin Clay of Brailes, Warwickshire (April 30, 1910). Sharp collected *"The Golden Glove"* from the seventy-seven-year-old singer. *(Reproduced by permission of the English Folk Dance and Song Society.)*

A. L. Lloyd and Ewan MacColl at the Centre 42 concert in Wellingborough, September 1962. *(Courtesy of Collections/Brian Shuel.)*

Shirley and Dolly Collins, Blackheath, London 1966. *(Courtesy of Collections/Brian Shuel.)*

Martin Carthy and Dave Swarbrick at the EFDSS Festival in the Royal Albert Hall, London, 1967. *(Courtesy of Collections/Brian Shuel.)*

Davy Graham in his flat in West London, 1966. *(Courtesy of Collections/Brian Shuel.)*

Transatlantic's announcement of Pentangle's first album (*Melody Maker*, May 18, 1968).

Inner record sleeve of Fairport Convention's *Liege & Lief* (Island Records, 1969) with references to various English traditions. (*Reproduced by permission of Island/Universal Records.*)

Pace-eggers

Pace-egging, an Easter custom in the North-West of England, uses the egg as a symbol of the springtime rebirth of life. Another symbolic rebirth depiction, the Mummers Play, is sometimes performed by the pace-eggers as they go a-begging for eggs. These plays involve usually a hero fighting evil, being killed and then being revived by a mock physician. The drawing shows pace-eggers from the Kirkby Stephen area, 1894.

Francis James Child

It is largely thanks to Prof. Francis James Child (1825–1896) that so many British ballads are known to us today. Born in Boston, Child came to England and the result of his studies was "English & Scottish Popular Ballads," the definitive collection, never to be superseded. Before Child, accurate editions of ballad texts were few and far between.

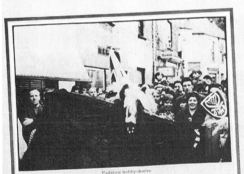

Padstow hobby-horse

At midnight on the eve of May Day, the Padstow hobby-horse may be seen going round the houses of the town with its attendants of men and women dressed as sailors singing songs of joy at the coming of summer. The hobby-horse is actually a man underneath a covered hoop, topped by a grotesque head with a long, pointed cap. In a final dance, the death of the horse is depicted and, next day, a second procession visits houses inviting alms.

Burry man

The Burry Man (a boy in white flannel covered with burrs from the wild burdock) can be seen at the annual fair on the second Friday in August at South Queensferry, West Lothian. He also has a floral head-dress and carries flower-decked staves. He tours the town in silence; he cannot and must not be drawn into speech. The custom is said to have originated with the Scottish King Malcolm who camouflaged himself in burrs to escape from the English.

Pentangle in London, 1967 (clockwise from top): Bert Jansch, John Renbourn, Terry Cox, Danny Thompson, and Jacqui McShee. *(Courtesy of Collections/Brian Shuel.)*

Fairport Convention (summer 1969), from the Fairley Chamberlayne photo session (from left to right): Dave Mattacks, Richard Thompson, Simon Nicol, Dave Swarbrick, Ashley Hutchings, and Sandy Denny. *(Courtesy of Ashley Hutchings.)*

Early poster of the 1970–71 Steeleye Span lineup that recorded *Please to See the King* and *Ten Man Mop*: Maddy Prior, Martin Carthy, Tim Hart, Ashley Hutchings, and Peter Knight. (*Courtesy of Ashley Hutchings.*)

Ian Telfer and John Jones from the Oysterband.
(*Courtesy of Andrew Cleal.*)

FIVE

THE MUSIC
A General Overview

> When I first joined Steeleye I didn't really appreciate the adherence to a tune and a scale I wasn't familiar working with. And I remember the fiddle player saying to me at one point, "You keep playing thirds, please don't play thirds, because it's not what we do in English traditional music." RICK KEMP

Rick Kemp's initial problems with Steeleye Span's approach reflected the complexities of electric folk's stylistic makeup. Based on popular music genres, it is nevertheless different from contemporary styles because of its traditional roots, evident in the tunes, harmonies, and lyrics. Conversely, electric folk is not simply a traditional tune set to a rock beat. Rather, it is the result of different musical styles and elements being fused together into something new, including the performance practice. Despite various American influences, the music has maintained a markedly English character, owing to the traditional material and the incorporation of traditional vocal and instrumental styles. Before taking a look at the general musical features of electric folk, I will begin with a brief excursion into the characteristics of the English tradition. Chapter 6 focuses on more detailed analyses of selected performers and approaches.

ENGLISH TRADITIONAL MUSIC

The focal points of both the revival and the electric folk movement have been the traditional songs and ballads. By contrast, dance material, although also a popular part of the repertoire, has been adopted to a much smaller degree and will not be touched on here. To summarize the writings of Cecil Sharp (1907) and his former assistant Maud Karpeles (1987), four general song types have been prevalent in England until the present day:

1. The classic ballads, embodied in the Child ballads. Addressing central human conflicts as in "Matty Groves," they have been categorized as "nonfunc-

tional," that is, not related to any working or seasonal context (Karpeles 1987: chap. 6).

2. The broadsides, which are more focused on historical events, told in sentimental language, and often include an explicit moral. For example, the nineteenth-century transport ballad "Van Diemen's Land," sung by Shirley Collins on *No Roses*, concludes with the advice "Lay by your dog and snare / To you I do speak plain / If you knew the hardships we endure / You'll never poach [i.e., take game illegally] again." Mainly written for commercial purposes, broadsides were distributed on sheets, often written by professional songwriters and set to well-known dance tunes of the time.

3. Work songs and songs associated with calendar customs, such as harvest and wassailing songs, sometimes still with pagan content, as evident in the winter ritual of the hunting of the wren.

4. Carols. Although Christmas songs have become the best-known form, this category comprises a broad range of popular songs "appropriated to some special season of the ecclesiastical or natural year" (H. R. Bramley in Karpeles 1987: 56). These include folk songs with a religious orientation (occasionally of balladlike character), dance songs that were popular in medieval times, and songs related to the midwinter custom of wassailing—wishes of good health that were sung by small groups on house-to-house visits between Christmas and Epiphany.[1]

These musical types, in particular the ballads, can be found all over the British Isles, although the regions of England, Scotland, Wales, and Ireland are each distinguished by particular variants, singing and playing styles, and other specific forms. The Gaelic-speaking areas have built up an especially distinct repertoire: Scotland and Ireland differ from the English region in the occurrence of fragments of epics, laments, mouth music,[2] and waulking songs (Hebrides).[3] Likewise, although jigs and reels can be found all over the British Isles, each region has developed particular forms, such as the ritual English morris dance, which also includes sword dances and mummers' plays. The differences are especially obvious in the various instrumental and ornamental techniques. The Scottish Travellers, for example, tend to sing in a highly ornamented style and create a very intense sound that is the result of tight vocal cords. Irish singers not only have developed their own styles like the nasal sean-nós, but they also sing highly ornamented lines, yet less intensely than Scottish singers, with a less throaty voice. English singing, in contrast, is less embellished than in the Gaelic areas, and the voice is often less intense and more closely related to the speaking voice.

As Sharp and Karpeles outlined further, English folk song is based on modal scales; most common is the Ionian mode, although Aeolian, Mixolydian, and Dorian can also be found. Pure pentatonic scales are rare, in contrast with Scottish folk song, although one can frequently discover hexatonic ones (i.e., without the sixth [as in most cases], third, or seventh degrees).

According to Sharp, the traditional vocal music of the British Islands was mostly sung unaccompanied. Whether or not this was his own idealized impression (see the "Harmony Singing" section below), the accompaniment was indeed often nearly non-existent with those songs that were recited in a parlando-rubato style. Yet these only made up a part of the traditional material—many songs and ballads, often depending on the content, were recited in a metrically clear style that was oriented in the dance tradition and would have allowed accompaniment. However, even here, as is clearly evident on the recordings Peter Kennedy made for the BBC, the occasionally existing accompaniment was in most cases subordinated in the form of a drone.[4]

The focus was instead on the melody. Traditional performers of the British Isles, who normally sing using a nontempered scale, often vary the melody or emphasize certain lines with ornaments such as slides, turns, or arabesques. These ornaments, the occasional shortening and lengthening of verse line endings, and the parlando-rubato recital style with its tempo fluctuations often result in an elongation and shortening of measures of an otherwise regular duple or triple meter. These irregularities make an accurate transcription occasionally difficult, with quintuple meters as a compound of 2 + 3 and changes of meter (e.g., 3/4 + 4/4) being fairly common, as are stresses on unusual measures.

Although Sharp insisted that his informants sing unaccompanied, he himself published these songs for the general public with piano arrangements that became quite popular; see, for example, his *One Hundred English Folksongs* (1916). Partly as a reaction against the first revivalists' practices and partly as a result of being sensitive to the original style, Peggy Seeger and Ewan MacColl recommended in *The Singing Island* that collectors and performers refrain from metrically or harmonically restrictive arrangements. Seeger and MacColl (1960: 2) clearly realized that the tradition had developed a predominantly monophonic singing style with complicated rhythmic and linear structures, inflections, decorations "and similar subtleties that could easily be drowned out or leveled out by accompaniment." They recommended that the voice "should not be hampered by instruments" and gave the advice to add an accompaniment cautiously, "so as not to rob the song of its fundamental characteristics or independence,"[5] that is, as a background against which one could sing freely or in a style that emphasized the song's rhythm. At the same time, the harmonies should be kept as simple as possible, without diminished or augmented forms; even seventh chords should be used carefully. Seeger and MacColl suggested traditional instruments like the fiddle, flutes, pipes, concertina, and melodeon, while discouraging guitars and banjos as foreign to the tradition. These rules—which were taken up by the core of the Second Revival—sometimes resulted in a restrictive practice, being applied much more strictly than within the original performance practice of the tradition itself.— Moreover, MacColl's rejection of the guitar and the banjo inevitably led to conflicts with the majority of the younger audiences, who preferred American-style accompaniments.

A GENERAL DESCRIPTION OF THE FUSION STYLES

"Electric folk" has become the collective name of various approaches mixing traditional and modern music. None of these groups and musicians merely played a fiddle or a bagpipe tune on a contemporary instrument like an electric guitar, or simply amplified an acoustic instrument. Rather, they fused traditional music with various contemporary elements, thus creating something completely new. The American electric folk musician Jennifer Cutting (1993) defined electric folk as "a syncretic music formed by the combination of melodic and harmonic elements from songs and tunes of the tradition, with the harmonic and rhythmic conventions of rock and other popular music forms, and played with a combination of acoustic and electric instruments."

The musical arrangement process has varied markedly among the groups, depending on their musical backgrounds (rock, blues, jazz) and the instruments they have used. While Fairport Convention started as a rock band, playing in places of the London underground scene, Steeleye Span began as a lineup of folk musicians who adapted rock elements, and Pentangle was a mixture of folk, folk blues, and jazz musicians. Of these groups, only the music of Fairport Convention and Steeleye Span was electric folk in the strictest sense of folk plus rock. Pentangle, often included under this label, was purely acoustic, apart from amplifying the instruments via microphones and a brief experiment with the electric guitar; it always maintained its acoustic, yet percussive and metallic, sound). Despite this obvious contradiction, this study still includes a large number of acoustic fusion musicians like Shirley and Dolly Collins or the folk baroque direction, as they have all anticipated or paralleled several characteristics of the electric bands.

Adaptations from the Tradition

Electric folk, and to some extent also the folk rock direction, is clearly differentiated from other popular music forms by its inclusion of traditional songs (predominantly ballads and broadsides, with occasional work and holiday songs but few carols), distinguished by tunes with a modal structure and texts with a characteristic ("traditional") language. The performers have also adapted traditionally oriented singing and playing techniques, such as Richard Thompson's imitation of the bagpipe sound, as well as structural elements like drone accompaniments and unusual rhythmic and metric forms. The latter includes imperfect meters (Fairport Convention, "Bonny Black Hare" in 5/4), meter changes (Fairport Convention, "Tam Lin") and unusual rhythmic accentuations combined with syncopated structures (Steeleye Span, "The Blacksmith" in 4/4 with stresses on either beats 2 or 3).

These elements were to some degree already inherent in the original music, although often not with the extreme clarity heard in revival and electric folk perform-ances.[6] The awareness of the rhythmic and metric peculiarities can especially be traced back to A. L. Lloyd, who had done fieldwork in Albania. Lloyd not only showed a clear preference for irregular accentuations in English folk music, but he also incorporated elements of Eastern European music into the English tradition, al-though in a very subtle way, as he stressed only those elements that were already in-herent in the original material. References to the parlando-rubato style, with inherent tempo fluctuations, are especially evident in early recordings by Fairport Convention like "A Sailor's Life," while later, with the straighter drumming style of Dave Mattacks, this feature became less important. Such is also the case with other, more dance-oriented bands like Steeleye Span or the Oysterband.[7]

Borrowings from Modern Music Forms

Elements this genre has adapted from rock music included—apart from the in-struments—rhythmic devices like the backbeat and arrangement techniques like the hook/riff and ostinato accompaniment (Cutting 1993), as well as irregular song struc-tures departing from the simple alternation between verse and refrain. Progressive rock, which developed almost at the same time, opened up further structural, instru-mental, and technical possibilities and thus became highly influential on the musical development of electric folk. This applies particularly to the Incredible String Band, which has occupied a position between the two genres. From jazz, electric folk appro-priated long improvisational segments, particularly apparent with Pentangle.

American influence was evident in the initial stages of the Second British Folk Re-vival and in various popular music styles before 1965. It was especially reflected in the repertoire and the instrumentation of the acoustic performers; guitars, banjos, and dulcimers were adapted after the music of the American folk revival had become popular in Europe. Despite Fairport Convention's cover versions of Bob Dylan and Joni Mitchell songs, the impact of American music became less obvious with the fusion styles that emerged as British groups began developing their own musical identities.

Hybrid Characteristics

The result of this fusion was a vast structural and musical variety that surpassed anything that had been going on in the folk clubs, especially in terms of tonal colors. A lineup mixing contemporary rock components (electric and acoustic guitar, electric bass, drums, and sometimes keyboards) with traditional instruments like fiddle, melodeon, plucked dulcimer, and (later) brass, or with a combination of traditional and early music instruments, has become typical of this genre. The most characteristic instrument has probably been the amplified fiddle. Even the Oysterband, which has long since gone in a different, more rock-oriented songwriting direction, is still identi-fied with that the electric folk scene because of the fiddle, as Ian Telfer pointed out:

Bands with a fiddle are going to be called folk or folk rock, even if they have no connection with folk music at all. And we, obviously, have lots of connections. The fiddle is a very useful instrument for electric music, in that it's rhythmic but also has infinite sustain. So you can do what a keyboard does in some other kinds of music, which is to sustain a note for as long as you want it *against* the percussive things. Or you can actually play it in a rhythmically alive way that meshes with the other rhythmic elements of music.

Another fusion characteristic is metric complexity. In some cases electric folk performers set the melodic line—already unusually structured and accentuated—against an independent rhythmic line in the accompaniment; this can be heard in Fairport Convention's interpretation of "She Moves through the Fair." Later, the increasingly backbeat-dominated folk rock bands would prefer simpler rhythmic structures that would encourage their audiences to dance.

STRUCTURAL ASPECTS

A creative variety of musical approaches is reflected in electric folk music's treatment of its source material, which can be roughly subdivided into four main categories, with many further combinations possible (see fig. 5.1). (For the treatment of the original sources, see chapter 7; newly composed material will be discussed in chapter 6.)

The arrangement process depends on the technical skills of the individual performers. For example, John Renbourn, who studied orchestration and composition in the 1980s at Dartington College of Arts, prepared his arrangements in an almost classical way:

Usually the folk tunes/songs are a blend from different sources. Most often I hear a tune in a club/pub or from a friend that sparks off a familiarity. "John Barleycorn," for example, I must have heard a thousand times over the years. Usually I find myself running over the melody in my mind from memory, and then when I get a chance looking at any printed sources—i.e., Lloyd's *Folk Song in England*, Chappell's *Music of the Olden Time*, and so on. I have a big collection of old books, but I may go to Cecil Sharp House or Westminster Library if I am in the area. Printed and recorded versions may throw up a different twist in a line or two, but often the tune is already in my mind. And I look at it in a fairly detached way—considering the scale/mode, general shape, and possible way of arranging it. A lot of the arranging goes on in the head, after which I put down ideas so I won't forget. I always have a lot of tunes in the rough stage, only a few get to see the light of day in a real arrangement.

This time lapse between the first impression of a song and its actual live performance was confirmed by Simon Nicol. The musical approach taken also depends on the character of an individual piece, as indicated in his recollection of the arrangement process for *Liege & Lief*:

I Text and tune traditional

II Text and tune traditional but collated: mixtures of different material

1) tune as a collation
    a) of two or more different songs or ballads
    b) merged with newly composed passages

2) text as a collation
    a) of two or more different songs or ballads
    b) merged with own textual passages   *Especially the music of Steeleye Span*

III Tune or text traditional

1) traditional music/new text   *"Farewell, Farewell"* (Fairport Convention)
2) traditional text/ new music   *"Polly on the Shore"* (Fairport Convention)

IV Newly composed pieces

1) new text compositions in a neo-
   traditional style
    a) text traditional with traditional/   *"Crazy Man Michael"* (Fairport
       old-style tune   Convention)

    b) modernised text with traditional/ old   Calling-On-Songs of Fairport
       style tune   Convention and Steeleye Span

2) modern content/language with references
   to the tradition
    a) shaped by old musical forms (e.g. ballad)   *"Wounded Whale"* (Fairport Convention)
    b) modern content/ event depicted in
       traditional images, symbols, forms   *"Walk Awhile"* (Fairport Convention)
    c) modern content but distinct atmosphere
       derived from traditional songs   Sandy Denny's songwriting
    d) folk/traditional instruments   (Levellers, Oysterband)

FIGURE 5.1. Musical and textual sources in electric folk

A song like "Tam Lin," although it's not very much longer than "Matty Groves," is a much more interesting story—and a longer story. That required a structure. So that was fairly formally arranged. You'd decide, once you get the general feeling, the theme of it; you then have to break it down into sections and say, well, you have to emphasize this point, bring this out, rush through that bit—that was what we did. So really that was kind of worked out in advance, and then we learned it. And the other songs like "Crazy Man Michael," "Farewell, Farewell," they were straightforward songs, and you'd find out the way that made them sound as interesting and enjoyable as possible.

The ballads, in which sixteen or more verses are based on a single melody, especially require other means to build and sustain musical tension. The bands hence developed a broad range of structural and stylistic possibilities, illustrated in figure 5.2.

1)   *unaccompanied singing*
            often with extra reverberation

2)   *harmony singing* (either a cappella or accompanied)
        a) alternating verse lines   *"Cutty Wren"* (Steeleye Span)
        b) responsorial forms (one (or more) verse(s)
            solo – refrain tutti)   *"Gaudete"* (Steeleye Span)
        c) polyphonic forms   *"Twa Corbies"* (Steeleye Span)

3)   *(subordinated) chordal accompaniment*
            i.e. instrument is clearly subordinated, as with
            chordal guitar accompaniment), few interludes   *"Pretty Polly"* (Sandy Denny)

4)   *drone accompaniment*
            drone (by acoustic or electric instruments, later
            predominantly synthesiser layer); voices free above
            with tempo-fluctuations, little instrumental
            improvisation; often: clear successive form
            (without interludes)   *"Nottamun Town"*, *"Flowers of the
                                                                      Forest"* (Fairport Convention)

5)   *improvisational forms*
            overall form fixed; independent lines, tempo-
            fluctuations; voice: parlando-style (embellished,
            lengthening of single tones); instruments improvised,
            provide vague metrical framework, onomatopoetic
            elements. Often with ballads like   *"She Moves Through the Fair"*,
                                                                      "A Sailor's Life, *"Reynardine"*
                                                                      (Fairport Convention)

6)   *hook/riff arrangements*
            straight tempo; fixed form with instrumental
            interludes; one instrument/voice leading,
            musical accompaniment separated from
            content of the piece, partly also from the tune;
            later often predominance of back beat.

6a) *song arrangements*
            3-6 verses, resembling rock/pop arrangements   *"Sir Patrick Spens"*
                                                                      (Fairport Convention)

6b) *ballad arrangements*
            (longer than 6a); longer instrumental interludes
            that structure the narrative   *"Matty Groves"*, *"Tam Lin"*
                                                                      (Fairport Convention)

FIGURE 5.2. The different arrangement possibilities

Particularly on Fairport Convention's early recordings, which were still influenced by the progressive rock movement, one can hear drone accompaniments, improvisatory forms with a fixed upper singing voice, and various combinations of riffs, hooks, and interludes that break up longer song/ballad structures. Despite this initial wide range of arranging possibilities, however, electric folk gradually became structurally much more limited. "Electric folk" in the sense of folk plus rock left little room for the rhythmic freedom that had been especially evident with Terry Cox's sophisticated drumming for Pentangle or with Martin Lamble's filigreed style for the early Fairport Convention. As the groups became more dance-oriented, they began to give up the freer parlando-rubato style and preferred to play with regular rhythmic patterns. Dave Mattacks's simple and straightforward drumming style for Fairport in the 1970s and late '80s, which was also characteristic of Steeleye Span, is especially effective on the dance-oriented instrumentals. These pieces require a more exact and measured style, which is further intensified by the amplification; the cumulative effect helps explain why Ashley Hutchings was so successful in reviving morris dance with electric instruments.

Nevertheless, many critics believed that the music, even if it still included unusual rhythmic patterns, lost much of its original quality in the later electric folk arrangements. The free singing style, with its metric subtleties and internal tempo fluctuations, was especially vulnerable to being smoothed out by the accompaniment of a constant drum pulse. This difference can be heard by comparing A. L. Lloyd's and Fairport Convention's interpretations of "Tam Lin": while Lloyd's parlando-rubato style is based on a looser metric organization, Fairport's drums tighten the rhythmic feel.

Something similar is occasionally evident in John Renbourn's and Pentangle's later work, which was more centered on instrumental textures and melodies than on the rhythmic side, thus losing much of the internal tension that was part of the fascination of the earlier works. While Bert Jansch's "Blackwaterside" is complex in its metric organization, Renbourn's interpretation of the same work on *A Maid in Bedlam* has lost this inherent tension; its rhythmic irregularities are minimized, partly due to the relatively homogenous tabla layer that levels out any differences.

HARMONIC PATTERNS

Because electric folk performers work with modal scales, their harmonic configurations differ from those of rock or classical music, which are based on the major/minor tonal system. This is especially evident with songs that use the Dorian and Mixolydian modes. In the Ionian and Lydian modes, the dominant is a major triad with a strong cadential character in progressions like I–IV–V–I (and related variants) that are common in classical as well as rock music. Rock also uses other harmonic patterns such as the major triad built on the seventh degree, which occurs only with Mixolydian, Dorian, and Aeolian modes—all essential for electric folk, where this cadential pattern also occurs frequently. However, the modal character can be easily destroyed by putting these modal structures into a major/minor context, because the modality relies on intervals and chords built on progressions that are not found in tonal harmony. Seeger/MacColl (1960) were probably aware of this problem when recommending that accompanying instruments should be used carefully, for modal distortions had characterized the arrangements of the earlier collectors. Although he conformed with the musical thinking of the late nineteenth century, even Cecil Sharp was nevertheless aware of this problem as well. In his arrangement of the Dorian "Bruton Town" (Sharp 1916) he followed contemporary musical conventions by notating the song in D minor, but he then canceled the key signature and devised a nontraditional harmonic arrangement deviating from the classic tonic-subdominant-dominant-tonic scheme. Similarly, many electric groups tried to maintain the spirit of modality by working linearly; instead of approaching a piece from a chordal level, they used drone structures (Fairport Convention, "Nottamun Town") and unusual harmonic progressions (see fig. 5.3).

Thus chordal thinking, as in jazz or some types of rock music, is more the exception than the rule in electric folk. Most musicians reported that they usually work and think melodically, John Renbourn commented:

> The old modal tunes have a lot of character and can be ruined by a bad setting. Sticking to the mode is a basic principle but not a cast-iron one. Moving lines that share the melodic characteristics of the original can be complementary—they don't actually "harmonize" in the eighteenth-century sense (although they can). So I tend to set them as part of a contrapuntal texture. The best blues bands I know of (even into electric Chicago blues), Muddy Waters, etc., all play *lines*—a type of American counterpoint. Even the Alan Lomax recordings—"Murder's Home" of convicts singing—show a mass of moving parts rather than a formalized chord structure.

Martin Carthy, who was especially referred to as an authority on this subject, admitted frankly that he could not say anything about chordal structures, as his perception of the music was clearly focused on the melodic lines. Not without reason, however:

> I think you actually get a better idea of this music if you approach it from a nonharmonic way, in a nonorchestral way. I think the difference between a normally tuned guitar and the way I tune the guitar is just that. If you have a normally tuned guitar, what you have in your hands is an orchestra. With these songs that are so melodic if you retune the guitar, it's an older way of doing things. A lot of folk instruments from all over the world have in common the fact that sometimes the strings are tuned a tone apart—with strings that then drone. That's how I tune. It's mountain banjo tuning in America; you'll find the oud tuned like that. It's a mistake to believe that those people who play like this don't play

<u>Fairport Convention</u>: simple but unusual patterns (different from contemporary songwriting, which uses much more complex 7th chords) with traditional pieces:

"Matty Groves": tune
Dorian

D5	C	D5	C	D5
I	VII	I	VII	I

"Tam Lin": tune
Aeolian

Em	D	G	Em	D	Em	D	G	Em	D	Em
i	VII	III	i	VII	i	VII	III	i	VII	i

<u>Steeleye Span</u>: symmetric forms as well as completely unstructured ones or drone forms:

"Cold Hayly, Windy Night":

Cm	Eb	Fm	C	Eb	Fm	Cm
i	III	iv	I	III	iv	i

"Cam Ye":

Cm	Fm	Cm	Bb	Ab	Cm	Bb	Cm	Fm	Cm	Bb	G	Ab
i	iv	i	VII	VI	i	VII	i	iv	i	VII	V	VI

"Lovely on the Water":

Cm	Fm	Cm	Eb	Cm	Bb	Cm	Eb	Fm	Bb	Eb	Bb	Cm	Fm	Cm
i	iv	i	III	i	VII	i	III	iv	VII	III	VII	i	iv	i

"Prince Charlie":   F-drone

"Boys of Bedlam":   Dm-G: drone-like character

FIGURE 5.3. Examples of harmonic progressions

harmonically—because they do! They're after an effect, and you get an effect when two notes clash. And you're trying to achieve that. You get it *all* the time; listening to the uilleann pipes you get these collisions, they're not just clashes, they are collisions of notes and that's what I find really thrilling.

This preference for these "clashes" in electric folk is also evident with other performers like Sandy Denny or Maddy Prior, who would also sometimes incorporate elements of Bulgarian polyphony.

THE SINGING

With the songs and ballads being a focal point of the revival and electric folk genres, a closer investigation of the vocal aspect has to be a central part of any musical analysis.

The traditional singing style, including harmony singing, has remained a defining characteristic of this music, distinguishing it from other popular music forms.

Vocal Styles: Physical Aspects

English traditional singing is, in general, much softer and more breathy in its overall sound than Irish, Scottish, or American traditional styles. The performers often use their head voice, with relatively open vocal cords, thereby using a register akin to the speaking voice, as can be heard on the recordings of Walter Pardon and Harry Cox. In this respect, the extremely soft voice of folksinger Anne Briggs is quite close to the traditional English singing style. Because the vocal cords are not usually constricted in order to produce a stronger sound, higher notes cannot always be pitched perfectly—especially if the musician is nervous or pregnant, the latter having been the case with Briggs's solo album *Anne Briggs* (Topic, 1971) which contains popular traditional songs like "Willy O' Winsbury" or "Reynardine."

The singing of the Travellers from Scotland differs clearly from other British folk cultures not only in terms of repertoire but also on a technical level. A voice like Jeannie Robertson's is based on a strong sound production similar to the American style presented by Carolyn Hester or Joan Baez. American singers, including older traditional performers, tend to sing with much tighter vocal cords, allowing them to pitch high notes clearly and strongly, even in advanced age. However, the aural impression of Robertson's voice is much fuller, as she, like many other Travellers, predominantly used the chest voice, in which the vocal cords vibrate to their full extent.[8] Because the Scottish singers are more in control of the physical side of sound production, including the muscles around the vocal cords and the diaphragm, the manipulation of vocal quality is an integral part of their musical interpretation. Depending on the content and atmosphere of the song, the singer may change the seat of the epiglottis, and thus the volume of the pharyngeal cavity and the vibration of the vocal cords. Consciously or unconsciously, the singer thus builds up a physical tension to enhance the dramatic content of the song, as is evident in Robertson's interpretation of "Lord Lovat."

Likewise, ornaments sung by Scottish performers consist not only of melodic additions, as in English folk music, but also of physical techniques like glottal stops and sobs that are produced in the throat. Individual singers' voices may, of course, differ. Phoebe Smith, for instance, tends to produce a very "earthy" but at the same time more nasal and more focused sound, with less corresponding body resonance than Jeannie Robertson. Yet these techniques, including the strong vocal production and the audible breaks between the differently used registers of the vocal range (e.g., chest and head voice), are still similar among many Traveller singers.[9]

As will be further discussed in chapter 7, the vocal styles of revival and electric folk singers have been—owing to a clearly comprehensible transformation process—a mixture of various elements, although one can detect some common features. The voices are softer than the strong and full ones of Scottish or the hard ones of American folksingers, as the performers tend to sing with less tension in the vocal cords, yet at the same time they are not so light as those of the Sussex singers, for instance. In some cases a relationship to traditional models is clearly discernible. Martin Carthy initially started singing in a church choir, at that time having "a sort of falsetto produced with a very wide, open throat" (Dallas 1977: 8). Although he would later prefer to sing with tight vocal cords, one can still hear a softer, breathier element in his singing; this is a clear reference to Joseph Taylor's style, whose phrasing he has adopted and whom he has always cited as a model.

Occasionally, elements of Irish sean-nós singing were incorporated within the revival style, although rarely as a complete technique. In the Irish tradition the nasalization of the sean-nós (the result of a high position of the epiglottis and the use of resonance spaces in the nasal cavity) is only used on isolated, emphasized notes (O'Riada 1962). With revival singers, it often became more of a sound color than a means of interpretation. This was especially evident with Ewan MacColl, who lapsed frequently into a sean-nós technique when singing long notes, as in "Shoal of the Herring," and in the early 1970s with Martin Carthy on recordings like *Crown of the Horn*. As can also be heard on his shaping of words in "Shepherd, O Shepherd" (*Sweet Wivelsfield*), Carthy occasionally combined this technique with the tendency to slide up to these notes. This element, which can also be observed with Maddy Prior's singing, seems to have been inspired by the playing style of traditional instruments such as bagpipes and whistle, also evident in Dave Swarbrick's fiddling style. Sometimes, as with Bert Jansch, the influence of American blues singing is also evident. Jansch, whose singing is close to his speaking voice, performs in a lightly nasal style, combined with an occasionally unclear pronunciation and a slightly delayed attack of individual notes that are often approached from a semitone above.

A remarkable stylistic variety can especially be observed among the female singers of the revival and electric folk scenes. Prior, for instance, sings with extremely tight vocal cords, resulting in a very clear, direct sound. Her unusual control enables her to make the differences between the vocal registers quite even. In contrast, Jacqui McShee's delicate, clear voice does not come down very low, although she can produce the notes directly without any extra pressure. Hence her softer head voice, which already starts at g', is clearly dominant, while the middle voice is hard and precisely pitched. To adjust to the different atmospheres of the songs, McShee uses also other techniques, such as very breathy singing with a higher portion of air in the sound production to make her voice sound darker, as in "Will the Circle Be Unbroken" on *Reflection*. Shirley Collins, who came out of the Sussex tradition, sang in a style close to her soft speaking voice. In order to give her voice a more characteristic "English" sound, as a contrast to American voices, she intensified the elements that were already inherent in the Sussex tradition: her voice is even more open than Briggs's—sometimes so open that she, especially on later recordings, seemed to have had difficulties raising her generally low voice to a higher pitch level.[10]

Only a few singers were able to play with stylistic elements and vocal techniques as easily as Sandy Denny, with the exception of folksinger Frankie Armstrong. Denny used melodic ornaments and the throaty effects of the Scottish Travellers side by side with the hard, metallic sound production of American performers and breathy English singing. Like many British revival and electric folk singers, her basic voice was quite relaxed, open, and breathy, although her middle register was unusually well supported, which enabled her to produce a round sound in all registers. Moreover, from early on she incorporated other vocal effects into her performances, using tightly closed vocal cords to produce a different, more American sound in several recordings from 1967 (*The Original Sandy Denny; Sandy Denny and the Strawbs*). On these recordings she was still singing with little diaphragm control ("Pretty Polly"), and her voice would often break at the higher register ("Two Weeks"), with the head voice still clearly separated from the middle register. Surprisingly, the next recordings, produced about two years later, presented a Denny who was clearly in control of her voice, even when singing breathily. She not only managed to balance the different voice registers, but she applied various vocal techniques to enhance her musical interpretations, including elements from the Scottish traditional style. A good example of her high level of technical variety, with an almost natural oscillation between the narrower head voice and the broader chest voice, can be heard in "She Moves through the Fair" on Fairport Convention's *What We Did on Our Holidays*.

Vocal Styles: Ornamental Techniques

As pointed out in the second chapter, the collectors around Cecil Sharp only slowly recognized the integral role of ornamental techniques in performance practice. Percy Grainger (1908: 159) emphasized that ornaments "are always boldly attacked (often being sung rather louder than the rest of the phrases in which they occur), and are, I am convinced, not merely the quaverings of old and shaky voices, but are introduced, like other ornaments, to give point and flourish."

Many revival and electric folk singers showed a clear fascination with these embellishments, which became particularly evident with Anne Briggs (Hunt 1989). Diverse styles of ornamentation were adapted, including melodic devices (slides, grace notes, turns, and so on) and physical techniques (like glottal stops). Other techniques learned from traditional singers, such as intervallic variation, lengthening of notes, rhythmic variation, and changes of tempo, have also become an integral part of performance practice. Often these elements have been so thoroughly mixed that the results cannot be traced back to individual singers or styles. Especially with Sandy Denny, it is impossible to identify the actual sources (if any).

The approaches varied with the individual performers. Jacqui McShee and Anne Briggs showed a clear liking for melodic ornaments, while Maddy Prior also adapted distinctly Irish elements like slides and Sandy Denny integrated difficult physical techniques like glottal stops. The results were highly differentiated singing styles.

Listening carefully to Jacqui McShee's singing on "When I Was in My Prime" (Pentangle, *Cruel Sister*), one discovers a preference for syncopations or slight delays in the attack of accentuated notes. This characteristic is combined with a precise and secure rhythmic delivery. McShee's phrasing, strongly oriented to the textual structure, is similarly clear, while her melodic ornamentation shows a preference for auxiliary notes. McShee makes only little use of variation here, repeating the same ornaments for the various verses. Her ornaments are used as a coloristic effect, in contrast to Irish sean-nós, where no two verses are sung the same way and the application of ornament is highly adapted to the content.

Maddy Prior's general singing is similarly precise, but with less rhythmic elasticity. Her phrasing is clear and balanced, and, like McShee, she tends to choose one overall vocal style related to the overall atmosphere of a song. Contrary to McShee, however, the focus is on applying a large variety of ornaments, which are an essential part of Prior's creative process. She uses primarily three forms: upward or downward slides over a large intervallic range, melismatic melodic ornaments, and, occasionally, physical ornaments like glottal stops.

Shirley Collins's singing, in contrast, remains close to a normal talking or recitative-like style. With the focus on the narrative, the structuring of the verse lines is much more important than the application of ornaments, which she smoothly integrates into the singing line. Likewise, Collins's phrasing is quite even, with little differentiation within one piece.

Like Jeannie Robertson, Sandy Denny showed a strong sense of phrasing, using an extremely differentiated variety of vocal effects combined with a broad dynamic range. A large repertoire of ornamental devices was already present in Denny's early singing in the form of arpeggios, tremolos, and scales. She would later integrate slides and glottal stops, applying them over larger intervals than the traditional singers. An interesting example is Denny's interpretation of Richard Fariña's "The Quiet Joys of Brotherhood," on which she sings her ornaments in the throat, but with little pressure. Although she later stopped performing traditional songs in public, she still used these ornaments in her singing, expanding them even further, as can be heard in her interpretation of her song "Who Knows Where the Time Goes?" (*The Attic Tracks*).

Denny not only demonstrated a clear rhythmic feeling; at the same time she maintained the lightness of natural speech rhythms (i.e., with syncopated phrases), evident on Fairport Convention's version of "She Moves through the Fair." Another characteristic of her singing was the use of long sustained notes at focal points, combined with changes of the initial metric structure. This technique, which could also be heard in Anne Briggs's singing, was especially displayed in slow, lyrical pieces that allowed her to apply her elaborate ornamental technique. At the same time, these sustained notes had a transparency that allowed the instruments to be heard through the voice, which was usually in the foreground.

Denny's interpretations of "A Sailor's Life" and "Reynardine" displayed extreme

variations from verse to verse with tempo, meter, and syncopation. Yet the songs retained their fundamental form owing to the verse structure and to focal points with
notes that were sung with rhythmic precision. The performance versions of each piece
sometimes differed greatly from concert to concert, although a basic pattern was recognizable, as a comparison of an uncut version of "A Sailor's Life" on Richard Thompson's *Watching the Dark* and the officially published one on *Unhalfbricking* reveals.
Denny would often ornament the same sections, especially pivotal parts, and lengthen
the same notes at highly dramatic points. The degree of ornamentation often depended on the general content and atmosphere of the song or ballad. While Denny's
interpretation of "Reynardine," mainly a dialogue between a girl and "werefox" Reynardine, would be extremely ornamented and varied, "Matty Groves" and "Tam Lin," both
highly dramatic narratives that leave little room for ornamentation, were sung in a
very straightforward style.

This range of vocal and ornamental techniques is also evident on Frankie Armstrong's album *Till the Grass O'ergrew the Corn*, one of the recent interpretations of
Child ballads. Singers like Armstrong often experiment with ornaments for a long
time to see what fits a song: "I can spend hours working on the phrasing of a song I'm
learning. I want to make sure that the tune works intelligently with the words. I need
to stress the words internally in a way that doesn't distort them. I find this process
very exciting!" Depending on the content of the ballads, she displays a range of vocal
approaches similar to that of many singers in classical art song: "Broomfield Hill" is recited in a soft voice with open vocal cords, while "Lady Diamond" is sung with a hard,
delayed attack. With "Fair Lizzie," Armstrong's voice is much deeper in the throat than
usual, incorporating many ornaments. In contrast, "Proud Girl" is performed almost
with a speaking voice, while the "Wife of Usher's Well" is strikingly hard, with an almost breaking voice and few ornaments.

Harmony Singing

A characteristic device of the folk and electric folk genres is a distinctive style of
harmony singing, often with harmonic combinations not generally in classical music,
such as parallel fourths and fifths or dissonant second intervals. Despite the predominance of monophonic ballad singing in the British Isles, harmony singing has not
been completely unknown in the tradition; in fact, it seems to have been more common than usually indicated in the literature.[11] The best-known early example was the
singing of the Copper Family, whose interpretation of "Claudy Banks" was not only
printed in the first *Journal of the Folk-Song Society* in 1899 but was also said to be the earliest song collected for the newly established Folk Song Society. Their particular
singing style, with parallel octaves, fourths, and fifths, was extensively described by A.
L. Lloyd, who suspected that it was probably influenced by an acquaintance with classical harmony. As he pointed out, the style was "seemingly based on book standards,
and as such it probably represents a survival of a practice once much widespread in

rural England" (Lloyd 1954: 149). Many performers at that time were also choir singers and knew how to differentiate between traditional and classical choir singing. Lloyd recalled a visit to a Cornish pub, where he heard fishermen singing three-part harmony:

> They were members of a choir, and some of the folk songs which they sang from print they also knew from tradition. I asked one whether he did not find it confusing to sing one set of harmonies on the platform another, quite different, in the pub. His answer was: "We know our own way, and we know the other way. We'd rather sing our own way every time. Some of these composers, why, they bass a tune as if they'd never sung a note in their lives." (Lloyd 1954: 149)

This observation was confirmed during my interview with Shirley Collins. Her family always sang harmony at church and therefore was familiar with classical singing styles, performing them regularly. Likewise, polyphonic carol singing has always been part of the annual calendar in the Sheffield area (Russell 1994). Whether harmony singing can be called "true" traditional music or not, Lloyd observed clear differences from classical music in the preference for parallel singing, the application of striking dissonances, and the often dronelike role of the bass, while countermelodies in the lower voices are in most cases missing.

Many of these elements were adapted by several vocal groups of the folk revival—notably the Watersons and the Young Tradition, who particularly put a strong emphasis on "archaic" sounds like the medieval parallel fourths or fifths, combined with a distinct choice of repertoire. The Watersons became aware of religious and even pagan elements in the music during a visit to Padstow and built up an unusual repertoire of pagan songs that they recorded on the album *Frost and Fire*. Alternating changes between solo and ensemble singing ("Hal-an-Tow") were characteristic of their arrangements. While the group structured the verses with clear phrasing that emphasized the rhythm, the voice leading seemed to be very deliberate, though one could detect a preference for parallel movements, including the extremely biting sound of parallel seconds. Truly contrapuntal singing was rare; instead, one voice often functioned as a drone, such as Mike Waterson's voice line in "The Broom of Cowdenknowes" (*New Voices*). The "Souling Song" is probably the most unusual example, with a range not surpassing a minor third, sung in strict parallel thirds. The resulting sound of this song, which was performed in the Midlands and the Northwest around Halloween, All Saints, and All Souls,[12] is unusually striking because the four Watersons often sang in just two vocal parts, instead of the three that are the minimum for classical harmony singing.

The Young Tradition created an even more extreme sound. Their three-part harmony singing carried a harsh sound resulting from an unusual voice order (Peter Bellamy would often sing the upper vocal line, while Heather Wood tended to stay at middle range, thus occasionally going below Bellamy), combined with a very broad, almost ponderous singing style and striking harmonies. "Byker Hill," for instance, begins in parallel fifths and fourths, alternating with sections of parallel thirds. The group would also often use dissonances like seconds and sevenths, as in the "Lyke Wake Dirge."

Harmony singing has also been an integral part of the music of electric folk groups like Pentangle. Despite the use of similar harmonies, including many parallel octaves, fourths, and fifths, the effect of Pentangle's interpretation of the "Lyke Wake Dirge" is much smoother because more reverb was used on the vocals. A stronger unity is also achieved through the additional rhythmic accentuation and structuring provided by Terry Cox's hand drum.

Fairport Convention and particularly Steeleye Span also adapted this kind of singing in their music. Steeleye Span had one of its largest successes with the a cappella song "Gaudete," a sixteenth-century Christmas carol from *Piae Cantiones* (1582), which guitarist Bob Johnson had discovered "at a folk-carol service in his father-in-law's church in Cambridge" (Irwin 1973). Johnson persuaded the students to send him a copy of the carol, which was then arranged by the band. The musicians of Steeleye also showed a strong preference for singing in parallel fourths and fifths ("King Henry"). Their singing did not follow a predictable pattern, as Maddy Prior pointed out:

> If you actually analyze the harmonies, they were all over the shop. Because nobody was organized. And if somebody said, "Oh, I'm singing that!," you would be singing something else. There was no question of somebody singing at the third or doing a counterpoint, I mean they were all counterpoint-ishly kind of parallel-ishly with fourths and fifths.

Due to the stylistic elements previously mentioned, this seemingly irregular approach nevertheless resulted in a recognizable style.

ASPECTS OF PERFORMANCE PRACTICE

Contrary to conventional notions of individual ownership, traditional songs are often seen as common property that can be adapted by anyone into something personal. Many songs have thus been sung by several performers—like "Tam Lin" and "Willie o' Winsbury"—although the electric bands have usually avoided playing songs that are closely connected with other performers. The lengthy ballad "Matty Groves" has always been closely associated with Fairport Convention, although it was never released as a single.[13] Steeleye Span, in contrast, has been associated with songs like "Twa Corbies" and "All around My Hat," which was moreover such an extensive rewrite that it would have been hard for any other group lay claim.

With a predetermined source of material and the aspect of re-creation being essential, electric folk musicians often prefer the intimacy of live performances to studio recordings. Consequently, the relationship with the musical material is different from that of many rock bands, whose musical output is album-oriented—especially the case with the highly elaborated sound of contemporary progressive bands such as Yes. As Ashley Hutchings pointed out:

> I *enjoy* performing live more than recording. I love the immediacy, I love to be able to see and relate to the audience directly. And I love playing for dancing, for people to dance to, which is an even more direct form of expression. But recording is . . . very important, be-cause when live gigs are forgotten the albums are still there for posterity.

This preference for live performances is occasionally also apparent in the quality of the recordings. Especially with Steeleye Span, the backbeat that sometimes can have a slightly monotonous effect on perfectly produced studio recordings develops a strong driving effect on live recordings such as *Tonight's the Night*, giving a piece like "All around My Hat" momentum. Likewise, Steeleye's strong and colorful vocals to some extent create even more dramatic tension in a live performance than on studio record-ings, as is evident with "Cam Ye o'er frae France." Furthermore, as fiddler Ian Telfer pointed out, groups like the Oysterband are musically more flexible than many hit-oriented groups of the pop spectrum, whose fans associate them with a fixed ideal sound: "Perhaps because we've never had any hits, we've never had particular songs which are what people only think of, . . . [which] are automatically identified with us. So we can keep writing and keep changing the exact nature of what we do."

The individual performance patterns vary. With Fairport Convention, improvisa-tion and variation are among the central elements of performance, while others like Steeleye Span and Martin Carthy have worked with a much more fixed scheme. Nev-ertheless, the aspect of re-creation has been a focal point for almost all groups, with the best example probably being the ballad "Matty Groves," retold by Fairport Con-vention in numerous variants.

Moreover, many bands did not rehearse but instead used the gigs as public re-hearsals. John Renbourn's recollection is typical:

> We didn't often have any full band rehearsals as such. In the early days all rehearsals hap-pened on the stand—and not much changed in later years. Most "rehearsals" happened in later years in hotels on tour and were informal affairs. By and large the music was worked out by a process of osmosis; if the gig paid for us all to be together, then we spent time play-ing and listening.

Although Fairport Convention, Steeleye Span, and Pentangle tended to stay within a general framework of an arrangement, it could change over the years, even if it was fixed on disc. Due to the considerable number of member changes, different ap-proaches have inevitably been brought in, as Steeleye singer Maddy Prior explained: "Bob [Johnson], when he came in, it changed again. When Ashley and Martin left, it changed again. I remember that we did 'Rosebud in June' as a harmony, and I thought that it was very lush harmony, compared to what we had done before."

If a piece has not been played for a long period and is picked up again, it often happens that the original version has been forgotten. Such was often the case with the complex harmony singing Steeleye did, as Prior recalled: "[The recorded versions] are probably fixed to some degree, inasmuch as we could remember them. If we didn't do them for a while, there was every possibility we'd forget. Or I would forget." Remembering lengthy ballads or longer arrangements is a frequent problem during a concert performance, which is almost natural, as Jacqui McShee pointed out:

> If you are *very* tired, and you're singing a song and you've been singing that song for years and years, if you start to relax too much you are going to make mistakes. And it *will* sound different. And you do lose the freshness . . . because you think, "Oh, you know this song inside out because you have sung it for so many years, how can you possibly make a mistake?" But if you lose concentration, you do.

I have occasionally heard traditional singers forget a verse or mix up the structure. When performing in the club at Cecil Sharp House, Freddy MacKay, a Northern Ireland singer, scrambled some verses and was immediately corrected by the folk club community. And on the Peter Kennedy recording of "She Moves through the Fair," Belle Stewart switched the positions of the second and third verses. Thus the expectation of perfection that is an element of media-dominated popular music is also transferred to live performances of electric folk. When I talked with Simon Nicol a week before the Cropredy Festival, he was a bit concerned about forgetting lengthy song texts: "I have a bad reputation for forgetting the words of things—but they should try it is all I can say. OK? So I screwed up on 'Wat Tyler' once, but is it any wonder?"

The Cropredy concert sets also last longer than the usual ninety minutes or two-hour sets (sometimes up to three or four hours), and during the second half, the number of mistakes naturally increases. Similarly, the use of computer technology such as preprogrammed sequencers might be of help—but only if none of the performers makes any mistakes, as Nicol added: "No worry about the [Wounded] 'Whale'—it's a sequence track, all of the strings are on a sequencer. So once it starts, that's it. You cannot lose your place. [It's also] relentless. It's gonna go until it finishes it, and you hopefully are all gonna finish in the same place."

With groups and musicians performing predominantly live, electric folk in its various forms has always had to deal with the problems of amplifying both acoustic and electric instruments. While visiting the Cropredy Festivals, my positive impression was, among other things, based on the extremely well-balanced sound. Visiting other concerts, I realized that Cropredy's sound engineering was not the norm. Sound problems related to the different acoustic qualities of the amplified instruments are very common. The discrepancy between the intended sound and the sound actually heard was extremely obvious during a Levellers concert at the Große Freiheit in Hamburg. I saw the musicians tuning their large variety of instruments carefully, but during the performance none of this variety could be heard. I made a similar observation when the Oysterband played in the Camden Town Hall at the Second Camden Ceilidh Night in North London, where it was impossible to hear many of the acoustic instruments even when close to the stage.

These situations raised the question of whether there was any sense at all in having such colorful instrumentation in electric folk or folk rock if it could not be heard, particularly in live performance. I thus wanted to know how the musicians would describe these problems. There was, first of all, the volume level—one of the major things that changed (upward) when traditional or folk songs were taken up by electric bands, since most folk clubs do not need electric amplification or extreme voice projection. The problem seems not to have been the mere fact that electric instruments were used, but the ways in which they were used. As Maddy Prior recalled, being loud—thus reaching the rock audience—was a basic intention of the folk performers who first picked up electric instruments. Volume was also one of the reasons why so many from the folk club scene were taken aback, even if they were interested in the music, like Frankie Armstrong:

> I just don't like loud noise. I love good jazz drumming, but I find many rock drummers boring because they result in the volume being upped so that everyone can be heard over them. The older I get, the more interested I am in intimacy—the process of being able to hear the audience breathing with you, *sensing* the audience breathing with you, is very moving. For me it's about the nakedness of the human voice, the silence and the space between me and the audience. This subtlety must be impossible for a rock group to sense.

Together with the growth in volume, the expectation of instrumental virtuosity increased as well, often equated with tempo. In Fairport Convention's interpretation of "Matty Groves" on *Live at the L.A. Troubadour*, the improvisational passage becomes a musical duel of sheer speed between Thompson and Swarbrick.

In many cases, electric folk performers have played both acoustic and electric instruments. Ashley Hutchings, for instance, had two bands in 1996: the Albion Band, a concert band that played acoustic, and the Ashley Hutchings Dance Band, an electric group that played a large instrumental repertoire especially for dancing. Most musicians describe the contrast between electric and acoustic not as one of easy versus difficult, but as two different forms of playing that require different skills. As Rick Kemp pointed out:

> Electric instruments are very, very difficult to control. And it takes a very special person to move from acoustic to electric for that reason. It's a very special skill to play an acoustic and it's a very, very special skill to play an electric in terms of being able to control the power. To make nice noises on electric, you need a very special skill which isn't prevalent at all on an acoustic instrument.

The use of the electric instruments has also influenced musicians' acoustic playing, as Martin Carthy emphasized:

Apart from the fact that one is measurably louder, you have to play much more delicately on an electric. And you can play much less on an electric. Much less. In fact that was the big lesson when I started first playing acoustic guitar in the folk clubs—to play less. I obviously played more than I would play on an electric. But I went in playing acoustic guitar much more busily than I did when I came out. . . . It taught me economy.

As Ian Telfer added, electric instruments have proved advantageous in several ways for playing in a larger band, although it also can change the status of the acoustic instruments:

Electricity is addictive, anyway. Once you have been loud, so that you don't have to worry about projecting the sound any more, there's no going back, really. I don't play very much acoustically at the moment. Playing amplified with a band is a different experience, because you are then not competing so much with other instruments in the same range of pitch. And so the violin is then perhaps filling a different role. But electric or acoustic, the subjective experience of playing is just the same.

The change to an electric sound was especially difficult for the singers at first, as they suddenly had to sing with a microphone. Being used to filling the room with their voices alone, it took some time to adjust to the fact that they now had to hold back the voice. Playing for larger audiences also resulted in a new communication situation, which became particularly challenging in the case of Pentangle, since improvisation was an essential part of the group's performance practice. During their period of international success, Pentangle played in many large venues, which was not without problems in that early time of sound technology. John Renbourn recalled:

In solo if you leave room for improvisation and it goes well (a lot depends on situation—sound system, etc.), it can lift your own playing and means that you play better that night. In group stuff it can lift the whole spirit of the ensemble. In Pentangle we used to leave whole sections open. It didn't always work—but when it did it pushed us on to greater heights. But being able to hear well on the stage and interact is often not the case in practice.

Although, as Renbourn explained further, the band tried to make the best out of difficult acoustic situations by cross-linking the amplifiers, the balance between drums/bass and guitars often remained problematic. The result affected performers and audiences alike, as Jacqui McShee remembered: "It was quite difficult at times to hear the guitars. It was easier to hear Bert because his playing is very percussive. But John's was very delicate, and sometimes I couldn't hear him at all. I remember seeing an article—it said we were the quietest band onstage but the loudest offstage."

Even for Fairport Convention—which has played as an electric band for a long time—the stage communication was better during its acoustic period. As Simon Nicol pointed out, "you are very close to each other onstage, and if somebody plays something you can immediately respond to, your own communication is very much better in an acoustic thing than it is electrically."

The musicians did not always intend to be loud. Finding the right volume level on-stage required considerable patience, McShee said:

> If you can't hear each other onstage, then the monitors are not balanced properly. They need to be turned down. And what happens is—I've seen it, it happened to us—you have a sound check, somebody says, "Oh, I can't hear so and so—can you turn it up?" That means, that monitor's gone up a bit. "Oh no, I can't hear the . . ." and gradually everybody is just having their monitors turned up. Instead of saying, "Right, what I hear mostly in my moni-tor is—that. So take that down." The band that we have now, we decided that we'd have the monitors as low as possible.

Much of a well-balanced sound thus depends on carefully calibrated amplification and most especially on a good sound engineer. Many groups today, if they can afford it, travel with their own sound engineer. Rick Kemp commented that, if one cannot hear anything in the audience,

> that's usually because they haven't got their own sound person. If a band is just playing with acoustic instruments and electric instruments mixed—or even just with drums, where the drummer is a sort of rock drummer, it's very difficult if they haven't got somebody that knows what they do in great detail. So if they're using the house PA man, it's almost impos-sible for that man.

Kemp explained that a thorough sound check for an electric folk group requires much more time than one for a purely acoustic or purely electric group, and demands considerable patience from both sound engineer and musicians:

> You need a lot more time before the gig. They have to do a three- or four-hour sound check. And most bands wouldn't like to do that anyway. Even if it was gonna be much, much bet-ter on the night. Most bands couldn't stand to have that length of sound check that would be necessary to get what they wanted. So it's not just the fault of the house PA man; on a one- or two-night situation, it is very typical to arrive at midday, you know, and everybody's tired, it sort of gets in the realms of hoping and wishing.

The various instruments pose different problems, as Ian Telfer illustrated in the case of the electric guitar and the melodeon:

> People often think that electric guitars will dominate because of the power that's there in the amplifiers; but actually it's more difficult for the front-of-house engineer to make an electric guitar distinct than a violin, for example, or a voice. It depends on the complexity of the waveshapes generated. The melodeon is quite a difficult instrument to amplify. John [Jones] has sometimes problems with that, even though it seems to be the instrument you can always hear—when it's played by the singer, who is always going to be in the center of

attention, there may be psychological factors in that perception. The problem is, you have to decide where to put the microphone. It's still mechanical, it's still the same as holding the instrument next to a microphone and playing it. It's just that when you put the microphone inside, you have to be careful to put it where you can then hear the whole instrument and not just a part of it.[14]

Moving from folk to rock not only meant changing performance venues and technical means, but also experiencing a different communication situation with the audience. While the intimate atmosphere of the acoustic folk clubs fostered a close interaction with the audience, the electric folk bands playing in stadiums or on larger stages encountered vast distances that made the interaction between the musicians and the audience problematic. This led to a different stage behavior more oriented toward the event, show elements (in the case of Steeleye Span), and a focus on the sound quality. As Martin Carthy stressed:

That [large venues] in itself needn't be a bad thing; it means that the musicians themselves have to be a bit more responsible. They have to learn to take control of what they do, and they have to try and maintain some kind of contact with their audience, a real contact— talking to people, not becoming alienated from their audience.

Wanting to be close to the audience, to interact and to communicate, remains a critical aspect for many electric folk performers. Jacqui McShee, for instance, emphasized that she needed a response from the audience, yet she did not like the extreme intimacy of the folk clubs:

I'm too nervous. I mean, you do get people that just sit there and go [imitates a staring face]. You do! It's very disconcerting, because you cannot stop looking at them. I'd rather play at a festival than at a folk club. Because although you have all the nerves before you go on, they're that much farther away. And yet I like the atmosphere in a club.

Owing to the hybrid nature of electric folk, the musicians' behavior and the expectations of their audiences sometimes collide in misunderstanding. Fiddler Eliza Carthy's performance with the Kings of Calicutt at the 1997 Cropredy Festival was characteristic: The audience, used to seeing the musicians tune their instruments either before the gig or unnoticeably during the performance, was confused when Carthy had to retune her relatively sensitive acoustic instrument between each piece—a common practice and part of the performance experience in classical (especially early music) or acoustic folk music. Conversely, Carthy, usually quite self-confident on stage, felt the need to apologize to the audience.

Playing acoustically or electrically also influences the repertoire, because some arrangements cannot be adapted. When Fairport Convention went on an "unplugged" acoustic tour, several songs that had been worked out electrically had to be excluded. In general, dance music, based on a consistent rhythm, responds especially well to an electric arrangement that enhances the rhythmic pulse. This observation was confirmed by Ashley Hutchings: "What worked very well, totally successful, is dance music of all kinds, whether it's jigs, reels, morris tunes! I think that was a great marriage, the marriage of electric instruments and traditional instrumental dance tunes. That always seems to work."

Hutchings also denied any lasting negative impact from using electric instruments with traditional material:

> I think traditional music is so adaptable. It is so flexible that it can take almost any kind of arrangement, everything from orchestral to electric instruments. So I wouldn't say that there is anything particularly unsuitable. A wonderful thing about traditional music is that it has a life of its own, no matter what you do to it. You can ruin a song with some kind of crass rock treatment, but that will be forgotten and the song will carry on. And the next person will come along and do something else with it—maybe doing an orchestral arrangement. So the music lives on. I don't think the music is damaged by folk rock or anything.

Interestingly, Maddy Prior, who had made a statement similar to Hutchings's, later disagreed. While in 1995 in an interview with Rob Weir in *Sing Out* she had commented that with an electric rhythm section she "could now dance to the music," she argued one year later that a straight rhythm section could indeed destroy something of the vocal music, which was based on a parlando-like recitative style: "Sometimes you had to be very careful with traditional music, because it is a bit like a butterfly, you can pin it to the wall if you're not careful, sometimes it needs more room to breathe and move. And Nigel [Pegrum] was a very rocky drummer, very straight, so there were some times they would be too pinned down."

Yet, as Ian Telfer pointed out correctly, with that kind of thinking, making music can lose something of its spontaneity:

> If you take traditional songs seriously, if you love them enough, then you want to behave respectfully towards them. I don't mean as if they were delicate, fragile pieces of ceramics that you can't use or touch, but you want to do the right thing by them. If you think of them that way you find yourself being careful and analytic in approach. On the other hand, the songs will survive any outlandish arrangements or performances you may inflict on them, so really the only harm you can do to a traditional song is not to sing it at all.

SIX

INDIVIDUAL MUSICAL APPROACHES

I played an awful lot of notes.   RICK KEMP

Within the framework of electric folk's general stylistic devices, the various performers and groups have displayed a large range of individual styles. It is therefore worthwhile to take a closer look at the vast range of musical possibilities explored by contemporary performers when working with traditional music.

FUSIONS OF TRADITIONAL MUSIC WITH ROCK AND JAZZ

Fairport Convention

Fairport Convention occupies a key position among the groups and performers described here, as almost the entire British electric folk scene is connected to the band through former members founding new groups or guesting in other groups, as well as through sheer musical impact and influence. The band has undergone many stylistic changes and hence reflects a broad spectrum of arrangement techniques that can be taken as models for various acoustic and electric approaches.

Groups like Fairport Convention, Steeleye Span, and Pentangle represented a different idea of originality in musical performance than the majority of popular music performers from the 1970s up until mid-1990s, who considered the songwriters or related groups to be the ones best able to interpret and understand their own written music.[1] Fairport Convention started, like most of its contemporaries, by playing cover versions, not only to acquire a basic repertoire but also as a means of getting booked on radio and television. Yet from early on, Fairport did not restrict itself to simply copying the original performers or songwriters, but instead took the original piece as a basis or structural skeleton upon which a unique musical interpretation could be built. The band's version of "Suzanne" (on *Heyday*), for example, was not a mere duplication of Leonard Cohen's song but instead became a piece clearly distinguishable by Thompson's guitar accompaniment and an original way of structuring the text through Sandy Denny's and Ian Matthew's alternate vocals. This was acknowledged by listeners at the time, as is evident from a reader's letter titled "Fairport Convention Disprove the Original Myth" in *Melody Maker* (November 2, 1968). As the reader remarked, "the rhythmic drumming in their arrangement creates a suitable hypnotic effect which is supplementary to the poetry of 'Suzanne' and I must say I find their version more enjoyable than the original."

The group built a large early repertoire of songs by Joni Mitchell, Bob Dylan, and Richard Fariña—material that, like the traditional singing repertoire, offered a high potential for reinterpretation. The lyrics were, despite first-person narrators, characterized by a universal perspective that could easily be adapted by other performers, partly because of their a high metaphoric content and partly because they were written at a very general, almost abstract level. Set to simple, catchy melodies and in a form similar in length and structure to ballads (Dylan's "Percy's Song" included sixteen verses), these songs were only a small step away from Fairport's subsequent reinterpretations of British traditional material.

Improvisation has always been an essential element of Fairport Convention's musical identity, as Martin Carthy pointed out:

> Fairport always used to play everything differently. It is a talent, but it is also a habit you get into. The whole band were of that mindset, they walked on the stage and [said], "We'll do such and such a tune. Let's start playing it!" Ashley was sort of fooling here and Richard fooling over there and you know, as long as you began together and stopped together and played the break where it was supposed to come—that's all. There is a definition of good acting, saying "All you have to worry about in acting is you never forget your lines and don't bump into the furniture!" And as far as Fairport were concerned, that was the rule of fun about music! Don't bump into the furniture, stop and start at the right time. And everything else is fine!

Because of its extremely improvisational structure, "A Sailor's Life" became one of the cornerstones in the development of electric folk—although it was different from what followed. Fairport's recorded versions of various pieces represent only one variant among many; over the years they have taken a wide range of approaches to "Matty Groves," for example. Studio recordings can therefore give us only a partial glimpse of the group's style, although studio efforts make up a major portion of their earlier recordings.

Fairport Convention's attitude toward the traditional material can be characterized as pragmatic. Although Ashley Hutchings later developed an almost excessive scholarly approach, trying to play the most accurate or "authentic" version possible (i.e., closest to what he could find in the printed sources), historical reconstruction was only of minor importance to most of the performers. Fairport Convention was not afraid to combine the old material with contemporary music, instruments, and texts. When Sandy Denny could not recall the whole text of the ballad "Willie o' Winsbury" (an ancient love tale between a queen's daughter and a poet/bard),[2] Richard Thompson—instead of researching—wrote a new text so that it became the parting song "Farewell, Farewell" on *Liege & Lief* (Humphries 1997: 57).

Despite many personnel and stylistic changes, the musical style of Fairport is still associated with "folk rock" as a literally equal fusion of folk and rock. This style was the result of the contributions of a particular constellation of performers: Sandy Denny blended modern chansonlike elements with traditional ornamentation and metrically free passages in her singing and also brought the traditional material she had acquired in the folk clubs ("She Moves through the Fair," "A Sailor's Life"), as well as her own songs, into the band's repertoire. Dave Swarbrick changed the band's sound by introducing the fiddle, a characteristic folk instrument, along with his extensive folk repertoire and musical experience. Richard Thompson became important to Fairport's modern sound with his distinctive electric guitar style, as did Dave Mattacks, who developed a similarly distinctive drumming style with the traditional material. Bassist and organizer Ashley Hutchings described Fairport's musical approach as "a very *organic* way of working. We didn't say: 'Let's do such and such.' And that's how the traditional material, and with the electric instruments, developed, because the instruments we *had* to pick up weren't fiddle, they were bass guitar and electric guitar and so on—and drums."

With the early Fairport, one can observe a shift from American impressions ("Reno, Nevada" by Fariña and various Dylan songs) toward more English images on *What We Did on Our Holidays*. The latter included modern texts like "Mr. Lacy" as well as songs with historical content like "Fotheringay"[3] and traditional repertoire such as the ghostly love story "She Moves through the Fair."[4] Fairport was thus selecting neutral, timeless stories (i.e., fewer historical ones related to a specific event) with vivid, often action-packed narratives, as was the case especially with classic ballads like the bloody tale of "Matty Groves." Tragedy, evident in many traditional songs, also became a perennial subject, already present in Denny's early repertoire of songs such as "Pretty Polly" and the grim story of love and death on the ocean, "A Sailor's Life." The band sometimes played obscure material like "Nottamun Town," as well as songs with texts that use metaphors to explore sexuality (e.g., the firing at the "Bonny Black Hare" or the seducing fox "Reynardine"). Except for "Tam Lin," rarely were there stories of elves and knights or romanticized pictures of nature or country life.

With its initial lineup of singer, guitars (solo and rhythm), bass, and drums, Fairport followed the classic rock lineup of the 1950s and 1960s. However, for its later folk rock sound that started with the guest appearances of Dave Swarbrick, a distinct mixture of electric (guitar, bass, drums) and acoustic (guitar, fiddle, mandolin, dulcimer, etc.) instruments became essential. The fiddle occupied an unusual middle function; on the one hand, it was an acoustic instrument with traditional playing techniques; on the other hand, when amplified it took on a specific tonal color that was, due to the limited sound engineering possibilities at that early stage, very close to that of the electric guitar.

At this early point in the group's evolution, the narrative was still the major focus. In the case of "A Sailor's Life," the instruments were very restrained, with the voice kept in the foreground. The band occasionally incorporated other sounds like that of a sitar, but Fairport in general stayed with its "trad./rock" combination. "Exotic" instruments, if used at all, were played like guitars, and were used for their tonal color rather than played with their own techniques. A synthesizer was not used until the 1980s. Special sound effects, except for a stronger delay and reverb with unaccompanied songs, played only a marginal role.

The folk instruments, especially the fiddle, mandolin, and dulcimer, were not used for mere tonal color, but rather were treated as highly individual instruments (the fiddle sometimes taking over the improvisational solo guitar part), which is another proof of a deeper musical transformation. The instruments and instrumental sections had various functions: (1) reinforcing the metric framework, especially with Denny's free singing and tempo fluctuations, to which the band had to set a counterpart; (2) interpreting the song's content, as with "A Sailor's Life," on which the bass "paints" the rhythm of the waves; (3) providing the musical continuation of the song's or ballad's narration in improvisational or jam session passages ("Matty Groves"); (4) structuring the longer ballads through interludes ("Tam Lin"); (5) offering a colorful accompaniment, often by setting a rhythmic counterpoint to the tune (especially in "She Moves through the Fair").

The fiddle often took over the melodic role of the electric guitar by playing hooks or rock figures such as rhythmic tone repetitions. The rock elements were obvious not only in the incorporated electric instruments (without synthesizer) but also in the straight metric frame of the rhythm section, with a preference for syncopated parts ("She Moves through the Fair"), metrically intriguing sections ("Tam Lin," "The Bonny Black Hare"), and unusual accentuations. Traditional and modern pieces were treated similarly. The melody line was the focal point, clearly accentuated. The accompanying instruments often received extra space within the piece—in the early days usually at the end—for so-called free jam sessions, group improvisations normally based around a fixed chord sequence (occasionally even just one chord) to allow free expression.

The drums were especially important as the keeper of the meter, emphasizing accents already inherent in text and melody or providing a counterpoint to Denny's free singing. One can hear a clear difference between Martin Lamble's and Dave Mattacks's playing, however. While Lamble's playing was rather restrained, with improvisational passages that incorporated many percussive tonal colors, Mattacks's style was much more straightforward, with a constant pulsation that offered a less flexible ground for a parlando-rubato delivery, although still with more space than a constant upbeat or downbeat. Without any background in traditional English music, Mattacks approached the old dances from a modern angle:

> If you look at 6/8, I saw it basically as a shuffle, which is a mid-tempo blues rhythm. It was just the way that the accents were broken up, but I didn't consider it particularly odd. Like 9/8, to me, was just a semi-jazzy waltz time. . . . I did it as a one, two, three, four—it's like nine but I just counted it as one-two-three, one-two-three, with a shuffle, just a 3/4 with a dotted feel to it. A triplet as opposed to one-and, two-and, three-and—it was just one-two-three, like that. (Dallas 1980b: 21)

As Mattacks pointed out further, he was always careful to learn the tune to find the correct placement of the downbeat, which is especially critical for metrically irregular pieces. He also often created a general percussive line independent from the inherent rhythmic structure of the text. "Matty Groves," set in 4/4 meter, was accentuated on the third beat by the snare drum, which gave the piece a strong drive. This accentuation of the third or fourth beat was also evident in pieces like "Tam Lin" which became so characteristic of Fairport's style that later groups like the Oysterband chose an upbeat-oriented percussive framework; although more restricting, this option reduced the aural associations with Fairport.[5] Mattacks often also displayed a much more sensitive, colorful side in pieces like "The Flowers of the Forest" and "The Quiet Joys of Brotherhood," on which the drum played small, almost motivic fragments.

The role of the electric bass was similar to the drums: on the one hand part of the rhythm section, on the other hand also used for instrumental color, as in "A Sailor's Life." Fairport's sound changed significantly when Dave Pegg replaced Hutchings on bass. Pegg added a much stronger virtuoso dimension, whereas Hutchings had preferred simpler structures and harmonies, while still providing vivid sonic portraits as in "A Sailor's Life."

FAIRPORT UNDERWENT several stylistic changes. Its first album, *Fairport Convention*, was still a mixture of American rock and folk ("Jack O'Diamonds"), Dylan and Mitchell songs ("Chelsea Morning"), and progressive pieces ("Decameron") with surrealistic texts. Much of what would later be characteristic of electric folk was already inherent in the latter pieces, where the instruments were not solely accompaniment but also interpreted the text. For example, the improvisational accompaniment for "The Lobster" consists less of actual hooks, motives, and riffs than of smaller segments—a cell of two notes in the beginning. Endlessly repeated with increasing speed and added complexity, thus slowly building up a momentum so that the piece seems to come from out of nowhere, this performance style closely resembled to what the band would later do in "A Sailor's Life."

One can likewise hear foundations for the later electric folk style in Sandy Denny's early traditional recordings on *The Original Sandy Denny* (1967), where she already displayed a preference for sustaining notes at key points of the text. This technique was only possible given a stable basis, provided here with a rather simple accompaniment and harmonization.[6] These vocals clearly differed from an unaccompanied version that had to carry the meter within itself. The guitar provided not only harmonic accompaniment but also an affective quality that could not be expressed by the voice alone. In "Pretty Polly" the growing tension of Polly's murder was reflected in both Denny's tightening voice and in small motives that were repeated on the guitar.

Fairport's second album, *What We Did on Our Holidays* (1969), included two traditional pieces that were arranged differently. While "Nottamun Town" is carried by a relatively simple, dronelike accompaniment, with the harmonies always on D, "She Moves through the Fair"[7] shows the instrumental improvisation and highly embellished, rhythmically complex vocals that would be identified with Fairport. The instruments provide a framework for the voice rather than playing an independent role. Bass and drums sustain the rhythm, but the accents are quite subdued, partly the result of Lamble's extremely filigreed and delicate drumming. Both instruments improvise like the melody instruments, instead of restricting themselves to the metric framework. The cymbals of the drums contribute to the atmosphere, as do the reverb and the electric guitar, which punctuates the vocal line with melodic fragments. The meter is also softened by the syncopated playing of the lead guitar and Denny's syncopated singing.

Fairport's third album, *Unhalfbricking* (1969), contained only one traditional song, "A Sailor's Life." Based on the version in Vaughan Williams and Lloyd 1959, the piece is improvisational, although the instrumental possibilities are not exclusively limited to textual interpretation. Rhythmic freedom is created on various levels: The structure of the verses is asymmetrical, varying extremely in length due to Denny's long sustained notes. The metric pulsation is additionally blurred by her syncopated and highly ornamented singing style. Because the singing offers considerable space for improvisation, especially in the first part, the instruments (including the rhythm section) create a compelling atmosphere that far exceeds a merely metric frame. The fiddle, the only traditional instrument in this piece, is played very "untraditionally" (from verse 3, Swarbrick plays mainly rhythmic improvisations on a single note).

In the first part (verses 1–3) one can hear the instruments playing onomatopoeic movements behind Denny's singing, instead of the usual hooks or riffs: the floating and movement of the waves is suggested by a flickering and fluctuating bass figure that accelerates and decelerates, thus interpreting the text. For example, "to move" is taken up by a triplet, and the word "float" is depicted by an up-and-down movement. Something similar is also evident in the guitar line. The cymbals, played with a brush, imitate the sound of roaring waves. The second part (verses 4–6), introduced by an interlude, is held within a clear rhythmic framework by a riff in the bass, although the music still retains its improvisational character. It is concluded by a jam session. A comparison with the version of "A Sailor's Life" on Richard Thompson's *Watching the Dark* reveals that the overall framework for the song is fixed, as are some basic ideas like the three-part structure, the triplets in Hutchings's bass in the beginning, and the idea of a gradual development by adding new instruments. Everything else, including the position and form of Denny's ornaments, is relatively free. The harmony stands in clear contrast to the complex form, as the whole piece is set in E minor only.

Apart from Fairport Convention's and Sandy Denny's metrically free parlando-rubato interpretation of Richard Fariña's "The Quiet Joys of Brotherhood," this approach was never expanded. *Liege & Lief* went in another musical direction. The reasons can only be guessed. Perhaps the group felt that the "Sailor's Life" approach, still close to the tradition, was too restricting. Work with onomatopoeic elements and a blurring of the metric framework as in "A Sailor's Life" and "She Moves through the Fair" would only have been possible on a limited number of pieces without becoming monotonous. Moreover, Fairport played for an audience that also wanted to dance. The approach that would be used for "Matty Groves" was more abstract and could be transferred to any piece, although Thompson preferred "A Sailor's Life" to the selections on *Liege & Lief* (1969), missing the liveliness and spontaneity from the earlier recording.

The character of *Liege & Lief* is evident in the first track, "Come All Ye," created as a calling-on song in the morris dance tradition. (Each dance team had its own song with which the team captains prefaced the dancing by introducing the fictive characters represented by the performers, with the length of the text depending on the time it took the audience to assemble.) Here the song was used to introduce the band members with their instruments and to emphasize their purpose of not only reviving but revitalizing the music. Steeleye Span would also use a calling-on song," modeled on the "Earlsdon Sword Song," already recorded by the Watersons on *Frost and Fire* (1965).

"Reynardine" is the only *Liege & Lief* song in the improvisational and rhythmically free style of the earlier songs. With the following song, "Matty Groves," a new approach was introduced—probably the most obvious mixture of folk and rock to date. "Matty Groves" (also known as "Little Musgrave and Lady Barnard," recorded by Carthy/Swarbrick the same year) belongs to the corpus of the Child ballads, containing a characteristically densely packed story of love, adultery, betrayal, duel, and death. This ballad, with its tense story line, had already been a favorite among ballad singers before it was adapted by Fairport Convention; the Vaughan Williams Memorial Library includes a large number of collected versions. Set to the tune of "Shady Grove" and reduced to nineteen verses—Fairport abbreviated the content to its essence—"Matty Groves" remains the band's most popular traditional piece, although the story is (even for folk standards) quite long, and the content rather grisly.

The piece is divided into two major parts: the ballad itself (preceded by an intro) and a longer improvisational sequence. This second part, which again resembles a jam session, serves to relieve the tension built by the story. It is based on an A-major variant of the "Matty Groves" tune, with a central dialogue or duel between fiddle and guitar. The expression "duel" fits well here, as Swarbrick's and Thompson's improvisations are based on different musical styles. While Swarbrick plays predominantly traditional motives and figures, leaving the fundamental very quickly and thus creating stronger harmonic tensions, Thompson focuses much more on the fundamental and harmonically related notes playing rhythmic one-tone variations and melodic figures within a smaller range, while also using more syncopation. The meter (4/4) and harmonic structure remain relatively simple, providing the framework for a straightforward telling of the story. Denny sings the ballad almost without any ornaments, as the content leaves little room for them. The story is structured by interludes and framed by a distinctive hook, while the rhythm section, using dotted quarter notes on the third beat, plays a key role by pushing the song forward.

Since *Liege & Lief* Fairport has performed "Matty Groves" at almost every gig. Simon Nicol still describes the singing of it as an always fresh challenge, as each re-creation results in something new. On various recordings, one can hear the piece becoming more varied, with more interpretive elements added over the years. While the *Liege & Lief* studio recording sounds quite polished, the 1969 live version on *Live at the L.A. Troubadour* comes much closer to a rock sound, with the fiddle sounding even more like an electric guitar and the drums stronger and more colorful. All the instruments are centered around the rhythm of the bass, which gives the piece, played at a high tempo, a strong drive. The improvisations, with scales, one-note rhythmic repetitions, and traditional-sounding motive fragments, are much simpler than on the studio recording. On *Fairport Convention: Live* (1974), the melodic line has been reduced even further, but one can discern more improvisational details as the instruments start to interpret the text more—such as the fiddle tremolos behind the phrase "I'll kill you" (verse 14).

Many of these elements are kept in later versions, especially the two-part form, the distinct intro, and the role of the fiddle as commentator. With Simon Nicol as the new singer, a slight change in words occurred, as *Moat on the Ledge* (1987) demonstrates; the female servant, for instance, has now turned into a male. On *In Real Time*, a live recording from the 1987 Cropredy Festival, further subtle text variants occur in Nicol's singing: "And there she saw little Matty Groves" (verse 2) is changed to "spied little Matty Groves," and "you are Lord Darnell's wife" is transformed to "that you are my master's wife" (verse 5). On this recording "Matty Groves" is part of a medley, and the initial instrumental jam session part is absent. Instead, its function as a tension reliever is taken up by another, purely traditional instrumental selection.

Another important Fairport piece that should be briefly mentioned is the ballad "Tam Lin." The tale of Janet or Lady Margaret freeing her love Tam Lin from the elfin queen's enchantment is another part of the Child canon. An ancient Scottish ballad (mentioned in 1550 as "The tayl of the young Tamlene" in Robert Wederburn's [or Vedderburn's] *The Complaynt of Scotland*) that also appears in Scandinavia, it has remained relatively popular among singers and became particularly known in the version by Robert Burns from 1792. The introductory hook that holds the piece together is an abstracted version of the melodic phrase "you maidens" from verse 1, unusual in the way that bass and guitar play the melodic line in unison within a deceptively tight rhythmic framework. The interludes are crucial in breaking up the extremely long ballad (which was shortened to twenty-one verses) according to the content. Fairport chose an unusual narrative perspective that is similar to the one A. L. Lloyd and Anne Briggs performed: the events are told indirectly beforehand through Tam Lin's giving advice to Janet, while the actual drama (the shape changing) is relatively short, thus resembling Child's version A or Bronson's version 2.1. As in "Matty Groves," the vocals are straightforward, with few ornaments and rather plain harmonies. The fiddle has again taken on the role of a commentator.

"Tam Lin" is considered one of the most difficult ballads of the traditional repertoire, demanding a delivery close to speech-song or inflected speech.[8] The problem of maintaining its metric structure also reflects its extreme length and the complexity of the story. Lloyd, for instance, worked with focal points and fermatas, but was free with rhythmic variation in every verse, depending on content and word stresses. Briggs's version resembles Lloyd's but is melodically stronger. For Fairport Denny sings quite straightforwardly, with few ornaments but with variations of the verse rhythm. "Tam Lin" was one of the few pieces Fairport rarely performed after Denny's departure. Nicol remarked about the difference between "Matty Groves" and "Tam Lin": "It's more a story sung in the head, you have to think about it more, whereas 'Matty Groves' is a very simple, gut-feeling kind of song. I think that is the difference—head and heart."

The difficulties of "Tam Lin" also become apparent when listening to the videotaped version Fairport performed in 1987 with folksinger June Tabor.[9] Whereas Lloyd, Briggs, and Denny had fully integrated the few ornaments they applied to this piece, Tabor here occasionally challenges the inherent metric framework by using an abundance of elaborate ornaments, almost stopping the narrative flow. However, "Tam Lin" is an exception; normally the problem of applying straight rock rhythms to traditional material, even if playing complex patterns, lies in the danger of leveling the differentiated rhythms of parlando-style singing. Although this danger had been imminent with Fairport Convention before, the problem of straight rock playing became particularly evident in Ashley Hutchings's subsequent projects. Later critics like Vic Gammon (1977: 13–14) would describe Hutchings's approach as a sort of straitjacket:

> The rock bass and drums place the emphasis on the on-beats of the bar, and not sufficiently on the off-beats where it naturally falls into this type of music: the combination of this type of backing coupled, I suspect, with Ashley's concern for order and tidiness, destroy much of the spontaneity of the music. . . . Ashley's total musical synthesis in fact works only by destroying much of the inherent nature and quality, both musical and social, of the material he works with.

The subsequent Fairport albums *Full House* (1970) and *Angel Delight* (1971) continued the direction the band had taken on *Liege & Lief*. *Full House* offered an especially effective example of the potential for folk/traditional material and rock music to be well fused into a new style—here probably even more apparent than on *Liege & Lief*, owing to the straight rock rhythms of a strong drum section and the fiddle's playing the same role as the solo electric guitar. As in *Liege & Lief*, the album also contains compositions in traditional style that are characterized by an almost playful casualness with which the folk/trad. instruments are integrated into the music making, rather than just being used as an exotic tonal color. In "Flowers of the Forest," for instance, the dulcimer provides a dronelike background with the drums adding sound colors—a simple but quite effective arrangement.

Later Fairport would drift off into rock music, playing increasingly more original compositions that, with the exception of a few pieces like "Hen's March through the Midden" (*Rosie*), lacked the melodic quality and rhythmic peculiarity of the traditional pieces. In recent years at Cropredy, Fairport has returned to its original strength as a highly skilled interpreter of songs by outside writers. The band often asks well-known songwriters such as Steve Tilston and Ralph McTell for material. The 2000 album, *The Wood and the Wire*, suggested some possible changes for the future, since fiddler Chris Leslie, a new band member, has also turned out to be a skilled songwriter. Fairport still searches the archives for traditional material, although it has become more difficult to find suitable songs recently, as Nicol confessed in his interview. As the folksingers in the 1960s would have done, the band still provides lengthy documentation with their albums, often including comments by the authors and composers.

Fairport's repertoire remains extremely broad, their selection criteria still focused on unusual and exciting story lines. For example, many songs on *Jewel in the Crown* (1995), like "Highwayman," as well as the instrumentals, are closely related to vivid folk images. The repertoire even encompasses some political ("Jewel in the Crown") and environmental songs ("Wounded Whale" and "The Islands," which refers to an oil freighter spill), often with double meanings. Traditional pieces represent only a minority of the songs, and the band does not play many long ballads anymore; most songs rarely extend more than five or six verses, although they are still longer than typical rock songs. The music's structural variety is less than it was twenty-five years ago; *Five Seasons* (1990), for instance, largely featured additive pieces like "Claudy Banks," in which the musical form is determined by a succession of different arrangements of the individual verses. Other Fairport novelties include the occasional use of synthesizers, as in "Hiring Fair" (*Gladys' Leap*) and on *Jewel in the Crown*.

Steeleye Span

In contrast with Fairport Convention, Steeleye Span worked with an almost exclusively traditional repertoire from the beginning. At the same time, the group was closer to the rock side of the genre, and it kept rock instruments and acoustic-electric effects much more in the foreground. Moreover, the group had a reputation of being loud—and thus of occasionally leveling dynamic nuances as well.

Steeleye also differed from Fairport in its attitude to traditional material; although the band was often extremely accurate about its sources, the performers simultaneously mixed different traditional pieces or composed new refrains if the old ones were felt to be unsuitable. The material stemmed partly from the members' own repertoire: the folk duo Maddy Prior and Tim Hart had already acquired a large English repertoire,[10] and Martin Carthy in particular became a good source. Another early source was Ewan MacColl's library, while the performers also undertook their own research later. The range of Steeleye's repertoire was much wider than Fairport's: "Fairport had this one album," Prior commented, "but it was a very particular area that they searched into, the ballads. Whereas we were much more wide-ranging on the musical approaches and styles."

Steeleye Span knew how to take advantage of the vast variety of traditional song types. Like Fairport, the musicians showed a preference for intricate stories with driving plots or meaningful content like "False Knight on the Road" (Child Ballad no. 3), classics such as Child Ballad no. 79, "The Wife of Usher's Well" (who so much wishes her dead children to return that they return from their graves for a last eerie visit), and the well-known symbolic song about the corn god, "John Barleycorn." The band also included popular songs like "The Lowlands of Holland" (a woman mourning for her drowned lover) and "All Things Are Quite Silent" about the dreaded press gangs who abducted even newly married men for war service, as well as a vast range of love songs like "Rosebud in June" and "The Lark in the Morning."

Steeleye's repertoire also included a large portion of songs with unusual content, often with double meanings and sometimes extremely obscure texts. Examples include the southern English song "The Blacksmith" (with the hammer as a phallic symbol); "Twa Corbies" (Child Ballad no. 26; the dinner conversation of two ravens over a slain knight); "Boys of Bedlam" (Bedlam was an early lunatic asylum); "King Henry" (Child Ballad no. 32), who, by his courteous behavior, redeems a lady who had been transformed into an ugly, ghostlike monster (Carthy remarked in the liner notes to *Sweet Wivelsfield* that it is "the Beauty and the Beast story, the only difference being that the sexes are reversed"); and the Christmas song "Gaudete," which became one of the band's biggest hits. The group sometimes took material from the pagan tradition ("The King," referring to the hunting of the wren) and with direct historical content. On *Parcel of Rogues* Steeleye chose Scottish material like "Cam Ye o'er frae France" (a satirical Jacobite song on King George I) and two songs from Hogg's *Jacobite Reliques*, "A Parcel of Rogues in a Nation" and "Prince Charlie Stuart." With these songs, the singers would also try to adapt to the regional style, as Hart (Tobler 1991: 29) recalled: "I'd put on an Irish accent if I was singing an Irish song, because the words are written in that accent and they work that way. Maddy sang a lot of songs with a Scottish accent—there was no way to sing them with an English accent, because they sound silly."

In general, however, songs referring to a single historical incident were rare. If fantasy elements were chosen, then the obscure ones or the ones with a general message were taken, as on *Now We Are Six* (1974). This album included the ecological horror story "Seven Hundred Elves"; "Thomas the Rhymer" (Child Ballad no. 37), who is abducted by an elf queen; and the erotic "metamorphosis fantasy" (Lloyd's description in the liner notes to *The Bird in the Bush*, 1966) "Two Magicians," in which a female sorcerer tries to escape her male pursuer through a succession of shape transformations (e.g., by becoming a mouse), but is always overpowered by his appearances (e.g., he turns into a cat and chases her).

The band dealt quite freely with the material, often collating versions if text and music did not fit together or if a text seemed to be incomplete or unsuitable. The result was a broad range of approaches: (1) collations from numerous variants, as in the case of "The Weaver and the Factory Maid" (*Parcel of Rogues*), with the main theme from A. L. Lloyd and other parts from a children's rhyme as well as from the vocals of Robert Cinnamond; (2) mixtures of two different songs, as with "All around My Hat"; (3) mixtures of traditional and their own composed elements, like "Demon Lover" and "Elf Call" (*Commoners Crown*); and (4) their own compositions combining electric and acoustic instruments, such as "Robbery with Violins," on which the fiddle plays a traditional melody against an electric bass line with syncopated offbeat accents in a funk style.

Despite a considerable number of member changes, Steeleye's stylistic characteristics (traditional repertoire, emphasis on vocals, rock elements) remained relatively constant. Selecting good melodies and strong vocals was crucial for the overall sound. The band members were—and are—good singers, well able to use different vocal colors. Polyphonic a cappella singing was a major characteristic of the group, as Prior emphasized: "The big thing with Steeleye, it's always been harmonies. It's always been the vocal strength."

Although some of the band's musicians were much more strongly rooted in the revival/folk scene than Fairport Convention's, elements of rock music were applied more consistently, the sound of the electric instruments being much broader and more dominant. The overall sound of Steeleye Span was sometimes not distinguishable from contemporary rock except for the use of a traditional text and tune, as can be heard with "Thomas the Rhymer." The backbeat dominated, with the rhythm section often being very tight, as on "Black Jack Davey" (*All around My Hat*), and the instruments playing a rhythmic counterpoint to the vocal line, thus creating a strong internal tension as on "Lovely on the Water."

Remarkably, Steeleye's early recordings, with the exception of their first album, *Hark! The Village Wait*, omitted drums. Consequently, the electric bass had to assume the role of the drums as keeper of the meter—as, for instance, with "Cold, Haily, Windy Night," on which the instrument has to put a much stronger emphasis than usual on beats 1 and 3 of the 4/4 meter. This could also be observed with the Etchingham Steam Band which also played without drums. Steeleye's bass player Rick Kemp did not always feel comfortable having to fill two musical positions:

> I played an awful lot of notes. And I played incredibly rhythmically, I think. And I played with the tune where I could. There are one or two pieces on early Steeleye recordings, for instance, where I'm playing in a very haphazard way. There's one that's called "Robbery with Violins," for instance, where it's just myself and the fiddle player throwing around lots of notes in the D scale. And very aggressive because that's the way I felt about it, and I found it limiting for quite a while. I found it was quite sort of stultifying in a way because there were not beats to get between as with the drummer, what I had to do was sort of make the drums and the beats in between. But then I got the hang of it after a while.

After *Parcel of Rogues* (1973), Steeleye had reached a point where the drums had to come in, as its lineup was felt to be too limited musically. Kemp obviously missed the groove—the pulse that is created by the close interaction of drums. Steeleye's new lineup was similar to Fairport Convention's, with singer(s), fiddle, acoustic and electric guitar, bass, and drums. As with Fairport, the fiddle had a double role as commentator and solo electric instrument, heard on "Black Jack Davey." The band also incorporated a large number of other instruments, experimenting with unusual combinations like an oboe played above a drum line as in "Drink Down the Moon" (*Now We Are Six*). The band also applied bagpipe effects (drone effects, combined with an embellished melody over the top, e.g., with grace notes one or more degrees above the melody note) as on "Prince Charlie Stewart" and "Cam Ye o'er frae France." On "Cam Ye o'er frae France," the drone in the second verse is produced by an accordion.

While Fairport's music was often described as "handmade" (i.e., without synthesizers or sound effects), Steeleye was much more experimental; its members were open to any new possibility in sound technology, using whatever means were available. This was even true for folk musician Martin Carthy, as Maddy Prior remembered:

> He'd come up with these different approaches. I remember singing in the back of a banjo! Why we were singing in the back of a banjo I have no idea, except that it was on "Boys of Bedlam," and the idea was to make the voices sound odd. Well, nowadays you'd just put a load of nonsense and that bought stuff, but then we hadn't that kind of thing, you see. So we sang in the back of a banjo. That's why it's got this strange vocal sound. Martin said, "Oh yes, this sounds great! Sounds like crazy lunatics." So I said, "All right! As long as somebody else holds the banjo and doesn't bang me on the nose." Very primitive stuff. It sounds odd. But it *was* fresh! That's the thing, isn't it?

Spatial effects, sound distortions, fade-ins, fade-outs, and the technical effects of the electric guitar and bass, like the wah-wah pedal on "Robbery with Violins" (*Parcel of Rogues*), or of the electric fiddle and bass on "Sum Waves" (*All around My Hat*) play a much more pivotal role than with Fairport. The effect of "Gaudete" (*Below the Salt*) came not only from the compelling melody and the haunting polyphonic singing, but also from its use of a constant fade-in until verse 4, after which the voices are removed from the listener through a fade-out. It is, perhaps, remarkable that the band had its first major hit with this piece, which was not even a traditional song in the strictest sense.

However, Steeleye Span's music was more limited structurally than Fairport Convention's. Parlando-style singing is missing, and the general form was much more fixed, as Carthy confirmed: "No—almost no improvisation. There was one song we used to do which did have quite a bit of improvisation, and that was 'When I Was on Horseback'—we did the song and gave ourselves some room to move, and Peter was the one who was given his head. I was never an improvising player, and I've never had the confidence to do it."

Improvisational passages were thus restricted to small segments, similar to the popular music of the 1970s that often consisted of two sung and one instrumental verse. Yet within this structural framework, Steeleye Span explored the rock-based possibilities of the traditional material in greater depth than any other group. It worked out a large variety of different hooks, which are sometimes highly elaborate, as for "Lovely on the Water," or rhythmically or instrumentally unusual, like the military drum style on "Cam Ye o'er frae France," set against completely different instrumental and vocal lines. This diversity made it impossible for listeners to predict any development from one piece to the next.

The effect of Steeleye's arrangements was not only based on carefully selected melodies and elaborate hooks, but was also the result of unusual and intriguing rhythmic patterns, such as the syncopated figure at the end of the verse lines of "The Blacksmith," set against a rhythmically different and irregularly accentuated bass line, or unexpected meter changes as at the ending of "Cam Ye o'er frae France."[11] The band's colorful arrangements often varied extremely between the verses, as in "King Henry" (*Below the Salt*).

An indirect explanation for Steeleye's musical colorfulness and the unpredictability of its musical development was suggested in Prior's description of the group's working style:

> There is a certain anarchic quality to Steeleye that it wouldn't follow any rules, except its own. And nobody knows what they are—and that includes me. But even if you thought of something and it feels uncomfortable, it'll go ahead because somebody else wants it to go ahead. And to some extent it's weight of numbers, weight of passion, or it's all the sensitivities to someone else's desires if they've written a song they really like. It's not your place to say no. So there is a lot of give and take.

This approach could work with Steeleye, because the band was still always guided by a shared general idea of the basis of traditional music—very much in contrast to Sandy Denny's Fotheringay, whose democratic approach failed because Denny was always regarded as the soloist (Heylin 2000: 117).

Pentangle

Pentangle can be described as the popular sideline of five very different musicians, all of whom were individually active as solo and studio performers. The band's music combined the textual complexity of jazz and the clarity of the folk baroque style. Its repertoire was an eclectic mixture of jazz, medieval, traditional, and blues material, as well as original songs by Bert Jansch such as "A Woman Like You" (*Sweet Child*).

The majority of Pentangle's material grew out of the repertoire of Jansch and John Renbourn. This was especially the case with traditional repertoire such as "Bruton Town" (*The Pentangle*) and with the large medieval repertoire. Unlike Fairport Convention or Steeleye Span, which often looked for specific variants, Pentangle mainly stayed with the classic versions of songs as popularized in the *Penguin Book*, like "The Trees They Grow High" (*Sweet Child*). Many of these songs were current in the folk scene and were often picked up orally; for example, Jansch learned several pieces from folksinger Anne Briggs. The traditional repertoire was not exclusively restricted to English material; "Omie Wise" (*Reflection*) was, for instance, an American version of "Pretty Polly." Occasionally the group would perform different versions of a song such as "Bruton Town." Likewise, Jansch would later record a more complete and tragic version of Pentangle's rather romantic version of "Once I Had a Sweetheart" (*Basket of Light*), entitled "Sylvie" (*Rosemary Lane*). Although the band sought compelling stories (in "Bruton Town," two brothers murder the servant lover of their sister, while "The House Carpenter" [*Basket of Light*] recalls the fate of a woman entangled with a demon lover), the melodic quality, the basis for the instrumental sections, was at least as important as the text.

Because of its ties to jazz, Pentangle differed from other groups in its overall sound color and musical style. The tonal color was generally quite transparent and metallic, the result of a precise playing style combined with a highly nuanced instrumental articulation and a distinctive choice of instruments. "Once I Had a Sweetheart" combined glockenspiel and sitar, while the sound of "Cruel Sister" was a mixture of sitar, guitar, and dulcimer. Drummer Terry Cox often used the complete percussive spectrum, and this metallic effect was further enhanced by the frequently heavy touch in the instrumental playing, especially through Jansch's strong guitar style, and the bowing technique of the acoustic bass. Used extensively and often in a virtuoso style, Renbourn's sitar played an important role in Pentangle's sound. Rather than just being strummed to provide an atmospheric background, it was treated as a fully integrated instrument, carrying hooks or melodic lines as in "House Carpenter," which is arranged as a dialogue between Jansch and Jacqui McShee.

The drums were almost treated as a melody instrument, playing highly varied figures on the whole range of the percussive apparatus. And although Cox's drumming was as metrically clear as Dave Mattacks's, it was much more transparent, with a wider dynamic range, which gave the songs more openness. A central Pentangle feature was its metrically intricate playing and singing, featuring syncopated rhythm patterns and frequent time changes. Combined with clear accentuations and a precise playing style, these elements highlighted the rhythmic profile of the pieces much more strongly than in any other electric folk group's performances. "Bruton Town," for instance, is characterized by a syncopated rhythm and sharp accentuations,[12] further complicated by the instruments playing musical counterpoints to the melody. Even the guitars were sometimes used more as rhythm than melody instruments, as can be heard in "Let No Man Steal Your Thyme" (*The Pentangle*). In contrast with this metric complexity, the harmonic dimension, especially in the improvisational sections, remains quite simple (in "Let No Man Steal Your Thyme," only tonic and dominant formulations), unlike the band's jazz pieces.

Pentangle's traditional material was often arranged simply, using additive forms ("Once I Had a Sweetheart") and clear harmonic progressions. The accompaniment did not interpret the textual content; instead, the musical devices alone were the focal point for the performers, the basis for the improvisations that were a central part of Pentangle's music making.[13] The arrangements were often developed during rehearsals or even during concerts, as Renbourn pointed out:

> "Bruton Town" was an old song that we three all kind of knew; Bert made the main arrangement. "House Carpenter" was a song that Jacqui did—via I guess Jean Ritchie. "Trees Grow" was a song Jacqui taught me, and I made a guitar part. "Cruel Sister" was a song that I put together on guitar—I showed Bert and then arranged it with some vocal parts. Songs such as these were rehearsed outside of band time and brought in on the night. I think a certain amount of Pentangle's material was generated in a loose way by various members knotting/forming ideas into a loose shape and then the whole band giving it a go on the stand. I did put forward some arrangements like "Lyke Wake Dirge," but by and large the music was worked out by a process of osmosis. If the gig paid for us all to be together then we spent time, playing and listening.

As Jacqui McShee recalled, Pentangle's improvisational work was sometimes affected by the stress of the concert tours:

> Danny and Terry usually improvised; John's guitar parts were usually improvised. But Bert would always work out his part that would be like the solid guitar part. And I have to admit, in later days, on very long tours, when you were playing every night, you do tend to stick to the same thing. Sometimes they did, but I think there would always be sections in the songs, instrumental sections, that would be improvised.

The band made use of the technical possibilities of that time, using fade-ins and overdubs of McShee's voice as in "Once I Had a Sweetheart," and occasionally adding a lot of reverb as on "The Lyke Wake Dirge" (*Basket of Light*). However, Pentangle also incorporated sound effects that were created by acoustic means, like the strumming sound of the bass in "Let No Man Steal Your Thyme."

Pentangle has often been criticized for having presented a too-perfect, nonindividual sound that was the result of five distinct and very different performers whose common musical ground seemed to be too general. Despite the rhythmic sharpness, many edges of the original sources were indeed rounded out on the studio recordings; the story, for instance, is often told in one line without much contrast in the voice. The live recordings like *Sweet Child*, in contrast, reveal Pentangle as a strong, characterful band. The later Pentangle and related solo projects presented an even broader sound that also smoothed out the rhythmic sharpness of the earlier playing; "Reynardine" (*A Maid in Bedlam*) by the John Renbourn Group sounds much more simplified than Jansch's earlier version due to the missing percussive edges. Yet the earlier approach was taken up again on McShee's 1985 solo recording *About Thyme*, on which the preference for metallic sounds and transparent arrangements reappeared.

ACOUSTIC EXPERIMENTAL AND FUSION STYLES

A musical portrayal of electric folk would be incomplete without an overview of the range of acoustic arrangements of traditional material. The largest and most prominent group is represented by the British guitarists, but it is also worth reviewing lesser-known approaches like Dolly Collins's combinations of folk with early music or the various attempts to merge folk with baroque material and stylistic elements. All of these experiments have added various new angles of musical arrangement possibilities to traditional material.

British Guitar Styles and "Folk Baroque"

The most unusual observation that the distinguished white American blues guitarist and music publisher Stefan Grossman (1990: 3) recalled about his visit to England in 1967 was that "guitar players not only picked their instruments but also sang!" Although British performers usually tried to copy American folk and blues musicians in the beginning, a characteristic guitar style soon started to develop in Britain, alongside the interpretations of traditional songs. Davy Graham, Bert Jansch, John Renbourn, and Martin Carthy were central figures in what came to be known as the British guitar style or "folk baroque." This direction was distinguished by a polyphonic texture, often with baroquelike ornaments and grace notes and a playing technique with inherently percussive and blues-derived elements. Furthermore, the open tunings involved a technical simplification for guitarists playing or accompanying these traditional songs in a style that was focused on melodic rather than on chordal thinking.

Open tunings, as well as percussive playing techniques, had been picked up from American blues musicians like Charlie Patton and Willie Brown. Probably during the first decade of the twentieth century, open tuning had been adapted from the banjo, which used so-called open strings, allowing retuning to play different chords in higher or lower registers.[14] Tuning a guitar in open D and G made playing easier, as the open strings could be strummed to produce a full-sounding chord. These possibilities had been limited with the original EADGBE tuning, unless one used complicated barrée techniques. The alternative tunings were therefore not only a technical simplification (blues, especially solo segments, is often played in the lower register because the distance between frets is smaller further down the neck), but they also opened a vast range of new finger-picking possibilities and slide (bottleneck) techniques. Combined with other elements, this led to what is now known as Mississippi delta blues. These techniques seemed to have been forgotten after the blues had reached its high point between 1920 and 1940, but within the American folk revival of the 1950s the blues repertoire and its variety of tunings were taken up again. The old open G and D tunings spurred the development of many new tunings that again provided a technical simplification and created a distinctive sound.

Several folk baroque performers like medieval/renaissance specialist John Renbourn are also highly skilled interpreters of American blues. The origins of the British blues scene, headed by the highly influential Alexis Korner, can be traced back to the late 1950s. The blues style that emerged in Britain—the starting point was skiffle—was predominantly shaped by the American "folk blues," represented first by the playing of Blind Boy Fuller and Blind Lemon Jefferson and later by Big Bill Broonzy and Brownie McGhee. The British adaptation is often not recognized as blues, as it is a rather smoothed-out version, based on clear, elaborate finger picking, a syncopated yet regular melody rhythm, and a constant rhythm in the bass, hence occasionally lacking the spontaneous element that is an integral part of African American blues (Oliver 1998; Siniveer 1981). These elements, however, provided an ideal basis for the accompaniment of English folk songs.

Like other folk guitarists, Martin Carthy, for instance, started by copying Big Bill Broonzy's sound. Yet, as a result of listening to folk instruments like the uilleann pipes and the fiddle, he subsequently developed a highly individual style that differed from American models by adapting the melodic role of the fiddle and transferring the drone from the pipes to the bass string (Grossman 1977: 15). The open DADEAD tuning enabled him to move away from American guitar playing, which is much more based on a harmonic approach. It is difficult to determine who finally developed the EADEAE tuning that would become particularly helpful for playing medieval and Irish melodies, since Carthy and Davy Graham both attribute this innovation to each other.

Most significant, the open tunings enabled the playing of a drone, an effective and appropriate device for traditional pieces based on a modal scale. The drone function is for the most part taken over by the two lower strings: Carthy's "Siege of Delhi" has a G drone throughout that is played on the open fifth string. Grossman (1977: 15) later compared this sound to "a very grand dulcimer." Yet despite this common ground, Carthy, Graham, Jansch, and Renbourn each developed highly individual approaches.

Martin Carthy

Carthy has developed a percussive yet transparent and almost sparse guitar style that always emphasizes the melody. This is not only evident in his solo recordings but also in the collaborations with his musical partner, fiddler Dave Swarbrick. Likewise a distinguished singer, Carthy learned many traditional songs in the mid-1960s (including pieces like "Byker Hill" and "Sovay" with unusual rhythmic elements) from A. L. Lloyd. Although his repertoire is regionally quite diverse, he still understands his style as urban English: "I use a lot of Scottish, Irish, and some Breton and American tunes, but I play them like an Englishman, and in a city context" (Kennedy 1987: 7).

Carthy's guitar style has frequently been copied in the folk scene. When *Martin Carthy: A Guitar in Folk Music*, a collection of his songs, was published, he refused to include the guitar accompaniments except for tunings and chord clues—partly "because of the Carthy clone syndrome" (Kennedy 1987: 4), partly because his accompaniments follow clear patterns that can be worked out easily. The basic assumption of Carthy's approach is that the tune is the most important element and has to be enhanced. Thus, even when sung, the melody is always also played on the guitar, which may then embellish, ornament, or improvise. The accompaniment is always kept rather simple to avoid distraction from the tune. Carthy often adds a dronelike bass line, mostly played with the thumb. Further notes might be filled in, but other than the melody only the bass can always clearly be heard, supporting the melody. Because Carthy thinks melodically, harmonic considerations play only a minor role when working out the guitar arrangement. Rather than setting up chord progressions, he develops and elaborates the melodic lines.

Carthy's playing is highly percussive, reflecting its adaptation from blues techniques with a loud, percussive bass and slides. On "The Bedmaking" (*Crown of the Horn*), for instance, the rhythmic element is almost stronger than the melodic one owing to Carthy's hard attack, enhanced by cutting off the sustain of the guitar strings. He also adds an intro and instrumental sections between the verses (the length varying from two measures to the length of the entire tune), mostly by using tune-related material.

After having worked out an approach, Carthy usually stays within the overall pattern for the piece, although

I basically *don't* do arrangements of songs, so in that sense it's not fixed. What I try and do is find out how to play the tune and then any variations of the tune, because the words of the song will actually affect the way the tune goes. So you have a basic model, and then because of the words you might have to go down there or put a twiddle in there or an extra bar or [take] a bar out, maybe. But once I've decided on what's in and what's out, that will stay the same pretty much—unless I want to do a little bit of adjusting. I don't think of myself as being a person who improvises as he sings or improvises on the guitar as I sing, because that's not what interests me. I'm interested in the two working together. The thing that makes it different for me these days when I'm performing solo is, it's to speed up and slow down. You can do that whenever you want. Playing with Dave Swarbrick is great fun, but the one drawback is that you set the tempo and you've got to stick with it.

When singing and playing with Swarbrick, Carthy changes very little of his overall musical approach—while Swarbrick's fiddle playing often gives the impression of the instrument commenting on the content or telling its own story behind Carthy. This effect can be heard on the album *Prince Heathen*. On "Arthur McBride and the Sergeant," the fiddle first plays the tune or parts of it as an intro and then improvises around the voice line with melodic phrases. Swarbrick is not afraid of adding striking dissonances, as "Reynardine" demonstrates. Improvisation plays a much stronger role in Swarbrick's playing, as Carthy pointed out:

> When we do songs we don't rehearse either—except a tiny bit on a couple of songs where we set up a signpost, say, you work towards the signpost and then you go off there and then you come back to the song. Basically what Dave will do is learn a song, and he will learn the way I sing it as we go along. Because I do quite a lot of variation. And once he's got it, he then starts to improvise. . . . Occasionally he will actually set himself, find something that he likes, and he'll stick with that. But, generally speaking, what he's doing is just playing extensively round the melody and listening to the words at the same time. And he actually plays with the song—better than anybody that I've ever met. And has a breadth of imagination that's . . . maybe he got that from twelve, fifteen years with Fairport and having been the front man and having to improvise.

Playing with Fairport Convention seemed to have still another impact on Swarbrick's playing, as he learned to play rocklike intros, that is, with material different from the tune, as in "The Rainbow"—a good example of the creative interplay between acoustic and electric styles.

Davy Graham

Graham has developed an eclectic style that mixes various elements from North African and Indian music to blues, jazz, and folk. Long before the Beatles introduced the sitar to a large pop audience, Graham had already incorporated elements of Indian music into his playing, creating idiosyncratic sounds even when he did not have the original instruments at hand. This stylistic adventurousness was also characteristic of John Renbourn, especially when playing with Pentangle.

The instrumental "She Moves through the Fair" (*The Thamesiders and Davy Graham*) offers a good example of his fusion style. As Karl Dallas points out in the CD booklet for *New Electric Muse*, Graham noticed very early the striking similarity of this piece's Mixolydian scale to the Indian raga scale That Kambaj (or That Kammaj). Transforming the Irish piece into an Indian mini-raga interpretation seemed to be only a small step. Similar to a first *áláp* section, the first verse is turned into a slowed-down introduction with descending raglike scales at the end of each verse. It is followed by a quicker, rhythmically stricter section (the *jor*), in which Graham plays with the melodic theme, and is the piece concludes with a slowed-down section similar to the beginning. The effect is further intensified by Graham's percussive playing, which gives the guitar a very metallic sound, and the bending of the bass strings.

Graham's (for that time) experimental, daring style was not only evident in his solo recordings, but especially on *Folk Roots, New Routes* with Shirley Collins. "Pretty Saro," for instance, follows the same basic idea as the previous piece: Graham only intensifies elements that were already inherent in the song. The mode is again Mixolydian and thus related to the Indian That Kambaj, which makes a transformation into raga reminiscences very easy. Moreover, the original variants of the pieces are, as in Alan Lomax's *Penguin Book of American Folk Songs* (1964), already rhythmically unusual in the notated version, where the meter changes between 3/4 and 4/4 (the latter characterized by the rhythmic sequence of quarter note–half note–quarter note, which adds a slightly syncopated feel). The Graham/Collins collaboration dissolves the metric framework even further through the extremely reduced speed and the prolonged rests that provide room for the ragalike introduction and interlude with scales and short ornaments. Thus, while maintaining the original framework, the piece has been transformed into something completely new.

Bert Jansch

Jansch's guitar style can be lyrical as well as percussive. Yet the salient characteristic of his style is the metallic sound that results from his way of attacking the strings. Jansch has large hands and often plays with his nails. He emphasized in an interview with Stefan Grossman (1990: 48) that he has never been influenced by American playing styles, although he has brought a predominantly jazz-oriented accompaniment to the traditional material. Instead, he learned clawhammer techniques in Scotland (from Scots, as he stressed to Grossman) and developed his distinctly percussive guitar style, which Grossman relates to the Mississippi delta, out of sheer aggression: "If the club was noisy you were trying to get as much out of the strings as possible. In the old days, I used to actually break the strings, I'd get so angry" (ibid.: 49).[15] He subsequently started to use this aggressiveness as a dynamic element in his arrangements.

Jansch honed his arrangement style on Davy Graham instrumentals like "Angi." While Graham had kept "Angi" relatively simple and clear by predominantly playing chords, Jansch applied an individual coloring with his strong attacks that emphasized the rhythms, and also added interludes and virtuoso elements like ornaments and rapid scale passages.

A good example of this highly elaborate and complex style can also be heard in his interpretation of "Blackwaterside," a traditional piece he learned from Anne Briggs. As he recalled in the Grossman interview, "It may have been one of the first times that I had actually sat down and tried to take a number . . . that had a definite melody line that I couldn't change—it's a traditional thing—and actually consciously sit down and create a backing to go with that particular tune" (ibid.: 48–49). On this piece, Jansch works with brief segments that are applied as patterns. In contrast with Carthy, the bass line and middle voice are much more complex, while the overall rhythmic structure is dominated by meter changes (4/4, 5/4, 2/4) and syncopations. As Sandy Denny does in her singing, Jansch uses long sustained notes that give room for the elaborate passages. Although he is a good musical storyteller, the accompaniment is at least as important as the story. As in the playing of Graham and Carthy, Jansch's bass string sounds a drone on D, while the harmonic progressions remain relatively basic, although from the second verse on they drift increasingly into more complicated seventh chord structures.

Traditional songs make up only a small part of his repertoire, since Jansch is also a highly acclaimed songwriter, his texts often inspired by events around him. He tends to neutralize the personal experience behind the texts without losing their emotional impact, which gives his songs a timeless character.

Jansch has integrated traditional pieces into his repertoire by giving them his distinct timbre and a highly personal, expressive touch. He sings the love tale of "Blackwaterside" as if he had really experienced it, which is part of the reason this song is still identified with him. His music making contains a constant element, and some of the pieces do not seem to change over the years. "Blackwaterside," first recorded on *Jack Orion* in 1966, was recorded again on *Heartbreak* in 1982 and is still performed almost any night that Jansch plays, but does not differ substantially from the first recording, in contrast with the successive recordings of Steeleye Span and Maddy Prior.

Shirley and Dolly Collins

Shirley Collins's recordings were distinguished by an individual singing style and by an unusual variety of material that stemmed predominantly from the English (Sussex) tradition. She could fall back on a broad repertoire, partly acquired at home from her family as well as from visitors and partly collected during her field trips in the States with Alan Lomax. Collins did not confine herself to these direct sources but expanded her repertoire further by adopting material recorded by contemporary fieldworkers (e.g., songs recorded by Peter Kennedy, such as "The Blacksmith") and archival material. The booklet texts and interviews reveal an attitude toward the music that clearly differed from that of many electric folk musicians, being characterized by a deep respect for the tradition and the people carrying it on. This concern was also reflected in the extreme care she took to name the sources of her songs; Collins often exposed an almost personal relationship to the pieces she sometimes acquired from the living tradition.

A characteristic feature of her recordings was her sister's accompaniment style. As Dolly Collins pointed out, the idea to base the arrangements on already inherent melodic material could be traced back to her composition teacher, Alan Bush:

He really taught me to look at the material presented to you like the tune of a folk song, find out what there was in it and use that material that's already there in the accompaniment, so that you don't actually bring any alien material into the work. . . . Whatever you do with that theme, if you turn it upside down or whatever, it's always got some association with the song. So my first lessons were on writing accompaniments to folk songs, on actually writing a "folk song" or something like that, but I never went as far ahead as I would have liked to have done, because . . . I just could not afford to continue the lessons. (Hunt 1979: 6)

Dolly Collins's arrangements clearly refrained from the romanticizations evident in Cecil Sharp's piano arrangements for his *One Hundred English Folksongs*. Comparing the settings for "Death and the Lady," one can see that Sharp's accompaniments are, generally speaking, carefully worked out with dynamic prescriptions, comparatively complex harmonic progressions (he uses seventh chords), and musically independent motives in the piano. In contrast, Dolly Collins's arrangements are rather sparse, economic, and almost simple, yet effective. Although she rarely doubled the melodic line, the accompaniment never distracted from the tune—singer and song remained always in the foreground.

Like Carthy, Dolly Collins did not work from a chordal viewpoint but developed the accompaniment from the melodic material: she took small modular elements from the melody and placed them at focal points of the piece, as with "Death and the Lady," for which she worked out a hooklike intro that keeps the verses of the piece together. Similarly, the intro and interludes to "All Things Are Quite Silent" (*The Sweet Primeroses* [sic]) have almost the same effect as a rock hook, as they include a returning figure that appears at the ends of lines or verses. This figure serves as a musical cornerstone or anchor for the voice and reinforces the motion between the verses. At the same time, these sparse arrangements gave a singer enough space for orientation, especially for someone not accustomed to singing with a classical or romantic accompaniment containing material different from the tune. Shirley Collins described it as "music she could lean against" while singing: Dolly "seemed to have the same understanding of the tunes that I had, and she had a wonderful sense of harmony. And what was lovely about her arrangements as well, that you got the introduction, you could just launch yourself on these songs."

Although Dolly Collins was extremely consistent in her composition style, it was also characterized by considerable flexibility and structural variety. One can find abstract hooklike intros ("Sweet Primeroses") as well as imitated traditional elements, such as an abstracted, dronelike bass reminiscent of the sound of bagpipes. She strove to achieve an idiomatic musical sound and style. The medieval spirit of the religious carol "Down in Yon Forest" (*Sweet Primeroses*), for instance, is expressed through an accompaniment that approximates a fifteenth- or sixteenth-century style. Similarly, "A Song-Story" (*Anthems in Eden*) combines the modality of the songs with typical elements from the medieval/early music repertoire such as period instruments and stylistic devices like syncopations, cadenzas, and ornaments. "Go from My Window," in contrast, is arranged in an additive form. The accompaniment builds up—and thus changes—with each new verse, using restrained percussion and bass.

Dolly Collins also tried to catch the original spirit of each piece with a well-thought-out instrumental selection. If the piano was used, it would be quite restrained. She often experimented with new tonal colors and unusual instrumentations: "Death and the Lady," for example, is sung against a basic ensemble of sackbut, bass viol, rebec, and violone—a sound much more transparent than with later classical instruments. She later worked occasionally with the Incredible String Band, which also experimented with unusual tonal colors.

INSTRUMENTAL FUSIONS AND CONCEPT ALBUMS

As is the case for its neighbors Ireland and Scotland, England's traditional music includes a vast range of dance pieces, jigs, and reels in 6/8 or 9/8. While heavy percussion has occasionally proven problematic with vocal music characterized by tempo fluctuations, electric arrangements have worked especially well as instrumentals. Since dance music requires a regular beat, the use of electric instruments was not so dramatic a change as for those ballads and songs that were performed in a parlando-rubato style. Fairport especially incorporated dance-based instrumental material into their repertoire. It also worked out new instrumental combinations and possibilities, as in "The Brilliancy Medley" (*Nine*), which combines guitar and fiddle, followed by a guitar section and a mandolin solo.

More than any other electric folk performer, Ashley Hutchings became known for instrumentally intensive concept albums like *Morris On* (1972) and *Son of Morris On* (1976), with which he highlighted a traditional element of English social life that had long been neglected and almost forgotten: morris dance. England had developed many complex processional and ritual dances with fixed dance figures that were important parts of May Day, midwinter season, and other calendar celebrations. The best known forms were the morris dances, which followed varying regional forms, although nowadays the term "morris dance" is particularly related to a dance performed in the Cotswolds. It is usually danced in groups (or sets) of six male dancers (who often hold handkerchiefs in their hands and wear white trousers and shirts decorated with colored ribbons, plus bell pads tied to their lower legs), arranged in two rows of three. In addition to the dancers, a morris team includes musicians and occasionally figures for comic relief like a fool (sometimes dressed up in women's clothes) and a morris beast (i.e., a hobbyhorse). The melodies, played fast and vigorously at an even meter (originally by pipe and tabor, later also with other instruments such as fiddle, concertina, and melodeon), are usually folk tunes, yet can also include folk opera melodies of the seventeenth through nineteenth centuries and bawdy songs. Morris dance was common in England until the nineteenth century. Since its revival around 1900, it has been cultivated in morris guilds.[16]

Hutchings's albums present a varied mixture of traditional morris dances and new morris compositions like the "Cotswold Tune" (*Son of Morris On*), along with broadsides and pastoral dialogues. The dance element clearly stands in the foreground on these recordings: while drums sometimes compromised the flexibility of the parlando style in ballads, here the accurate time keeping is essential to maintain the dance rhythms. A good example is Hutchings's variant of "Greensleeves" (*Morris On*), featuring simple harmonies and clear metric accentuations. Despite the modern instruments, the connection to the living tradition was made obvious through the participation of real morris teams or "sides." Unlike other folk or electric folk recordings, Hutchings's dance albums had a strong impact on the tradition, stimulating a revival of several morris dancing groups. The spoken segments played an important part as well on both these recordings and others such as Hutchings's *Compleat Dancing Master*.

Apart from dance albums, several dramatic concept albums such as *Babbacombe Lee* (1971) by Dave Swarbrick/Fairport Convention and its acoustic counterpart *The Transports* (1977) by Peter Bellamy were produced. *Babbacombe Lee* tells the tale of a murderer who was sentenced to death but survived his hanging when the mechanism of the scaffold failed three times. Described by Denselow (Laing et al. 1975: 162) as "the first folk-rock opera," it was highly promoted on its release. Based on a true story (as is Bellamy's *Transports*), the tale was presented via a cycle of new compositions in the style of broadside ballads, linked by narrative passages. Close to a musical, *Babbacombe Lee* contained traditional, acoustic folk, and rock music, but the clear focus was on rock, for only one piece was truly traditional. The melodic color that is so characteristic of the English tradition was missing, which seemed to have been one reason for its sparse sales.[17] Another problem with *Babbacombe Lee* was the impossibility of a staged performance; it was conceived as a one-person psychograph of Babbacombe Lee, without any real action. The record sleeve provided a great deal of background information, without which the piece would have been difficult to understand.

Bellamy's ballad opera *The Transports*, concerning a young convict couple transported to Australia, was arranged by Dolly Collins in a style similar to the arrangements she prepared for her sister. It is often reminiscent of Brecht/Weill's *Threepenny Opera* and the eighteenth-century ballad operas that incorporated folk songs or songs composed in a folk song style, of which John Gay's *The Beggar's Opera* is still the best known.[18] The orchestra, consisting of the instruments most probably played in the eighteenth century, like those in church bands, underlines the overall period feeling. The music follows late baroque forms, with the score completely independent from the song text. Bellamy and Collins were clearly looking for an unusual sound; often, as in the *Threepenny Opera*, the instruments are not intended to be played with complete accuracy. The work's appeal lies in its effective combination of diverse folksingers with different singing and accompaniment styles: June Tabor, for instance, sings unaccompanied, while Norma Waterson, who predominantly uses Irish-style slides in her singing, is accompanied in Collins's neobaroque style.

Both *Babbacombe Lee* and *The Transports* fascinated critics, and Bellamy's work was revived at the Whitby Folk Festival in 1992. Yet neither album sold well, and these approaches have only been continued to a small extent, particularly in Ashley Hutchings's various projects.

BEYOND THE MERE INTERPRETATION
OF TRADITIONAL SONGS

The approaches mentioned above were mainly based on traditional song material. However, electric folk did not stop there. Some performers not only imitated and adapted traditional stylistic devices but also transferred these elements into new musical creations. This was true for their own songwriting as well as for other new directions, such as the Pogues-era folk rock. There have also been periodic fusions with other genres such as progressive rock and early music, which have opened up further musical possibilities.

The Adaptation of Traditional Elements into Modern Songwriting

In many cases, as with Steeleye Span, songwriting would come much later—or not at all, as with singers like Shirley Collins and June Tabor. Yet when electric folk musicians have started to write their own music, it has often been reminiscent of the tradition. The adaptation of traditional elements into modern songwriting has transpired quite subtly, for many folk and electric folk musicians regard songwriting or the incorporation of modern songs as a natural continuation of their involvement with traditional material. One example is Maddy Prior's solo album *Year* (1993), on which she explicitly dealt with English topics. Prior does not, however, often sing music written by other songwriters:

> It's only traditional music I can sing. I can actually sing songs that people I know have written because I can identify with them, but I don't know what it is that draws me to songs to sing them. . . . June [Tabor] and I have very different approaches to this, because she sings other people's songs a lot. That just never occurs to me! I like what they do, but all I could do would be a pale imitation because I wouldn't rethink it. I've tried singing other people's songs, and they die on me very quickly.

Fairport Convention, especially in their early stage, had strong songwriters in Richard Thompson and Sandy Denny, and their best songs could easily be detached from their personalities and were soon interpreted by many other performers. The case of the Oysterband is different. When moving into a more rock-oriented sphere, the band would almost exclusively fall back on their own songwriting, especially that of Ian Telfer. Their songwriting has clearly been influenced both textually and musically by their previous involvement with traditional material. This influence is also evident with many other performers, even if it has been on a subconscious level. Rick Kemp, for example, recalled that another factor in his frustration with electric folk was that "if I was writing something, which I did towards the end, I couldn't write what I wanted to write. I was governed by these strictures which were part of the baggage of the band."

There have been a broad range of forms of adaptations, especially on a textual level:

1. New textual compositions in a neotraditional style
   (a) *Texts in traditional song or ballad style with traditional or old-style tunes.* "Crazy Man Michael," written by Richard Thompson for Fairport Convention to a tune from Dave Swarbrick, adapted a characteristic ballad plot with the sequence of prophecy-fate-redemption-moral like that of "The House Carpenter." It tells the story of Michael, of whom a dark fate is foretold by a raven—which turns out, when killed by Michael, to be his love. Thompson has assimilated elements of the traditional language with characteristic expressions ("Crazy Michael will cursed be"), phrases ("out upon the sea"), rhetorical grammatical figures (sentences beginning with conjunctions like "And"), repetitions ("Michael he . . . , Michael he"), inversions ("your future I will tell unto you"), similes ("with eyes black as coals"), and distinct traditional word images (sea, evil, dagger, raven, curse). Thompson thus created a story that has become a classic part of Fairport Convention's repertoire. Ralph McTell chose a different approach for "Hiring Fair." This love story centers around a historical sociological subject: the hiring fair, a rural employment fair where laborers could offer themselves as seasonal workers. McTell uses traditional images and phrases ("a maid in the very next row"), but the song is modern insofar as individual feelings are clearly described and depicted by a first-person narrator, which is rare in the tradition. The result is a much more hybrid work.
   (b) *Modern texts combined with traditional or old-style tunes.* Examples include Fairport Convention's and Steeleye Span's calling-on songs, as well as Fairport's "Farewell, Farewell."
2. Modern content, perspective, or language (e.g., individual feelings), mostly combined with new musical compositions
   (a) *New works shaped by old musical forms (particularly ballad form).* One example is Archie Fisher's "Wounded Whale," which was interpreted by Fairport.

In form and length almost balladic and also using traditional phrases ("Hark from the masthead"), it is still a modern song with extended descriptions of the whale and her death that would not have been present in traditional song material.

(b) *Modern content/event that is depicted in old (English/British) images, symbols, and forms (particularly shorter song forms).* Electric folk musicians' original love songs have rarely been straightforward, and instead have been embellished with traditional language, images, and symbols. "Walk Awhile" (Fairport Convention, *Full House*) uses traditional images ("with another tale to tell," "down the road") while creating an overall contemporary picture. Likewise, in "White Dress" Dave Swarbrick uses classical phrases from traditional songs ("how the wind blows").

(c) *Modern content combined with a distinct atmosphere derived from the traditional songs.* Sandy Denny's songwriting often included a traditional framework (phrases, pictures, and images—especially long scenic descriptions), combined with a modern perspective related through a first-person narrator. Although she borrowed well-known images from the tradition ("It Suits Me Well" centers around a romanticized picture of a gypsy), she often used these elements, predominantly natural images like the sea, to create vivid descriptions of the inner psychic state of the narrator or the acting figures. She sometimes also adapted traditional attitudes like the strong fatalism inherent in many traditional songs, evident in the phrase "that's the way it is" for "Rising for the Moon."

The short-lived group Mr. Fox experimented regularly with these combinations of modern yet traditionally grounded approaches. Although Bob and Carole Pegg wrote completely new pieces with traditional content or references to the tradition, the results were far removed from pure romanticism. The band used idiomatic, sometimes almost identical titles ("Salisbury Plain") and similar forms, such as ballads with idiomatic phrases, but behind these formal similarities lurked unusual, dark stories of a distinctly modern sensibility. One example was the sinister story of "Mr. Fox." As with "Reynardine," the fox still represents a sly, devious character, seducing and killing innocent women; the female narrator, however, is not a spineless victim, but instead knows how to drive Mr. Fox out of town. In addition, the band juggled with topics familiar to the folk scene, as with "Aunt Lucy Broadwood," the folk song collector, who experiences a surrealistic dream.

Electric folk groups would often compose new pieces, as did traditional and folk musicians, to be used especially for dancing, like the "Cotswold Tune" (*Son of Morris On*) by Ric Sanders. The musicians would sometimes go further by incorporating a contemporary sound into their music making, as in "Crazy Man Michael," which combined Swarbrick's amplified fiddle with Simon Nicol's acoustic guitar. Even when traditional pieces were absent, as on Fairport's *Rising for the Moon*, the influences could still be heard in the images created in the texts, as well as in the sound combinations like mandolin and drums or unusual rhythmic accentuations that distinguish this music from other rock music.

A forerunner in this respect was again Mr. Fox. As Carole Pegg (CD 1996) later emphasized, in the early 1970s "we were the only group using English traditional instrumental sounds, rather than just the texts of English folk songs." The band worked with idiomatic melodies, motives, ornaments, and instrumental colors and also added a new element with Carole Pegg's fiddling that was—unlike that of other electric folk bands—a conscious mixture of different styles. "My fiddling," she said, "was an amalgamation of styles learned from 'old boys' in the Yorkshire Dales and from traditional fiddlers in other areas, such as Jinky Wells and Harry Cox" (ibid.). Writing in a neo-traditional style does not have to be a museum-like regression, as can be heard in Mr. Fox's "Aunt Lucy Broadwood." Lucy's surreal dream is told in a raplike talking style, accompanied by hand drums and choral singing in archaic-sounding parallel fourths and fifths.

Richard Thompson's songwriting offers an especially rich example of the adaptation of traditional elements into contemporary musical language. Thompson, who had already written some poignant songs during his time with Fairport, emerged after his separation from the group as an internationally acclaimed songwriter of exceptional skill. He includes relatively few traditional pieces in his solo repertoire, as most of his songs address contemporary or psychological issues. Yet he has often integrated elements from British folk or electric folk into his music, which was most obvious in his first solo album, *Henry the Human Fly!* This borrowing later became more subtle, sometimes almost unnoticeable.

Henry the Human Fly! (1972) consists of newly composed pieces that addressing issues from the tradition, but with a modern twist. The songs are often multilayered like "The New St. George," which became one of his most popular pieces (see chapter 7). This fusion also occurred on a musical level: Thompson merged characteristic English elements (not only from the tradition but also from English rock 'n' roll) with American rock. These elements included characteristic instruments like brass, fiddle, and the melodeon; folklike tunes; typical motives or near abstractions of traditional-sounding melodies; and imitations of uilleann pipes on electric guitar by playing traditional ornaments and slides. Dronelike sounds are frequent, as on "Roll Over Vaughan Williams," created by sustained notes lasting a full measure or longer. This piece reflects on the dilemma of a British composer representing the English tradition (Humphries 1996: 132–33). The clash of two distinct musical styles (Vaughan Williams and Chuck Berry) is underlined by a traditional-sounding motive and a dronelike bass, combined with a rock rhythm. *Beat the Retreat* (1994) likewise proves that a fresh interpretation of old elements can lead to something new, for Thompson always makes economic but extremely effective use of these elements. They never call attention to themselves.

THE SOUND OF THE FIDDLE: MODERN FOLK ROCK

The principal difference between electric folk and "modern" folk rock as played by groups, such as the Pogues, relates to the different sources of the music. The term "folk rock," originally coined for Bob Dylan and the Byrds, refers to newly composed songs whose form is loosely based on traditional ballads and songs. The relationship to folk can be heard in the use of instruments like the fiddle and accordion, but otherwise this music has primarily spoken the rock language.

British and Irish folk rock developed only a bit later than English electric folk: English bands like Lindisfarne and Irish groups like Horslips had already moved in that direction from 1970 on. The connection was particularly evident in the instruments; Horslips used uilleann pipes, bodhrán, tin whistle, and also keyboard, although its individual tonal color was especially a result of the flute. Likewise, the Strawbs used banjo and mandolin, and, as evident on *Preserves Uncanned* (1991), which was originally recorded between 1966 and 1968, also made references to the open guitar tunings of Jansch and Renbourn. The band occasionally included some traditional material: "October to May," for instance, was based on a Russian folk tune, while "Blantyre Explosion" was an obvious reference to Ewan MacColl (guitarist Dave Cousins had also played in the folk clubs). The majority of the Strawbs' repertoire, however, was modern compositions. Likewise, the Home Service, which included several former Albion Band members, played contemporary rock with folk instrumentations, preferably using brass; again, traditional songs played only a minor role—songwriting was much more important.

It was particularly the Pogues who gave British folk rock a new meaning. In contrast with the electric folk bands, their repertoire contained only a few traditional songs, and their contemporary, often socially critical texts had a different kind of authenticity than the traditional material. A refined singing style was of no importance to the Pogues. However, despite their punk-based background (evident in the use of hard rock instruments, technical effects, and a backbeat-dominated, hook/riff-based musical language), the folk influence was still present in the distinct acoustic tonal color of fiddle (usually cast in the role of the electric guitar), mandolin, accordion, melodeon, and banjo, as well as in the incorporation of fragments of traditional melodies.

The Levellers went in a similar direction, incorporating a large variety of acoustic instruments, although they have been using a smaller spectrum of folklike melodies, increasingly relying on more stereotyped melodic motives. Tonal colors play a particular key role with the Levellers; the acoustic instruments give the intros and interludes a distinctive sound, occasionally combined with technical effects as in "Liberty Song" (*Levelling the Land*). These instruments also fulfill certain standard functions; the acoustic guitar, for instance, is frequently used with rock ballads.

The Oysterband fits midway between electric folk and folk rock. Like the other modern folk rock bands, it has found a niche in popular music through its particular tonal color (predominantly John Jones's accordion and Ian Telfer's fiddle), catchy folk-related melodies, and a more elaborate singing style. Playing dance music is still a major intention of the group, which started as a céilidh band and can still readily turn to acoustic instruments.[19] Yet the musical means have changed: the band's playing today is metrically straight and backbeat-dominant, the predominant rhythmic stresses falling, as with the Pogues and the Levellers, on the second and fourth beats. Ian Telfer argued that the problem younger electric bands like the Oysterband faced was the idiosyncratic style of Dave Mattacks's drumming, which made any successors sound like a copy: "What Fairport did is all, for me, founded on the drummer. Mattacks invented the backbeat as applied to traditional song, so you have that slow 2–2 bar, that *boom*-ta-ta-*tsch*-t-t-t-*dum*-ta-ta-*tsch*, and that is so distinctive that anyone who played British traditional songs to that feel immediately sounded like Mattacks and Fairport."

The Oysterband plays at a much higher speed than other electric folk groups, hence giving its music a stronger drive but also reducing the complexly ornamented melodies into a single, direct line. A good example is the Child ballad "Dives and Lazarus" (*Freedom and Rain*), where June Tabor, usually known for her highly ornamented style, sings the biblical tale in a very straightforward manner. In this version, melody and dance rhythm are more important than the song's narrative. This is also the case with the band's modern songwriting. Telfer has become a highly skilled songwriter with a preference for texts with socially critical content. Yet in a concert performance a full understanding of the text is of secondary importance for the audience, as Telfer admitted. At the same time, he emphasized that "one of the most distinctive features of British traditional music is the rhythms. The songs that we do still have quite strong dance feels in them, I would say. Whether people dance to them or not— that's a different question. But there are applied dance rhythms in there, varieties of polka particularly."[20]

Likewise, although Telfer writes about contemporary events and problems, a subtle textual connection to the tradition is still apparent, as he pointed out: "British traditional song is narrative, it's all narrative, almost without exception. Most of our material isn't narrative, not in a straightforward story-telling way, but I think the songs we write have some of the impersonality of traditional songs."

All told, the Oysterband's dance music and original songs offer perhaps the best examples of how traditional devices can continue to exist in new music, even if they are almost unrecognizable at first hearing.

THE RELATIONSHIP WITH OTHER GENRES:
EARLY MUSIC AND PROGRESSIVE ROCK

Fusions with Early Music

An affinity for the early music repertoire has always been characteristic of folk and electric folk musicians, who made it available to a completely different audience. To Shirley Collins, the connection between folk and early music was almost natural:

> Early music was the other music that satisfied my soul. I've got all the Monteverdi, I've got Praetorius. That's what I listen to for pleasure, and have done it for years. And it had an authentic feel to me as well. There was this robustness of those instruments, the roughness in the authentic instruments as well. [They] seemed to me to marry so well in a music that was equally robust because it's survived for so long. Equally beautiful in its melodies. And with a roughness that wasn't a sophisticated, a polished thing.

The use of accompanying medieval and renaissance instruments was almost obvious, for instruments like the organ or brass were played by traditional musicians at church, and they seemed in some ways much closer to the tradition than instruments introduced later like the accordion or guitar. Early music sometimes even directly entered the electric folk repertoire, as when Shirley Collins incorporated songs of the troubadours and trouvères.

Dolly Collins's work with acoustic tonal colors was in many ways equal to that of the electric goups. She worked with David Munrow's Early Music Consort on *Anthems in Eden* (1969), the first complete album that combined traditional songs with early music instruments. Denselow (Laing et al. 1975: 146) later said that the instrumental combinations "gave the songs a toughness, a vitality, and an element of surprise that literally shook them into life. The album's 'theme,' a thin one of love, death and reawakening, could have sounded fey, but the overall effect of the album was anything but."[21] This roughness even became a major conceptual element, as on *Love, Death, and the Lady* (1970) where the sparse arrangement of the period instruments created a chilling texture that suited the album's dark topic. The tonal color and instruments she used for Peter Bellamy's ballad opera *The Transports* were in many aspects reminiscent of Brecht/Weill's *Threepenny Opera*. Yet the overall sound was even coarser, as Collins chose a different form of musical "authenticity" by incorporating instruments common at the time of the drama, such as bass and organ, and by embellishing the accompaniments in a neobaroque style. She later often connected the various genres through a combination of traditional, early music, and electric instruments. In the case of "Fare Thee Well My Dearest Dear" (*Amaranth*), she combined the folk instrument concertina with the early music virginal and electric guitar.

The small portative organ Shirley and Dolly Collins used for their concerts was another outcome of this close encounter between these two styles and musical scenes.

Constructed by the church organ builder Noel Mander, it was a modern, mechanically blown reproduction of a similar, hand-pumped instrument built in 1684 by the German craftsman Hase. Unusual because of its distinctly reedy sound, it also allowed more possibilities than a Victorian or Romantic piano accompaniment style, as it could produce sustained dronelike notes and chords. As Shirley recalled: "I think we heard the flute organ at one of the Musica Reservata rehearsals—and I fell in love with the soul of it. It had this breath around it as well. And we used to hire the thing and go around and do concerts in clubs with it." From a contemporary viewpoint it might be surprising that a portative organ could have been considered progressive, yet even if it was "acoustic" it was not so far away from the incorporation of the Hammond organ by progressive rock bands—and the sisters thereby created a special niche for themselves within the folk scene.

Guitarist John Renbourn also worked extensively with medieval and early Renaissance material, presenting it on his solo albums as well as with Pentangle alongside their arrangements of traditional and blues repertoire.[22] Although he was already a highly acclaimed guitarist in the early 1960s, Renbourn did not fully develop his style until he started to build up his medieval repertoire at the end of the decade. As a musician with a British-Irish folk repertoire, based on the so-called church modes, taking the steps to incorporate medieval material was almost natural for him: "I would think that any musician looking at 'Celtic' folk music could hardly fail to see connections with what has come down to us as medieval music. Also that the songs that have been seen as 'folk' songs often have direct antecedents in the popular songs of centuries ago."

In his musical attitude, however, Renbourn differs from many classically trained musicians. He shows a strong preference for dance tunes or songs with a strong rhythmic character. A favorite composer is Guillaume de Machaut (ca. 1300–77), whose harmonic work has particularly fascinated him. Renbourn considers the original source as first and foremost a musical matrix and thus only the starting point. Although he is careful to name the original sources in the accompanying liner notes and often prefers to go back to the original sources (as he did with the carol setting of "The Truth from Above" on *The Enchanted Garden*, instead of using Cecil Sharp's version), the accurate reconstruction of original sources is not the focal point. Instead his treatment of the music is similar to that of monophonically notated traditional music, as Renbourn explains: "'Nacht Tanz/Schaeffertanz' are from [Tielman] Susato and were already set in 4/5 parts. I used those parts but allowed for a looser format. In such instances I would keep the basic harmonization, divided the parts that have ornamentation/improv. in one or two of the parts. Not all, usually upper lines."

In many cases, as in Machaut's "Douce Dame Jolie" (*The Enchanted Garden*), the only original part that remains unchanged is the melody line (with polyphonic music, also the harmonic progression and/or the bass line), and, as evident with other arrangements, even that is sometimes only incorporated in parts. Keeping that voice, Renbourn then adds new counterlines or uses the melody line as the basis for improvisations. He sees this kind of polyphonic writing as a natural extension of his original guitar work:

> It's like a separate bass and a separate melody, which is a step away from the picking style, which is like an alternate bass. It's more like a single-line thing. This is particularly like the way Bert plays "Blackwaterside," for example. . . . I think I was anxious to keep the lines and perhaps restrict the guitar playing to, say, two lines and then maybe have recorders or another instrument playing a separate line. (Grossman 1990: 87)

Another example of Renbourn's approach is his treatment of "My Lady Carey's Dompe" (*The Nine Maidens*).[23] He has taken only the melody and the bass line from the original source. The melody line from the guitar provides the basis for several variations in which he has added the other voices. Another interesting piece that occupies the borderline between medieval and folk music is the "Circle Dance" (*The Nine Maidens*): The main part of the arrangement is based on the original tune, a fourteenth-century saltarello based on a 12/8 estampie, which is slowed down in the introduction. In the next part, while this melody is played at the original tempo, a countermelody played on sopranino recorder is added, a conflation of a thirteenth-century English tune "Stantipes" and the Irish jig "Pipe on the Hob." The effect of this mixture is intriguing to the ear, as the jig and the medieval material take turns in the foreground. This blurring of the differences between traditional and early music can also be heard in the slowed-down introduction, played on Northumbrian small pipes. Yet these notated arrangements allow less freedom than in Renbourn's traditional musical arrangements:

> None of them, in fact, allows for anything ever to go wrong. There's no room for improvisation in any of them, whereas a lot of the instrumentals I used to play were a bit of a constructed tune followed by more or less an improvisation, not freely improvised, but nevertheless with a lot of stock phrases that may or may be not used depending on how I felt. (Grossman 1990: 90)

Renbourn has used a large variety of instruments, including Northumbrian bagpipes and sitar. In the case of "My Lady Carey's Dompe," he also achieved new tone color effects with the use of an "acoustic guitar with overdubbed electric guitar in harmonics put through a harmonizer"[24] that were combined with recorders. Another sound effect was created by the use of Padstow drums (originally used for the May Day processions), which emphasized the dance character by accentuating the first beat of each measure. Many of Renbourn's pieces are accompanied by tablas as well. However, his instrumental choices are often made by chance:

> I am not too interested in the exotic for its own sake. A sitar will practically provide a modal middle line—like a big dulcimer. Tablas can reproduce rhythmic patterns with greater finesse than a kit drum. It's really a matter of texture and what works best for the

music. If the instrument is capable of providing the right notes and sits well in an ensemble (most will in a studio), then all are welcome.

Renbourn has been quick to use some of the stylistic idioms of early music in his own compositions. Various neobaroque impressions are further enhanced by his imitation of idiomatic tonal colors, produced, for instance, by a longer sustain of the guitar strings (as on "The Nine Maidens") or by retuning the guitar.

A more recent example of a similar musical synthesis is Maddy Prior's collaboration with the Carnival Band on *A Tapestry of Carols* (1987). The musicians again present a mixture of traditional (e.g., bagpipes) and early music (lute, baroque guitar, bassoon, recorder) instruments, complemented by Prior's relatively unornamented vocal style. The sound of this modern collaboration is quite different from earlier approaches. At the time that Shirley and Dolly Collins experimented with new sounds, early music groups such as the Early Music Consort seemed more interested in creating unusual sounds than in performance practice. The Carnival Band and other contemporary early music groups now seem to place a greater emphasis on musical expression than on the effect of unusual tonal colors, thus creating a fine, transparent sound. The recording with Prior is also unusual in that it focuses on carols, which occupy the borderline between traditional and early music material and have been neglected for a long time by both the folk revival as well as by electric folk musicians.

Further surprises may still lie ahead in this area of collaboration between electric folk and early music. In 1998 Richard Thompson and recorder player Phil Pickett joined forces for an album entitled *The Bones of All Men*. The highly acclaimed album demonstrates convincingly how to create a carefully balanced sound texture based on two completely different electric-acoustic instrumental groups. The period instruments around Pickett and Thompson's rock & roll line-up seem to merge effortlessly—not least due to Dave Mattack's colorful and understated drumming.

Electric Folk and Psychedelic/Progressive Rock

Macan (1997: chap. 2) saw the connection between electric folk and psychedelic/progressive rock primarily in the juxtaposition of acoustic and electric instruments and in a shared affinity for early music (as evident with Shirley and Dolly Collins and Pentangle on the electric folk front, and bands like Gryphon on the progressive front).[25] Yet the connection lies even deeper, because both genres, due to their parallel and partly interrelated development, had a similar base. Macan differentiated three branches of psychedelic music, which then formed the roots for subsequent progressive rock groups. These elements could also be found in electric folk music of that time.

The first branch, represented by the Cream, the Yardbirds, and Jimi Hendrix, was characterized by the heavy, electric reinterpretation of blues—with blues-based progressions, repetitive rhythm-section riffs of two to four measures, driving backbeat, open fifths, guitar feedback, and long instrumental sections. The classic pre-1965 lineup with one or two electric guitars, bass, drums, and voice remained predominant until the late 1960s. Electric folk likewise had an early strain that was related to the reinterpretation of blues with similar instrumental lineups, as evident with Fairport Convention.

Macan's second branch was strongly influenced by jazz sources, with virtuoso solos, complex chord changes and rhythmic patterns, and instruments such as saxophones, flutes, and, keyboard, as heard with the Soft Machine. Pentangle was a clear counterpart of this second strain, although the element of virtuosity was also represented by performers like Dave Swarbrick who were largely outside the jazz influence.

The third psychedelic direction, represented by groups like Pink Floyd and Procul Harum, worked with concept albums and large-scale structures. The phenomenon of concept and drama albums also existed within electric folk (e.g., *Babbacombe Lee* by Fairport Convention), yet in a different format and on a much smaller scale.

Although the general development of electric folk took a different path—so that Macan's categories are much more overlapping—both genres also resembled one another in overall stylistic devices, such as the preference for lengthy pieces. In the case of electric folk, this preference was partly due to the lengthy ballad texts and partly due to the extensive instrumentals. Like electric folk, progressive rock bands also experimented with fusing elements of rhythm and blues, jazz, classical, and Indian styles. Thus, many common features can be recognized, including ostinato patterns, drones, unusual meters, and the melodic doubling/unison playing of electric and bass guitar. These were evident in Fairport Convention's riff for "Tam Lin" and other instrumental combinations (Fairport was particularly influenced by progressive rock during its time at the underground UFO Club). In both electric folk and progressive rock, the melody or tune provides the principal structural framework, not the bass or harmonic progressions.

Other resemblances could also be observed on an instrumental level. The Hammond organ played a key role in progressive rock because it could be flexibly used to play sustained notes as well as virtuoso passages, often carrying the thematic material. Dolly Collins's portative organ fulfilled functions similar to those of its electric counterparts. As Macan's analysis also demonstrates, progressive musicians predominantly used the upper part of the drum set (snare, toms, cymbals, high hat) to create an intricate set of rhythmic patterns that contradicted the downbeat; they also used other tuned (timpani, chimes) and untuned (gongs, cowbells, wood blocks) percussion instruments. All of these elements were likewise evident with Pentangle. The inclusion of various instruments from outside contemporary rock music was also common with both genres: while progressive rock gave flute and violin a central role, this practice had clearly been preceded by the electric folk sound, with fiddle, melodeon, and early music instruments playing the same central role.[26]

Electric folk clearly differed from progressive rock in its material and its attitude toward the music, as well as in the overall sound. It made much less use of synthesizers and differed also in the vocal styles. While progressive rock was primarily limited to male voices, electric folk developed a much broader range, particularly with harmony singing, owing to the presence of female voices from high sopranos to low altos (like June Tabor).

Nevertheless, progressive rock had an impact on electric folk's fusion experiments, especially through the Incredible String Band. In the late 1960s and early '70s this group pioneered new musical directions and alternatives to the then-dominant rigid pop formulas, on both instrumental and structural levels. It developed a sound based on "exotic" instruments predominantly borrowed from Asian countries, combined with an overall gentle sound that lacked any hard percussive effects. This smooth impression was further enhanced by surrealistic speech experiments that put stresses on normally unaccentuated prepositions or conjunctions and resulted in irregular time lengths. Robin Williamson and Mike Heron also introduced to a large audience a variety of classical instruments unusual in folk performances at that time, such as harpsichord, organ, and harp, as well as instrumental combinations like vielle/guitar or organ/electric bass—combinations that were later adopted by the electric folk movement, most notably by Steeleye Span, but which were already paralleled in the experiments of Dolly Collins.

The Incredible String Band did not merely create an exotic sound for its own sake, but also mastered its instruments technically. A close hearing of *The 5000 Spirits or the Layers of the Onion* (1967) reveals the group's extreme security when mixing blues idioms with Indian elements on "No Sleep Blues" or singing in Indian style as on "Painting Box." The band rarely used repetitive forms or strict verse-refrain schemes; instead, additive or asymmetrical forms were predominant on their recordings. Not afraid of dissonances, parallel chord progressions, or unusual rhythmic elements (as the highly syncopated accompaniment of "Little Cloud" demonstrates), the Incredible String Band thus became a significant musical influence for many rock groups, including the Rolling Stones.

It is, of course, occasionally difficult to determine who has influenced whom. Progressive rock and electric folk emerged within the same general time span, and electric folk adopted many elements from the English tradition, such as the drone, that could have come from progressive music as well. This is also the case for the use of church modes, which replaced the tonic-subdominant-dominant blues progressions and gave both genres greater tonal flexibility.

OUTLOOK: CURRENT TENDENCIES

The question of electric versus acoustic appears not to be a problem for many of the still-active electric folk performers who have always played both. Yet it seems to me that these boundaries have also been further blurred on recent recordings, hence emphasizing that "electric" and "acoustic" indeed cannot be used as musical quality crite-ria. For example, Fairport Convention played many electric favorites, such as "Matty Groves" or "Crazy Man Michael," with such an energetic freshness and groove on their acoustic CD *Old–New–Borrowed–Blue* (1996) that it could compete with any dance-oriented rock performance. Likewise, although one would still categorize the record-ings of Jacqui McShee's Pentangle as electric (with keyboards and percussion), the in-struments are nevertheless played in such a restrained manner that they almost seem acoustic.

Most recent recordings have been, partly due to more careful production, distin-guished by higher technical and musical quality than in the late 1960s and '70s, while they also seem to echo the musical experiences made in that era. A good example is *common tongue* (1997) by Waterson: Carthy, who use understated but expressive musi-cal means that are further enhanced by the combination of voice, fiddle, and guitar (pioneered by Carthy and Swarbrick), plus dulcimer on "Lowlands of Holland" (pre-viously heard on Fairport Convention's "Flowers of the Forest"), creating a percussive, metallic sound that was earlier evident with both the "folk baroque" direction and Pen-tangle. It is nevertheless an acoustic folk album that stresses Englishness through the use of distinctive tonal colors; vocal styles (Norma Waterson's voice is strong, yet she sings with the characteristic high-air portion and with very few ornaments); the choice of material found in England; and English musicians.

Unusual instrumental combinations have remained characteristic of many modern electric and folk recordings; for example, on her solo album *Year* (1993), Maddy Prior is accompanied by brass on the track "Supper." The bands and soloists continue to reinterpret old favorites. Prior recorded a new version of Steeleye's classic "Twa Cor-bies" with organ accompaniment on *Year*; another recent version can be found on Steeleye's *Time*. On the latter recording, fronted by founding member Gay Woods, the use of audio signal processing effects has become greater, although the emphasis is still on the vocals. With "Cutty Wren," the band follows Clannad in its use of lush har-monic effects (created with a greater use of reverb), although—and this seems to be characteristic of the English bands—the rhythmic peculiarities are much more strongly accentuated, which makes the pieces edgier than the Celtic songs.

Although one will still find rock-oriented pieces with a strong rhythm section, the handling of the metric side has become more varied and sophisticated. A group illus-trating this trend is Brass Monkey, formed by Martin Carthy and John Kirkpatrick in the first half of the 1980s and revived in the late 1990s. Although the band had a per-cussion section, Brass Monkey replaced the usual combination of electric guitar and bass with trumpet and trombone, thus gaining a fresh sound and considerable arrang-ing flexibility. The brass instruments also provided a historical connection to the brass bands of the English tradition. Another special feature of this group has been the un-usual instrumental combination of guitar, concertina/melodeon, saxophone, trom-bone, and percussion.[27] The trombone often has a drone function, as on "Waterman's

Hornpipe," while the guitar is used primarily as a rhythm instrument, as on the group's version of "Sovay." Yet Brass Monkey did not abandon the rock element completely. Contemporary folk-rock songs such as Richard Thompson's "Bad News" are part of its repertoire, as well as traditional ballads. The group has also adopted additive instrumentation and rock improvisational techniques, such as the trumpet's playing rhythmic figures on one note in "Jolly Bold Robber."

In summary, groups such as Brass Monkey, the most recent incarnations of Steeleye Span, and Waterson:Carthy demonstrate that the musical development that has continued since the early days of electric folk and progressive rock is not over. More surprises are likely for the future.[28]

PART III

THE TRANSFORMATION AND ADAPTATION PROCESS

SEVEN

MUSICAL GHOSTS THAT BECOME MEANS TO A NEW IDENTITY

I think most countries have a cycle that when they have a big change like a revolution or an opening up to outside influence, everybody immediately rushes for rock 'n' roll and then, after a certain period of time, people look back over their shoulders and they start to miss their own culture. Then they go back to rediscover it. And you'll get a revival of interest in the pure tradition. And the problem comes that you start to have most of the musicians playing traditional music [who] are no longer from the countryside, they are educated people from the city. This changes the music and makes it more self-aware and not as free and not as powerful. There is the big danger that by the time a country realizes what they're missing, all the best ones have died. And people are learning from records and learning from other sources.   JOE BOYD

Joe Boyd's description sums up the situation of present revival generations, which have often grown up without an initial connection to the tradition. Generally speaking, the modern revival of a traditional music appears to be accompanied by a shift in the sociocultural network of which the original music had been a part. This pattern could be observed in the postwar American folk revival, during which rural music cultures such as the Appalachian ballad repertoire were adapted by an urban, university-based subculture with a different performance practice, behavior, and social codes. In England, as discussed in chapter 4, the location of the folk revival shifted from an oral, intimate performance situation to large festival stages with a comparatively distanced and passive performer-audience relationship.

Depending on the cultural presence of a traditional music in a society prior to a revival, there is a more or less clear gap between the traditional and the revival cultures. Consequently, the traditional and the revival cultures often represent two completely different sociomusical environments with little direct interchange. This seems to have especially been the case in England, where the gap was—in contrast with neighboring Scotland and Ireland—extremely large. How, then, did the English revival generations of the 1950s and 1960s rediscover the tradition, and to what degree did the performers adapt it for themselves as a means of cultural identity? This chapter will explore some of these pathways of change to examine how these transformations came about. At the same time, it will demonstrate how traditional music can regain a new importance from these processes.

THE INITIAL RELATIONSHIP TO THE TRADITION AND REDISCOVERY

A close look at individual biographies reveals that only few electric folk performers had an initial connection to the tradition. Singers like Shirley Collins, who came from a family that was still fostering the traditional repertoire, or Ian Telfer, who grew up in Aberdeen where traditional music was a "very ordinary part of things," clearly represent a minority in the folk and electric folk scenes. The majority of performers did not grow up with what would later become the basis of their musical identity.

Alienation from the Tradition

The prior break with the tradition can be observed in the generation of these musicians' parents. By 1950, English traditional music had slipped to a large extent from public notice, being not only reduced to the more private realms of individual performers but also disappearing within the spheres of traditional communities. Of course, the decline had started long before the war: the emigration to the cities during the Industrial Revolution, the introduction of the church organ that took away the livelihood of many local English bands (which had earned their main income from playing for church services), and the gradual replacement of oral forms of transmission by modern media are only some of the multiple reasons for this development. Since the 1920s, however, one major factor seems to have been that British people increasingly felt that traditional music, like unfashionable old clothing, was an obstacle to their access to a modern life of progress embodied by elements of American culture, especially music (Boyes 1993). This aspect became even stronger after World War II. As discussed in chapter 2, for traditional performers the old ballads and dance tunes have always been one form of music among many, yet they now started to lose their initial predominant position to American-oriented popular music. Hence, even if parents and grandparents had once been close to traditional music, they passed it on only in fragments, like Martin Carthy's mother, who had been involved on the fringes of the First Revival. As a result, the next generation did not have a repertoire to draw on.

The disappearance of this repertoire was sometimes also the outcome of a conscious break with the tradition, which was the case with several performers who came from families that had emigrated from Ireland to Britain in the previous century. Although certain immigrant communities strongly cultivated Irish traditional music, as in Camden Town during the 1950s, for most of this population, survival in British so-

ciety depended upon assimilation. Having arrived in England as illiterate, cheap workers since the nineteenth century, the Irish were often met with antipathy, although
today they are viewed as the strongest assimilated subculture (Händel and Gossel
1994). Thus, by trying to integrate into British society, this immigrant generation consciously attempted to conceal their cultural background from outsiders as well as from
their children. Martin Carthy's family dropped the "Mac" to become anglicized, and
his father would not confess until much later, when Martin was already established as
a folk musician, that he had played the fiddle in his youth and was familiar with some
of the Irish repertoire played by revival performers. Despite his Irish roots, Carthy can
therefore be considered an English musician, since he grew up in an emphatically English cultural environment.

Thus estranged from their parents' heritage, the young revival generation would
also naturally reject, partly unconsciously, traditional musical and other devices as
anachronisms that did not fit the times and places they were growing up in. Maddy
Prior, for instance, recalled that she realized only a few years ago that she had been
raised in a tradition of the northeast ("Geordie country"). But growing up in Blackpool on the west coast, she viewed it as detached from her own life, being only "one of
Dad's idiosyncrasies."

The rejection of folk music also seems to have been an outcome of the way the performers had been exposed to the tradition at school. Several decades previously, Cecil
Sharp had emphasized the value of English folk songs "as an education force. They are,
moreover, attractive to children, easy to comprehend and easily learned by them. The
songs must, of course, be chosen with discrimination; the compass of the tunes must
be within the range of young voices, and the words adapted to the understanding of
immature minds" (Sharp 1907: 134).

Besides their pedagogic efficiency, Sharp also saw the introduction of folk songs
into school curriculums as a means to "stimulate the growth of the feeling of patriotism" (ibid.), and folk songs indeed became part of music lessons at that time. Because
folk songs remained in school curriculums long after the English Folk Dance and
Song Society (EFDSS) had lost its widest influence, most of folk and electric folk
musicians experienced some early contact with traditional music. Yet the effect was
rather often the opposite of Sharp's intentions, mainly due to the way in which the
music was taught. Many songs were presented in an extremely edited, almost artificial
form, together with the material that was contained in the *National Songbook* (originally published in 1906 by Charles Villiers Stanford), such as "The Land of Hope and
Glory" or "Rule Britannia." Accordingly, Maddy Prior would describe the major portion of the songs she learned as a child as being "allowable English traditional songs
which we were taught by these old maiden ladies at school," a comment reflecting an
image folk music has retained until the present day for many people I met in England.
As Jacqui McShee remembered, the songs were stripped of the historical background
that would allow a connection back to the original tradition:

It was almost as though the songs were diluted at school, they were very diluted—and you wouldn't be taught about the history of them, or where they came from. It would be just an exercise for you to learn a song, write it down in your music books, the notes, but—that would be it! They wouldn't say to you "This is an English song from Somerset, there are several different versions." They are the basic songs. Even my daughter, even now, she might come home and say, "We had to learn that really stupid song today," and I would say, "Oh, I can remember learning that at school!" So you come out of school having quite a bad idea of what is in this country. In those days, it wouldn't make you go and find out more. But hearing people sing them in folk clubs, where they had obviously researched the songs and adapted them to their own playing, guitar playing or banjo playing, they just seemed very different.

The Impact of American Music

School and family background apparently only played a minor role compared to the influence of the popular music sphere at that time. The future folk and electric folk musicians, born in the late 1940s or early 1950s, grew up within the supercultural soundscape of a predominantly American-based popular culture. As could be inferred from my interviews, American popular music was almost automatically embraced, and consequently many British performers also became part of American-related subcultures.

American music—as well as films and plays—had become popular before and during World War II, increasingly replacing British popular music forms, as Boyes pointed out in her trenchant study *The Imagined Village*: "Dynamic, innovative, slick and irreverent, American presentations contrasted sharply with the inconsequential drawing-room comedies, sweetly-pretty musicals and remnants of music hall filling the generality of English stages" (1993: 204). This trend would also affect the tradition, as new American dances like the fox trot and the Charleston or the Latin American samba replaced the old jigs and reels. In consequence, local dance bands playing the old repertoire became increasingly dispensable (Bartram 1996). The presence of American music increased further after World War II, when, via radio programs broadcast for the American troops, the British audience heard not only blues and jazz but also American folk music by Woody Guthrie and Pete Seeger.

Postwar Anglo-American popular music before the advent of rock 'n' roll was, generally speaking, an extremely artificial product. The majority of singers on both sides of the Atlantic relied on professional songwriters for material (in Britain either as cover versions of American songs or from the songwriters at Denmark Street) and titles such as "I Taught I Taw a Puddy Tat" were dominating British hit parades at that time. The situation changed with the appearance of skiffle and rock 'n' roll, which offered the emerging American-oriented youth culture its first alternatives to the lightweight material from the pop industry. Martin Carthy's early musical preferences were characteristic of those of many contemporaries:

The first three [records] I bought were the *Rock Island Line* by Lonnie Donegan, *Rock around the Clock* by Bill Haley, and *Heartbreak Hotel* by Elvis Presley. And that seems just to cover all of the popular music that was around at the time—the interesting popular music, but all the other music around at the time seemed to be "I'm a pink toothbrush, you're a blue toothbrush, won't you marry me someday?" I mean, that was the general level—or "How Much Is That Doggy in the Window?" That was the general thrust.

Carthy, like countless other future English folk and rock performers, had joined a skiffle band in the 1950s when musical instruments became affordable.[1] With skiffle, an Anglicized version of the original hybrid of African American blues, Anglo-American folk, and traditional jazz, many of these young musicians were exposed for the first time to traditional folk song material like "Jack O'Diamonds" or "This Train" from the repertoire of Lonnie Donegan. By tracing back to the original sources, they not only discovered singers like Leadbelly and Woody Guthrie but also began to build an initial traditional repertoire that was a mixture of white and black American music. Most of the performers, however, were at that time still unaware that part of this repertoire had originally been of British-Irish origin.

With the emergence of folk clubs, the perception of the tradition began to shift. Like several other performers, Carthy first came into contact with traditional English material by chance after the skiffle craze faded in 1958. The folk clubs provided the same kind of intimate atmosphere as the then-popular coffee bars and jazz clubs, and they offered former skiffle musicians opportunities to play and to learn new material. The clubs remained a popular alternative sphere well into the 1960s, when folk music would connect with the beatnik culture and later with the protest movements whose members would constitute part of the club audience. Jacqui McShee, for instance, discovered the folk clubs by chance while participating in a CND demonstration.

Despite the presence of a few folk performers with a British repertoire like Louis Killen, Shirley Collins, and the Campbells, the early English folk club scene was still dominated by an American repertoire, clearly continuing to reflect developments in popular music. This was even true of Ewan MacColl and his first folk club in 1953, the Ballads and Blues Club. Similarly, folk enthusiasts were more familiar with Carolyn Hester's singing of "She Moves through the Fair" than, for instance, with Margaret Barry's rendition. As Shirley Collins recalled, British musicians often adopted an American singing style at that time, imitating the hard, almost metallic sound that resulted from a predominant use of head voice and tight vocal cords. A review of the early 1960s issues of the major British popular music magazine, *Melody Maker*, reveals largely American-focused coverage, with American music being also regarded as a "trendsetter." A British band's success was often equated with their success in the States—even after the "British invasion," headed by the Beatles and the Rolling Stones, gave the British popular music scene a new self-confidence in 1964–65.

Rediscovery of the English Tradition

By the mid-1960s, British-Irish folk music had come to dominate England's folk clubs—so strongly that musicians even started to complain about the narrow-mindedness of the scene. And in the late 1960s the genre called electric folk or British folk rock began to raise a considerable amount of public attention, peaking with Steel-eye Span's commercial success with the English folk song "All around My Hat" in the mid-1970s.

How could the situation have changed so completely? American ethnomusicologist Mark Slobin (1993: 9) pointed out that, despite or because of the growth of mass media and the dominant Western popular music, musical subcultures (micromusics) are by no means disappearing. With a growing supercultural network, the feeling of loss of cultural identity seems to increase, producing a pressure to create a new (musical) identity. While members of an immigrant culture like the United States apparently tend to cling to their roots, the original cultures start to search for or reinvent their lost roots as a reaction against the growing dominance of the Americanized mainstream. Indeed, one of the major motivations for Ewan MacColl and A. L. Lloyd to start the British Second Folk Revival, apart from their political goals, had been to rediscover and reinvigorate Britain's cultural individuality. As Lloyd pointed out years later in Alun Howkins's television documentary *The Other Music* (1981), the British revival was set in motion by a contradictory situation: it was, on one hand, a defensive reaction against the domination of American culture, yet, on the other hand, it was also inspired by American models.

It was occasionally the visiting American performers themselves who put English musicians in contact with their own tradition again, as the Americans found it puzzling that the British had merely been imitating American music and singing styles instead of building on their own rich musical heritage. Maddy Prior, for instance, who had started to sing in the folk clubs in the mid-1960s, first developed a repertoire consisting mainly of songs performed by Bob Dylan, Joan Baez, and Peter, Paul, and Mary—material she regarded as folk music. At the time, she was also working as a chauffeur and guide for visiting American entertainers like the folk duo Sandy and Jeanie Darlington. When she performed some of her American songs for them, their reaction was rather devastating:

> They said, "For goodness' sake, stop singing that American stuff, it sounds awful!" They
> said, "Sing English!" And I said, "I don't know any!" But this couple had a lot of tapes, most
> of which they'd pirated from the EFDSS. And [they] also got quite a lot of material from
> Ewan [MacColl] . . . They'd go to his house, and he was quite happy to let anybody tape
> his material. So they played these tapes to me and I thought, "My word! They sound very
> *old*, these people!" And they were like, I've always described them as ghosts of voices. So
> they were very old voices, and there was also a particular style which I didn't recognize and
> wasn't familiar with. So I listened to these tapes, they were mixtures of field recordings

done by Lomax and Kennedy and people like that—and basically learnt the tradition from that.

Due to this generation's initial almost complete alienation from the tradition, the process of learning and absorbing it was by no means easy, as Carthy confirmed:

> It's a mistake to believe that because a person is English they have any understanding of English music. Because what we've been involved in over the last thirty, well in my case thirty-seven years, is a revival in English music, which means just what it says: that it was to all intents and purposes, certainly to city people, that it was lost. So to the uninitiated ear, which means most English people, all the tunes sound the same. When I first heard Irish fiddle music I thought all the tunes sounded the same. And then I got into it, and I realized that that wasn't all the same. It dawned on me later on that—English folk music—that's foreign to me as well!

The rediscovery of the old ballads and dance music was an encounter with a style that was felt to be strange and exotic. Having been a choir singer during his school days (which required extremely accurate singing), Carthy remembered his first encounter with the singer and bagpipe player Seamus Ennis as *the* decisive turning point that led him to play this material: "I went down to a place called the Troubadour in Earl's Court, and I walked in the door and I saw Seamus Ennis, and that was an incredibly important moment because the man was just astonishing! According to the rules as I knew them, he sang all wrong and he played all wrong, but the effect of it was just completely mesmerizing."

In these early stages of the revival the majority of the traditional models were of Scottish or—like Seamus Ennis—of Irish origin. Anne Briggs, although a native of Nottingham, discovered traditional music via Scottish singer and actress Isla Cameron:

> When I was about fifteen I heard a record of Isla Cameron's. . . . I'd heard various bits and pieces on the radio . . . and there was a certain type of song that I always was instantly drawn to. I had no idea what that type of music was called. Then I saw this record by this woman called Isla Cameron and I noticed that one of the songs she was singing on this record was one that I'd heard on the radio. I read the notes on the back of the sleeve and it was described as "folk music." I thought, "Ah, that's the sort of music that I really like." So I bought the record and played it. I started singing along with the songs that she'd recorded. (Hunt 1989: 9)

It was these Scottish and Irish musicians—and not English performers like the Coppers or Phil Tanner—who conveyed, often via the radio or recordings, the next generation's first impressions of traditional music. This reveals another problem of English folk song: in terms of style, English music not only had very much blended with other traditions but also seemed in its outer appearance less distinctive and accessible than the music of its Gaelic neighbors. When trying to transform the "musical ghosts" into something real, the aspiring performers needed recognizable elements and thus first picked out components from the Irish/Scottish music—and not from the more breathy English singing styles. The rediscovery of the actual English tradition, including Northumbrian bagpiping or southern English fiddling, as well as ritual elements and authentic source material, would come only at a later stage, when a revival performance style was already established.

These two steps—first, the imitation and adaptation of the dominant superculture to create a musical identity synonymous with the idea of a modern, future-oriented existence, and second, the counterreaction by using distinct elements from the native culture to create a new identity within the superculture—could be observed in the development of electric folk. Fairport Convention's recording, *Liege & Lief*, which was made with the clear intention of creating something genuinely English, was partly meant as a counterpart to *Music from Big Pink* by the American group The Band. While The Band effortlessly juggled characteristic American idioms of blues, gospel, and the sounds of harmonica and banjo, Fairport started to dig out the Child ballads, combining them with the sound of fiddle or imitated bagpipe drones. This new consciousness of the vernacular became particularly evident in the name of Ashley Hutchings's core group, the Albion (Country) Band, which has focused on playing predominantly English music like morris dances. Yet by working from the base of rock music's language, both bands are still connected to the original American models against which they created their musical identity.

THE INFLUENCE OF INDIVIDUALS: EWAN MACCOLL AND ALBERT LANCASTER LLOYD

As Anne Briggs's memories of her first Isla Cameron record suggest, many performers of the 1960s had to fall back upon indirect sources of transmission, such as recordings or written collections, along with learning material in the folk clubs. The gap between this generation and the original tradition was further widened by the fact that the Second Revival was not a completely natural development, but rather clearly planned; with most of the original music forgotten, outside forces were necessary to get the revival process going. Thus, before proceeding with a discussion of how these musicians dealt with the material and developed a new relationship with the tradition, it is necessary to understand how these partly underestimated outside influences worked and how they changed the perception of the tradition.

Two individuals, Ewan MacColl and A. L. Lloyd, contributed much to the rediscovery of the tradition, and they transformed it in the process. Both extensively used the mass media to raise public awareness; MacColl produced a landmark radio series, *Radio Ballads*, and Lloyd issued recordings such as *The Iron Muse* and *The Bird in the*

Bush on the Topic label. Both also had a strong direct influence on the revival performers, which is still evident in current repertoire, attitudes, and behavior, even though they chose two contrasting approaches.

Ewan MacColl

Though he was an active collector[2] and performer, MacColl is most remembered today as an organizer and a dogmatic authority figure in the clubs. He exerted his strong influence not only through his club but also by teaching or running ensembles like the Critics Group—a number of musicians who met frequently to study and discuss vocal techniques and theatrical styles, as well as to give individual performances. As the founder of one of the first folk clubs and later the organizer of one of the main performance venues, the Singers' Club, MacColl was responsible for setting up the rules that became so characteristic of the whole folk club scene.

After playing much American and skiffle music in the early stages of the revival, MacColl began to change the politics of his club radically in the late 1950s. Observing the performers, he realized that his efforts were heading in the wrong direction. He recalled in his autobiography that

> As the months went by, we found that we tired of singing songs in a language we didn't speak fluently or, sometimes, didn't understand at all. . . . We felt no real sense of identity with them. . . . Furthermore, Peggy found it difficult to keep a straight face when she heard Cockneys and Liverpudlians singing Leadbelly and Guthrie songs. (MacColl 1990: 288)

Hence, as he explained in an interview, the resident singers of the Ballad and Blues Club decided on the policy "that you sang the songs of the language you spoke or the language that you'd grown up with . . . we felt, rightly or wrongly, that it was necessary for us to develop a national identity" (Woods 1973b: 4). MacColl was clearly aware of the unpopularity of his decision, which reduced the audience to a minimum for weeks. Yet his idea seemed to prove right, as many clubs started to take up that rule—with the result that by the early 1970s not only was English-Irish material predominant in the clubs, but the characteristic performance practice adhered to MacColl's conception of an "authentic" unaccompanied style.

It is difficult, however, to determine retrospectively why the clubs became so narrow-minded about this performance practice, which did not leave much room for innovation and eventually led to a musical dead end. Many observers blame MacColl—and he indeed alienated performers not only by setting up the rules but also by being extremely dogmatic about them. Stories and comments I heard in my interviews suggest that he must have been a very difficult person. Several performers evidently fell out with him, as Frankie Armstrong, a long-time member of the Critics Group, recalled:

He did polarize people in a way that Bert [Lloyd] didn't. I think this was partly to do with his politics; Bert was a much more complex political thinker than Ewan. Ewan tended to be much more dogmatic about everything. There was a period when he tried to insist that people should only sing songs from their own region—he put many people's backs up because it was very rigid, very judgmental and prescriptive. There were those who would hold him in great respect and would still be influenced by him but find his dogmatism off-putting.

MacColl's own background contradicted the rules he advocated. Both of his parents had sung at home, yet he developed a completely different performance style that seemed to ignore his own background. Nevertheless, it should not be forgotten that MacColl had a sharp mind and vast knowledge, and he encouraged performers to research their music. Both Ashley Hutchings and Ian Telfer made extensive use of his vast library. Furthermore, as Martin Carthy pointed out, MacColl's dogma was not wholly restrictive; it also played an influential role in the rediscovery of truly English music and, therefore, in the development of electric folk:

> He was always vilified because he insisted that at his club English people sang English songs, Scottish people sang Scottish songs, Irish people sang Irish songs. Well, if it hadn't been for him, then people like me would not have gone looking for English songs. I didn't go to his club, but I was suddenly presented with this notion that if someone could stand up and sing English songs in his folk club, then there must be English songs to find! So I went looking for them.

Moreover, the problem of the often-mentioned narrow-mindedness within the scene was evidently not MacColl's fault alone but also a result of a general emerging dogmatism within the clubs, often in imitation of MacColl. The aspects so carefully crafted as recommendations—not as rules—in the introduction to the MacColl/ Seeger book *The Singing Island* were adopted in many clubs as the only possible "authentic" way to play the music, which made innovative approaches more difficult. Electric folk groups later encountered resistance partly because the MacColl ideals rejected electric instruments. Although, as discussed in chapter 4, some groups had played traditional music on electric instruments in the early 1960s, electric music was generally seen in the folk clubs as inauthentic and unnatural (Thompson 1977). The realization that the MacColl-based performance practices were not truly time-honored at all came quite late: Several of the instruments that were recommended as traditional had not been played until the nineteenth century, such as the accordion. And although an unaccompanied singing style had indeed been a general characteristic of the British vocal tradition, many traditional performers preferred to accompany themselves on whatever instrument was available. Belle Stewart's rendition of "She Moves through the Fair," as recorded by Peter Kennedy, was accompanied by a melodeon,[3] while Margaret Barry often accompanied herself on the banjo.

By that point, however, the clubs had already created their own tradition, including certain behaviors such as the "finger in the ear style"—originally a way a singer would correct the intonation by holding a hand behind one ear to hear himself or herself better. Much favored by MacColl, the gesture itself became a central part of his performance style. Adopted by many performers in the clubs, it became an often negative symbol of the almost ritualized behavior patterns of the scene. Looking back now, thirty years in retrospect, it seems obvious that these ideals would lead to a musical blind alley, spurring many innovative musicians out of the clubs and in many cases into part of what is now known as electric folk. Tim Hart's criticisms were characteristic of the attitude of several future electric folk performers who did not want to conform to the clubs' rules:

> I didn't like the folk clubs, I felt they were too introspective and too amateur and I didn't think they did the music any favours at all. It was a very eclectic little thing, folk music went on in upstairs rooms in pubs, and you had to sit very quietly through it. If you weren't the right sort of person, if you didn't fit, you couldn't listen to folk music—it was totally bloody silly. (Tobler 1991: 30)

Further musical development became almost impossible within the clubs, and performers later started to copy folk "stars" like Martin Carthy or June Tabor instead of creating individual new styles. Nevertheless, the majority of acoustic musicians remained dependent on the clubs as the principal performance venues. Likewise, leaving the folk club scene did not always mean that the performers could automatically leave its dogmas behind. Maddy Prior, for instance, recalled that she fought for a long time internally with the "little judgmental voice" that gave her the subliminal feeling of violating the unwritten rules of the scene. This "voice" remained with her until Steeleye Span made its first tour to the States.

A. L. Lloyd

Like MacColl, Lloyd made a lasting impact on the folk scene on multiple levels. Appointed artistic director of Topic Records around 1957, he not only conducted landmark recording projects such as *The Bird in the Bush* (1966) but was also in charge of selecting musicians who would take part in these productions. Many of these musicians, like Ray Fisher, Louis Killen, and Frankie Armstrong, would become well known this way, even outside the clubs. Lloyd's influence was especially apparent with Anne Briggs, whom MacColl had discovered when the Centre 42 project came to Nottingham. Through Lloyd she not only took part in several key recordings such as *The Bird in the Bush* and *The Iron Muse*, but also acquired the major portion of her early traditional repertoire. On her EP (extended-play) recording, *Hazards of Love*, for instance, almost all the songs came from Lloyd, who also wrote the introduction for the album.

Although usually described as a very private person, Lloyd long maintained a strong, partly provocative presence in the scene. His influence worked much more subtly than MacColl's, as Carthy remembered: "He did everything; he annoyed, he upset, he did things that you'd think, 'no that's wrong, you can't do that.' Then you'd find that you'd subconsciously investigated it and it had stuck right deep in" (Anderson and Holland 1985: 11). Lloyd is cited by several sources as having sustained a deep interest in all that was happening in the folk and electric folk scenes—for instance, calling or writing to the musicians when he liked an interpretation, or giving them additional verses, as in the cases of both Carthy and Armstrong. Because Lloyd knew that Armstrong had poor eyesight, he sang verses to her on the telephone.

Lloyd's strong—and generally positively judged—position in the scene also is reflected in the fact that at one point there had even been talk about his joining Fairport Convention. Much in contrast with MacColl, Lloyd was always respected for his openness to innovation. Ample proof of this can be found in his writings. For example, he and coeditor Vaughan Williams remarked in the *Penguin Book of English Folk Songs* that "The ideal way to sing an English folk song, of course, is unaccompanied. . . . However, for those to whom the unaccompanied voice seems naked, there is no harm in adding a few supporting chords on the pianoforte, guitar, or other instrument" (Vaughan Williams and Lloyd 1959: 9).

Carthy emphasized that Lloyd's open-mindedness regarding the question of instrumental accompaniment should not be confused with indifference toward this issue: "For him, if you'd sing unaccompanied the narrative thing was all, but if you were trying to accompany the thing, then something else was being made. So you ought to treat it on its own terms. Sing the song, give the song its respect and its niche, its place, and then if you want to play something to it, then just get down to it."

At a time when the traditional material and awareness of it was almost gone, Lloyd put a host of forgotten songs back into circulation—pieces that are nowadays taken for granted, such as the Scottish ballad "Tam Lin" (Child ballad no. 39). According to Carthy, Fairport Convention would not have recorded the ballad for *Liege & Lief* "had it not been for Bert. Nobody would have, the song was considered too big. After that you could sing a song of that length." Lloyd's influence often worked indirectly via individual performers with whom he worked: many of Anne Briggs's songs and versions such as "Reynardine," "Willie o' Winsbury," and "Blackwaterside" were taken up by other performers.

The development of this new line of transmission is especially apparent with Carthy and Dave Swarbrick. Early in their careers, both separately accompanied Lloyd on various recordings; Swarbrick, for instance, played the fiddle on pieces like "The Two Magicians" and "The Bonny Black Hare" for *The Bird in the Bush*. Later he and Carthy would use exactly this material and Lloyd's versions—also of songs like "Sovay" and "Byker Hill"—for their own highly influential series of recordings made between 1965 and 1970. They were careful to credit Lloyd in the liner notes. Both later brought several of these songs into the repertoire of the electric groups, after Swarbrick joined Fairport Convention in 1969 and Carthy became a Steeleye Span member in 1970. "The Bonny Black Hare," for instance, was recorded by Fairport in the same basic version as Swarbrick had acquired from Lloyd and played with Carthy.

Lloyd did not pass on these songs unaltered, however, but deliberately changed much of the material with the clear intention of making it more interesting for the performers of the Second Revival. As he remarked with gentle irony in the notes accompanying the recording of the ballad "The Two Magicians," "Eventually the ballad dwindled away, but it seemed too good a song to remain unused, so I brushed it up and fitted a tune and now it appears to have started a new life. Dr. Vaughan Williams once said: 'The practice of re-writing a folk song is abominable, and I wouldn't trust anyone to do it except myself.'" Performed by Carthy on his *Second Album* (1966), the piece became a standard in the folk clubs.

Lloyd's alterations—both textual and musical—were manifold. A performer himself, Lloyd naturally adapted the texts to his own speaking style, changing words that seemed to better suit his narrative. These changes are often hard to retrace, as Lloyd often did not reveal the sources of his songs. In the case of "Tam Lin," one can compare the various versions in Child's collection and find variants A (source: Robert Burns) and B (Glenriddell's MSS) similar to Lloyd's, but it is difficult to go any further.

It is similarly complicated to pinpoint the musical changes, although it is at least possible to isolate some general characteristics of the alterations, as with "Sovay" (also "Sylvie" or "The Female Highwayman"). This song about a woman who robs her beloved to prove his faithfulness was already popular when it was collected by Sharp and contemporaries. It later became a favorite of revival and electric folk performers like Martin Carthy and Pentangle in the version that Lloyd had been using.

Listening to Lloyd's version, it is evident that the song contains many rhythmic changes—which is in itself nothing extraordinary. Many British traditional songs are in 5/4 meter or are delivered in a rhythmically irregular parlando style, and likewise many variants of "Sovay" with rhythmic changes do exist. Yet Lloyd writes in his accompanying liner notes that "in a couple of places I've added a pinch of spice to the rhythm which seems to me to suit the character of both the song and its heroine." Carthy, who researched further back, gives some clearer indications in his note: "The tune was collected by Hammond in Dorset and slightly altered rhythmically by Bert Lloyd, giving it a somewhat Balkan lift."[4] Lloyd was quite interested in the traditional musics of southeastern Europe, where he also did extensive fieldwork,[5] and in the works of Constantin Brăiloiu ("Le rythme aksak," *Revue de Musicologie*, 1952). Carthy's remarks signify more precisely that Lloyd took the second Hammond version of "Sovay" ("Shilo"),[6] which itself is rather unusual due to the subsequent rhythmic stresses on 2 + 3 within the ternary metric structure (see fig. 7.1). Lloyd subsequently changed a part of the first two lines to a typical aksak rhythm,[7] here a 7/4 meter that combines binary and ternary units (the subdivision in this case is 2 + 3 + 2). "Byker Hill," another example, was a song Lloyd adapted from the Tyneside song "Me Ginny

H.E.D. Hammond: "Shiloh" (*Journal of the English Folk Song Society*, No. 11, second part of Vol. 3 (1907), 127

A.L. Lloyd: "Sovay" (*First Person*, Topic 1966)

FIGURE 7.1. The adaptation of "Sovay" by A. L. Lloyd

Sits Ower Late Up," turning it into a strictly isometric sequence of 2 + 2 + 2 + 3—a rhythmic pattern that is not common in Britain. Although these changes were rather subtle, they should not be overlooked, given that it was his versions that became prevalent in the revival and electric folk scenes. It is almost impossible, however, to estimate how much has been changed by Lloyd—probably a much larger portion than has been assumed.[8]

In addition to Lloyd, several English revival and electric folk musicians developed a particular liking for southeastern European music. The fascination for this music was not solely restricted to its rhythmic intricacies. Sandy Denny, for instance, emphasized in an interview with Dallas (1972d) that her arrangement of Richard Fariña's "The Quiet Joys of Brotherhood" had been strongly influenced "by some of those Eastern European groups like the Bulgarian State Ensemble. Not that I've tried to sound like them, but I've tried to capture some of the starkness of the singing in those groups." She achieved this effect by adding the characteristically "biting" sound of second dissonances, for which "Silly Sisters" June Tabor and Maddy Prior also showed a special fondness.[9] It seems that these performers wanted to give their songs a sharper, "archaic" edge by incorporating Balkan rhythms and dissonances as well as medieval parallel fourths and fifths—an aspect they apparently missed in their own traditional music (despite the harmony singing of traditional groups like the Coppers). This might also explain the appeal of Lloyd's arrangements.

MacColl's and Lloyd's status as musicians within the scene varied. Although many objected to MacColl's performance style, he was highly respected as a songwriter. In contrast, Lloyd was widely admired as a performer. Even though his voice was not as strong as MacColl's, interviewees always emphasized that he could "communicate a song," conveying the narratives in a way that approached the storytelling power of the best traditional singers. Furthermore, because of his broad range of scholarly publications, Lloyd—who in his later years also taught as an ethnomusicologist at King's College, London—was much more accepted as a researcher than MacColl, who never really entered academia. Ironically, Lloyd was subsequently much more strongly attacked by academia, primarily for the politics evident in his writing. The other points of criticism related to his methods: with his egalitarian attitude about the handling of the original sources, Lloyd often violated many unspoken rules that are almost imperative for ethnomusicologists, such as avoiding a personal influence on the music and the musical community as much as possible. However, he was doubtless aware that bringing traditional material back into circulation within a different musical and social culture would not have been possible if he had remained aloof from the performing scene or adhered strictly to the original sources—an attitude that was also shared by several performers.

Moreover, the First Revival had been even more extreme in violating the ideals of authenticity: as discussed in chapter 2, only few early collectors like Percy Grainger tried to transcribe the music accurately, while Cecil Sharp altered the music to fit it within the classical 2/4, 3/4, or 4/4 rhythmic structures and changed many texts to make them more compatible with late Victorian morality. The question is how important these matters ultimately are. The goal of what German musicologists call *Quellentreue*, the precise reproduction of notated sources, cannot be achieved within a living tradition whose collected versions can only mark a temporary state, particularly when this tradition has almost died away. Within the folk and electric folk scenes, this has never been an issue for criticism—many musicians re-researched their material anyway to find other text and tune variants. Nevertheless, some performers like Martin Carthy wished that Lloyd could have been a bit more candid about his sources.

In contrast with MacColl and Lloyd, Alan Lomax always remained very much in the background of the folk scene, despite his presence in the media and his enormous impact in the revival's early stages. It is interesting, however, to note the change in his reputation after his move to Britain. While in the States Lomax was seen "only" as a collector, in Britain, he was much more regarded as a "real" scholar, with a vast knowledge of traditional musics of the world and expansive theories of Cantometrics and Choreometrics that he taught to Ewan MacColl and Peggy Seeger. Yet Lomax was not without his critics in Britain. Shirley Collins, for instance, strongly disagreed with him about MacColl being "the greatest ballad singer he'd ever heard"—which points at a significant issue, for MacColl's performances (and those of Isla Cameron) indeed occupied a large space among Lomax's field recordings of English-Scottish music and had a decisive influence on the picture of traditional singing that was thus conveyed.[10]

THE ADAPTATION PROCESS: MODERN MASS MEDIA AND ARCHIVAL RESEARCH

Returning to the musicians' perspective, it might seem, at first glance, that the transmission of material in the folk clubs did not differ substantially from that of the original (oral) tradition: the revival performers learned the major portion of their repertoire by listening to fellow musicians at the clubs and picking up the music that was around. Yet the adaptation of the music became an extremely conscious process for this generation, which resulted in different performance practices, as discussed in chapters 5 and 6. This outcome was not only due to the Lloyd/MacColl influence and the discussions that evolved around these two personalities, but also due to the predominance of indirect source material.

Only a few bands and soloists could call upon a personal traditional repertoire. Singer and melodeon player John Jones, for instance, grew up in Yorkshire's hunting and mining communities, learning a number of regional songs that were later performed by the early Oysterband. Much more often the musicians had to consult indirect sources to develop an individual repertoire. This was largely the case even with those performers who had a traditional background. On *No Roses*, for example, Shirley Collins not only included songs she had learned via direct contact (with Bob and Ron Copper, and with her aunt), but also songs she had learned in the folk clubs (via A. L. Lloyd) and from recordings such as field tapes from the BBC archives (especially Peter Kennedy's material, but also the old Joseph Taylor recordings).

With the few exceptions of "concept albums" like Frankie Armstrong's collection of Child ballads, *Till the Grass O'ergrew the Corn*, folk and electric folk musicians would rarely consult only a single source. The prominent Child and Bronson collections were only one option. For instance, on their first album, *Hark! The Village Wait*, Steeleye Span included songs from various print sources such as the *Folk Song Journals* ("The Blacksmith") and collections ("My Johnny" from Colm O'Lochlainn's *Irish Street Ballads*, vol. 2), as well as from the personal repertoires of the Irish duo Gay and Terry Woods and of Ashley Hutchings, who had acquired some songs from MacColl.

The Involvement of Modern Mass Media: The Aural Process

Modern mass media thus became instrumental in the development of a distinctly English (i.e., non-Gaelic) material and style. Radio (e.g., Peter Kennedy's *As I Roved Out*) and recordings in particular (semicommercial recordings of contemporary singers on Topic as well as field recordings in archives) provided in many cases the first real contact with traditional singing and playing styles.[11] The small, affordable paperback, *The Penguin Book of English Folk Songs*, edited by Lloyd and Ralph Vaughan Williams, made an enormous impact on the repertoire. As pointed out in the book's introduction (1959: 7), these songs had all been taken from the *Journal of the Folk Song Society* and its successor, the *Journal of the English Folk Dance and Song Society*, predominantly "songs and variants unpublished outside the pages of the journals." Intended as a "book to sing from" (ibid.), the songs were published undecorated but otherwise unchanged, except for some textual completions and some shortenings of long variants. Many songs that were in circulation in the revival and electric folk scene can be traced back to this source, even if the performers usually referred to the original sources rather than to the book itself. Despite many changes and collations, the underlying textual and melodic versions are often still recognizable as the versions published in the *Penguin Book*, as is the case with Fairport Convention's "A Sailor's Life."

Pondering these indirect ways of transmission, Fred Woods (1979: 24) wondered: "is a revivalist singer who learns his songs from the records of a traditional singer actually a traditional singer or a revivalist?" Woods's poignant question does not really get to the heart of the problem; aural and written media always seem to have been involved in the musical transmission process. As pointed out in chapter 2, Irish Traveller and singer Margaret Barry often learned songs from the most popular recordings to respond to the demands of her audience, also picking up song texts that were printed in newspapers. In contrast, Dick Gaughan learned much of his material at home— but was, like other revival performers, not called a traditional singer, owing to the different musical environment in which he performed. The performance context and style are key to answering Woods's question.

It is true, however, that the media became the primary sources for the musical learning process in the initial stage of the Second Revival. This resulted in a different mechanism of selection, for the music—on recordings, on the radio, in book form— was distributed over a much larger area than before. The emerging generation of folk and electric folk musicians were thereby exposed to a much wider range of material, individual styles, and versions than earlier performers. Yet in many cases the recordings were rather old (e.g., originally on wax cylinders, such as the Joseph Taylor recordings) or by elderly musicians, allowing only a faint glimpse of the original style—what Maddy Prior described as hearing "ghosts of voices."

Some musicians, like folksinger Peta Webb, tried to mimic the traditional style as closely as possible. Likewise, Martin Carthy in the late 1960s assimilated Joseph Taylor's singing, especially noticeable in his recording of "Brigg Fair" (*Byker Hill*), where even the ornaments are quite close to Taylor's version from 1907. In most cases, however, the performers of the Second Revival developed a broad range of individual styles by combining various traditional techniques with other elements and styles they had developed before their exposure to the traditional material. A good example is the "folk baroque" guitar style, which—notwithstanding the baroque countermelodies— was clearly based on blues techniques.

Female singers in particular explored a large and eclectic variety of models and influences. Prior would especially refer to Brigid Tunney and Mary Doran, while folksinger Frankie Armstrong developed her sound as an amalgam of the styles she had encountered. After listening to Jeannie Robertson, the Stewarts of Blair, and Irish Travellers, she discovered the "basic" (chest) voice. Shirley Collins, in contrast, adopted a traditional Sussex singing style but was also influenced by her U.S. fieldwork experiences with Alan Lomax in the 1950s. First attracted to the harsher American singing style, she later created a more "English" voice by developing a softer style, based on leaving the vocal cords more open.

Archival Research and Fieldwork

Another significant feature of the modern folk scene has been the frequent use of archives. While the first aural sources were often commercial records that were available at the time, performers later started to explore the resources of various libraries and archives, many of them private. Although Ewan MacColl's private library served as a major resource for many performers, the principal source of material has been the Vaughan Williams Memorial Library of the EFDSS at Cecil Sharp House in London. The Society has also benefited from the musicians' research, since some public attention was thereby directed to the respected but secluded organization. With the growth of the folk revival and the success of groups like Fairport Convention and Steeleye Span, the EFDSS also found itself periodically mentioned in the British popular music papers *Melody Maker* and *New Musical Express*, the latter, for instance, describing it as the "British Museum of folk music" (Logan 1969). A certain detachment from English public life has always been associated with the Society; progressive rock author Paul Stump (1997: 333) equated Cecil Sharp House with an "altar of folk traditionalism and scholarship."

Although Ashley Hutchings became particularly known as a meticulous researcher, many revival and electric folk performers of his generation developed an almost academic approach to the notated material, comparing and collating sources, texts, and tunes. This intense preoccupation with the songs' historical background was reflected in the liner notes to the recordings, where the performers often described their sources extensively, partly adopting the scholarly annotation styles of MacColl, Lloyd, Lomax, and Kennedy. Shirley Collins disparaged the folk scene of the 1990s for its comparative lack of rigor:

> I think in many ways people are too lazy to look for traditional songs. Ashley [Hutchings] worked really hard when I first met him. He used to spend a lot of time in Cecil Sharp House in the Vaughan Williams Library, looking through the Chichester Library, and I myself spent so much of my youth looking for songs and listening to old traditional songs, and people just don't do it now.

The initial motivation for using the archives was often the intent to develop a unique repertoire that would set a performer or group apart from the mainstream. This also became the guideline for the choices that were made, as Prior pointed out in the case of Steeleye Span: "There was a criterion—but we were certainly unaware of it. But looking back on it, you wouldn't do resident songs, [or] if you did, you would do them so differently from the way everybody else did them. The idea was to choose obscure material which nobody else did."

Electric folk musicians have often been accused of treating traditional material in a superficial way, simply taking from the sources what they could find.[12] Although commercial considerations became indeed important for groups like Steeleye Span, it is not possible to draw any conclusions regarding their selection process, as it became increasingly complex. In Fairport Convention's *Liege & Lief*, for instance, the balance between traditional ballads, dance tunes, collations, and original songs was well planned in advance, as Simon Nicol recalled:

> We knew we wanted to include some tunes which showed off what the jigs and reels could do in an electric setting. So we had put a set of those in. And we knew we wanted to include some songs which borrowed very much from traditional themes and indigenous tunes and then added new lyrics, which could have almost been traditional, things like "Crazy Man Michael." So all that decision was made in advance. Oh—and we wanted a calling-on song because Ashley [Hutchings] was very keen on the way that morris dancers and mummers, theater people, would usually come on and introduce themselves to a crowd, just to wake people up and say "Well, this is what's gonna happen next." So that's how "Come All Ye" came about.

Although musicians like Prior would often start in an archive by browsing through the magazines, and although finding an unknown or obscure song might have been the initial and main motivation, these were not the sole criteria. Text and tune also had to be of a certain quality—and still do—as Prior herself pointed out: "Some people think that all traditional songs are good. They aren't. There are a lot of bad and wooly songs that don't go anywhere" (Weir 1995: 41). The narrative qualities of the songs have remained a key consideration, and often much emphasis is placed on finding and establishing a good text. As Martin Carthy cautioned, however, the combination with a good tune is of equal importance:

> I believe two things which contradict each other. I think you should aim at singing a good tune to a song. But I also believe that the tune doesn't matter. Because the tune is the vehicle for the words, you know. The words come first. Having said the tune doesn't matter, I don't [want to] sing a song to a lousy tune. Right? Who does? But that's a contradiction and I accept that.

A personal affinity with the material is also crucial to making a choice, as singer Frankie Armstrong remarked:

> It has to move me in some way; it could be to laughter, to tears, to anger. There has to be a reason for me to sing it. A song has to "call me" to sing it—there's lots of good songs, but if they don't somehow speak to me personally I don't learn them. If I learn a song from the singing of a source-traditional singer, then I just keep singing and singing it until it feels to be my own.

In most cases, however, the song versions performers come across through archival research are incomplete or would not make sense in their original form, and therefore have to be completed by other text and tune variants—or even rewritten, if no other material is available. Thus, selection and collation have become a pivotal part of the musical preparation process. Carthy in particular became adept at fusing various versions. "Byker Hill," for instance, is a mixture of a version he learned while playing with the Thameside Four and another he obtained from A. L. Lloyd. Carthy also would research songs he had acquired orally, as for his recording of "High Germany," a combination of the broadside version with some lines from a related version, "The Two Lovers." And even when musicians found a complete source, such as the three Child ballads on Fairport's *Liege & Lief* recording ("Reynardine," "Matty Groves," and "Tam Lin"), they would still collate it with other versions and change it later anyway.

Sometimes completely new versions developed in this way and became standard versions in the clubs, like the variant of "Willie o' Winsbury" that was recorded by Anne Briggs and Pentangle. As Briggs recalled in an interview with Hunt (1989: 13), the Irish musician Andy Irvine, who took the text from Child's *English and Scottish Ballads*, got the ballad number confused when looking up the melody in Bronson's collection of tunes for the Child ballads. He thus combined the text with an unrelated tune—yet it is this version that is cited in many folk song books of the present.

Maintaining an original version as had been previously fixed on a recording or transcribed—a practice adamantly promoted by Cecil Sharp and several hardcore members of the folk scene—has been of only minor importance in the electric folk scene. Such "fidelity" is often sacrificed for the sake of practical musical reasons. Alterations are sometimes made on a subtle textual level, as Jacqui McShee tends to do:

> I do change words to fit a melody. I think the sound of words is quite important. I know it's not a very traditional way of looking at things, it isn't at all. But it's just that I feel happier if they sound, if they flow nicely. I like words to flow into each other—not so that you lose the meaning. I suppose it's also to make the melody flow. There is the song "Lovely Joan," and it talks about the couple going to a sort of haystack, this is the "pokes of hay." That's what's in the original. When you sing it, it sounds sort of clumsy. So when I sing it, I've changed it to the "stookes of hay" because it flows from the word beforehand. I've smoothed it out, really. Because to suddenly say "pokes," saying things with "p" and "b" anyway, it's quite strong.

Steeleye Span went to a further extreme by even mixing completely different songs—which did not always meet with the approval of traditionalists. This was the case with the commercially successful "All around My Hat" for which the first verse, serving as introduction and refrain, was combined with three verses of a version of "Farewell He," as Prior related:

> We'd put them together, collate. Nothing purist there at all. "All around My Hat" is a prime example. I mean—two completely different sets of words that don't make any sense at all, but it works. Because "Farewell He" is one sort of song and "All around My Hat" is another sort of song—its verses were awful! Absolutely dreadful. And I knew "Farewell He," and I just thought it had lovely words—and with a lovely tune—that Archie Fisher did. So I just

took the words. And I did that with a lot of things, I would get the words from one place and the tune from somewhere else—or would write tunes.

Although this practice could be criticized from an editorial viewpoint, it was, in fact, the only logical consequence of what was previously mentioned regarding the interrelationship of text and tune: a bad tune can destroy a good text, and vice versa. Therefore, the only way to give the text or tune a new musical life is to separate it from the part that does not "work" anymore. This approach partly became an art in itself, best illustrated by John Renbourn's treatment of medieval or renaissance material. Mixing completely different sources, such as one bass line with another counter-melody, he thus created completely new variants out of the notated material.

Sometimes (at a later stage or in areas with a livelier tradition) a revival generation may establish a closer, more conservative relationship with the tradition—partly as a result of having become researchers themselves. The American singer Jean Ritchie, for instance, journeyed via a Fulbright Scholarship to the British Isles in the 1950s to explore the roots of her Kentucky mountain tradition. Likewise, Hungarian folksinger Márta Sebestyén (who became known internationally through the movie *The English Patient*) collects music herself, especially in Transylvania, to expand her repertoire. This development can occasionally be observed in England. Although the early revival scene to a large extent remained separated from the tradition, some individual performers will reach across the divide. When the highly respected traditional singer Walter Pardon died in 1996, for example, Martin Carthy attended the funeral along with representatives from the EFDSS.

A NEW RELATIONSHIP WITH THE TRADITION

We have examined the transformation process from various sides, but one essential question has still to be answered: What is the significance of the tradition for the performers? As previous studies have clearly demonstrated, a revival always results in a change of and a subsequent separation from a musical tradition. Yet I propose that one may posit a similar shift in the performers' personal and cultural identities. Even in the case of the electric folk bands that pursued wider commercial success, the music was not simply "stolen" from defenseless traditional communities, as some critics of this genre have claimed (Woods 1979), but rather was internalized through a complex inner adaptation process that gave the revival a completely new dimension.

The Fascination with Archaic Elements

It cannot be denied that electric folk musicians were indeed often fascinated by the exotic and grotesque and by mythic topics and symbols. The original cover of Fairport Convention's *Liege & Lief* presents a characteristic selection, with images of the north-western custom of pace-egging, the Padstow hobbyhorse, the Burry Man from Lothian, morris dancing, and the midwinter custom of "hunting the wren."[13] The wren is often interpreted as the totem symbol for the Celtic god Bren or Bran, and was, as a representation of the winter, hunted and killed around Christmas time. This custom, still alive in the nineteenth century, became a recurring theme with Steeleye Span—evident, for instance, in titles like *Please to See the King* (= the wren) as well as in the song "Cutty Wren" (*Time*). Another example is the "Lyke Wake Dirge" (collected by the antiquarian John Aubrey in the Cleveland District of Yorkshire in the seventeenth century), which has been in the repertoire of the Young Tradition, Pentangle, and Steeleye Span. The song, sung at wakes for the dead, refers to proto-Christian and late pagan beliefs (widespread across Europe) about the soul's dangerous otherworld journey to purgatory.[14] Many of A. L. Lloyd's textual interpretations of such songs were adopted by various performers, including the interpretation of the killing and resurrection of the ancient corn god in "John Barleycorn" by Martin Carthy and the Watersons.[15]

The Watersons' album *Frost and Fire* (Topic, 1965) was completely centered around pagan-derived seasonal material like the midwinter wassailing songs. Norma Waterson recalled in an interview with Colin Irwin (1997) that the group's fascination with this material started when visiting the May Day Eve festival at Padstow in Cornwall. May Day is still observed in the English rural calendar as the beginning of the summer season. In Padstow it is celebrated by street parades that include old traditions like the hobbyhorse as well as mixes of old dances set to new music, such as the Abbots Bromley Horn Dance. The impressions of this festival moved the Watersons to search further in their home region, Yorkshire, and led to some amazing discoveries as Norma Waterson remembered:

> We went down to Padstow in '62 and the whole thing was so explosive for us. . . . The fact that this still went on in England—we'd never come across anything like it. We then went out of our way to look for traditional ceremonies and music to go with it, and *Frost and Fire* came out of that. The roots are so deep I feel very, very connected whenever I go into one of these ceremonies. I feel almost that this is what it's all about. . . . From things like Padstow, . . . we've discovered little tiny ceremonies like the Penny Hedge thing which happens on Ascension Eve in Whitby. It's just three men building a little hedge and a horn-blower comes along and shouts "Out on ye, out on ye." The hedge has to last three tides and it's a penance for the descendants of three families. It's so strange and quirky and it's been going on for 900 years! (Irwin 1997: 37)

British folk and electric folk thus seemed to coincide with the ideologies of progressive rock, which drew strongly on symbolism taken from mythology, fantasy, and science-fiction literature. As Macan (1997: 73) explained, "Fantasy landscapes and medieval or Eastern imagery came to represent the idealized society—close to the earth, based on mutual dependence and a strong sense of community, linked with the past—to which the hippies aspired." Books such as J. R. R. Tolkien's Middle-earth cycle (*The Hobbit, The Lord of the Rings, The Silmarillion*) experienced an extreme popularity among the hippies. Indeed, there are a number of electric folk examples that correspond with the then-popular Tolkien imagery, like Fairport Convention's "Tam Lin," the tale of young Janet, who frees her love Tam Lin, captured by the elf queen, in a highly dramatic horseback ride. Likewise, "Let No Man Steal Your Thyme" and "Scarborough Fair," as popularized by Simon and Garfunkel, deal with the mystical powers or allegorical roles of herbs (with thyme as the symbol for virginity). Moreover, several songs such as "Willie o' Winsbury" and "The Trees They Grow High" are set in a medieval context, while Pentangle's name, as previously mentioned, was inspired by Arthurian mythology and probably also by John Renbourn's emerging interest in medieval music.

Generally speaking, however, fantasy images per se were rare in electric folk—or if used, then were often couched within an ironic context, as in Steeleye Span's eerie modern ecology song, "Seven Hundred Elves." Although a fascination for these topics is clear in the lengthy textual explanations accompanying the recordings, folk and electric folk performers never romanticized them as did their progressive rock counterparts. This attitude can also be inferred from the sleeve art, which was seldom as "mystical" as that of the progressive rock albums. Although relying strongly on pagan imagery, Fairport's cover of *Liege & Lief* conveys a down-to-earth impression due to the inclusion of realistic photos and explanatory descriptions. Mysticism was not the an extreme focal point for these English bands that it was for the Celtic movement, which later merged increasingly with the New Age scene. Often, pagan or arcane material appeared to be approached from a relatively sober angle, as in the case of the Watersons' *Frost and Fire*. A. L. Lloyd wrote in the liner notes that

> Just as one doesn't need to be an ancient Greek to be moved by the plays of Aeschylus, so it's not necessary to be anything other than an ordinary free-thinking twentieth-century urban western man with a proper regard for humankind, to appreciate the power of these songs. To our toiling ancestors they meant everything, and in a queer irrational way they can still mean much to us.

Similarly, the transfigured image of nature seems not to have been such a strong focal point with the modern English performers as it had been with Cecil Sharp, who, with his folk song theories, also fostered an idealized image of England that was subsequently adopted by American folk musicians and later by the hippies. While the American folksinger Joan Baez loved the Anglo-American ballads for their romantic tragedy (Cantwell 1996: 338), this attitude was less evident among English musicians.

Performers of an Unpopular Music

Mere romanticism or mysticism—nor commercialism, as writers like Stewart (1977) suggest—could thus not be enough to explain why these performers kept playing this music, in some cases for decades. Had it just been for commercial reasons, then many musicians simply would have turned to rock or jazz. Moreover, these performers have been playing a music that remains in both its forms—as traditional or revived folk music—extremely unpopular in mainstream England, despite the efforts of the EFDSS and the commercial success of some electric folk bands in the 1960s and 1970s. Some musicians therefore still doubt the long-term success of the English repertoire. As Oysterband melodeon player and singer John Jones, for example, told Sarah Coxson, "I question how much you'll ever sell British music to British people. The exotic is always going to interest them more than their homespun product. Being English can be the kiss of death. You've got to overcome so many things to actually make it feel radical and different and genuinely alternative" (Coxson 1990: 55).

This difficulty was evident during the early stages of the Second Revival. Alan Lomax observed in the 1950s that traditional music was often rejected in England. As he recalled about his field recording tour in the BBC documentary *The Other Muse*:

> I recorded with the help of Peter Kennedy, who had been surveying the ground. I recorded all over Britain . . . and so at the end of a year I knew what the map of British folk music was like. And I also knew how much it was disdained, these extraordinary sounds. People would say: "That's not singing! That old Charley Wills can't sing!" . . . And when I put Margaret Barry, the great Irish bard, on the air, we got indignant letters from the upper class saying: "We don't want a woman without teeth on our air. It's a disgrace to our nation!" (Howkins 1981)

Similarly, other traditional forms like morris dance were—especially before Ashley Hutchings's *Morris On*—little accepted in British society, except in a highly romanticized form, as Maddy Prior pointed out:

> We moved out of the country, out of this wonderfully idyllic scene, we moved into towns. And that's where most of the music disappeared. And also because of this massive move towards progress and industrialization, and nobody wanted to be left back with the smocks and straw in their hair and in their hat. They wanted to be where the bowlers and the waistcoats were. They wanted to move away from anything associated with it. And it still applies! People still feel like that. They say, "Oh, it's morris dance, this frilling about with those hankies!" Because they have no relationship to it. They sometimes look at them, but if you actually ask them, they think they're poofs, which is kind of weird, because have they been trying morris dance? It is hard, ardent work! And they don't see that kind of side, because they don't want that thing—except idealized as this cottage in the country. And it reflects a lot of it in the songs. What we've finished up with is the national songs and the songs that the ladies taught you in school because they were acceptable, nice pictures of people doing things in the countryside. And pretty tunes.

These negative impressions were reinforced by the amateurish side of the revival. The revival motivated many untrained people to start making music, and the uneven results that could be heard at some folk clubs created mixed feelings. Doubts were further fueled by the general low level of knowledge about traditional music. While I researched this book, English people tended to ask me, often ironically, whether there was really any such thing as traditional music in their country. Similarly, in Colin Irwin's article "England: Last Undiscovered Exotic Outpost of World Music" (1997), the author apparently felt—not without reason—the need to explain extensively why he had to write an article about this music.

The treatment by British public radio programs offers another indicator of traditional music's low status. Despite the early success of Peter Kennedy's *As I Roved Out* series on BBC radio, this music retained its marginal role in the media, being restricted either to local radio stations or to specialized radio shows like *Folk on Friday* (later *Folk on Sunday* and *Folk on Two*). Yet neither of these formats, as music journalist Andrew Means pointed out in 1972, made much use of the BBC archives, owing to internal policies. Former radio presenter Frances Line argued in Means's article (1972d) that relatively popular performers like Isla St. Clair were the nearest she could get to the tradition in her shows without endangering her audience share. At the time of this writing, English traditional music was almost completely absent from the BBC except on late-night shows with a small audience—in clear contrast with Scotland and Ireland, where traditional music receives much more media attention.

English musicians' dedication and perseverance in playing this music under these conditions thus suggests a much more profound but also reflective relationship to the tradition than may be evident at first sight.

A Conscious Relationship with the Tradition

Given the complex research needs and the extensive discussion that has surrounded the revival and electric folk, most performers have developed highly self-aware attitudes and well-articulated beliefs about their music. The musicians I interviewed were very aware of the gaps between the tradition and their revival culture, and of the stylistic limits. Jacqui McShee, for instance, clearly rejected the possibility of a style of slavish imitation, pointing out that her musical feel for ornamentation was different from the feel of Lizzie Higgins, one of her major models.

Many performers thus have intentionally developed a different style, as they felt too restricted by being merely imitators of the traditional singers, which would not have given them the identity they were seeking. Maddy Prior named Brigid Tunney and Mary Doran as models for ornamental techniques and phrasing, yet she did not consider them models for her whole vocal style. As pointed out previously, even Shirley Collins, who came out of the Sussex tradition, changed her style after her fieldwork in the States with Alan Lomax, making the English contrast with the harsher American singing style more obvious by further softening her voice.

This clear awareness of their position as revivalists was often combined with complicated conceptions of the terms "folk" and "traditional music." Rather than repeating any of the academic descriptions, the performers—when asked by the author about their idea of traditional music— each set different emphases on aspects mentioned in the "official" definition of the International Folk Music Council. Many have developed a relatively complex perception of traditional music, extending beyond musical or stylistic aspects, combined with a clear awareness of the many overtones or various academic definitions that superimposed their own perceptions. Frankie Armstrong, for instance, made a clear differentiation between "Tradition," meaning the oral process (independent from the material), and "tradition" as the "essence" or idea carried within the musical material. Rick Kemp and Ashley Hutchings, in contrast, focused on the element of age in connection with the notion of tradition, while Martin Carthy and Maddy Prior emphasized the process of change that, paradoxically, is closely linked with the element of constancy (the relationship between tune and text variants is still recognizable). Hutchings also pointed out the element of communal experience—the fact that oral transmission is a process in which many people are involved. Others, like Ian Telfer and Shirley Collins, indicated a specific performance situation that is also communal and oral in its transmission.

Whether or not they intended to consciously distance themselves from the romanticized ideas of the First Revivalists, none of the performers linked traditional music with specific subject matter. Only Shirley Collins defined the music as the expression of a certain (working) class—her own identity. She was thereby also trying to distance herself from Big Bill Broonzy's infamous remark, clearly recognizing that it has become the basis for a large range of overly general definitions that ultimately convey nothing: "When people say, 'well, a folk song is anything that people sing, because I've never heard a horse sing,' you know, it makes me so cross—it's just such a shallow answer. And I think that's partly why I am so keen to define it as mainly rural laboring classes' own music."

The Inner Side of the Relationship

The individual aspects mentioned above as part of a definition of traditional music are also expressions of those traditional elements internalized by the performers as an articulation of their own musical being. This highly philosophical level is often combined with other elements of possible meanings, for a performer's interest in this music often developed in several steps, progressing from (a) fascination with the tunes to (b) fascination with the texts—enabling one to "enter a whole other reality" (Frankie Armstrong), as well as with (c) the whole performance process. On a final level (d), the musician starts to discover other levels of the music, such as the archetypical aspect of the ballads.

The fascination with the modal tunes (step a) was mentioned by most of the performers at some point during their interviews. As Rick Kemp commented, the preoccupation with these tunes has partly permeated their work on an unconscious level, which became apparent to him when he wrote the material for his first solo album: "There is an English traditional tune which I love. I think I picked the tune up without knowing it. For instance, on the new album there is a thing called 'Waiting for a Miracle,' which I noticed is a fairly traditional-sounding tune. Which I didn't mean to do. It just happened that way."

This fascination was also transferred to the performance style. From early on, other images of the tradition, such as ideas of roughness, archaism, or naturalness, have permeated these musicians' perception of traditional music. Especially before rediscovering English folk music, "tradition" had a distinct meaning to these performers, clearly differing from later conceptions and scholarly writings. When asked about the first traditional music they had ever heard, most of them mentioned American blues musicians: Frankie Armstrong, for instance, recalled that "the first people I started listening to were Leadbelly, Big Bill Broonzy, Ma Rainey, Bessie Smith—and the Lomax recordings of people like Jean Ritchie and Woody Guthrie." Traditional (or "authentic") music was equated with a "raw" quality that was inherent in the physical performance style of blues musicians like Leadbelly, and also characteristic of the early Elvis Presley. It was often regarded as a contrast to the popular (= polished) music of the 1950s.

This could also explain why the performers were initially much more attracted to Irish-Scottish or Bulgarian singing styles than to their own. These styles are based on a closer relationship between the body and the voice, often using chest voice, which is perceived as much "earthier" and "rougher" than a pop-music singing style that tends to exclude the lower parts of the body. This body-voice relationship is similar to classical (i.e., operatic) singing, yet different, as it can be accessed outside the boundaries of a stylized high culture. At the same time, this "naturalness" and "directness" or "immediacy" is something completely different from the amateurish image the early Second Revival often conveyed. Within most traditions, a good performance still requires skills, even if they are acquired (often over a long time span) independently from an academic education.

Likewise, a fascination with the texts (step b)—on a narrative as well as on a sociohistorical level—has always been present. It is not without reason that a ballad like "Matty Groves," which contains in a highly condensed form a story of seduction, adultery, betrayal, challenge, duel, and murder, became so popular within the scene. The musicians also took a deep interest in the texts' sociohistorical background. In Frankie Armstrong's words, the songs gave her "the opportunity of entering a whole other reality, be it that of a milkmaid, be it that of a beggar man." Hutchings emphasized that these texts offered him access to English history in a way he could not find in history books: "I learnt about working-class history, about miners—all the old stories, you know, which I hadn't learnt at school I learnt from folk song."

Apart from the music's modal character and style, it was especially the performance aspects (step c) that set electric folk apart from other contemporary rock music. The creative challenge of retelling a story so that musically it turns out differently every time is clearly a major reason why groups like Fairport Convention have always returned to traditional material. Simon Nicol, for instance, remarked about performing "Matty Groves" that "it never feels the same to me doing it." Frankie Armstrong's described how the change of simple elements like extended or missing ornaments can alter the entire atmosphere of the song, and it is especially the ornamental dimension that has fascinated many performers.

Particularly through the narrative process, many performers have developed an intense relationship with the music, discovering further, much more complex and abstract levels (step d). This involvement was already evident with traditional singers like Jeannie Robertson, who often gave her own psychological explanation of the ballad characters' motivations (Porter and Gower 1995: 75). Similarly, the revival performers often began to interpret the multilayered content of the songs and ballads on a much more timeless, archetypical level, discovering basic patterns of human existence behind the outer narrative level that address "something very profound," as Armstrong remarked:

> There are always lessons to be learned from the songs. Some of the broadsides could be crass and cheaply sentimental, but in the great ballads, as in mythology, the lessons are much more subtle; you just live with them and they will gradually osmose into your consciousness. In them we can find immense compassion, imagination, and illumination of the human condition—in all its complexity and contradictions.

As Maddy Prior explained, the story of a young girl who becomes pregnant without anyone noticing it is independent from her wearing a traditional gown. It could also have happened in modern New York, with a sweater covering her belly. This interpretive insight often developed—and deepened—over the years. Armstrong, for example, only gradually arrived at her archetypical interpretation of the Child ballad "Child Waters" as an example of female strength: the story superficially is "about a seemingly cruel man and a woman who loves him so passionately that she's willing to run after him for days while he rides his horse. However, on a more mythic level it is she, close to nature and following her heart, who wins out over his attempt to follow the conventions of the time—i.e., that he must marry a woman of wealth and position."

The Political Side of Electric Folk

Although the focus of the performers I interviewed was clearly on English music, they rarely mentioned any nationalistic aspects—as would have been the case with the first revivalists in the nineteenth century or in other suppressed minority cultures or countries like Ireland. Developing a sense of Englishness was often rather seen as a step away from the partly still prevailing negative (colonial) connotations that are associated with the term "Britain." Ashley Hutchings, for instance, described the rediscovery of traditional English music—and especially of morris dance—as a journey back to his own roots, which also became evident later in his country clothing style.

Yet, very much in contrast with Britpop musicians, who have used symbols such as the Union Jack, Hutchings refrained from displaying political elements like the cross of Saint George.

Likewise, being political—in the sense of using traditional music as a vehicle for a political agenda—has never been common, at least not in the form it was for the Marxist revivalists. As with the progressive rock movement, British folk and especially electric folk musicians lacked the explicit political goals or ideals that were an integral part of the American folk movement. A. L. Lloyd and Ewan MacColl were known as stout Marxists, yet—viewed retrospectively—their political influence seems to have been restricted to the scene immediately around them. MacColl's political activities were often regarded with detachment by the performers I interviewed, clearly evident in the comments of Shirley Collins, whose family (including herself) was strongly socialist. Although she still defines traditional music as the music of the rural working classes, she never merged her traditional material with political activism—much in contrast with MacColl, who asked her to do so:

> I didn't want to sing for the Communist or the Labour Party. I wanted to do *music*, I didn't want to do *political music*. And I think that in a subtle way that a traditional song [which] talks about war, for instance, is much better than somebody who has written an antiwar song expecting to sing it. I'd rather let the people who suffered, I'd rather use *their* form of protest. . . . So this was partly why they disliked me—because I wasn't going to toe the party line with them or join in this political thing. Even though, as I say, I was a socialist. But that was a separate thing from my music.

American folk songs were part of the CND demonstrations, and several musicians like Sandy Denny performed in public at the rallies, yet most electric folk musicians did not include overt political references in their material. This clearly dovetails with Macan's observations about the apolitical character of progressive rock:

> Since Britain did not undergo the Vietnam experience, antiwar themes in the music in the British counterculture usually lack the urgency and stridency found in their American counterparts. . . . English bands tend to view war from a more philosophical, abstract viewpoint than their American counterparts, seeing it as the inevitable result of society's materialism and its attendant greed and lust for power. (Macan 1997: 78–79)

Macan points to Pink Floyd's "Us and Them," which treats war on a highly abstract level. The topic of war is indeed present in the folk repertoire, but as the bands used historical material, the songs were not related to current events. Songs like "The Deserter" (Fairport Convention), "The Banks of the Nile" (Fotheringay), or "High Germany" (Martin Carthy) dealt with dramatic situations, not historical facts. This did not mean, however, that these songs were seen as pastoral imagery. The content was often of timeless importance, as "The Twa Corbies," a central piece of Steeleye Span's and Maddy Prior's live repertoire, demonstrates. This song takes the perspective of two ravens or crows. Pecking at a dead knight's body, they cynically remark that nobody will ever find or miss him, neither his dog and hawk, nor his "lady fair," who already has another lover, concluding that "nane shall ken [know] where he is gane."

Referring to contemporary politics automatically meant the incorporation of individual songwriting. Although British folk and electric folk lacked the strong political edge that was characteristic of American singer/songwriters like Joan Baez and Bob Dylan, social criticism would later become an integral part of some groups. Richard Thompson wrote songs that criticized aspects of British politics and environmental pollution, often on a multilayered level, as in "The New St. George." The Oysterband and other groups performed the satirical songs of Leon Rosselson. Later groups of the more punk-oriented strain of folk rock, including the Pogues, the Levellers, and Billy Bragg, wrote extremely critical songs clearly directed against the Thatcher government.

The Tradition as a Means to a Cultural Identity

Joe Boyd concisely described traditional music as "an expression of national feeling which is positive," less a nationalistic or political vehicle than an expression of profound humanity that touches deep emotions. Singing or playing traditional music seems to be an articulation of the personal perception of human identity at various levels. For Shirley Collins, it is the expression of a whole class, while for Martin Carthy it represents the idea of continuity, the music providing a link between the past and the future that constitutes the essence of what it means to be human: "We're talking about identity, and we're talking about continuity. What interests me is forging a link with the past and—if you like to be overdramatic—holding out a hand to the hand in the future. That's what human beings are. If we are not that, then we are nothing."

When June Tabor announced at a concert at Hamburg's Fabrik that the song "Go from My Window" had been performed for more than 300 years, I saw the audience visibly holding its breath—although other traditional songs can be dated back even further, and this is a short time from the viewpoint of classical performers who sing masses by Guillaume Dufay or Josquin Desprez. Yet the awareness of music shared over many generations' time span, whether directed back to the past or toward the future, seems particularly intense among folk and traditional musicians and their listeners. The notion of traditional music is linked with an experience of community much stronger than in rock or classical music—owing to the minimal or nonexistent distance between the musicians and the listeners, as well as among the listeners themselves. This is especially the case if dance is involved. Ian Telfer cited the example of céilidh dancing: "It's a very collective thing, where age and sex and the other ways in which people are different hardly matter at all. It's a shared, a common experience. With this kind of dancing you must dance with someone else, even if you're on your own."

When Ashley Hutchings talks about the directness that attracted him to traditional music, he means not only the performance side, which in the 1950s and '60s was seen as freed from any artificial elements connected with commercial and classical music. He also points to the question of authorship, because the music has essentially become communal through its long oral transmission process, losing all traces of its original authors. For a performer of the early twenty-first century, it does not matter anymore whether a song was originally a commercial broadside of the eighteenth or nineteenth century. If the song has been transmitted for such a long time, it now seems to convey a meaning—or different levels of meanings—independent of its origin. Moreover, it seems to have a meaning for many people, which could also explain why it can become an expression of one's cultural roots, or the "pure expression of the nature of the people," as Boyd put it. That is also the reason why Harker's arguments—which rejected the concept of traditional music because of its predominantly commercial origins—are ultimately insignificant. In short, the multilayered levels of meaning that can be discovered in the traditional material are probably the main reasons why this music still holds such a powerful appeal in the present—even if the original forms have almost died away and have been replaced by revival forms.

EIGHT

MODERN REVIVAL AND FUSION PROCESSES

Traditional music will survive. Instead of oral transmission, it's transmitted by CD, it's transmitted by radio wave—it's in no danger of dying. It persists in ever-changing forms. The only thing that changes about traditional music is its setting—but it is still transmitted from mouth to mouth, ear to ear, person to person, whether it is learning it informally at someone's knee or whether it's hearing it on TV! There is a wonderful quote from Alfred Williams's *Folk Songs of the Upper Thames*, I think it was, that the old ballads should be used as a basis for future work. And that's what electric folk is about. That's the spirit of it.   JENNIFER CUTTING

In the twenty-first century, music revival processes are all around us—and it is probably not without reason that traditional music is being revived in many countries, for it offers a strong possibility of creating a tangible identity within an increasingly anonymous superculture. Jennifer Cutting, an American who performs English electric folk music, is thus right to emphasize that traditional musics are not static and exist in more than one form. This is not to deny the dominance of Western popular music on a supercultural level; both in the media and in the business, it continues to exert a strong impact on traditional music cultures. Yet we need more flexible models or schemes—such as those developed by Appadurai (1998) and Slobin (1993)—in order to grasp the complexity of modern musical interaction and transformation processes more comprehensively.

This chapter will thus review some of the related processes in the United States, Scotland, and Ireland that are all intertwined with electric folk developments in England. In this discussion, it is particularly the idea of cultural segments interacting with each other on various levels (taken from Slobin's microcultural model) that will help add a different, relativizing angle to the portrayal of electric folk.

Compared with how traditional music has fared ins other European countries, England's experience over the past half century has been in some ways unique: there are not many parallels for the extreme rejection of traditional music after World War II, the isolation of the English Folk Dance and Song Society (EFDSS), the initial dogmatism of the Second Revival scene, and the polarized debate about the use of electric instruments. However, because the English electric folk movement in particular has had a strong impact on other cultural regions, the chapter will conclude with a brief survey of selected developments in Scandinavia, Germany, and Eastern Europe.

ELECTRIC FOLK IN AMERICA

Even in England, where the tradition was extremely marginalized before the first revival movement of the 1930s and '40s, one could confirm Slobin's observation that, despite the growth of the supercultural network, cultural variety was changing but by no means completely disappearing. The British folk revival and electric folk initially emerged as a counterreaction to the dominating American music of some forty years ago. Exactly the same kind of counteractive musical movements in turn led to new means of cultural identification in the United States and Canada from the mid-1980s on.

English Music in the United States

The fact that it is nearly superfluous to point out that the United States is often regarded as synonymous with the so-called mainstream culture underlines how strongly the States embodies the classical model of a strong superculture on both an internal and a global level. Slobin's techno-, media-, and finanscape network (see this book's introduction) is very tight in the States. Social stereotypes, standardized styles, and elements of mass production have permeated every aspect of daily life during the last twenty or thirty years, as fast-food chains like McDonald's and omnipresent brands like Coca-Cola amply illustrate.

Consequently, the tendency to eliminate individual differences has grown enormously. This became especially evident to me when visiting American shopping malls. Whether located in Texas, Indiana, or Washington, D.C., they are all dominated by a small number of chain stores with identical branches—including identical arrangements of the interior, selection of goods, and staff uniforms. On one hand, this uniformity ensures equal shopping opportunities for everyone; on the other hand, it also increases a feeling of cultural anonymity. Similarly, most of the popular music that can be heard on the mediascape (as represented by the MTV channel) seems to be a unified "mainstream" sound that has, alongside other supercultural elements, also become the basis for a global network of popular culture embodied in the omnipresence of performers like Britney Spears and Metallica.

Inferring from these superficial impressions, however, that the United States presents only a unified music culture is a well-known misapprehension; on the contrary, it supports an impressive microcosm of musical subcultures that flourish beneath the supercultural level. A stroll through any large American city such as Chicago or New York reveals that urban musical microcultures—spanning a broad range from ethnic

Irish, Polish, Swedish, or Greek communities to the rap, jazz, and klezmer scenes—have an extremely strong presence. One can still find a large variety of European musical forms like Scottish pipe bands that have been preserved alongside emerging hybrid forms, such as mixtures of early music with Scottish/Irish repertoire, illustrated by the Ensemble Galilei (Winick 1996). This is even the case with English tradition: in addition to having metamorphosed into modified styles such as bluegrass or being integrated into the blues repertoire, parts of the material brought by early English immigrants are still being fostered. The best known remains probably the Appalachian tradition of ballad singing, but one can find various morris dance groups, Sacred Harp singing, and various other Anglo-American hymn traditions as well.[1]

Within an increasingly anonymous superculture, people tend to become more aware of their own cultural background—which, interestingly enough, is not usually seen as being related to the supercultural sphere (even if American stars like Bruce Springsteen have dealt with national or regional topics) but rather to the original immigrant culture, as far as it can be traced back. A flourishing interest in ancestral research, the strong fascination for collecting antiques, and the fostering of cultural remnants are good indications of that tendency in America (with stronger immigrant cultures, this trend would lead to the creation of Slobin's so-called diasporic interculture). Traditional and revival music plays an important part in that process, because cultural roots seem to be especially well expressed in the sound of traditional music. As Cutting explained: "For me [playing traditional music] is a connection to my past. Both grandfathers were born in Britain, so it's a connection to my past and it's also music that pleases me at every level."

Nevertheless, the case of English traditional music is much more complicated than most other microcultures in the States. Not only is it a comparatively small scene, but the strong association of the term "Child ballads" with the English element in the American culture, even if the original ballad was of Irish or Scottish origin, has partly been enforced from outside the tradition.[2]

I therefore would like to return to the history of Anglo-American folk song before the folk revival of the 1920s and '30s, for until the late nineteenth century, English music was just one of many traditional American immigrant music cultures. Interest in the musical material of the living American tradition was still limited then, as evidenced in Francis James Child's groundbreaking series, *The English and Scottish Popular Ballads*, published in five volumes between 1882 and 1889. He did not consider his ideal of the folk ballad to be represented in the American tradition but rather in the "original" English one, and he thus relied primarily on printed sources from British collectors like Scott, Percy, and Motherwell.[3] Child, a Harvard professor whose publications were aimed at a scholarly audience, treated the ballads as European literature of high art—printing the lyrics in Old English dialect and omitting the notation of their associated tunes (with the exception of the last volume that includes a few), which were not added until about sixty years later by B. H. Bronson between 1959 and 1972.

The living tradition had already been marginalized in England, however, while exactly the same ballads were still sung in America. Not only in remote areas of Appalachia but also in midwestern regions like Indiana, people had persevered with linguistic and song traditions that were long dead in England. Yet the interest in Appalachian folk music was still confined to a small group of enthusiasts in the early 1900s. It was British collector Cecil Sharp who jump-started the appreciation of Appalachian heritage, doing a major part of his fieldwork in the United States over the course of three visits between 1916 and 1918. Discovering much material that had already disappeared in the Old World, he not only popularized these folk songs in edited versions but also re-created the England he had never found at home from the cultures he encountered in the States. Sharp depicted the Appalachian mountaineers not as of varied British and African origins but as genuinely English, and their traditions became identified with the general American musical heritage for several decades, which strongly influenced the actions and motivations of later collectors (Filene 1995: 28–35).[4]

The Lomaxes subsequently tried to replace the Child canon with something more genuinely American, which John Avery Lomax found embodied first in the cowboy song, although the focus later shifted to the black blues and gospel traditions. For the Lomaxes, African American traditional music, particularly the repertoire of Huddie Ledbetter (Leadbelly), became a means of demonstrating that the United States had a folk song heritage independent of Britain. Within popular music, blues became an influential model for substantial further musical development.

Although music of British/English origin was still an integral part of the repertoire of the American revival performers of the 1960s such as Hedy West, Buffy Sainte-Marie, Judy Collins, and—most influential in this regard—Joan Baez, it seemed not to be a conscious element of identification with the original English culture anymore. Played on American folk instruments like guitar and banjo, it was, especially in the 1970s, increasingly replaced by the original songwriting of Joni Mitchell, Jackson Browne, and James Taylor. (This was not surprising, given the influence of Woody Guthrie and Bob Dylan in directing people's energies away from interpreting old songs and toward writing new ones.) In the meantime, American folk and folk rock were either on the decline or had already disappeared. Stars like Pete Seeger, Baez, and Dylan were still welcome guests at American and especially European festivals, yet the political folk song movement increasingly lost its importance after the Vietnam War and was further weakened by the suicide of Phil Ochs in 1976 (his voice had never recovered from an accident in Africa).

Punk rock and disco had a negative impact on the American folk and singer/songwriter scenes similar to their effects in Britain, and it was not until the mid-1980s when the singer/songwriter direction was newly revived by the popularity of artists such as Suzanne Vega and Tracy Chapman. In the meantime, the American folk scene underwent some major changes that became especially evident from the mid-1980s on: folk was no longer equated with a political counterculture but instead with an alternative cultural identity often to be found in the original immigrant cultures. This trend could be seen in the proliferation of morris dance groups, the popularity of contra dance, and in the founding of genuinely American Irish/Scottish/English-style folk and electric folk groups, among which the New St. George was one of the most prominent electric groups.

The New St. George: An American-English Electric Folk Group

During a stay in Washington, D.C., in 1997, I had the opportunity to interview Jennifer Cutting, a reference librarian at the Archive of Folk Culture in the Library of Congress and musician and leader of the now disbanded electric folk band he New St. George. The interview, around which the following parts of this chapter are centered, was of two-fold importance: Cutting was one of A. L. Lloyd's last students and confirmed many observations of Lloyd and the electric folk scene mentioned earlier. Furthermore, a review of the history of the New St. George offered insights into the character of the modern American folk/electric folk scenes, which are strongly focused on their European counterparts, and into the mechanisms of interaction among the various musical microcultures, especially the Irish and Celtic scenes.

Although she grew up in the United States, Cutting came from a British background. Possibly related to Francis Cutting, composer at the court of Henry VIII, she could look back on a lengthy musical history within her family: one of her grandfathers, born in Devon, came over to the States with his parents when he was a child and became a conductor of the NBC Symphony Orchestra in New York, while the other grandfather was a composer. Her mother was a concert guitarist who first exposed her to English folk music by playing tunes such as "Greensleeves."

After the death of her grandmother, who had worked as an editor on critical translations of Indian scriptures, Jennifer, then twelve years old, was raised by two Indian scholar/priests. During her teens Cutting thus grew up within an Indian American microculture that took its cultural models from Britain:

> I was sent to live at their ashram on a mango plantation in southern Florida. The whole community was vegetarian and celibate, and it was a very ascetic existence because it was, in fact, a monastery. My guardians spoke British, not American, English, and they saw to it that I did, too. I was educated at home by governesses. For many years I never saw the outside world—no television or radio or any other children. My environment was an exact replica of colonial India. Musically, I suppose the classical music I was studying during my piano lessons was melding with the Indian music I heard every Friday night, when live musicians treated us to sitar and tabla concerts.

Cutting would later reflect on this experience when writing the song, "All the Tea in India" for the New St. George. Like many fans of the post-1960s generation who discovered English folk musicians such as Martin Carthy through the popularity of the

Pogues or the Levellers, her curiosity about the background of electric folk led her into the study of the relatively unknown English folk music. Cutting's first encounter with electric folk was rather coincidental, as she recalled:

> When I was an undergraduate at Jacksonville University, Florida, I picked up a live album of Steeleye Span. I didn't even know who they were, and when I put it on the record player, it was love at first listen! So all through my first music degree, when I was studying music education, I listened to Steeleye Span. Then for my graduate degree I went to the University of London, King's College, to study. I had decided before going there that I wanted to study English folk music because I liked the Steeleye Span record so much! And Brian Trowell, who was professor there at the time, said, "Well, you are just in luck—how would you like to study with the father of the current, the modern English folk revival? He wrote the bible of English folk music, he wrote the book—*Folk Song in England*. His name is A. L. Lloyd." At that time I didn't know what a great honor it was to study with A. L. Lloyd—I didn't even know who A. L. Lloyd was. But I thought, if he is the best, then I want to study with him!

Cutting was encouraged by Lloyd to pick up the melodeon and subsequently she joined the New Espérance Morris Women in London. As she recalled: "They were very strict; they wouldn't let you play an instrument for the morris until you had danced for a couple of years—but I worked my way up to musician status." Returning to the States in 1984, after she received her master's degree, she started to work for the Smithsonian Institution's Office of Folklife Programs in Washington, D.C., and joined the less strict Rock Creek Morris Women, who were short of musicians at the time. Touring with the group, Cutting acquired a large repertoire of morris tunes. She subsequently became a member of the British-style electric folk band the New St. George, which was based in Washington, D.C.

The New St. George's first rehearsals took place in 1986, in the home of the English guitar player and singer Bob Hitchcock, who had come to New York in 1975. Having grown up in Brighton (Sussex), Hitchcock was quite familiar with the British folk club scene and local groups like the Copper Family, and as he said later in a *Dirty Linen* interview (Nelligan 1995), he had initially thought about forming an acoustic band like Pentangle. The lineup that would record *High Tea* in 1994 took shape around 1992 as an extremely varied cultural and musical mixture. The American singer Lisa Moscatiello, who replaced the band's first lead singer, Elise Kress, had discovered folk music via Celtic-Irish music, in particular the acoustic band Clannad. She had been playing in a "straight-ahead" Irish band when she heard the New St. George for the first time. As an electric, stage-oriented band, it offered her an alternative to the traditionalized, more "inward" way of playing (ibid.). Bass player Rico Petruccelli, in contrast, came from a jazz background, but had also been a fan of Fairport Convention and Richard Thompson for about ten years before joining the band. Likewise, drummer Juan Dudley had played in the Washington, D.C., jazz scene and had come into contact with the folk scene during college, cofounding a coffee house and playing in a local Celtic-oriented band.

It was Cutting, however, who became decisive for the band's direction. Like Hitchcock (the only remaining member of the original lineup), she had an English background that would influence the group's musical focus; she played button accordion and keyboards, and also brought in new repertoire and wrote the arrangements. As Cutting recalled, the band's sound developed gradually: "Bob and I were very into doing English repertoire. We weren't very electric at first, it was just an electric bass, but then gradually Bob began to pick up the electric guitar, and the real turning point was when I bought a synthesizer—and we added a drummer to the mix. And then we were a full-fledged electric folk band."

Cutting increasingly took up the band's management. She made use of her academic background and her job in the Smithsonian's Office of Folklife Programs and later in the Library of Congress's American Folklife Center to broaden the group's repertoire. As with their British counterparts, research was an integral part of making the music:

> A lot of our material came from the *Penguin Book of English Folk Songs*, which I'd got from Bert Lloyd—my own autographed copy. I used to sing those melodies to myself all the time, and then began imagining interesting chords that I could put with those melodies. And after that, when I was working here at the Archive of Folk Culture at the Library of Congress, I would begin to pull interesting books off the shelves and get songs from them.

The musical style of the New St. George was closely based on the British electric folk originals, especially the "classic" phase of Fairport Convention and Steeleye Span between 1969 and 1972. An analysis of the group's material on *High Tea*, as well as of Cutting's lecture from the 1996 Folk Alliance Panel, "Rocking the Folks" (Cutting 1996), reveals that the band had incorporated, somewhat consciously, the most idiomatic elements of this music: The repertoire on *High Tea* is characterized by catchy, distinctly British/English tunes combined with medieval/renaissance material, as Pentangle had done before. Lisa Moscatiello's singing style is close to Maddy Prior's, very direct but with less tension in the vocal cords than is usual among Americans, with a sparse but striking use of ornamentation. As with their English counterparts, a cappella sections, often with parallel singing as well as dronelike lines in the bass, were an integral part of the music. The rock music influence is evident in the characteristic backbeat and hooks that structure the songs.

The New St. George could therefore almost be described as a direct continuation of Fairport Convention and Steeleye Span, although the band maintained a distinctive sound color and style through its choice of instruments. Among the electric instruments, Cutting's keyboards played a prominent role, and the band also differed from its British counterparts in its selection of melodeon and flute/whistle as the primary melody instruments, rather than fiddle.

In contrast with most British folk and electric folk performers, Cutting is a professionally trained musician, which is apparent not only in her ability to verbalize her arrangements precisely but also in her harmonically based musical thinking. Although the arrangements are characterized by relatively complex harmonies and modulations, her starting point is always the melody line:

> I find the most original arrangements I've ever done have come from just going from only a melody line. Sometimes I'll alter it, like I'll flat the seventh scale degree if I don't like the way it sounds, or I'll take out a few passing tones. I do fiddle with the melodies sometimes to make what I think is an improvement on them, and then the next step is to add or vary interesting chords and chord substitutions—not just the obvious I–IV–V chords with the occasional sixth minor, but very, very creative chord voicings and substitutions.

She then works out general structural elements, before devising more detailed hooks and bridges and the instrumentation. The arrangement process is thus much more conscious and elaborate than that of many of the British performers. Despite her musicological education, however, the reconstruction of a "correct" ballad text plays only a minor role for Cutting. Finding a good, catchy tune is much more important to her:

> I'm much more compelled by the shape of the melody than by the story, and if something has a good melody you can always find a better lyric to go with it. I always look for a melody with good bones—with a good skeletal structure. If I don't like the lyrics that come with a particular melody, because I work in this archive, I can find ten other versions of that lyric until I find one that's good. Or do like Bert Lloyd: when I was doing "Time to Remember the Poor," which I found in Kidson's *Traditional Tunes*, I took a verse or two from a Nova Scotia version of "Time to Remember the Poor" and then conflated that text with the one that was in the Kidson book, and came up with what I thought was a better version of the tune all around. When we did "The Steggie," a traditional Scottish song, it wouldn't be appropriate for an American band to be doing something in thick Scots dialect that no one could understand. So I just reworked the lyrics—I substituted words, in fact, I rewrote some of the words. So you can always play with that! But you've got to find a really good melody because that's what hits people first, I think.

The debate about the legitimacy of electric instruments in traditional and folk music was already twenty years old when the New St. George was formed, yet this issue still came up in interviews with the band, although it was never as controversial as in England. For this generation of performers, the incorporation of electric instruments was rather a natural process. Bob Hitchcock suggested an analogy to the use of modern instruments in earlier epochs: "I think about how when George Wheatstone invented the concertina in 18-something, people went out and bought them and played them not because it was this old traditional instrument but because it was the slickest, latest, newest thing in the shops. It's the same with old blues musicians who played steel-bodied National resonator guitars" (Nelligan 1995: 25).

Since percussion instruments can be found in nearly all cultures since primeval times, drummer Juan Dudley likewise saw no contradiction in using a modern drum kit with folk music. In Cutting's eyes, the "electrification" of traditional and folk music does not imply a musical simplification, but instead invites a greater complexity of arrangement style and a broadening of repertoire, which echoes what Steeleye Span guitarist Rick Kemp said about the playing of electric instruments:

> Once the electric instruments were added, there was a certain level of sophistication that kept going up and up and up. And we left behind these chunkier, more traditional-sounding arrangements and went for more sort of polished pop- and rock-influenced arrangements. So in fact we stayed with British repertoire, but chose things that would be better set off by electric arrangements.

The New St. George won many awards and was highly successful on festival stages. Nothing in Tom Nelligan's article in *Dirty Linen* from April/May 1995 suggested that the group would play its last gig on October 7 in the same year and officially disband on April 16, 1996. The causes for the breakup were diverse. As Scott Miller points out in an Internet essay, "Too Many Dragons: A Historical Essay" (2003), the New St. George had experienced a series of management difficulties: signing with a small recording label that had little idea how to market electric folk; the misfiling of the band's CD *High Tea* in the stores; and the dismissal of the label's A&R man who had signed them, shortly after the CD was released. These misfortunes were disastrous in such a small-scale market. Cutting assumed all of the management and administrative work, in addition to the musical direction, until she could not cope with the workload anymore. She also reported that the technical problems of providing live sound reinforcement for a hybrid electric folk band took a severe financial toll:

> There is some added degree of difficulty, a strain imposed by carrying all that equipment around. It makes doing our job even tougher. If you are a famous rock band, and if you have all the roadies and techies in the world to help you, there isn't a strain in playing in the electric band—but folk rock bands, we always carry around our own things. We don't have roadies, no one can afford it. One of the added hardships is you not only have to split the money five or six ways between the members of the band, you also have to pay the sound engineer. And usually the sound engineer gets a cut equal to the band's, or a minimum of $100. And the band members have to lift all that heavy equipment, too. It's just a whole added layer of strain and difficulty. So electric folk bands are fragile and wonderful things—and because they may blow up at any moment, they should be appreciated while they are around![5]

In contrast with Britain, where the emerging progressive rock movement had provided performance spaces like smaller halls or universities for electric folk groups, the hybrid nature of electric folk caused problems for American bands, which could not build upon a corresponding existing network of venues. As Cutting explained:

> There was no network of such places. One had to be creative, one had to play at science fiction conventions and church concert series, and we just found all kinds of creative ways around this! One thing that did work in the folk scene was festival stages. Because generally festivals are an outdoor thing, you can be as loud as you want—and the volume was a big problem. When we would play the church basement folk clubs, it was usually too loud for the size of the room, and it was very difficult for a drummer to play his instrument properly while keeping the volume really low. Many of the small folk clubs were not suitable for this kind of music. So eventually we settled into outdoor concert series and festival stages as a great place for electric folk to flourish.

Although the New St. George appealed to an extremely varied audience with its danceable music, the band still faced the problem of being part of a small and specialized music scene on the East Coast. Most of the bands in the United States and Canada that have pursued a similar direction as the New St. George have focused on the Scottish/Irish (Celtic) side.

At the time of this writing, other than Cordelia's Dad, the group Tempest best represents the modern American electric folk generation, with a mixture of Celtic, Norwegian, and various European folk styles in a rock format. The band was founded in 1988 by Norwegian folk musician Lief Sorbye, who was strongly influenced at an early age by the Incredible String Band, Fairport Convention, and Steeleye Span. Their impact was clearly noticeable in his first electric folk band, Evil Delight, which also incorporated Norwegian folk music. Starting Tempest with a core group of San Francisco rock musicians, he later also added the multi-instrumentalist Ian Butler and fiddler Michael Mullen, who had previously played country music. The addition of a fiddler did not occur until 1992, for the band had wanted to avoid the "Fairport Convention sound" (Morman 1998: 21). Sorbye himself considers Tempest a progressive folk band rather than an electric folk or folk rock group. The group's highly successful concept album *Serrated Edge* (1992), for instance, combined traditional ballad characters like Tam Lin with elements from the novels of fantasy writer Mercedes Lackey.

This combination of rock with Celtic elements (i.e., elements from Gaelic-speaking areas) appears to occur much more frequently in Canada than in the United States. With a large number of Scottish and Irish immigrants, Canada hosts the highly vibrant folk scenes of Cape Breton and Newfoundland. These regions became a new home for Scottish refugees following the disaster of the Battle of Culloden in the mid-eighteenth century. Gaelic still spoken there, and traditional music is still well fostered. As is evident from the career of the Cape Breton fiddler Natalie MacMaster, these traditions have been passed on to the present generation. Although interest in traditional music declined in the early part of the twentieth century, from the 1950s on Canada has experienced a renewed interest in the tradition, especially in fiddling.

While Cape Breton has become well known for its acoustic folk music, the less orthodox Newfoundland has fostered several electric groups, the most popular being Figgy Duff (1974–93) and Great Big Sea, founded in 1993. The latter band's four singers and multi-instrumentalists Alan Doyle, Bob Hallett, Sean McCann, and Darrell Power grew up with traditional music on the Avalon Peninsula on the eastern part of the island. Mixing folk songs with modern instrumentation, the band soon expanded its following from the local clubs to Halifax and beyond, and by their second recording they had already signed with Warner. The distinctions between electric and acoustic or traditional and popular are less evident here; the band does not see itself as a rock band but instead describes itself as an "aggressive folk band that happens to be popular" (Nelligan 1999/2000). Apart from Great Big Sea, other popular Canadian electric folk bands are the Paperboys and Mad Pudding, both from Vancouver.

The Relationship of Electric Folk with Other American Microcultures: English, American, and Irish Identities

Facing a large number of different distinct microcultures and strong supercultural structures, the New St. George needed to set clear boundaries of identity to a much greater extent than its British counterparts. For this reason, the group intentionally set itself apart from the majority of Irish and Scottish (i.e., Celtic) groups by its repertoire and by its identity as an American-British electric folk band. While for Moscatiello, Petruccelli, and Dudley, the band's repertoire was just one music among others they played, for Cutting and probably also for Hitchcock the identification with the English tradition was quite strong. In contrast with their European predecessors, the American performers could clearly define the English elements of the repertoire. As Cutting remarked,

> With Celtic bands, dance tune medleys reign supreme. The tunes are normally played over and over again. With us and other English bands, the emphasis is on singing songs as opposed to playing instrumentals. A distinguishing feature of the English folk songs that we choose is that they have very stately melodies; there's an anthemic, noble quality to them. It isn't a flashy sort of thing at all, but a very subtle, quiet dignity. (Nelligan 1995: 25)

Cutting said that the melodeon is the most easily distinguished English instrument, in contrast to the Irish fiddle or Scottish bagpipes. Accordingly, the distinction between English and Irish does make sense for her, "because there is a way that dedicated Irish musicians master the Irish repertoire that people who are not of that tradition would never dream of going to that depth. It's a very difficult repertoire. It requires a lot of highly specific skills to do. It is a specialization, it is a genre apart unto itself, a tradition unto itself."

The name "New St. George" represented a link to the early British electric folk movement and to Fairport Convention and Richard Thompson in particular. Even to outsiders of the scene, the name of England's patron saint and the logo, the abstract of the cross of St. George,[6] were clear indications of the group's material and cultural interests: it was English and not Celtic/Gaelic. For insiders of the electric folk scene, the band's ties were even more obvious, since "The New St. George" was originally a song from Richard Thompson's first solo album, *Henry the Human Fly!* (1972). In an attempt to create a genuinely modern English music, Thompson combined contemporary (American/rock/popular) musical elements with the specifically English sounds of brass ensembles and accordion, and with lyrics addressing modern aspects of life. In an interview with Humphries (1996: 132), Thompson said that *Henry*'s introductory number, "Roll over Vaughn [*sic*] Williams," reflected the "dilemma of being a British musician who wants to represent British tradition in some way. If you want to be contemporary you can't ignore America and if you want to be true to your roots then you have to take that on board as well. It was having to fuse two cultures together—consciously and unconsciously."

Like other songs by Thompson, "The New St. George" is multilayered in its content. Written at a time when environmental protection was not yet taken for granted, the song can be understood as an early denunciation of environmental pollution, but it can also be read as a general criticism of British politics. Thompson remarked in a *Melody Maker* interview with Dallas (1972b) that "you can't just pitch on ecology and say this is bad without saying a lot of the other stuff's bad because it's the same thing." The meaning of the refrain "Leave the factory, leave the forge / dance to the New St. George" can be interpreted in different ways: as the demand for a "New England" or just as a call for a "re-establishing of traditional English values. More William Morris stuff," as suggested by Dallas (ibid.). Thompson was not happy with the overall style of *Henry the Human Fly!* and even received several negative reviews at the time. Today it is considered a classic recording, featuring many of the best performers from the British electric folk scene. "The New St. George" has subsequently been recorded by many musicians, including the Albion Country Band on *The Battle of the Field*,[7] and has also become a classic piece among the Thompson songs.

By establishing this connection to the mother culture of England, the New St. George unconsciously followed a clear pattern outlined by Slobin (1993: chap. 4), who pointed out that immigrant cultures are rarely isolated; there always still exists a clear interaction with the original mother culture that results in the emergence of the so-called diasporic interculture. Immigrant communities do not content themselves with merely playing their own music; rather, the presence of "original" musicians from the mother culture is also of great importance. From the beginning of the Second British Revival, a renewed strong presence and popularity of English/Irish groups could be observed in the United States. The music was swiftly noticed in American folk music magazines, as illustrated in issues of *Sing Out!* from 1965 to 1970. Various articles and advertisements reveal that the Copper Family from Sussex was as well known as Bert

Jansch, John Renbourn, and Pentangle, or Steeleye Span later on.[8] Likewise, English electric folk has always been extensively covered by the (younger) American folk magazine *Dirty Linen* (named after a Fairport Convention number). Many of its major articles focus on English groups, which seem to be almost as well known in America as in their country of origin.

The same seems to apply to recordings: as I observed during various visits to the States in the late 1990s, the selection in music shops is almost the same as in Britain. Joe Boyd's label, Hannibal Records, located in London and New York, has reissued many of the old Fairport and Thompson recordings, often with complete reprints of the original covers, which has not been the case in Britain. English groups retain a large following on the American folk circuit, which enables them to undertake extensive touring all over the country. In contrast to the mid-1960s, when Joan Baez's interpretation of "Matty Groves" was well known, it is now Fairport Convention's interpretation that is best known in the States, playing a key role in the American as well as in the English folk and electric folk scenes.[9]

The positive interaction between mother and immigrant culture does not always work well in both directions, however. American-English folk and electric folk groups, as well as the whole scene, tend to receive negative reviews from English music journalists, despite the reverse imitation and predominance of American supercultural elements in English music. A representative example is Ian A. Anderson's report (1994: 16) for *Folk Roots* on the 1994 North American Folk Alliance conference and performer showcase. The negative undertone begins with a description of the attendees as "almost exclusively white, middle-class, college-educated, past the first flush of youth, preoccupied." Fascinated by the Chinese yang-quin player Zhentin Zhang and the American punk/folk singer Ani DiFranco, Anderson describes the New St. George as "the second worst folk rock band I've ever heard" (ibid.),[10] very much in contrast with the enthusiastic American and Australian reviewers. When trying to reach a British audience, the New St. George found itself almost completely ignored by the British press and music scene; with the exception of *Living Tradition* and *English Dance & Song*, it could not even manage to get *High Tea* reviewed.

This rejection sometimes also works in reverse. With the exceptions of Davy Graham, Bert Jansch, and John Renbourn, who are acknowledged for their musicianship and for their creation of a unique fusion of American blues/jazz with British traditional elements, British acoustic blues musicians (as well as the skiffle movement back in the 1950s) are often not well regarded in the United States. American folk journalist Scott Miller (2003), for example, recently posted a satirical Internet analysis of a British blues imitator.

Apart from the interplay with the mother culture, microcultures also interact with adjacent microcultures. As the New St. George discovered, setting clear cultural boundaries was not sufficient to guarantee survival within a multiethnic society. With its distinctive English repertoire, the New St. George represented only a small musical minority among the Anglo-American groups. Irish music has always had a much stronger presence in America than English music. One simple reason is that music making has always been a central part of the social life of Irish Americans, as illustrated in Captain Francis O'Neill's collections.[11]

The strength of the Irish music scene is grounded in an extremely coherent subculture. Even in the late 1990s, one could still find a large variety of Irish pubs, shops, and neighborhoods in the United States. There are also a large number of Irish music festivals; leafing through *Dirty Linen*'s August/September 1996 issue, one could discover advertisements for events such as the North Texas Irish Festival (announced as the second largest festival in the nation), the Washington Irish Festival, Celtic Day, and so on. Some Irish microcultural elements have even reached a supercultural sphere. St. Patrick's Day (March 17), for instance, is celebrated by a large portion of the entire white population in the States in a lavish, large-scale way (with parades, media coverage, and so on) that has far exceeded the mother country's observance of it as a quiet family day.

The reasons for this strong presence are multilayered. The Irish population is among the largest of the immigrant cultures in the States, although its number does not surpass other West European populations.[12] Yet it has maintained much more distinct, identifiable cultural features than the other large European groups, as Cutting observed: "People could very easily tell you what was an Irish tune, more than they can tell you where the ballad 'Barbara Allen' came from—it's so easily graspable for people. It hasn't blended so much into the mainstream that it doesn't have its own character, whereas English ballads became Appalachian and other Anglo-American ballads."

Furthermore, in contrast with the British and German settlers, the Irish immigrants came later to the States (especially after the Great Famine of 1845–49), had been oppressed in Europe by the British, and were, as the poorest stratum of society, oppressed again in America. As a counterreaction, Irish people, discernible by name and accent, clung to their culture as a bulwark of their identity even more fiercely— sometimes replacing many historical facts with an intense nostalgia and mysticism.[13]

This strong Irish cultural identification caused problems for the New St. George. As an American-English band, the group had to depend on other, stronger microcultures and consequently played occasional gigs in the culturally related Irish subcultural sphere. Cutting remembered that the band sometimes collided with a strong anti-English sentiment still prevalent in the Irish scene:

> The nationalism among Irish Americans, it's the fiercest of all. There is an Irish bar in Baltimore that has a noose hanging on the wall. A noose for hanging! It's a plaque on the wall saying, "English necktie"! The New St. George, named after the patron saint of England— and our logo was the English flag, the red cross against a white background—was definitely not welcome in the hard-core Irish scene. There were festivals that we couldn't get in be-

cause of our name. You know, there is a strong anti-British sentiment. We lost our job at Flanagan's Irish Pub one time because somebody made a joke and played a bit of "Rule Britannia." Just as a joke! They never hired us again.

Cutting's story confirms Slobin's observations that many immigrant cultures continue to foster old negative political sentiments toward former enemies of their home countries—which, in a way, is also part of the process of establishing an identity within the diaspora (Slobin 1993: 66). Yet in the case of the New St. George, pragmatic considerations usually outweighed any political resentments. Because the Irish scene offered gigging possibilities, a certain level of adaptation was inevitable for the group, as Cutting recalled:

> We were trying to work in a completely Celtic-dominated music scene. If the booking person who could make the decision whether we would get the job or not asked, "Do you all play Irish music?" "Well—sure!" We have a set of Irish polkas, there was the odd Irish song in our repertoire, as there always was in the repertoire of Fairport Convention and Steeleye Span. Whenever they needed extended instrumentals, they always turned to Irish music. We relied on it less than they did—but there were the odd couple of Irish pieces.

As this comparison between the Irish American and English American cultures suggests, microcultures develop in different patterns. No surprise then, perhaps, that it is especially the stronger and better rooted microcultures that can provide the ground for the development of new micro-supercultures such as the Celtic music scene, inseparably connected with the revival of Scottish and Irish music in Europe.

THE EMERGENCE OF CELTIC MUSIC: A CURRENT MUSICAL FUSION FORM

Gaelic or Gaelic-sounding music has been used for many popular movies such as *Braveheart*, *Rob Roy*, and *Titanic*, thus reaching an extremely large audience. In addition, since the mid-1980s, elements of the strongly rooted and more accessible Irish as well as Scottish and Breton music cultures have been transformed into an easily adaptable (and commercial) concept of a Celtic tradition. Until the early 1990s, "Celtic" was basically another term for the music and artwork of Gaelic-speaking areas, while the distinctions between the different regions remained relatively clear-cut. Currently, "Celtic" is used as a very general term without any regional or stylistic distinctions, comprising not only the traditional musics, but also newly composed music in the style of Clannad's "Harry's Game."

Celtic music was not the first fusion of traditional Irish or Scottish music with popular music. Around the beginning of the twentieth century, the Irish music idiom had permeated to a popular level in the United States. In his study of Irish ethnic recordings, Moloney (1982) distinguished four separate, although overlapping, stages: (1) Largely romanticized or sentimental songs were composed by Anglo-Irish songwriters and interpreted by classically trained singers, among whom John McCormack was the most prominent. McCormack, who was a recording star between 1904 and 1941,[14] popularized "Danny Boy," which became emblematic of Irish music for this period. (2) Irish-style songs were used for minstrel-like stage shows between 1900 and 1940. (3) Traditional dance music was recorded in the wake of the huge popularity of ethnic recordings. Irish music played a dominant role within the large catalogue of recordings recorded by the major labels Columbia, Decca, and Victor in the 1920s and '30s. While Scottish pipe and fiddle music was also frequently recorded, English music, such as the Child ballads, was almost nonexistent in the States during this period. (4) A hybrid of the first three varieties emerged, often incorporating elements of contemporary popular music and instrumental combinations such as fiddle, flute, accordion, bass, and drums.

The major recording companies ceased producing Irish ethnic records in the 1940s. It was about twenty years later, when the American folk revival was at its peak, that Irish music reemerged. The cornerstone of this development was the appearance of the Clancy Brothers from Ireland's County Waterford on the Ed Sullivan Show in 1961 and at New York's Carnegie Hall in 1962. Using *the* instrument of the 1950s, the guitar, combined with harmonica and five-string banjo, the Clancy Brothers set the foundations for a renewed interest in the ballad singing. As Moloney (1982: 95) points out, this tradition was "largely unfamiliar to Irish-Americans from the second generation onward, whose concept of Irish music had been developed largely by commercial Irish-American recordings and particularly the nostalgic, sentimental material made popular by singers like Bing Crosby and Dennis Day."

The music of Tommy Makem from Armagh and the brothers Liam, Paddy, and Tom Clancy from Tipperary brought a much "rougher" music to American and Canadian audiences. Their impact was also evident on the other side of the Atlantic, for their success further ignited the emerging traditional music revival in Ireland. Despite similar features, the Irish revival would—like the Scottish revival—evolve in a substantially different direction than its English counterpart.

The Revivals in Scotland and Ireland after the Second World War: The Rediscovery of the Gaelic Cultures

The music revival in the Gaelic regions occurred in three stages. The first revival of the 1950s and 1960s, headed by groups such as the Chieftains, remained closely connected with developments in England and basically focused on instrumental music and material sung in the English language. The 1970s, by contrast, witnessed a growing interest in neglected Gaelic traditions, especially through the recordings of the Chieftains, Clannad, Planxty, De Dannan, and the Bothy Band as well as through harpist Alan Stivell from Brittany. The 1980s finally saw the emergence of the so-called Celtic movement, which took a distinctive shape with Clannad's synthesizer experiments and lush, reverb-laden vocal harmonies.

Traditional music had also been marginalized in Scotland and Ireland after World War II, yet the situation was different from that in England, as many people maintained a stronger relationship to the tradition. In Scotland the céilidh house[15] was still a part of rural life until the early 1950s, and traditional material was still performed by the older generation, although they were often met with a pitying smile from their children or neighbors, as Peter Kennedy pointed out in the introduction to his *Folksongs of Britain and Ireland* (1984: 2). Chieftains spokesman Paddy Moloney recalled in a *Dirty Linen* interview that playing traditional music, which was still fostered by the older Irish generation, was not considered "hip" among the young Irish in the 1950s; most people preferred to play skiffle and later rock 'n' roll (Winick 1998). As in England, radio had a strong impact in raising the awareness of this music at that time—especially through the collecting activities of Seamus Ennis and the weekly broadcast shows by Seán Mac Réamoinn, whose presentation of field recordings gave traditional performers a new self-confidence. And there was also Alan Lomax, who made extensive field recordings in England, Scotland, and the western counties of Ireland in 1951 that were issued by Columbia Records around 1955. Traditional music also found new visibility through the emerging music festivals, the first of which was the Fleadh Cheoil (Festival of Music) in 1951.

The young revival generation in Scotland and Ireland could still draw on a living tradition instead of having to use indirect forms of transmission like the mass media. Yet one could still observe the strong impact of individual figures. Apart from Seamus Ennis, who was also responsible for the renaissance of bagpipe playing, Seán Ó Riada (John Reidy) has to be credited for much of the renewed public interest in the Irish music tradition. Ó Riada (1931–71) greatly influenced the formation of the Chieftains, whose music making on traditional instruments such as pipes, fiddle, and whistle was rather unusual for its time.[16] Alongside the Clancy Brothers, the Chieftains, as well as the Dubliners (founded in 1962), were pivotal in the further development of the Irish revival by drawing outside attention to the music. Like many Irish bands, the Chieftains would remain part-time performers until the mid-1970s, when Jo Lustig took over their management. The Chieftains had already played as an opening act for electric folk groups like Fairport Convention in the late 1960s and early 1970s but, much in contrast with the British bands, would experience increasing international success from the mid-1970s on. Other Irish groups followed.

Scottish traditional music also underwent a revival process similar to the one in England in the early stages, with a number of radio broadcast series by Peter Kennedy, Hamish Henderson, and Alan Lomax raising awareness of this music. Of all of the series, Kennedy's *As I Roved Out*, which drew primarily from Scottish and Irish material, probably made the strongest impact, giving traditional singers a new, respected position within their own communities and creating broad national awareness of their music. The School of Scottish Studies, founded in 1951, also played a key role in reviving Scottish traditions, primarily through Hamish Henderson, who was appointed a research fellow in Scottish folk song that year. Henderson—who, like Ewan MacColl and A. L. Lloyd, had a strong commitment to socialism (he was not permitted to visit the United States until 1984)—established a number of field collections and promoted many traditional singers to a national audience. The most outstanding case was his "discovery" of the singer Jeannie Robertson. A Traveller singer from the northeast of Scotland, she became highly popular with audiences outside her community and was awarded an MBE (Member of the Order of the British Empire) in 1967 (Porter and Gower 1995).

As was the case in England, festivals like the Edinburgh People's Festival (1951–55) and Aberdeen (1963–), as well as the label Topic Records and Arnold Wesker's Centre 42, offered public platforms for traditional and revival musicians. Like their English counterparts, the Scottish performers and groups often started with skiffle (as did the Ian Campbell Folk Group). The early 1960s also witnessed a mushrooming folk club culture. With the background of the thriving living tradition, however, Scottish clubs were never as dogmatic as in England and always presented a mixture of American, Irish, Scottish, and English music. Early on, Scottish traditional singers like Donald Higgins or the Stewarts of Blair were guests in the clubs, side by side with English revival performers such as Davy Graham, Martin Carthy, and the Watersons, or with early Scottish revival groups like the Ian Campbell Folk Group, Robin Hall and Jimmie MacGregor, and the Corries (Munro 1996: 36). Conversely, several Scottish performers were extremely successful within the English sphere, most prominently the Incredible String Band and Bert Jansch. Scottish folk music, with groups like the Boys of the Lough (with Shetland fiddler Aly Bain) and the Battlefield Band, would also play an increasingly dominant role in Scotland itself and abroad from the 1970s on, further enhanced by the popularity of Celtic music.

The Rediscovery of Celtic Culture in the Mid-1970s

Although electric folk and folk rock groups also emerged in Scotland and Ireland—the most prominent being the Irish Horslips—the so-called Celtic direction proved much more important for further musical development. The term "Celtic" originally referred to all "members of a group of Indo-European peoples inhabiting the British Isles and large areas of west and central Europe in Antiquity."[17] Today it is usually restricted to Ireland, Scotland, the Isle of Man, Wales, Brittany (including the entire area, not only the purely Gaelic-speaking regions), Cornwall, and increasingly, with the emerging bagpipe revival in northern Spain, to Galicia as well.[18] "Celtic music" originally just meant traditional material from these areas but was later increasingly merged into a unified style.

Performers and groups from Brittany like Alan Stivell, Tri Yann, and La Bamboche were clear predecessors of the development that started with the Irish group Clannad in the 1980s. The Breton folk music revival in the mid-1960s was sparked by Alan Stivell (harp, bagpipes, Irish flute). Born Alan Cochvelou in Riom in 1944 (thus originally not from Brittany), he rediscovered the almost completely forgotten Celtic harp through his father, who had begun to reconstruct and rebuild this instrument. When only nine years old, Cochvelou presented the harp to a Breton audience and later started his popular music career as Alan Stivell[19] in Paris in 1966. Following the trend of that time, he played a considerable amount of American material. Yet only a few years later—the parallels with Britain are obvious—he initiated a revival of the interest in Breton music and Gaelic language with his recordings *Reflets* (1971) and, in particular, *Renaissance de la harpe celtique* (1972). Stivell's repertoire included a vast range of traditional Irish and Breton instrumentals, while his songwriting drew strongly on Celtic mythology, with characteristic topics and titles like "Ys" or "Broceliande." With guitarist Dan Ar Braz, Stivell created an electric folk sound that differed from the English groups in its stronger emphasis on Celtic instruments like the harp and, on the electric side, on synthesizers and sound effects, something that would become characteristic of the Celtic direction.[20]

Gaelic Music since the 1980s: The Celtic Fusion in Europe and in America

The Irish group Clannad from Donegal is largely responsible for the modern Celtic boom since the 1980s. Formed by family (clan) members of the Braonains and Dugains, the musicians had played together at school and made their first public appearances around 1970. In contrast with groups like the Chieftains or the Dubliners, whose repertoire consisted mainly of songs in the English language, at an early stage Clannad incorporated Gaelic material that at that time had only a small audience.[21] The early Clannad was one of the most innovative Irish bands, combining traditional pieces with modern acoustic arrangements. It struggled in the beginning, encountering disapproval from the traditional scene and a lack of support from the almost nonexistent Irish folk rock scene. However, the situation changed completely with the growing general popularity of Irish and Scottish music after 1975, and Clannad became one of the most successful and enduring Irish acts.

In 1983 the group wrote "Harry's Game" for the Yorkshire Television adaptation of a North Ireland–based thriller by Gerald Seymour. "Harry's Game" appeared on *Magical Ring*, the group's first album on an international label (RCA). It marked the beginning of a new style: until then Clannad had remained acoustic, apart from the occasional incorporation of synthesizers played by a cousin, Eithne Ní Bhraonáin, who as Enya would later become a highly successful solo musician. With *Magical Ring*, Clannad started to develop a more rock-oriented sound, combined with its own songwriting. This style is characterized by the use of traditional and modern Gaelic texts or phrases, often of mythic content, that are combined with catchy melodies in a traditional style.

These are built up as multilayered vocal or instrumental structures with much reverberation to create a lush sound. This style, which has been imitated by many other Irish and Scottish singing groups, has become associated with both the terms "Celtic" and "New Age" (under which Enya's recordings are frequently shelved in stores).

Although Clannad has been attacked for this approach, musical crossovers are quite common in Ireland, with its relatively small, closed community of musicians. The guest appearance of U2's lead singer Bono on Clannad's *Macalla* (1985) and the a cappella ensemble Voice Squad backing popular star Sinéad O'Connor—who also guested on recordings of the Chieftains[22]—are nothing unusual in the Irish context.

"Harry's Game" marked the beginning of an international career for Clannad; it won the Ivor Novello Award for best television soundtrack and also entered the British pop charts—which was even more remarkable at that time, as Gaelic was still considered suspect in many segments of British society (Bond 1993: 52). Following Clannad's international success, many Irish groups started to perform in Gaelic. Scotland also witnessed a revival in Gaelic song, partly set in motion by the British revival.[23] As in Ireland, Gaelic language and culture had been disappearing. Related musical material, such as waulking songs and laments, had been strongly marginalized; the working context was disappearing, and the music was also rejected by many communities as an expression of an outmoded lifestyle people wanted to leave behind. Although the collecting activities of the School of Scottish Studies raised a new awareness of this material, it was especially the Celtic folk rock and electric folk groups of the 1980s and '90s like Runrig and Capercaillie that revived widespread interest in Scotland's musical heritage. Both Runrig and Capercaillie started as dance bands, but they soon included Gaelic song material as well, probably partly because of Clannad's huge success.

Scotland has always produced extremely successful popular or rock music performers such as Rod Stewart or the Simple Minds. These musicians drew occasionally on traditional melodic and instrumental elements but were otherwise much like other mainstream rock or pop groups. Founded in 1978, Runrig, in contrast, wrote a major portion of its material in Gaelic from the beginning. Capercaillie, whose sound was more traditional than the rock-oriented Runrig, also incorporated Gaelic material from early on. Using a musical language similar to Clannad in its early stages—especially with its arrangements of laments—for a long time Capercaillie was tagged as a Clannad copy. But while Clannad stayed with the formula it had worked out for "Harry's Game," Capercaillie (which also gained wider popularity through the soundtrack for the film *Rob Roy*) developed its approach further, incorporating African elements as well. Runrig and Capercaillie have not only contributed to the international success and awareness of Celtic music (Runrig easily fills halls with more than 40,000 listeners) but have also revived interest in the Scottish-Gaelic tradition in Scotland (MacLeod in Munro 1996).

The Appeal of Celtic Music

The Celtic style has been copied in other countries as well, particularly if sacred or ritual music is involved,[24] and has evolved in a New Age direction with Enya, whose connection with the original tradition now lies primarily in her use of the Gaelic language and melodic elements. Clannad exerted a strong influence on the development of Celtic-influenced music in the United States. In 1992–93, approximately ten years after its first European success, "Harry's Game" appeared in the film *Patriot Games* and was also used for a U.S. advertising campaign for Volkswagen.[25] From then on, the popularity of Celtic music increased in the States and in Canada.

One of the best-known Canadian artists is Loreena McKennitt, a harpist, singer, and composer. Although she uses traditional British and Irish songs, she often embeds them in her own songwriting. She eclectically combines various Celtic elements and myths with musical styles and instruments from all over the world; her recordings and posters feature colorful artwork and design. Probably out of confusion regarding how her hybrid style should be categorized, she has often been tagged as New Age.

The combination of music, a recognizable graphics style, and mysticism seems to be attractive to a broad range of people. This is reflected not only in the large numbers of albums sold by Clannad, Enya, and McKennitt but also in the changing advertising style in the American folk magazine *Dirty Linen*. Around 1992 only a few ads labeled music as "Celtic,"[26] and the announcements were differentiated, describing "Music from Scotland" or "Irish-American bands." Within three years almost everything, including the majority of the festivals, was labeled "Celtic." This successful marketing strategy also exerted an influence upon the presentation of English music: Steeleye Span was suddenly promoted as "Celtic Rock at its best."[27]

As far as Britain itself is concerned, however, "Celtic" has rarely found favor with the electric folk bands. As Oysterband fiddler Ian Telfer mused:

I think "Celtic" is a fiction. It's a label of convenience. It's anything you want it to be. It's like the word "alternative" in marketing—anything that wants to claim authenticity or credibility labels itself "alternative," no matter which global capitalist megacorporation owns it. And similarly, whatever wants to invoke passion or inspiration or rebelliousness nowadays calls itself "Celtic." But historically it's entirely fake. There are states and there are cultures and ethnicities and languages and artistic styles and forms of social organization, and they all overlap; but they're far from identical, and the relations between them are subtle and complicated and shift hugely over time. I could easily defend the proposition that England is a Celtic country, for example, insofar as the term means anything at all. So to jump straight from the Book of Kells to U2 (or even the Dubliners) is just laughable.

The potential for nationalistic symbolism can occasionally be observed in Europe as well, although it is still difficult to draw any definite conclusions from the following incident: After their stylistic change from an acoustic dance band to a modern folk rock group, the Oysterband started to use Celtic artwork and designs for their CDs and other merchandise. As Telfer recalled, the band suddenly found itself a point of interest for what he described as "fascist groups" in Europe, although these people disappeared when they found out that the band played sociocritical English music:

> In fact the idea of "Celticness" is quite double-edged. I didn't notice until we went on a tour to Germany with the Pogues some years ago, and to my surprise some young fascists turned up at the shows. They soon realized they were at the wrong gig, but if you think about it—the Celts were "white" and allegedly pan-European, artistic but (we are told) warlike, and there's so little written historical evidence [that] you can make it all up. You can see the possible appeal to a certain mentality. So I'm very skeptical about Celts and Celticness, even though I suppose many people would consider I am one. It's just too convenient: let's not be boring old Spaniards, let's be hip Galician Celts! And in little valleys in Switzerland, and in Belgium and Germany and the Czech Republic, people are busy with rediscovering their "Celtic roots."

REVIVAL PROCESSES AND ELECTRIC FOLK: BEYOND FAIRPORT CONVENTION

Although the Irish and Scottish groups are currently much better known internationally than the English ones, the historical importance of the English electric folk movement cannot be emphasized strongly enough. It was predominantly these groups that set many subsequent European revivals of traditional music in motion. Especially after the success of Pentangle, Fairport Convention, and Steeleye Span, similar revival processes occurred in other European countries and regions like Scandinavia, Holland, Belgium, France, and Germany. Woods (1979: 69) observed that "all the European revivals started by using British material, usually sung in English and sometimes even with the appropriate regional accent."[28] Only as a second step did these groups and performers begin to explore their own traditions, although acoustic and electric musical arrangements often still showed the influence of British electric folk.

The imitation of British groups, predominantly Fairport Convention and Steeleye Span, was obvious with the early Swedish groups such as Folk och Rackare and Kebnekajse. However, with a ballad tradition similar to that in England, it was only a small step for the Scandinavian revival performers to develop completely individual styles. The difference between Scandinavian and British groups has more to do with the instrumentation and singing techniques than with the musical arrangement structure. The Swedish electric folk group Garmarna, for instance, gave its interpretation of the ballad "Herr Holger" a modern rock backing—with upbeat drums, a strong bass sound, and a catchy hook—that is quite close to British styles. Yet it still differs because its sound is dominated by fiddle, hurdy-gurdy, and a falsetto-like singing style.

Scandinavia also offers a good example of how the terms "folk rock" and "electric folk" have partly become expressions that no longer refer to a specific regional musical style but rather to a general practice of playing traditional music with electric instruments. During the WDR Folkfestival 1995 in Cologne, one member of the Norwegian group Chateau Neuf Spelemannslag[29] told me that—much to his displeasure—many people described the music of his band with the general term "folk rock," even though it mixes traditional instrumental music and ballad singing with elements of jazz and classical music that have little to do with a mere fusion of folk and rock.

As Woods pointed out, many German revival performers started by imitating Irish and Scottish groups, developing an interest in their own music only as a second step, as in the case of Fiedel Michel or Liederjan. In contrast with other countries, however, German folk groups often stayed with these models: a significant feature of the German folk/electric folk scene was that, apart from a strongly politically oriented direction shaped by the so-called 1968 movement, the German-Irish/Scottish groups or bands differed from the British groups in the songs and languages used but not in instruments or musical style. The major problem this revival movement faced was that, although the musicians could call upon a broad range of German material, especially from the archive of folk music in Freiburg, these sources were mainly in written form only. Recordings, especially of clearly distinguished performance practices, were either few or difficult to access, and the living tradition was almost completely gone, with a few exceptions in the Alpine region that witnessed a revival in the late 1980s as "Neue Volksmusik."

Groups like the Bavarian Hundsbuam Miserablige and the Austrian duo Attwenger have created punklike music with overdubbed accordion, bass, and vocal layers, suggesting that the Alpine region might also come up with further experiments in the future. Many non-Alpine German groups nevertheless have stayed with Anglo-American (supercultural) performance styles. The German-Irish folk group Wild Silk, for instance, partly uses British and Irish songs and ballads that closely resemble the versions performed by Steeleye Span and Pentangle. Their emphasis is on the melodic sound rather than on the storytelling characteristic of their British or Irish counterparts. The group's arrangement of "Let No Man Steal Your Thyme," for instance, includes only the first three verses of the song, which are, without any ornamentation, repeated several times. Yet the group is not a mere copy; despite the strong presence of Irish fiddling, Wild Silk has developed an individual sound color by incorporating highly skilled recorder playing as well as Middle Eastern instruments. It also performs German traditional songs and original songs, often written in English.

Another musical direction was initiated by the German electric folk band Ougenweide from Hamburg. Named after a poem by the medieval minnesinger Neidhart von Reuental, the group, founded in 1971, plays predominantly secular medieval songs from minnesingers or heathen material like the "Merseburger Zaubersprüche" ("spells from Merseburg"), an approach that has also been taken up by several younger groups like Estampie and Schandmaul.

Electric Folk in the Context of World Music Fusions

Space does not permit a comprehensive overview of musical fusions outside Europe. As a glance at any recent issue of *Folk Roots* will confirm, today almost all non-Western countries combine their own folk music with modern (western) instruments and music styles. Moreover, the fusion of traditional musics with popular music elements is not new: blues and jazz, as well as other traditional styles like Cajun music and zydeco have always incorporated contemporaneous elements. Similarly, bhangra, the fusion of Indian/Pakistan traditions with British popular music, can be traced back to the 1950s, while South Africa's vibrant jazz scene is almost as old as its counterparts in the United States. South Africa's urban environments have been the basis for a large number of tradition/pop fusions, such as the keyboard-based bubblegum that emerged in the 1980s and '90s.

These interactions of traditional music with contemporary forms of popular music can be described as a natural process, and as Slobin (1993) pointed out, many new musical forms and subcultures emerge this way. Yet owing to the increasing dominance of global mass media networks, the danger has increased of further homogenizing living traditions. Western popular music—as represented by the recording conglomerates Warner, BMG, and Universal—has become an international superculture that can reach almost any region. Many local cultures would rather follow Westernized music trends and tastes than foster traditions that are perceived as old-fashioned.

This situation is reflected in the sleeve notes of the singer/instrumentalist Hanitra, leader of Madagascar's most popular group, Tarika, on the recording *Soul Makassar* (2002). The group plays a partly electric fusion style, yet the search for more original traditional sounds resulted in a trip to Indonesia, from whence the first settlers of Madagascar had come 1,500 years ago. Hanitra had hoped to find a wealth of traditional material, since the Indonesian culture was older than Madagascar's. She learned much to her disappointment, however, that the situation in Indonesia was not much different from Madagascar's own, with traditional music not considered fashionable at all. Only a little public money was available to support the preservation and cultivation of traditional music.

How, then, should the original British electric folk movement be understood within these global developments? Every revival of a traditional music always entails losses from as well as additions to the original material, and revivalists always move between these two extremes, whether they are aware of it or not. Yet electric music and the marginalization of a tradition are nevertheless two different issues. The fragile relationship between these two spheres is indeed problematic (and one might well argue that there is a danger of one drawing talent from the other), yet electric or fusion music is not always a destructive element; rather, it is extremely dependent on the original tradition for its success as a musical style.

To make this point clear, I would like to cite a final example from Bulgaria that Joe

Boyd mentioned in his interview. One of his Hannibal Records acts was the modern clarinetist Ivo Papasov, who plays a mixture of complex Bulgarian rhythms and jazzy improvisations. With his electric band, which includes clarinet, saxophone, accordion, and keyboard, Papasov encountered the same kind of opposition from acoustic performers as had the early English electric folk bands. Boyd recalled that "the acoustic musicians that I have recorded like the Balkana group were horrified when they heard that I was making a record with Ivo Papasov. They hate Ivo Papasov, and they feared that he'd destroy their folk music. But the fact is that Ivo Papasov is very popular with the people and he's a very big star in the countryside, and it's real—to me."

Although Boyd works with many musicians who experiment with their traditional music, he still rejects much of the modern "world music" fusions: "Most I hear are upside down to me. They take an exotic melody and put it over a kind of mid-Atlantic rhythm, and to me that's a peanut butter sandwich fallen on the carpet" (Nelligan 1996: 24). Neither the involvement of electric instruments per se nor the popularity, and thus commerciality, is the central problem. The problem is rather that many modern approaches tend to ignore the original stylistic sources. Quoting Boyd again:

> If you listen to Jimi Hendrix—he was a genius! And now you listen to some heavy metal guitar player playing in a Jimi Hendrix style: it's very depressing, because it has the sound of it without any of the feeling. And I think the same thing has happened with folk rock in a way. When I hear Ashley MacIsaac and his band playing jigs and reels with a drummer, an electric bass player, and a guitar player and the violin, I find it very difficult to listen to because to me it's very loud and very fast for the sake of being loud and fast. Instead of going back to the source and trying to invent something fresh from the source, a lot of groups have taken the approach that Fairport did to those kinds of dance melodies and just imitated Fairport or imitated Steeleye Span. . . . It's kind of the form of it without the essence.

As long as musicians maintain the cultural integrity of their music, which—for Boyd—is basically expressed in the rhythm, these fusions pose no danger for the original tradition: "Ivo Papasov can play 'Yankee Doodle' but keeps that 11/8 or 9/8 rhythm going, and it's authentically Bulgarian. So any fusions that I get involved in have that basis—to take music on its own rhythmic terms" (Nelligan 1996: 24).

With a revival music, indirect forms of transmission like transcriptions and recordings play an essential role. Even if only a few fragments are left, a knowledge of their content still offers a possibility to express the material with new or more intense musical and stylistic means. The various original singing styles, including the tempo fluctuations of the parlando-rubato style, as marginal as they seem, are an integral part of the music; when it is played mainly for dance purposes, it inevitably loses many subtle elements. If there is something that English electric folk could be accused of, it is of having ironed out some of the more complex vocal elements, especially in the early years of the late 1960s and early '70s. This "leveling" effect was partly due to limited technical recording possibilities, partly due to a mere lack of knowledge. On the other hand, work with traditional sources should not and cannot imply a historicized, museum-like attitude that only allows the music to be played in its "original" form (i.e., in the form in which it has been recorded), as happened in the English folk clubs. As Joe Boyd reflected,

> I have no feelings that folk music has to be stuck in a museum—it has to change. Some folk music lives in the rhythm, and that's one thing I have learned from Fairport—that the essence comes from the rhythms. Most kinds of fusions or modernizations take a kind of mid-Atlantic rhythm and put a decoration of folk music on top like melodies and instruments and things, but the rhythm isn't really the folk music. To me that is pretty boring and uninteresting and very destructive. Whereas if you do something in dance, even if it's extreme and loud and electric like Ivo Papasov, you get people to dance to it, people from the tradition, country people, then, to me, you still have your feet on the ground, then you still are in touch with what music really is—even if you're playing electric instruments on top of it.

The same applies to the early English electric folk, which, despite all its external and internal struggles, nowadays stands as a paradigm of the interaction of traditional and popular music in a Western European country. It is a music in its own right within Western popular music styles, but, at the same time, its maintains a tie to the tradition that has helped to strengthen its place in modern society.

NINE

POSTLUDE 2003

Was electric folk a typical product of the 1960s youth cultures? The question is difficult to answer, because the Second Folk Revival in England had been active long before folk music became associated with middle-class youth countercultures. Several attempts to fuse traditional and contemporary music had already occurred in the early 1960s, and many performers were already experimenting with new approaches. However, the structural conditions that facilitated the development of this genre—such as John Peel's radio show, independent record companies, and an audience open to musical experimentation—first emerged with the counterculture of the late 1960s.

English electric folk had its peak between 1969 and 1975. The disappearance of this music from the most mainstream popular spheres does not necessarily portend its complete disappearance. Looking back on the developments of the 1990s, I believe that this music will continue to survive and develop, building on its established audience, festivals, and network of specialist recording companies, magazines, and Web sites. Groups like Steeleye Span, Fairport Convention, and Pentangle have recently been even more creative than during the previous ten years, releasing a number of high-quality recordings, albeit on a small scale. It is not likely that any of the older performers—who long ago became institutions—will (or can) retire in the near future.

From a musical viewpoint, the development could go into several directions—in part owing to the ongoing exchange of performers, as was especially evident with Steeleye Span in 2000–2001. Generally speaking, the sound, due to better recording technology, has become much more transparent, with a less heavy bass or guitar sound. Many performers and groups such as Fairport Convention increasingly incorporate modern songwriting, although traditional material will always play an essential role in their repertoire. Moreover, the folk scene is by no means as restrictive as it was twenty years ago, and so many musical innovations can also be expected from that side. Hence, I suspect that many creative developments in traditional music will be more acoustically based, as suggested by recent recordings of Waterson:Carthy, June Tabor, and Maddy Prior. However, electric folk has surprised us before and will likely continue to do so.

WHAT ABOUT THE "first generation" of electric folk, then? It is surprising how easily these musicians returned to a noncelebrity lifestyle when the popularity of electric folk declined after 1975. Yet their stardom was never as excessively celebrated as with rock music. The performers have always remained accessible, as journalist John Tobler explained:

> I can phone most of these people up. I know where they are living. Folk people are not usually stars; they like to be stars, but they know they are not. These are very ordinary people. These are not Mick Jagger. Someone like Ashley Hutchings is about the same age as me—it's just he went into one direction, he went into music, and I went doing what I do. But I suppose he probably didn't imagine that he was still gonna do it thirty years later, and still have to be running the Albion Band and putting out records.

It seems that only a few—if not to say none—of the musicians made enough money during the 1960s and 1970s to enable them to stop performing. Almost all the performers are still active in the music sector, although outside the popular music venues. The annual timetable is still similar to what Simon Nicol described in 1996:

> We have Cropredy in August, and then we have a British winter tour in January/February, and then the rest of it depends on if the individuals are available. If we've got time to make a record, we'll make one. If we've got time to make a record, then that probably means we'll get a chance to get to America with it, but you need some help from an American record company to promote a new product. So that's why we are going in October.

Several performers also work for other groups or as studio musicians, but it is difficult to estimate how well they can live off their music. Tobler suggested that several performers also depend on the incomes of their spouses. Living solely from music requires a punishing working schedule as he pointed out:

> Some of them, the best ones, can make a living. Dave Pegg was in Jethro Tull, which was a very big-paying job: an American tour and an English tour every year, an album. So he was making a lot of money off Jethro Tull. Fairport—they get some money out of Cropredy. But it's very expensive to put on: putting a stage on, just the security people, catering a lot, hiring the field. You have to work hard. It's by no means an easy option to be a professional musician.

Each performer seems to have found a different solution. Most of the Fairport musicians live near Banbury (Oxfordshire), working, as Nicol does, as full-time musicians. Having previously drummed for Chris Rea, Alison Moyet, and Brian Eno, Dave Mattacks left Fairport in 1997–98 and is working successfully as a much-requested freelance studio musician. (As Fairport had been on an unplugged tour anyway, the subsequent change to former Pentangle drummer Gerry Conway was rather smooth.)

Dave Swarbrick returned to England after a brief intermission in Australia from 1993 to 1996. Despite poor health (on April 20, 1999, he found himself prematurely honored by an obituary in the *Daily Telegraph*), he occasionally performs in the scene, sometimes teaming up with Martin Carthy as well as making frequent guest appearances in Cropredy. He was living in Coventry at the time of this writing. In November 2002 he was awarded the English Folk Dance and Song Society's Gold Badge for his contributions to folk music. The EFDSS hereby not only recognized his immense musical influence on a vast range of performers, but also the fact that his modern approach has attracted many listeners and performers back to the English tradition. As Beryl Marriott (2003: 10) enthused in her laudatory speech, "Dave Swarbrick is one of the most influential, most universally loved and—most important—surely one of the most deserving recipients of the Gold Badge of the EFDSS."

Of all of the Fairport Convention members, Richard Thompson has probably had the most successful career as a highly acclaimed songwriter and guitarist. He now lives in both Los Angeles and London's Hampstead area. Ashley Hutchings still performs with his Albion Band, both acoustically and electrically, still with constant changes. Living in Stockport, near Manchester, he was also working in 1996 on radio shows such as a survey of the music of Manchester. In 2002 Fairport Convention was honored with the Lifetime Achievement Award at the BBC Radio 2 Folk Awards.

Joe Boyd created Hannibal Records, a label that has become important for raising awareness of Eastern European music in the West. Too small to survive in a larger market, Hannibal was sold to Rykodisc several years ago, and Boyd worked as senior vice president and A&R man for Hannibal/Rykodisc, which has its European basis in London. He not only remains an authority in the field of British electric folk (Hannibal has reissued several old recordings by Boyd artists Fairport Convention, Richard Thompson, Fotheringay, and Nick Drake), but has also become an expert on the rather sensitive challenges of marketing traditional/folk music in general. In early 2001, at Hannibal's twentieth anniversary, Boyd left his job for the label.

In 2000 Maddy Prior was awarded an MBE (Member of the Order of the British Empire) in recognition of her service to folk music. She lives with her husband Rick Kemp near Carlisle and still works as a full-time musician. She left Steeleye Span in 1998 to have more time for her solo career as well as for individual projects such as recordings and tours with the Carnival Band. Her recent albums *Flesh & Blood* (1998) and *Ravenchild* (1999), as well as her solo performances, have been warmly received by critics. Likewise, Kemp, who was not able to play bass for a while because of an injury, has recorded two more rock-oriented solo works, *Escape* and *Spies*, since 1996. He was also running a music club and teaching at the local college in Carlisle at the time of our interview:

> I wouldn't have to do it. I think I'm doing it because I'm interested in teaching and ways of going about it. It fascinates me the way that people feed me, when I'm supposed to be teaching them. And they feed me all the time. It's extraordinary the amount that I learn in a day. If I'm passing on a fraction of that to other people in another way, then I'm happy. Because I get so much from this.

After Gay Woods left Steeleye Span at the end of 2000, Tim Harries and Peter Knight decided to continue with the band and asked Rick Kemp in again. In 2002 Prior returned to Steeleye as well. Her "Silly Sisters" partner, June Tabor, originally an Oxford-educated librarian, turned professional only a few years ago after various restaurant projects. Increasingly incorporating more jazz and singer/songwriter material into her repertoire, she has managed to appeal to an audience outside the clubs as well.

Jacqui McShee lives with Gerry Conway in Redhill (Surrey) near London. When I visited her for the interview, she had just produced her first solo recording, *About Thyme*, with Conway and Spencer Cozens. As the only founding member of Pentangle who has carried on with the group over the years, she was at that time thinking about continuing the group with her *Thyme* lineup and Alan Thompson on guitar: "We are actually going to call us Jacqui McShee's Pentangle. It's the last thing I wanted to do. With 'the new Pentangle' you are gonna be associated with the early years."

Two years later, the band produced a new album, *Passe Avante*. Conway is also much in demand with other electric folk projects: after Mattacks left Fairport Convention in 1998, he took over as drummer and likewise played drums for the new Steeleye Span record *Horkstow Grange* (1998) after drummer Liam Genockey left. McShee also occasionally gigs with John Renbourn, who continues to perform in the Anglo-American music scene. At the time of these interviews, Bert Jansch was regularly gigging at the London Twelve Bar music club, as well as playing at festivals and occasionally recording. His album *Crimson Moon*, released in 2000, received enthusiastic reviews both inside and outside Britain.

Martin Carthy, who was awarded an MBE in 1998 for his "services to English folk music" and an honorary Ph.D. from Sheffield University in 2002, remains a tireless performer who does numerous gigs every year. When I interviewed him at his house at Robin Hood's Bay, he was home only for a few days before heading off again. His touring calendar was full of dates abroad in Spain and Japan with his wife and daughter as Waterson:Carthy.

At that time, the Watersons were receiving renewed public attention. Carthy's wife Norma Waterson had just produced a highly celebrated and commercially successful album with interpretations of traditional songs and rock songs (the album, *Norma Waterson*, was also nominated for the Mercury Award in 1996, which included a televised appearance at the award ceremony). She won the BBC Radio 2 Folk Award 2001 in the category "Singer of the Year." Norma's sister, Lal Waterson, who died in 1998 of cancer, had in 1996 released a new solo album, *Once in a Blue Moon*, with her son Oliver Knight, a rock guitarist and music producer. The greatest attention, however, is now focused on Carthy's daughter, Eliza Carthy, who plays fiddle and sings. Able to draw upon the rich musical background and connections of her family, she experiments a great deal, either solo, with her family, or with new folk rock groups like the Kings of Calicutt. She was awarded the BBC Radio 2 Folk Award 2003 in the categories of both "Singer of the Year" and "Album of the Year" for her album *Anglicana*, released in 2002.

Shirley Collins was living in Brighton at the time of our interview. Still shattered by the death of Dolly, she was working through a number of her sister's unpublished songs. In 1998 *Harking Back*, a collection of live recordings, was published. She also lectures and has been working on a book about her U.S. fieldwork with Alan Lomax, *America Over the Water*, which was published in 2004.

The members of the Oysterband are full-time professional musicians. Although closer to the rock sector, they occasionally revisit their acoustic roots. The night before my interview at Ian Telfer's house in London, I heard the Oysterband as a céilidh band in Camden. Telfer pointed out the next day that the group had been worried about having forgotten their old repertoire: "Of course we'd remember all the tunes, but we couldn't remember the names of them, so it was hard to communicate to each other what we wanted to play next. So me and John and Alan know an enormous number of dance tunes, but we don't play them often. But they're in there somewhere." In 2003 the Oysterband won a BBC Radio 2 Folk Good Tradition Award.

It hence seems that all these performers will remain musically active as long as possible—and most likely the scene's outlook will have changed again by the time this book appears.

PERSONNEL LISTINGS AND SELECTED DISCOGRAPHY

Any Internet search engine will easily reveal several extensive fan sites with much more comprehensive discographies than the following list, which aims to provide only a representative selection. A detailed compilation of LP/CD release data is extremely difficult because of the vast number of reissues (often edited), sold recording labels, and foreign-country releases. I have therefore decided to list only the first release dates for the original British labels.

Likewise, I have included only those artists who have been covered in the text. I have thus had to omit or include only one or two recordings by such distinguished artists as Bob Davenport, Robin and Barry Dransfield, Ray and Archie Fisher, Nic Jones, Louis Killen, Martin Simpson, and Peta Webb, as well as singer/songwriter Ralph McTell and guitarists like Stefan Grossman and Wizz Jones. Because I also wanted to draw attention to the English material, I have, with a few exceptions, omitted the major portion of Scottish and Irish recordings. The albums are listed chronologically within each subcategory.

For a complete discography of Shirley Collins, see Hunt (1980a); for Fairport Convention, see Humphries (1997); for Richard Thompson, see Humphries (1996), and for Sandy Denny, see Heylin (2000).

THE MAJOR ELECTRIC FOLK GROUPS

In order to provide a better historical orientation, I have combined this selected discography of the major British electric folk groups—Pentangle, Fairport Convention, Steeleye Span, and the Oysterband—with the personnel lineups. With the exception of Fairport Convention, which experienced many well-documented personnel changes in its early stages, I mainly list the years in which the lineups changed.

The instrumental lists have been kept as close as possible to the original liner notes, with a few alterations: "Guitars" signifies the use of both electric and acoustic guitars, while "guitar" signifies the acoustic instrument only. If only an electric guitar was used, it is signified by "electric guitar." As keyboards have played only a marginal role in British electric folk, I have not included this term. The term "drums" usually includes the kit and any other percussion instrument the drummer might use, although in some cases specific percussion instruments, if unusual, have been listed.

Pentangle

Lineup 1 (1967–end of 1972)

ALBUMS

The Pentangle (Transatlantic, 1968)

Sweet Child (Transatlantic, 1968)

Basket of Light (Transatlantic, 1969)

Cruel Sister (Transatlantic, 1970)

Reflection (Transatlantic, 1971)

Solomon's Seal (Reprise, 1972)

Pentangle on Air (BBC 1969–72) (Strange Fruit, 1997). The album contains also some tracks of *Solomon's Seal*, of which the master tapes have been reported missing (Tony Dale, CD booklet).

Jacqui McShee—lead vocals

Bert Jansch—lead vocals, acoustic guitar, dulcimer, concertina, recorder

John Renbourn—vocals, guitars, sitar

Danny Thompson—double bass

Terry Cox—drums, percussion, glockenspiel, dulcitone

Lineup 2 (1982–1984)

ALBUMS

Open the Door (Spindrift, 1984)

Jacqui McShee—lead vocals

Bert Jansch—lead vocals, guitar

Mike Piggott—guitar, fiddle

Danny Thompson—bass

Terry Cox—drums

Lineup 3 (1984–1986)

ALBUM

In the Round (Pläne, 1986)

Jacqui McShee—lead vocals

Bert Jansch—lead vocals, guitar

Mike Piggott—guitar, fiddle

Nigel Portman-Smith—bass, keyboards

Terry Cox—drums

Lineup 4 (1988–1991)

ALBUM

So Early in the Spring (Pläne, 1988)

Jacqui McShee—lead vocals
Bert Jansch—lead vocals, guitar
Rod Clements—electric guitar, mandolin
Nigel Portman-Smith—bass, keyboards
Gerry Conway—drums
guest: Tony Roberts—flute, whistle

Lineup 5 (1991–1995)

ALBUMS
Think of Tomorrow (Hypertension, 1991)
One More Road (Permanent, 1993)
Live 1994 (Hypertension, 1995)

Jacqui McShee—lead vocals
Bert Jansch—lead vocals, guitar
Peter Kirtley—guitar
Nigel Portman-Smith—bass, keyboard
Gerry Conway—drums, percussion

Jacqui McShee, Gerry Conway, Spencer Cozens

ALBUM
About Thyme (Hypertension, 1995)

Jacqui McShee—lead vocals
Spencer Cozens—keyboards
Gerry Conway (and guests)—drums

Jacqui McShee's Pentangle (from 1998 on)

ALBUMS
Passe Avant (Park Records, 1998)
At the Little Theatre (Park Records, 2000)

Jacqui McShee—lead vocals
Spencer Cozens—keyboards
Jerry Underwood—saxophone
Alan Thomson—bass, guitar
Gerry Conway—drums

Fairport Convention

See also Frame (1994: 15) for a detailed lineup, which was presented in shortened form as "Fairport Confusion" as part of the liner notes/CD booklet for *History of Fairport Convention*).

Lineup 1 (November 1967–May 1968)

ALBUM

Fairport Convention (Polydor, 1968)

Judy Dyble—lead vocals, autoharp, piano, recorder
Ian Matthews—lead vocals
Richard Thompson—vocals, guitars
Simon Nicol—vocals, guitars
Ashley Hutchings—vocals, bass
Martin Lamble—drums

Lineup 2 (May 1968–June 1969)

ALBUMS

Heyday: BBC Radio Sessions (BBC 1968–69) (Rykodisc, 1987)
What We Did on Our Holidays (Island, 1969)
Unhalfbricking (Island, 1969)

Sandy Denny—lead vocals, guitar
Ian Matthews (left to form [Matthew's]) Southern Comfort)—
    lead vocals
Richard Thompson—vocals, guitars
Simon Nicol—vocals, guitars
Ashley Hutchings—vocals, bass
Martin Lamble (died in an accident in June 1969)—drums

Lineup 3 (September 1969–November 1969)

ALBUM

Liege & Lief (Island, 1969)

Sandy Denny (left to form Fotheringay)—lead vocals, guitar
Dave Swarbrick—fiddle, mandolin, vocals
Richard Thompson—vocals, guitars
Simon Nicol—vocals, guitars
Ashley Hutchings (left to form Steeleye Span)—vocals, bass
Dave Mattacks—drums

Lineup 4 (December 1969–January 1971)

ALBUMS

Full House (Island, 1970)
Live at the L.A. Troubadour (1970, Island 1976)

Dave Swarbrick—lead vocals, fiddle, viola, mandolin

Richard Thompson (left to continue as a solo/session-musician)—lead vocals, lead guitar

Simon Nicol—vocals, guitars, mandolin, dulcimer

Dave Pegg—vocals, bass guitar, mandolin

Dave Mattacks—drums, harmonium, boran [*sic*]

Lineup 5 (January 1971–December 1971)

ALBUMS

Angel Delight (Island, 1971)

Babbacombe Lee (Island, 1971)

Dave Swarbrick—lead vocals, fiddle, mandolin

Simon Nicol (joined Albion Country Band)—vocals, guitars, viola, dulcimer

Dave Pegg—vocals, bass, mandolin, viola

Dave Mattacks—drums, electric piano, bass, vocals

Lineup 6 (December 1971–February 1972)

Dave Swarbrick—lead vocals, fiddle, mandolin

Roger Hill—vocals, guitars

Dave Pegg—vocals, bass, mandolin

Dave Mattacks—drums

Lineup 7 (February 1972)

Dave Swarbrick—lead vocals, fiddle, mandolin

Trevor Lucas—guitars, vocals (from Fotheringay)

Jerry Donahue—guitars, vocals (from Fotheringay)

Dave Pegg—vocals, bass, mandolin

Tom Farnell—drums

Lineup 8 (March–June 1972)

Dave Swarbrick—lead vocals, fiddle, mandolin

Roger Hill—guitars, vocals

Dave Pegg—vocals, bass, mandolin

Tom Farnell—drums

Lineup 9 (June–July 1972)

Dave Swarbrick—lead vocals, fiddle, mandolin

David Rea—guitars

Dave Pegg—vocals, bass, mandolin

Tom Farnell—drums

Lineup 10 (August 1972–February 1974)

ALBUMS

Rosie (Island, 1973)

Nine (Island, 1973)

Dave Swarbrick—lead vocals, fiddle, viola, mandolin

Trevor Lucas—lead vocals, guitar

Jerry Donahue—guitars

Dave Pegg—vocals, bass, mandolin

Dave Mattacks—drums, percussion, keyboards, bass guitar

Lineup 11 (March 1974–January 1975)

Sandy Denny—lead vocals, guitar

Dave Swarbrick—lead vocals, fiddle, mandolin

Trevor Lucas—vocals, guitars

Jerry Donahue—guitars

Dave Pegg—vocals, bass, mandolin

Dave Mattacks—drums

Lineup 12 (January–February 1975)

Sandy Denny—lead vocals, guitar

Dave Swarbrick—lead vocals, fiddle, mandolin

Trevor Lucas—vocals, acoustic guitars

Jerry Donahue—guitars

Dave Pegg—vocals, bass, mandolin

Paul Warren—drums

Lineup 13 (February 1975–January 1976)

ALBUM

Rising for the Moon (Island, 1975)

Sandy Denny—lead vocals, guitar, electric and acoustic piano

Dave Swarbrick—lead vocals, fiddle, viola, mandolin, autoharp, guitar, dulcimer

Trevor Lucas—vocals, guitar, harmonica

Jerry Donahue—electric, acoustic, slide guitars

Dave Pegg—vocals, bass, mandolin

Bruce Rowland/Dave Mattacks—drums, percussion

Lineup 14 (February–August 1976)

ALBUM

Gottle O' Geer (Island, 1976)

Dave Swarbrick—lead vocals, fiddle
Bob Brady—piano
Dan Ar Bras—guitars (joined Alan Stivell's band)
Roger Burridge—mandolin, fiddle (joined Alan Stivell's band)
Dave Pegg—vocals, bass, mandolin
Bruce Rowland—drums

Lineup 15 (September 1976–August 1979)
ALBUMS
Bonny Bunch of Roses (Vertigo, 1977)
Tipplers Tales (Vertigo, 1978)
Farewell, Farewell (Woodworm, 1979)

Dave Swarbrick—lead vocals, fiddle
Simon Nicol—vocals, guitars
Dave Pegg—vocals, bass, mandolin
Bruce Rowland—drums
Since 1980, annual meetings of the band and former members have occurred at the Cropredy Festival (lineups are not counted). The 1981 meeting took place at Broughton Castle and was recorded on *Moat on the Ledge: Live at Broughton Castle* (Woodworm, 1982).

Lineup 16
ALBUM
Gladys' Leap (Woodworm, 1985)

Simon Nicol—lead vocals, guitar
Dave Pegg—bass guitar, acoustic basses, mandolin, bouzouki, vocals
Dave Mattacks—drums, keyboards
guests: Cathy Lesurf—vocals, Richard Thompson—guitar, Ric Sanders—violin

Lineup 17 (1985–1996)
ALBUMS
Expletive Delighted (Woodworm, 1986)
In Real Time: Live '87 (Island, 1987)
Red & Gold (New Routes, 1989)
The Five Seasons (New Routes, 1991)
The Woodworm Years (Woodworm, 1992)
Jewel in the Crown (Woodworm, 1995)
Old, New, Borrowed, Blue (Woodworm, 1996) [without Mattacks as Fairport Acoustic
   Convention]

Simon Nicol—lead vocals, guitars
Maartin Allcock—guitars, bouzár, tambourine, accordion, keyboards, vocals, percussion
Rick Sanders—violins
Dave Pegg—vocals, bass, guitar, mandolin
Dave Mattacks—drums, percussion, glockenspiel, crotales, organ, synthesizer

Lineup 18 (since 1997)

ALBUMS

Who Knows Where the Time Goes? (Woodworm, 1997)
The Woodworm Years (Silver Mist, 1997)
The Cropredy Box (Woodworm, 1998)
Close to the Wind (Mooncrest, 1998)
The Wood and the Wire (Woodworm, 2000)
XXXV (Woodworm, 2001)

Simon Nicol—lead vocals, guitars
Rick Sanders—violin
Chris Leslie—fiddle, mandolin
Dave Pegg—vocals, bass, mandolin
Gerry Conway—drums

Steeleye Span

Lineup 1 (December 1969–March 1970)

ALBUM

Hark! The Village Wait (RCA, 1970)

Maddy Prior—lead vocals, five-string banjo, step dancing
Gay Woods—lead vocals, concertina, autoharp, bodhrán, step dancing
Tim Hart—vocals, guitars, mandolin, electric dulcimer, fiddle, five-string banjo, harmonium
Terry Woods—vocals, guitars, concertina, mandola, five-string banjo
Ashley Hutchings—vocals, bass
(Dave Mattacks/Gerry Conway guesting on drums)

Lineup 2 (April 1970–November 1971)

ALBUMS

Please to See the King (B & C, 1971)
Ten Man Mop or Mr. Reservoir Butler Rides Again (B & C, 1971)

Maddy Prior—lead vocals, spoons, tabor, tambourine, bells
Tim Hart—lead vocals, guitars, dulcimer, bells

Peter Knight—vocals, fiddle, mandolin, organ, bass guitar, bells
Martin Carthy—lead vocals, guitars, banjo, organ, bells (left to play solo)
Ashley Hutchings—vocals, bass (left to form the Albion Country Band)

Lineup 3 (December 1971–May 1973)
ALBUMS
Below the Salt (Chrysalis, 1972)
Parcel of Rogues (Chrysalis, 1973)

Maddy Prior—lead vocals, morrisette
Tim Hart—lead vocals, guitars, mandolin, dulcimer, tabor, spoon
Peter Knight—vocals, fiddles, viola, mandolin, tenor banjo, piano
Bob Johnson—vocals, guitars
Rick Kemp—bass

Lineup 4 (June 1973–January 1977)
ALBUMS
Now We Are Six (Chrysalis, 1974) [with David Bowie, alto saxophone]
Commoners Crown (Chrysalis, 1975) [with Peter Sellers, ukulele]
All around My Hat (Chrysalis, 1975)
Rocket Cottage (Chrysalis, 1976)

Maddy Prior—lead vocals
Tim Hart—lead vocals, guitars, mandolin, electric dulcimer
Peter Knight—fiddle, mandolins, tenor banjo, recorders
Bob Johnson—vocals, guitars
Rick Kemp—bass and acoustic guitar, vocals
Nigel Pegrum—drums, tambourine, recorder, oboe

Lineup 5 (January 1977–March 1978)
ALBUMS
Storm Force Ten (Chrysalis, 1977)
Live at Last! (Chrysalis, 1978). (The band disbanded after this album.)

Maddy Prior—lead vocals
Tim Hart—lead vocals, guitars, mandolin
Martin Carthy—vocals, guitars
John Kirkpatrick—melodeon
Rick Kemp—bass
Nigel Pegrum—drums

Lineup 6 (1980) (= lineup 4)

ALBUM

Sails of Silver (Chrysalis, 1980)

Maddy Prior—lead vocals
Tim Hart—lead vocals, mandolin
Peter Knight—fiddle
Bob Johnson—vocals, guitars
Rick Kemp—bass
Nigel Pegrum—drums

Lineup 7 (1984–1986)

ALBUM

Back in Line (Flutterby, 1986)

Maddy Prior—lead vocals
Peter Knight—fiddle
Bob Johnson—vocals, guitars
Rick Kemp—bass (had to give up playing and left in 1986. Replaced by Mark
    Williamson [1986] and Chris Staines [1986–87], yet these lineups [nos. 8 and 9]
    recorded no albums).
Nigel Pegrum—drums
Vince Gross—synthesizer

Lineup 10 (1989)

ALBUM

Tempted and Tried (Dover, 1989) [with Martin Ditchum, percussion]

Maddy Prior—lead vocals
Peter Knight—vocals, violin
Bob Johnson—vocals, electric guitar
Tim Harries—vocals, bass, keyboard
Nigel Pegrum—drums

Lineup 11 (September 1989–1995)

ALBUM

Tonight's the Night . . . Live (Shanachie, 1992)

Maddy Prior—lead vocals
Peter Knight—vocals, violin

Bob Johnson—vocals, electric guitar
Tim Harries—vocals, bass, keyboard
Liam Genockey—drums, percussion

Lineup 12 (1996–October 1997)
ALBUM
Time (Park Records, 1996)

Maddy Prior—lead vocals (left in 1997 to do solo work)
Gay Woods—lead vocals and bodhrán
Bob Johnson—vocals, electric guitar
Peter Knight—vocals, violin
Tim Harries—bass, keyboards, vocals
Liam Genockey—drums, percussion

Lineup 13 (November 1997–September 2000)
ALBUMS
Horkstow Grange (Park Records, 1998)
Bedlam Born (Park Records, 2000)

Gay Woods—lead vocals
Bob Johnson—vocals, electric guitar (left after *Bedlam Born*)
Peter Knight—vocals, violin
Tim Harries—bass, keyboards, vocals
Guest: Dave Mattacks—drums

Lineup 14 (September 2000–January 2001)
Gay Woods—lead vocals
Peter Knight—vocals, violin
Rick Kemp—bass
Tim Harries—bass, keyboards, vocals

Lineup 15 (2001)
Peter Knight—vocals, violin
Rick Kemp—bass
Tim Harries—bass, keyboards, vocals

Lineup 16 (since 2002)
ALBUM
Present—The Very Best of Steeleye Span (Park Records, 2002)

Maddy Prior—vocals
Peter Knight—vocals, violin
Bob Johnson—electric guitar
Rick Kemp—bass
Liam Genockey—drums, percussion

The Oysterband

Lineup 1: Oyster Ceilidh Band (various lineups, 1976–1980)

ALBUM

Jack's Alive (Dingle's, 1980)

Cathy Lesurf—lead vocals
John Jones—lead vocals, melodeon, piano
Ian Telfer—fiddle, viola, concertina
Alan Prosser—guitar, fiddle, bones, bowed psaltery, vocals
Chris Taylor—bouzouki, mandola, guitar, jaw harp, melodeon, harmonica
Chris Wood—bass, percussion, vocals
Will Ward—bassoon, recorder, crumhorn, synthesizer
(Telfer, Prosser, Lesurf, and Wood played also in Fiddler's Dram [*To See the Play*,
    Dingle's, 1979; *Fiddler's Dram*, Dingle's 1980]).

Lineup 2: Oyster Band (1981–1984)

ALBUMS

English Rock 'n' Roll: The Early Years, 1800–1850 (Pukka Records, 1982) [with Cathy Lesurf,
    vocals]
Lie Back and Think of England (Pukka Records, 1983)
Twenty Golden Tie-Slackeners (Pukka Records, 1984)

John Jones—lead vocals, melodeon
Ian Telfer—fiddle, viola, concertina, alto and G tenor saxophone, organ
Chris Taylor—bouzouki, mandola, guitar, jaw harp, melodeon
Alan Prosser—guitars, synthesizer, bones
Ian Keary—bass, twelve-string/acoustic/slide guitar, épinette, autoharp

Lineup 3 (1984–1985)

ALBUM

Liberty Hall (Pukka Records, 1985) [with Martin Brinsford, percussion; Ron Elliott,
    Northumbrian pipes; Rod Elliott, trumpet; Chris Taylor, harmonica, jaw harp]

John Jones—lead vocals, melodeon
Ian Telfer—fiddle, keyboards, saxophone

Alan Prosser—vocals, guitars, synthesizer

Ian Keary—vocals, bass

Lineup 4 (1986–1988)

ALBUMS

Step Outside (Cooking Vinyl, 1986) [with Clive Gregson, backing keyboards]

Wide Blue Yonder (Cooking Vinyl, 1987) [with Kathryn Tickell, Northumbrian bagpipes]

John Jones—lead vocals, melodeon

Ian Telfer—fiddle, tenor sax, concertina, keyboards

Alan Prosser—guitar, vocals

Ian Keary—bass, twelve-string guitar, banjo, vocals

Russell Lax—drums, percussion

Lineup 5 (1988–1992)

ALBUMS

Ride (Cooking Vinyl, 1989)

Little Rock to Leipzig (Cooking Vinyl, 1990)

Freedom and Rain (Cooking Vinyl, 1990) [with June Tabor]

John Jones—lead vocals, melodeon, accordion

Ian Telfer—fiddle, alto saxophone, organ

Alan Prosser—guitar, vocals, mandolin, bowed psaltery

Chopper—bass guitar, vocals, electric and acoustic cello

Russell Lax—drums

Lineup 6: Oysterband (since 1992)

ALBUMS

Deserters (Cooking Vinyl, 1992) [with Tomas Lynch, whistle, pipes; Rory McLeod, harmonica]

Holy Bandits (Cooking Vinyl, 1993) [with Sarah Allen, whistles; Jackie Sheridan, backing vocals]

The Shouting End of Life (Cooking Vinyl, 1995) [with Sarah Allen, whistle; Kathryn Tickell, Northumbrian bagpipes; Chris Batchelor/Expensive Mustapha, trumpets]

Alive & Shouting (Running Man, 1996) [with Alan Scott, twelve-string guitar, bass guitar, mandolin, octave mandola, percussion]

Deep Dark Ocean (Cooking Vinyl, 1997)

Alive and Acoustic (Running Man, 1998)

Here I Stand (Running Man, 1999)

Rise Above (Pläne, 2002)

John Jones—lead vocals, melodeons
Ian Telfer—fiddle, English and tenor concertina, viola
Alan Prosser—guitars, banjo, vocals
Chopper—bass guitar, vocals, cello
Lee—drums, bodhrán, percussion, hammer

ELECTRIC FOLK / FOLK ROCK AND RECORDINGS OF INDIVIDUAL BAND MEMBERS

Albion Band, *Rise Up Like the Sun* (Harvest/EMI, 1978)
——, *Stella Maris* (Making Waves, 1987)
Albion Country Band, *Battle of the Field* (Island, 1976)
The Albion Dance Band, *The Prospect before Us* (Harvest, 1976)
——, *I Got New Shoes* (Spindrift, 1987)
——, *1990* (Topic, 1990)
——, *An Hour with Cecil Sharp* (Dambuster, 1986)
——, *Songs from the Shows*, vol. 1 (Albino Music, 1990)
——, *Songs from the Shows*, vol. 2 (Albino Music, 1992)
——, *Acousticity* (HTD, 1993)
——, *Albion Heart* (HTD, 1995)
——, *Demi Paradise* (HTD, 1996)
——, *The Acoustic Years, 1993–97* (HTD, 1998)
——, *Happy Accident* (HTD, 1998)
——, *Before Us Stands Yesterday* (HTD, 1999)
Blowzabella, *Bobbityshooty* (Plant Life, 1984)
——, *The Blowzabella Wall of Sound* (Plant Life, 1986)
——, *A Richer Dust* (Plant Life, 1988)
Brass Monkey, *Brass Monkey* (Topic, 1983)
——, *See How It Runs* (Topic, 1986)
——, *Sound and Rumour* (Topic, 1998)
Shirley Collins, *Sweet England* (ARGO, 1959)
——, *False True Lovers* (Folkways, 1960)
——, *Heroes in Love* (EP, Topic, 1963)
——, *English Songs*, vol. 1 (Selection Jeb, 1964)
——, *English Songs*, vol. 2 (Selection Jeb, 1964)
——, *The Sweet Primeroses* (Topic, 1967)
——, *The Power of the True Love Knot* (Polydor, 1968)
——, *Adieu to Old England* (Topic, 1974)
Shirley Collins and the Albion Country Band, *No Roses* (B & C, 1971)
Shirley and Dolly Collins, *Love, Death, and the Lady* (EMI/Harvest, 1970)
——, *Anthems in Eden* (EMI/Harvest, 1969)

————, *Amaranth* (EMI/Harvest, 1976)

————, *For As Many As Will* (Topic, 1978)

————, *Harking Back* (Durtro, 1998)

Cordelia's Dad, *Comet* (Normal, 1995)

————, *Road Kill* (Scenescof, 1997)

————, *Spine* (Appleseed, 1998)

Sandy Denny, *The North Star Grassman and the Ravens* (Island, 1971)

————, *Sandy* (Island, 1972)

————, *Like an Old Fashioned Waltz* (Island, 1973)

————, *Rendezvous* (Island, 1973)

————, *The Original Sandy Denny* (B & C, 1978, recorded in 1967)

————, *Who Knows Where the Time Goes?* (Hannibal, 1985)

————, *"Gold Dust"—Live at the Royalty* (Island, 1998, recorded in 1978)

Sandy Denny and the Strawbs, *All Our Own Work* (Sonet Dansk Grammofon A/S, 1973) [different compilation: Rykodisc, 1991]

Sandy Denny, Trevor Lucas, and Friends, *The Attic Tracks* (1972–84) (Special Delivery, 1994)

Edward II, *Zest* (Ock, 1996)

————, *The Way Up* (Ock, 1998)

The Etchingham Steam Band, *The Etchingham Steam Band* (live recordings from 1974–75) (Fledg'ling, 1995)

Fotheringay, *Fotheringay* (Island, 1970)

Gryphon, *Gryphon* (Transatlantic, 1973)

————, *Midnight Mushrumps* (Transatlantic, 1974)

Tim Hart and Maddy Prior, *Folk Songs of Olde England*, vol. 1 (TeePee, 1968)

————, *Folk Songs of Olde England*, vol. 2 (TeePee, 1969)

————, *Summer Solstice* (B & C, 1971)

Home Service, *The Mysteries* (Fledg'ling, 1985)

————, *Alright Jack* (Making Waves, 1986)

————, *Wild Life* (Fledg'ling, 1995)

————, *Early Transmissions* (Road Goes On Forever, 1996)

Ashley Hutchings (Morris On Band), *Morris On* (Island, 1972)

————, *Son of Morris On* (Harvest/EMI, 1976)

————, *Rattlebone & Ploughjack* (Island, 1976)

————, *Kickin' Up the Sawdust* (Harvest/EMI, 1977)

————, *By Gloucester Docks I Sat Down and Wept* (Paradise and Thomas, 1987) [live version from 1988 released on RGOF]

————, *The Guv'nor*, vols. 1–4 (HTD, 1998)

Ashley Hutchings and John Kirkpatrick, *The Compleat Dancing Master* (Island, 1974)

The Ashley Hutchings Dance Band, *A Better Pudding for John Keats* (HTD, 1996)

The Incredible String Band, *The Incredible String Band* (Elektra, 1966)

————, *5000 Spirits or the Layers of the Onion* (Elektra, 1967)

————, *The Hangman's Beautiful Daughter* (Elektra, 1968)

————, *Wee Tam and the Big Huge* (Elektra, 1968)

————, *Be Glad for the Song Has No Ending* (Island UK, 1970)

————, *No Ruinous Feud* (Island UK, 1973)

The Levellers, *A Weapon Called the Word* (Musidisc, 1990)

————, *Levelling the Land* (China Records, 1991)

————, *Special Brew* (Hag, 1988–93)

————, *The Levellers* (China Records, 1993)

————, *Zeitgeist* (China Records, 1995)

Lindisfarne, *Nicely out of Tune* (Charisma, 1970)

————, *Fog on the Tyne* (Charisma, 1971)

The Man They Couldn't Hang, *Majestic Grill* (Demon, 1998)

Mr. Fox, *Mr. Fox* (Transatlantic, 1970)

————, *The Gypsy* (Transatlantic, 1971)

The Pogues, *Red Roses for Me* (WEA, 1984)

————, *Rum, Sodomy & the Lash* (WEA, 1985)

————, *If I Should Fall from Grace with God* (WEA, 1987)

————, *Peace and Love* (WEA, 1989)

————, *Hell's Ditch* (WEA, 1990)

————, *Waiting for Herb* (WEA, 1993)

————, *Pogue Mahone* (WEA, 1996)

The Pressgang, *Burning Boats* (Twah!, 1995)

————, *Fire* (Twah!, 1995)

Maddy Prior, *Changing Winds* (Chrysalis, 1978)

————, *Year* (Park Records, 1993)

————, *Flesh & Blood* (Park Records, 1997)

————, *Ravenchild* (Park Records, 1999)

————, *Ballads & Candles* (Park Records, 2000)

Maddy Prior and the Carnival Band, *A Tapestry of Carols* (Saydisc, 1987)

————, *Sing Lustily & with Good Courage* (Saydisc, 1990)

————, *Hang Up Sorrow & Care* (Park Records, 1995)

————, *Carols at Christmas* (Park Records, 1999)

Silly Sisters [Maddy Prior and June Tabor], *Silly Sisters* (Chrysalis, 1976)

————, *No More to the Dance* (Topic, 1988)

Dave Swarbrick, *Rags, Reels, and Airs* (Polydor, 1967)

————, *Swarbrick* (Transatlantic, 1976)

————, *Swarbrick 2* (Transatlantic, 1977)

————, *Flittin'* (Transatlantic, 1981)

————, *Smiddyburn* (Transatlantic, 1981)

————, *Folk on 2* (Cooking Vinyl, 1996)

Richard Thompson, *Henry the Human Fly!* (Island, 1972)

———, *(guitar, vocal)* (Island, 1976)

———, *Strict Tempo* (Elixir, 1981)

———, *Hand of Kindness* (Hannibal, 1983)

———, *First Light* (Hannibal, 1984)

———, *Across a Crowded Room* (Polygram, 1985)

———, *Daring Adventures* (Polygram, 1986)

———, *Amnesia* (Capitol, 1988)

———, *Rumor and Sigh* (Capitol, 1991)

———, *Watching the Dark: The History of Richard Thompson* (Rykodisc/Hannibal, 1993)

———, *Mirror Blue* (Capitol, 1994)

———, *you? me? us?* (Capitol, 1996)

———, *Mock Tudor* (Capitol, 2000)

Richard and Linda Thompson, *I Want to See the Bright Lights Tonight* (Island, 1974)

———, *Hokey Pokey* (Island, 1975)

———, *Pour Down Like Silver* (Island, 1975)

———, *First Light* (Chrysalis, 1978)

———, *Sunnyvista* (Chrysalis, 1979)

———, *Shoot Out the Lights* (Hannibal, 1982)

Richard Thompson and Philip Pickett, *The Bones of All Men* (Hannibal, 1998)

Various, *The Electric Muse* (Transatlantic, 1975)

Various, *New Electric Muse: The Story of Folk into Rock* (Essential, 1996)

Various, *New Electric Muse II: The Continuing Story of Folk into Rock* (Essential, 1997)

Various, *Troubadours of British Folk* (Rhino, 1996)

Whippersnapper, *Promises* (WPS, 1985)

———, *Tsubo* (WPS, 1988)

———, *Fortune* (Celtic Music, 1989)

———, *Stories* (WPS, 1991)

Wood, Wilson, Carthy, *Wood Wilson Carthy* (R.U.F., 1998)

Gay and Terry Woods, *Backwoods* (Polydor, 1975)

———, *Renowned* (Polydor, 1976)

The Woods Band, *The Woods Band* (Greenwich, 1971)

The Guitarists

Martin Carthy, *Hootenanny in London* (Decca, 1964) [as member of 3 City 4]

———, *Martin Carthy* (Fontana/Polygram, 1965)

———, *Landfall* (Philips, 1971)

———, *Shearwater* (Pegasus, 1972)

———, *Sweet Wivelsfield* (Deram Records, 1974)

———, *Crown of the Horn* (Topic, 1976)

———, *Because It's There* (Topic, 1979)

————, *Out of the Cut* (Gama/Topic, 1982)

————, *Right of Passage* (Topic, 1988)

————, *Signs of Life* (Topic, 1998)

Martin Carthy with Dave Swarbrick, *Second Album* (Fontana/Polygram, 1966)

————, *Byker Hill* (Fontana/Polygram, 1967)

————, *But Two Came By* (Fontana, 1968)

Martin Carthy and Dave Swarbrick, *Prince Heathen* (Fontana/Polygram, 1969)

————, *Life and Limb* (Special Delivery/Topic, 1990)

————, *Skin and Bone* (Special Delivery, 1992)

Davy Graham, *3/4 AD* (EP, Topic, 1961)

————, *The Thamesiders and Davy Graham* (EP, Decca, 1963)

————, *The Guitar Player* (Golden Guinea/Pye, 1963)

————, *Folk, Blues & Beyond* (Decca, 1964)

————, *Folk Roots, New Routes* (Decca, 1965)

————, *Midnight Man* (Decca, 1966)

————, *Large as Life and Twice as Natural* (Decca, 1968)

————, *Hat* (Decca, 1969)

————, *Holly Kaleidoscope* (Decca, 1970)

————, *All That Moody* (Eron, 1976)

————, *The Complete Guitarist* (Kicking Mule Records, 1979)

————, *Dance for Two People* (Kicking Mule Records, 1979)

Dorris Henderson and John Renbourn, *There You Go!* (Columbia, 1965).

Bert Jansch, *Bert Jansch* (Transatlantic, 1965)

————, *Jack Orion* (Transatlantic, 1966)

————, *It Don't Bother Me* (Transatlantic, 1966)

————, *Nicola* (Transatlantic, 1967)

————, *Birthday Blues* (Transatlantic, 1969)

————, *Rosemary Lane* (Line, 1971)

————, *A Rare Conundrum* (Charisma, 1977)

————, *Avocet* (Charisma, 1979)

————, *Heartbreak* (Logo, 1982)

————, *From the Outside* (Castle, 1985)

————, *Sketches* (Hypertension, 1990)

————, *When the Circus Comes to Town* (Cooking Vinyl, 1995)

————, *Toy Balloon* (Cooking Vinyl, 1998)

————, *Crimson Moon* (Castle Music, 2000)

Bert Jansch and John Renbourn, *Bert and John* (Transatlantic, 1966)

Bert Jansch Conundrum, *Thirteen Down* (Kicking Mule, 1980)

John Renbourn, *John Renbourn* (Transatlantic, 1965)

————, *Another Monday* (Transatlantic, 1967)

————, *Sir John Alot of Merrie Englandes Musyk Thynge and ye Grene Knyghte* (Transatlantic, 1968)

————, *The Lady and the Unicorn* (Transatlantic, 1970)

————, *Faro Annie* (Transatlantic, 1971)

————, *The Hermit* (Transatlantic, 1976)

————, *The Black Balloon* (Electric Muse, 1986)

————, *Ship of Fools* (Flying Fish, 1988)

————, *The Nine Maidens* (Making Waves, 1985)

John Renbourn Group, *A Maid in Bedlam* (Transatlantic, 1977)

————, *The Enchanted Garden* (Transatlantic, 1980)

————, *Live in America* (Flying Fish, 1982)

John Renbourn and Stefan Grossman, *John Renbourn & Stefan Grossman* (Sonet, 1978)

————, *Acoustic Guitar* (Sonet, 1979)

————, *Live . . . in Concert* (Spin, 1983)

————, *The Three Kingdoms* (Shanachie, 1987)

The Revival Performers and Groups

Frankie Armstrong, *Lovely on the Water* (Topic, 1972)

————, *I Heard a Woman Sing* (Fuse Records, 1985)

————, *Till the Grass O'ergrew the Corn: A Collection of Traditional Ballads* (Fellside, 1997)

Peter Bellamy, *The Transports* (Free Reed, 1977)

Anne Briggs, *Anne Briggs* (Topic, 1971)

————, *The Time Has Come* (CBS, 1971)

The Ian Campbell Folk Group, *This Is the Ian Campbell Folk Group* (Transatlantic, 1963)

————, *Across the Hills* (Transatlantic, 1964)

————, *Contemporary Campbells* (Transatlantic, 1966)

Jackson C. Frank, *Jackson C. Frank* (Columbia, 1965); reissued as *Blues Run the Game* (Mooncrest, 1996)

Louis Killen, *Ballads and Broadsides* (Topic, 1965)

A. L. Lloyd, *English Drinking Songs* (Riverside, 1959)

————, *All for Me Grog* (Topic, 1961)

————, *English & Scottish Folk Ballads* (Topic, 1964)

————, *First Person* (Topic, 1966)

————, *Leviathan!* (Topic, 1967)

————, *Classic A. L. Lloyd* (Fellside, 1994) [compilation]

A. L. Lloyd and Alf Edwards, *A Selection from the Penguin Book of English Folk Songs* (Folk Lyric, 1960)

A. L. Lloyd, Ewan MacColl, and Harry H. Corbett, *Blow the Man Down* (EP, Topic, 1956)

Ewan MacColl, *The English and Scottish Popular Ballads (Child Ballads)* (Folkways, 1961)

———, *Broadside Ballads*, vols. 1 and 2 (Folkways, 1962)

———, *British Industrial Folk Songs* (Stinson, 1963)

———, *The Angry Muse* (Argo, 1968)

Ewan MacColl, Charles Parker, and Peggy Seeger, *A Hundred Years Ago* (Topic, 1956)

———, *Bold Sportsmen All* (Topic, 1958)

———, *A Sailor's Garland* (Transatlantic, 1966)

———, *Blow, Boys, Blow* (Transatlantic, 1967)

———, *Classic Scots Ballads* (Transatlantic, 1967)

———, *The Wanton Muse* (Argo, 1968)

———, *Whaling Ballads* (Washington, 1974)

———, *The Radio Ballads*, 8 vols. (Topic, 1999)

Ewan MacColl with Peggy Seeger, *Chorus from the Gallows* (Topic, 1960)

June Tabor, *Airs and Graces* (Topic, 1976)

———, *Ashes and Diamonds* (Topic, 1977)

———, *Aqaba* (Topic, 1988)

———, *Angel Tiger* (Cooking Vinyl, 1992)

———, *Aleyn* (Topic, 1997)

———, *A Quiet Eye* (Topic, 2000)

Various, *The Bird in the Bush: Traditional Songs of Love and Lust* (Topic, 1966)

Various, *Blow Down the Man: A Collection of Sea Songs and Shanties* (Topic, 1964)

Various, *The Iron Muse: A Panorama of Industrial Folk Music* (Topic, 1956)

The Watersons, *New Voices* (Topic, 1965)

———, *The Watersons* (Topic, 1966)

———, *A Yorkshire Garland* (Topic, 1966)

———, *Frost and Fire* (Topic, 1965)

———, *For Pence and Spicy Ale* (Topic, 1975)

———, *Green Fields* (Topic, 1980)

Lal and Mike Waterson, *Bright Phoebus* (Trailer, 1972)

Lal Waterson and Oliver Knight, *Once in a Blue Moon* (Topic, 1995)

Mike Waterson, *Mike Waterson* (Topic, 1977)

Norma Waterson, *Norma Waterson* (Hannibal, 1997)

———, *Bright Shiny Morning* (Hannibal, 2000)

Waterson:Carthy, *Waterson:Carthy* (Topic, 1994)

———, *Common Tongue* (Topic, 1997)

———, *Broken Ground* (Topic, 2000)

The Young Tradition, *The Young Tradition* (Transatlantic, 1966)

———, *So Cheerfully Round* (Transatlantic, 1967)

The Young Tradition with Shirley and Dolly Collins, *The Holly Bears the Crown* (Argo, 1969, unreleased; Fledg'ling, 1995)

Traditional and Field Recordings

Margaret Barry and Michael Gorman, *Her Mantle So Green* (Topic, 1958)

Jeannie Robertson, *Jeannie Robertson: The Great Scots Traditional Ballad Singer* (Topic, 1959)

Belle Stewart, *Queen among the Heather* (Topic, 1977)

Various, *A Century of Song: A Celebration of Traditional Singers since 1898* (EFDSS, 1998)

Various, *The Folk Songs of Britain*, vols. 4 and 5: *The Child Ballads* I/II (Topic, 1961)

Various, *Hidden English: A Celebration of English Traditional Music* (Topic, 1996)

Various, *Songs of the Travelling People* (recorded by Peter Kennedy, 1951–68) (Saydisc, 1995)

Various, *World Library of Folk and Primitive Music*, compiled and edited by Alan Lomax.
  vol. 1: *England* (1939–51); vol. 2: *Ireland* (1951); vol. 3: *Scotland* (1951) (Rounder, 1998)

Various, *The Voice of the People*. 20 vols. (Topic, 1998)

Electric Folk and Folk Rock: United States, "Celtic," and Other Countries

Capercaillie, *Beautiful Wasteland* (Rykodisc, 1998)

Chateau Neuf Spelemannslag, *Spell* (Hello, 1995)

The Chieftains, *The Long Black Veil* (BMG, 1995)

Clannad, *Magical Ring* (RCA, 1983)

———, *Macalla* (RCA, 1985)

———, *Anam* (BMG, 1990)

Enya, *Watermark* (WEA, 1988)

Figgy Duff, *Figgy Duff: A Retrospective, 1974–1993* (Amber Music, 1996)

Garmarna, *Guds Speleman* (Massproduktion, 1996)

Mad Pudding, *Bruce's Vegetable Garden* (Fiendish Records, 1995)

———, *Dirt & Stone* (Fiendish Records, 1996)

The New St. George, *High Tea* (Folk Era, 1994)

Ougenweide, *Liederbuch* (Polydor, n.d.)

The Paperboys, *Late as Usual* (Stompy Discs, 1996)

Runrig, *Searchlight* (Chrysalis, 1989)

Alan Stivell, *Renaissance de la harpe celtique* (Fontana, 1970)

Tempest, *Serrated Edge* (Firebird Arts & Music, 1992)

———, *Sunken Treasures* (Firebird Arts & Music, 1993)

———, *The Gravel Walk* (Magna Carta, 1997)

Tri Yann, *La découverte ou l'ignorance* (Phonogram, 1976)

Wolfstone, *The Half Tail* (Green Linnet, 1996)

———, *This Strange Place* (Green Linnet, 1998)

NOTES

INTRODUCTION

1. Acculturation can be defined as the process of adopting the cultural traits, social patterns, or, as in this case, music of another group, especially a dominant one (such as Western popular or rock music), resulting in a restructuring or blending of (music) cultures and the development of hybrid (music) forms.

2. By "English" I mean predominantly non-Gaelic material. For a closer discussion of the notion of Englishness in traditional music, see chapters 1, 5, and 7. I am neglecting the American side of folk rock here, as this topic would require another comprehensive study. See chapter 1 for a roughly sketched background.

3. For a further discussion of the terms "electric folk" and "folk rock" see chapter 1.

4. Frey and Siniveer 1987 provides a good example: basically a documentation of the history of German folk music, the book devotes several chapters to the Anglo-American development.

5. The authors were Dave Laing, rock editor and writer; Karl Dallas, regular contributor to *Melody Maker* and rock/folk writer; Robin Denselow, BBC film director, former folksinger, and folk and rock critic for the *Guardian*; and Robert Shelton, folk, country, and rock critic for the *New York Times* from 1958 to 1968.

6. A slightly revised compilation with the title *New Electric Muse: The Story of Folk into Rock* was reissued on CD in 1996, followed by another compilation, *New Electric Muse II: The Continuing Story of Folk into Rock* (1997), both of which added more recent musical approaches.

7. See, for instance, the review by Peter Bellamy (1975). Similarly, Dallas's theoretical chapter was later subjected to strong criticism, as evident in Middleton (1995: 74–75). See also chapter 2, this volume.

8. See Humphries (1996 and 1997), Harper (2000), and Heylin (2000).

9. Enya's first record, *Enya (The Celts)*, was produced in 1987 and comprised a selection of original compositions heard in the BBC-TV series *The Celts*.

10. I do not want to be unfair to Maud Karpeles, who—having also collected songs with Cecil Sharp in the Appalachians in the early 1900s and from 1929 to 1939 in Newfoundland—was an important figure in the history of English folk song scholarship. Having been a part of the romanticized era of English folk song collecting, her efforts to preserve the "purity" of folk song were apparently likewise shaped by the early attempts to make the songs fit into parlor-style arrangements of the early twentieth century. This purist view has been significant for many studies of folk song.

11. "Traditional music" and "folk music" are often used synonymously to refer to the original, orally transmitted style and material—which in this context also includes commercial material such as broadsides, as this music was part of a distinct culture. I prefer "traditional music" to

"folk music" when referring to the original cultures, as the latter expression, similar to expressions like "folk revival" and "folk clubs," is also used for the music and culture of the Second Revival generation of the 1950s and '60s.

12. The singer Carolyn Hester was from Austin, Texas, but the folk rock development within the States was of major importance for English music journalism at that time.

13. This layering even applies to the sociocultural context, for several of the early collectors were related to each other. Maud Karpeles's sister Helen was married to EFDSS director Douglas Kennedy; their son was collector Peter Kennedy, who became famous through his TV documentary *As I Roved Out*.

14. Historically speaking, this direction first emerged with groups like Lindisfarne or the Strawbs nearly at the same time as the electric folk genre in the early 1970s. Yet, it became particularly popular with the Pogues in the 1980s.

15. Merriam (1964: 305) is referring here to Melville J. Herskovits, *Man and His works* (New York: Alfred A. Knopf, 1948).

16. See "Thick Description: Toward an Interpretive Theory of Culture" in Geertz (1973: 3–30). See also Bruno Nettl, "Recent Directions in Ethnomusicology" in Myers (1992: 375–400). In contrast with Geertz, however, who focuses on the intertwined symbolic and conceptual thought structures of a cultural system, I have adapted a more general approach, trying to disentangle the various layers of music, history, and performers' relationships with the tradition and American musical models.

17. Metanarrative is a term Hamm (1995) derived from David Harvey and Jean-François Lyotard, thereby denoting generalized statements or hypotheses ("broad, all-encompassing schemes," ibid.: 1)—in this case referring to popular music—that claim to represent the truth, although they are not verified. These metanarratives are rarely challenged because they have been extremely popularized. See also chapter 2, this volume.

18. As Slobin (1993: 12) emphasized, his approach neither follows a fixed model nor offers one-sentence definitions. A model for Slobin was, among others, Arjun Appadurai, "Disjuncture and Difference in the Global Cultural Economy," *Public Culture* 2 (1990), 1–24, which described the five dimensions of global flow as ethnoscapes, mediascapes, technoscapes, finanscapes, and ideoscapes. See also Appadurai (1998).

19. This tendency is still evident in the German folk magazine *Folk MICHEL*. See, for instance, Ulrich Schnabel, "John Renbourn: Ein aufrechter Typ und vielsaitiger Musiker" *Folk MICHEL*, no. 4 (July/August 1989), 22–25.

20. Details about the emic/etic distinction, developed by Kenneth Pike in *Language in Relation to a Unified Theory of the Structure of Human Behavior* (Glendale, Calif.: Summer Institute of Linguistics, 1954), can be found in Myers (1992).

21. For a further discussion of interview methodologies, see Flick (1995). See also Merton and Kendall (1946).

CHAPTER 1

1. I am greatly indebted to Jennifer Cutting, who pointed me to Bruce Jackson's report and transcription. This case is also a good reminder that even long-established written contemporaneous accounts cannot always (or maybe never) be trusted. Another example is the true background of Sandy Denny's death, which had always been protected by the tale of her having

accidentally fallen down the stairs at a friend's house, an explanation that became part of accepted (folk) rock history. The actual—even more tragic—facts were never publicly revealed until Clinton Heylin's biography (2000) was published.

2. See Wilson (1969b) and Dallas (1970g).

3. This distinction was already pointed out by Cutting (1993). The magazine *Folk Roots* tried to find a solution by using "roots music" from the 1990s on. Yet "roots music" is also a problematic expression, for every music has roots. The term is often applied to contemporary music with traditional elements that are often not easily discernible.

4. See Filene (1995) for further details. For a more detailed description of the processes summarized here, see Rosenberg (1993), Lieberman (1995), and Cantwell (1996).

5. One of Seeger's most popular songs was "The Bells of Rhymney." Based on a text by the Welsh poet Idris Davies, it addressed the decline of the coal mining industry.

6. The group nevertheless had a best-selling hit with the Leadbelly song "Goodnight Irene," probably originally a Tin Pan Alley Song from 1886, as Cantwell (1996: 179) has suggested.

7. Harry Belafonte and American Folklife Festival founder Ralph Rinzler both reportedly searched out material through the Library of Congress's Archive of Folk Song.

8. The Grand Ole Opry was established in Nashville, Tennessee, in 1925, and has remained one of the most popular American radio (today also television) shows, featuring a live country music program.

9. See Cantwell (1996) for a detailed account.

10. See chap. 8, "Anthems from Eden," in Boyes (1993).

11. See Woods (1973a–c), MacColl (1990), and Winter (1990).

12. For a further background about the label's history, see Winter (1994: 24). MacColl was Topic's top recording artist for a long time. Both MacColl and Lloyd also made many recordings for the American label Riverside, which was partly commissioned by Topic.

13. See Pelletier (1992), McAleer (1993), and Laing et al. (1975).

14. Originally included in Barber's 1954 album, "Rock Island Line" was subsequently issued as a single by Decca and credited to the Lonnie Donegan Skiffle Group.

15. Although Dallas (Laing et al. 1975: 89) described the clubs as a continuation of the old music halls, they should instead be considered in conjunction with the coffee bars, where the early folk clubs had often taken place, as MacKinnon (1993: 24) pointed out.

16. See, for instance, MacKinnon (1993) and Denselow (in Laing et al. 1975), as well as various individual biographies of the folk and electric folk artists.

17. See, for instance, Denselow (in Laing et al. 1975: 138) and MacKinnon (1993: 23–24).

18. MacColl not only objected to American accents and slang, but also to songs in Russian, Spanish, Italian, and French (see MacColl 1990: 287).

19. "Traveller" (sometimes also "Tinker") refers to a member of the various itinerant peoples of the British Isles, comprising both people of Romany origin and native groups.

20. This notion that any group that becomes commercial inevitably loses its artistic integrity was also developed by popular music theorists; see, for instance, Flender and Rauhe (1989).

CHAPTER 2

1. D'Urfey also seems to have included material from street singing and tavern songs. See Harker (1985) and particularly Myers (1993: 129–33) for further printed sources.

2. See Hughes and Stradling (2001: 77–79) for more details about the ideas of the England-based German exile Carl Engel.

3. For a further discussion, see Bohlman (1988: 6–9).

4. See, for instance, Sharp (1907: 137) and Pearsall (1973). This strict separation is still evident, yet in a much more adapted form, in Maud Karpeles's preface to the revised third edition of *English Folk-Song: Some Conclusions* (p. xi), where she points out that "it is not the popularity of a tune that makes it a folk tune, neither does a popular 'composed' tune automatically become a folk tune by being adopted by country singers or instrumentalists, although it may become so after it has been submitted throughout generations to the gradual moulding process of oral transmission."

5. As Chris Bearman (1998) demonstrated in a paper presented at the 100th anniversary of the founding of the Fock Song Society, Harker's arguments are also occasionally based on incorrect numbers.

6. This custom had also been the practice in other countries such as Germany for many centuries, especially for secular music.

7. Middleton (1995: 13) has correctly pointed out that around 1840 musical production was in the hands of or mediated by commercial music publishers, concert organizers, promoters, and so on. However, this period was neither the first time that music was bought, nor the strict beginning of commercialization of traditional (Scottish-Irish) songs, as Middleton assumes.

8. For a complete description of the music halls, see Russell (1987: 72–130).

9. "My Lagan Love" set words by Joseph Campbell to a traditional air collected by Herbert Hughes, first published in 1905. Hall (1994) argues that Barry's version is closer to the 1948 recorded version by Richard Hayward than to John McCormack's from 1910.

10. Grainger's 216 surviving cylinders are now stored in the Library of Congress, Washington, D.C. See Yates (1982) for a further discussion of early field recordings. For example, American Jessie Walter Fewkes recorded songs of the Zuni and Passamaquoddy Indians as early as 1889.

11. Interestingly, Harker's theories have strongly permeated popular music theory. While Middleton (1995: 127–35), for instance, criticizes Lloyd and others for having adopted elements of Sharp unconsciously, he himself adopts Harker's arguments without much scrutiny. Boyes (1993), although a highly important work that adds many new facets to Harker, is not discussed further here. Generally speaking, Boyes comes to similar conclusions as Harker—that the tradition was an invented construct.

12. See Rosenberg (1993) and Filene (1995: 80–97), for a further discussion.

13. See *The Gutenberg Galaxy: The Making of Topographic Man* (Toronto: University of Toronto Press, 1962), *Understanding Media: The Extensions of Man* (New York: McGraw-Hill, 1964), and *The Medium Is the Message: An Inventory of Effects* (New York: Bantam, 1967).

14. Jon Landau, *It's Too Late to Stop Now: A Rock and Roll Journal* (San Francisco: Straight Arrow Books, 1972: 130), cited in Frith (1981: 159). Frith adopted this definition as the basis for his argument.

15. Even more cautious or neutral definitions like Barre Toelken's, defining traditional song as "any song that has been shaped and given a cultural (rather than a personal, individualized) sense of meaning derived from the live, performance context of oral circulation" (Toelken 1995: 12), still lack the awareness that traditional music, even if it is predominantly orally transmitted, also contains other components.

CHAPTER 3

1. See Hunt (1979, 1980a, and 1980b) and Dallas (1978c).

2. This series was first issued on the New York–based label Caedmon and later issued in Britain on Topic. It was reissued in a revised and expanded series, *Voice of the People*, by Topic in 1998.

3. Austin John Marshall was also the author of "Whitsun Dance" (set to the tune of "The False Bride"), which Shirley Collins recorded for *Anthems in Eden* (produced by Marshall). This song referred to the devastating impact of World War I on morris dancing, leaving many widows who continued to dance for their lost ones.

4. The album was released for the first time in 1995 by Fledg'ling Records.

5. This account of Carthy's career is based on Dallas (1977), Anderson and Holland (1985), Kennedy (1987), and various CD booklets.

6. See the 1994 Ossian CD *The Singing Campbells: Traditions of an Aberdeen Family*.

7. Simon also recorded songs by other British performers, such as Davy Graham's "Angi." Carthy also became friendly with Bob Dylan. The widespread rumor, however, that Dylan stayed with Carthy when he first came to England was denied by Carthy (Dallas 1977: 10)

8. "Morris" is the term for a rural folk dance of northern English origin, performed by costumed dancers.

9. For a further history, see Suff (1993a).

10. See Grossman (1990), Hunt (1997a), and Leigh (1990).

11. Known as the "father of British blues," guitarist, singer, and bandleader Alexis Korner (1928–84) played a major role in developing the British rhythm-and-blues scene of the 1950s and '60s. Having played in Ken Coyler's skiffle band, alongside Lonnie Donegan and Chris Barber, he subsequently set the British blues revival in motion and had a direct influence on various British rock performers, including some members of the Rolling Stones.

12. I basically refer to Harper's (2000) detailed biography—which also clarifies various myths, such as Jansch being falsely reported to be the only person in Britain suffering from scurvy.

13. See chapter 4 for a further description of this alternative concert project.

14. This album has been reissued by Topic as *Anne Briggs: A Collection*.

15. Grossman thereby agrees with Dallas, who would later coin the expression "folk baroque school" in connection with Jansch for this kind of decorative style (see also Dallas 1966c).

16. Unsigned review of *Bert Jansch* in *Melody Maker*, August 28, 1965, 12.

17. See also Holland (1993) as the second principal source for this biographical account.

18. Average weekly earnings in the British manufacturing industry were about £23 around 1968. See also Butler and Sloman (1980).

19. See Humphries (1997) for further details.

20. See the CD *Heyday: BBC Radio Sessions 1968–69* (Rykodisc, 1987).

21. According to Humphries (1997), sales have exceeded 100,000 copies—a large number for this kind of music.

22. For a detailed account of Fairport's activities in the 1980s and early 1990s, see Redwood and Woodward (1996).

23. For Denny's career history I have primarily referred to Heylin (2000).

24. See the albums *The Original Sandy Denny* (produced during 1967 at Saga Studios

in Hampstead, London) and *Jackson C. Frank* (Columbia, 1965). Frank was "rediscovered" by T. J. McGrath in an American nursing home, but he died in 1999 of the long-term effects of injuries he had suffered in a childhood fire; see McGrath (1995).

25. See, for instance, the articles in *Folk Roots/fRoots* and *Dirty Linen* and Humphries (1997), whose book on Fairport's early period is not without reason subtitled "The Classic Years."

26. BBC:Folk on 2, *Sandy Denny—Who Knows Where the Time Goes: A Radio 2 Tribute*, April 20, 1988. This retrospective was broadcast ten years after her death.

27. Ibid. See also Heylin (2000: 110–24).

28. See the sleeve notes of the CD reissue of *Sandy*, based on information by Pete Frame and Patrick Humphries.

29. See also Humphries (1996 and 1997).

30. Shirley Collins, quoted in the CD booklet for *No Roses*.

31. Phil Pickett is the director of the New London Consort and the Musicians of the Globe.

32. The EFDSS reissued the Kimber recordings on the CD album *Absolutely Classic: The Music of William Kimber* in 1999.

33. See Jones (1995a).

34. See John Tobler's liner notes for the Steeleye Span CD reissues. Generally speaking, one also has to distinguish between the early Steeleye, which played traditional style on electric instruments, and the later lineups that incorporated more rock rhythms.

35. With Christy Moore, Liam O'Flynn, and Donal Lunny, Andy Irvine founded the highly successful Irish band Planxty in 1972. Lunny later became the producer of Irish groups such as Clannad).

36. Terry Woods became a member of Doctor Strangely Strange before he founded the Woods Band with his wife in 1972.

CHAPTER 4

1. As with to punk, one of the main features of the ideology of folk was that there should be no authority figures. Yet some musicians—with a performing history of nearly fifty years from the mid-1950s to early 2003—have almost involuntarily acquired this status.

2. See Davis (1990: 180–82) for a further discussion of these aspects.

3. "Jagger Swipes at Folk Fakers—After Dylan What?" *Melody Maker*, June 12, 1965, 1. The revival was not hesitant to give a sharp reply two weeks later ("Folk Star Ian Slams Back at Mick Jagger," *Melody Maker*, June 26, 1965, 4): "It seems comical to hear Mick Jagger talking about folk 'fakers.' Is there nothing fake about an English ex–grammar school boy trying to sound like a Southern Negro farmhand? It was precisely this phony Americanism that many young people were protesting against when they created the British folk music revival."

4. This is a reason why Thompson (1977) regards the Albion Dance Band, more than other groups or performers, as a successor of the early Scottish electric bands.

5. Although a *Time* magazine article (April 15, 1966) is usually credited with coining the "swinging London" sobriquet, a feature article by American journalist John Crosby in the *Weekend Telegraph* of April, 16, 1965, previously gave a detailed description of the city at that time. See Connolly (1995: 77–82), in which the Crosby article is reprinted.

6. See Howkins (1981) and Frith (1984: 143).

7. I refer here to Schaffner (1991), who pointed out that the owner of the Roundhouse was

at that time Arnold Wesker, a pivotal figure for the Centre 42 projects. See also Macan (1997) for a further discussion of the progressive rock scene.

8. This festival (after 1962 renamed the Sidmouth Folk Festival) takes place on the August Bank Holiday, which is the first Monday in the month. See Schofield (1990, 1994a, and 1994b).

9. See also Shaar Murray (1991, chap. 1).

10. The importance of these stations also became apparent with Fairport Convention. As Humphries (1996: 39-40) has pointed out, these programs were an inspiration to young bands who were not yet writing songs of their own. Thus, after the closure, Fairport again had to fall back upon friends' record collections to expand their repertoire.

11. Some of Fairport's early live radio material was reissued on CD as *Heyday: BBC Radio Sessions 1968-69* (Hannibal, 1987). It provides a good indication of the band's repertoire at that time, which still predominantly consisted of American covers. Fairport's extensive practice playing cover versions laid the foundation for the band's subsequent highly original interpretations of traditional material (which, from a rock perspective, were also cover versions).

12. "Trend 1969: Student Power Is the Music Business," *Melody Maker*, January 11, 1969, 7.

13. Hunt (1991) includes a similar account of Martin Carthy's and Dave Swarbrick's early recording experiences.

14. The video *Travelling for a Living* (1966) provides a good overview of the Watersons' lifestyle in the 1960s.

15. Another reason that electric folk groups turned professional might be that electric bands were expensive. Acoustic players just needed a guitar (if they did not perform completely a cappella), while an electric band required expensive instruments, equipment, roadies, and a van.

16. Bronson (1988) and Fuller (1998). The latter article includes more detailed information about Chrysalis's history.

17. Financial problems were also caused by other excessively expensive actions, for example, the album cover design for *Ten Man Mop* (1971). With a golden record sleeve and extensive booklet, the design and manufacturing costs for this album far exceeded the royalties. See also Tobler (1992), where Hart recalled that Steeleye Span ended up losing "money on every record sold."

18. When Fairport's first singer, Judy Dyble, was asked to leave the group, a new female singer was engaged, mainly because the group was regarded as a counterpart to the American band Jefferson Airplane, which was centered around Grace Slick.

19. After the band struggled for about two years without a female lead singer, Prior returned to Steeleye Span in 2002.

20. For scholarly publications on English folk music, see Atkinson (1996). It is also characteristic that representatives of the EFDSS and not academic researchers (musicologists) have been active at the meetings of the International Folk Music Council and were also responsible for the prevailing definition of folk music. Scotland, Ireland, and Wales have their own institutions focused on vernacular music.

21. See Stump (1997: 131-35) for a further discussion of this aspect.

22. This is even more remarkable when considering, as pointed out by Porter and Gower (1995: xxiv-xxvi), that in Traveller communities men usually deal with the public sphere, while women are discouraged "because their sexuality, as central to their identity, affects their musicality." Hence, many of the female Traveller performers were older (Jeannie Robertson became widely known when she was in her late forties).

23. The Poozies (formed in 1989) consist of Patsy Seddon and Mary MacMaster (from

Sileas), accordion player Karen Tweed, and Eilidh Shaw (successor of the singer/songwriters Sally Barker and Kate Rusby).

24. There are also a few alternative stations and Internet programs that offer broadcasting niches. The issues of *fRoots* offer listings of the various programs (including "world music," which faces a similar problem).

25. Malcolm Taylor, Ralph Vaughan Williams Memorial Library, personal communication, 2003.

CHAPTER 5

1. Wassailing (linguistically of Saxon origin: *wes hál*, i.e., be hale, be of good health) originally involved a toast or wish of good health. See also Karpeles (1987: 60). Similar traditions are still evident in northern Germany (although dying out), such as in the northernmost county, Schleswig-Holstein, where they are called "Rummelpott."

2. Mouth music is dance music that is sung by syllables.

3. These songs were sung during the *waulking*, a communal procedure in which tweed was cleaned, thickened, and shrunk. Women pounded the wet cloth, using rhythmic work songs with call-and-response patterns to organize the labor.

4. Examples can be heard on *Songs of the Travelling People (1951–68)*, reissued by Saydisc in 1995.

5. As Michael Verrier has suggested in a paper delivered at the EFDSS centenary conference *Folksong: Tradition and Revival* (July 10–12, 1998), the former actor MacColl was at the same time strongly influenced by Brecht's epic theater, which also shaped his work on the BBC radio ballads of the late 1950s and early 1960s.

6. Given the rhythmic and metric freedom in traditional singing, however, it is difficult to determine to what extent these irregularities were already part of the music and to what extent they were part of individual (recorded or transcribed) interpretations.

7. Robert Burns (not the Scottish Bard) demonstrated in a computer analysis in his paper "Where Are the Borderlines of Folk and Rock?" at the 1998 EFDSS *Folksong: Tradition and Revival* conference, that the rhythmic and metric structures of traditional music became much more fixed in later electric folk adaptations.

8. These observations confirm the physical aspects of Alan Lomax's systematization of folk song styles. Lomax categorized western and northern English singing as Old European, in which the voice is produced from a relaxed throat, while he categorized the singing of Scotland (one might include the Travellers here) and colonial America as Modern European, favoring a harsh, hard vocal production. A closer look at the singing styles suggests that these categories (which were, of course, shaped by the selected material Lomax studied) ought to be further differentiated. Lomax, for example, included southern and eastern England within the Modern European style (Lomax 1959: 927–54). This oversimplification has been criticized by Gregory (2002: 162) as well.

9. See Munro (1996), especially the description of singer Sheila MacGregor (p. 61). Munro also described the singing as "traditional bel canto art."

10. Collins's interpretation of "Pretty Saro," sung with much tighter vocal cords, demonstrates that her style was not the result of limited technical abilities.

11. See Sharp (1907), Karpeles (1987), and Nettl (1990).

12. These are three consecutive dates. October 31: Halloween [(All) Hallow(s) + E(v)en], the evening of All Saint's Day. November 1: All Saint's (i.e., Allhallows). November 2: All Souls (in Christian traditions reserved for prayers for all dead persons).

13. According to the single releases listed in Humphries (1997), the early Fairport never released singles with traditional A-sides.

14. The problem with amplification is particularly obvious with younger, less experienced electric folk or folk rock bands.

CHAPTER 6

1. This attitude changed completely when groups in the 1990s started to reinterpret songs from the 1960s through the 1980s.

2. Walton (1983: 100) points out that Winsbury's red gown indicated that he was a bard or poet.

3. Fotheringay was the castle where Mary Queen of Scots spent her last days before she was executed.

4. The tune of this song (other variants are known as "Our Wedding Day" or "Out of the Window") was first adapted by Padraig Colum from a collected instrumental fiddle tune in County Donegal, while the lyrics are based on an old ballad (see Kennedy 1984: 384). Colum's version of "She Moves through the Fair" was first published in Hughes (1909–36, vol. 1, p. 46) and has been adapted by many folk and traditional singers.

5. With his various Albion Bands, Ashley Hutchings would later play on-beat (i.e., emphasizing the first and third beat in a quadruple meter) as well.

6. Denny's accompaniments on this album are close to what has been suggested for song no. 152 in Kennedy (1984): 352.

7. This song is also known as "Our Wedding Day." Denny's version is based on Hughes (1909–36, vol. 1, 46). Hughes's published words were apparently adapted by Padraig Colum from an old ballad, although they differ little from other recorded versions.

8. This speech-song character is particularly obvious with Lloyd's recording.

9. *Fairport Convention: It All Comes 'Round Again* (video, Island, 1987).

10. See, for instance, Hart and Prior's pre-Steeleye recordings, *Folk Songs of Olde England*, vols. 1 and 2.

11. "Gaudete" was perceived by guitarist Davy Graham (Leigh, CD 1990) as 7/4, for instance.

12. These rhythmic features are also evident in the version published by Sharp (1916).

13. Sandy Denny's interpretation of "Bruton Town" (*Who Knows Where the Time Goes*, 1992) offers a clear contrast with Pentangle's version.

14. See Grossman (1992), on which this part of the chapter is based.

15. This memory is probably no exaggeration. Having seen Jansch in the Twelve Moon Bar, I can confirm that he can get rather angry at guests who talk too loudly while he is playing (or trying to concentrate).

16. The term "morris" was mentioned by Shakespeare. The origins of the name are still unclear; according to one theory, recently dismissed, it referred to the dance Moresca (known to exist in Burgundy in 1427, but with origins in the fourteenth century), which became one of the most popular dances of the fifteenth century and was even incorporated in Monteverdi's

Orfeo. Sword dancing is of later origin but is often danced in conjunction with morris; likewise, the dance teams occasionally also performed so-called mummers' plays. See Murray Winters (1996) and Forrest (1984), who suggested that the Cotswold morris and the Spanish-originated matachin might be the same dance, which furthers the theory that morris might have been of Arabian ("Moores") origin. The term also later referred to certain grotesque court dances with bizarre costumes in the seventeenth century. A helpful recorded introduction to the various British dance traditions can be heard in volume 16 (*You Lazy Lot of Bone-shakers: Songs and Dance Tunes of Seasonal Events*) of Reg Hall's twenty-volume CD anthology, *The Voice of the People* (Topic Records, 1998).

17. Denselow (Laing et al. 1975: 62) opined that with "Just a touch of Richard Thompson, . . . it could have been the folk world's *Tommy.*"

18. Bellamy's work differs, however, from Brecht/Weill in its form of social criticism; although it describes the situation and political injustice of a couple being transported to Australia, the content never becomes overly political.

19. *Little Rock to Leipzig* includes some good examples of the Oysterband's early dance music, such as "Johnny Mickey Barry's."

20. As Ian Telfer added in 2003, "Or at least that was true of Oysterband songs for many years; by the end of the 1990s, I feel our music had begun to evolve beyond that somewhat."

21. As Suff and Tobler added in the CD booklet for the reissued *Anthems in Eden* (Harvest, 1993), the album provided the groundwork for many subsequent musical experiments: "Several critics have suggested that it is impossible to imagine that electric accompaniment for traditional song, as successfully purveyed by Fairport Convention and Steeleye Span, could have developed quite as it did without the pioneering 'Anthems in Eden.'"

22. See, for instance, *The Enchanted Garden* (1980), recorded by the John Renbourn Group.

23. HS BM Royal App. 58 (ca. 1525), sometimes attributed to Hugh Aston. This is an early virginal piece in the style of the hornpipe, anticipating the scale techniques of the later virginal repertoire.

24. Renbourn in the CD booklet for *The Nine Maidens* (1985).

25. Although basically referring to U.S. West Coast bands of the late 1960s, whose music making suggested hallucinatory drug effects (extensive, distorted structures, work with the wah-wah pedal, etc.), the term "psychedelic rock" is also used to describe the early British progressive groups such as Pink Floyd. The experiments these groups undertook with musical structures, sound effects, and so on became the basis for more elaborate later rock styles.

26. The flute was less essential for English groups but became important for Irish groups like the Horslips and Clannad.

27. Carthy had already used similar tonal colors with trumpet and accordion/ concertina on *Because It's There* (1979) and trombone and accordion on *Out of the Cut* (1982).

28. Musical innovations continue within the rock world as well. In 2002 the independent band Chumbawamba released a highly acclaimed CD, *Readymades*, that works with song samples from the English tradition and folk scene. For example, the track "Jacob's Ladder" combines the traditional performer Harry Cox singing the refrain from "Pretty Ploughboy" ("And they sent him to the wars to be slain") with Davy Graham's "Angi." This song is a critical reflection on the sacrifice of British seamen during the evacuation of Norway's king during World War II; as the band points out in the liner notes, a modern interpretation could also refer to the Russian *Kursk* disaster.

CHAPTER 7

1. The recollections I heard in interviews with Rick Kemp, Frankie Armstrong, John Renbourn, and the Watersons all closely resembled Carthy's.

2. MacColl made many recordings with eminent traditional performers like Margaret Barry.

3. *Songs of the Travelling People* (1961; reissued in 1995).

4. Martin Carthy, liner notes to *Martin Carthy* (Topic, 1965). Lloyd's source is included in H. E. D. Hammond, ed., *Journal of the Folk Song Society*, No. 11, second part of Vol. 3 (1907: 127).

5. See his recording of *Music from Albania* (Topic, 1956).

6. Lloyd took this version and not the first one attributed to Marina Russell, as Carthy writes in the liner notes to his first recording, *Martin Carthy* (1965).

7. The term "aksak" (from the Turkish word for "stumbling" or "limping") was introduced by the Romanian musicologist Constantin Brăiloiu in 1952 to describe additive rhythmic forms like 2 + 2 + 3, thus replacing the expression "Bulgarian rhythm."

8. The likelihood of a substantial number of Lloyd modifcations was suggested by Martin Carthy, interview with author, October 20, 1996.

9. Listen, for instance, to "Blood and Gold" on *No More to the Dance* (1988).

10. For a comprehensive study and discussion of Lomax's activities in the British Isles between 1950 and 1958, see Gregory (2002).

11. Many of the recordings played by Peter Kennedy on the BBC radio in the 1950s were transcribed for *Folksongs of Britain and Ireland*, which was first published in 1976 and was later reissued by Oak Publications in 1984. It was thus less the book than the recordings that made the initial and critical impact on the revival process.

12. See, for instance, Weir (1995) and Watson (1983).

13. See also Stewart (1977) for further interpretations of songs like "Bruton Town" or "Edward."

14. The "Lyke Wake Dirge" refers to the medieval "ars moriendi," the preparation during life for the soul's way to heaven—in this case, for instance, the idea that if, during one's lifetime, one had given shoes to beggars, the soul would also have shoes to cross the dangerous Whinny (i.e., "thorny") Moor.

15. See Carthy's early album, *Martin Carthy* (1965), and the Watersons' *Frost and Fire* (1965).

CHAPTER 8

1. In Britain today there are around 500 Morris teams (ca. 5,000–7,500 dancers), while in the United States and Canada there are around 150 dancing teams with 1,500–2,000 people (Murray Winters 1996).

2. Liz Milner, one of my American manuscript reviewers, has even observed a surprising amount of resentment toward the English for being the dominant culture in the States. As she remarked, English folk songs are often rejected by American folksingers as being too close to high culture (personal communication, June 2003).

3. See Harker (1985: 113) and especially Filene (1995: 12–36) for a further discussion of these aspects.

4. Sharp insisted that Appalachian people were 100 percent English, while in fact 13 percent

were black (Filene 1995: 35). As Filene points out further, although black vernacular music had been a point of fascination for northerners in the 1870s, it was not until the writings and activities of Carl Sandburg and Robert Winslow Gordon (and later also John Lomax) that African American songs became generally accepted as America's musical heritage (ibid.: 62).

5. Taking a hiatus from regular performing at the time of this writing, Jennifer Cutting remains a moving force in electric folk as a writer/producer with her own transatlantic production company, which specializes in bringing British and American musicians together in the studio. Her recent productions have included Maddy Prior, Dave Mattacks, Peter Knight, Polly Bolton, and Troy Donockley.

6. British/English musicians have never used the image of the Union Jack to indicate their cultural/musical allegiance.

7. See also the appendix in Humphries (1996).

8. See notice on Bob and Ron Copper, "On English Shepherd and Farming" (Folk Legacy FSB-19), 1965, Sing Out! 15 no. 3 (July); "The Copper Family of Sussex," introduced by Peter Bellamy, Sing Out! 20 no. 1 (Feb./March); section "From Britain," Sing Out! 20 no. 4 (September); review of Steeleye Span, Sing Out! 22 no. 6 (Dec.).

9. See also Owston (1992).

10. I was later told by an informant that Anderson considered Tempest to be the worst one.

11. O'Neill amassed one of the largest Irish music collections in the States in the early twentieth century, gathering a substantial amount of material from Chicago's Irish Music Club, an establishment that had replaced originally informal session meetings with more regular meetings and social activities around the turn of the century.

12. The 1990 U.S. census counted the five largest (self-identified) ancestry groups as: German: 57,947,000; Irish: 38,736,000; English: 32,652,000; African American: 23,777,000; Italian: 14,665,000. (Population total: 248,710,000.) Based on the *Statistical Abstract of the United States 1993* (Stevenson 1996: 16).

13. Moloney (2002) presents a detailed description of Irish immigration as reflected in song.

14. See Worth and Cartwright (1986) and Cohen and Wells (1982) for further details concerning McCormack's recordings.

15. Céilidh houses were neighborhood meetings with singing, poetry recital, storytelling, and discussions that could take place in any household.

16. Ennis and Ó Riada's influence corresponds with the observations of Livingston (1999), who argues that in most cases a group of individuals starts a music revival.

17. Definition from *Random House Webster's College Dictionary* (New York: Random House, 1991).

18. The revival of Galician bagpipe playing was especially initiated by the success of Carlos Nunes's album *A Irmandade das Estrellas* (1997) and Hevia's even more popular album *Tierra de Nadie* (1999). Other notable performers are Susana Seivante and Xosé Manuel Budiño. See also Andrew Cronshaw, "Stars & Gaitas," *Folk Roots* 201 (March 2000), 20–25.

19. "Stivell" is the Breton word for "fountain" or "spring."

20. Stivell and Ar Braz continued their careers separately. Stivell drifted increasingly in esoteric directions, while Ar Braz, who played with various bands, was at one point a member of Fairport Convention.

21. See the early recordings *Clannad 2* (1974), *Dúlamán* ("Seaweed," 1976), *Crann Ull* ("The Apple Tree," 1980), and *Fuaim* (1982).

22. See the Chieftains' *The Long Black Veil* (1995), which features guests like Sinéad O'Connor, Van Morrison, Sting, and the Rolling Stones.

23. See Morag MacLeod, "Folk Revival in Gaelic Song," in Munro (1996: 124–37).

24. Celtic techniques have been used for shaman songs performed by Native American groups and for other songs with a pagan content, particularly by the Latvian group Ilgi.

25. It thus became known in the States as "the Volkswagen song." See Bond (1993).

26. See, for instance, *Dirty Linen* 47 (August/September 1993).

27. From a CD review, cited in an ad in *Dirty Linen* 65 (August/September 1996), 24.

28. Some examples, partly also listed by Woods, include *Belgium*: Rum/t'Kliekske/Wanners van der Welde, Hubert Boone, Roland; *Holland*: Scheepesbeschuit; *Germany*: Singspiel, Elster Silberflug, Fidel Michel, Hannes Wader, Knut Kiesewetter, Ougenweide, Liederjan, and Helmut Debus.

29. The name of the group, which comprises about twenty members (mainly music school graduates), refers to Spelemannslag, a traditional large ensemble.

REFERENCES

The distinctions between academic and journalistic sources in this reference list are not meant to imply a qualitative differentiation. Yet because magazines and newspapers like *Folk Roots* (*fRoots* since 2000) and *Melody Maker* tend to publish interviews primarily, a separation seemed to be reasonable. These areas do overlap, particularly in the case of *English Dance & Song*: although written by folk music insiders and aimed at "amateurs," it includes well-researched historical articles. I have thus included articles from this publication under both "Articles and Papers" and "Magazines and Periodicals."

PRINTED MUSIC

Allcock, Maartin, and David Gleeson. 1993. *Fairport Convention Songbook: 42 Things from 25 Years.* Banbury, UK: Woodworm Music.

Bronson, Bertrand Harris. 1959–72. *The Traditional Tunes of the Child Ballads.* 4 vols. Princeton: Princeton University Press.

Child, Francis James, ed. 1882–98. *The English and Scottish Popular Ballads.* 5 vols. Boston: Houghton Mifflin.

Denselow, Robin, and Bill Pitt. 1975. *Steeleye Span Songbook.* London: Wise Publications.

Grossman, Stefan. 1990. *British Fingerpicking Guitar.* Pacific, MO: Mel Bay.

———, 1992. *Fingerstyle Guitar Solos in Open Tunings.* Pacific, MO: Mel Bay.

———, 1995. *Fingerstyle Guitar: New Dimensions and Exploitations.* Pacific, MO: Mel Bay.

Hoffmann, Gisela, ed. 1982. *Englische und amerikanische Balladen.* Stuttgart: Reclam.

Kennedy, Doug. 1987. *Martin Carthy: A Guitar in Folk Music.* Petersham, UK: New Punchbowl Music.

Kennedy, Peter, ed. [1975] 1984. *Folksongs of Britain and Ireland.* New York: Oak Publications.

Hughes, Herbert. 1909–36. *Irish Country Songs.* 4 vols. London: Boosey.

Lloyd, Albert Lancaster. [1952] 1978. *Come All Ye Bold Miners: Ballads and Songs of the Coalfields.* London: Lawrence and Wishart.

Lomax, Alan. 1960. *The Folk Songs of North America.* Garden City, NY: Doubleday.

Ritchie, Jean. 1965. *Folk Songs of the Southern Appalachians as Sung by Jean Ritchie.* New York: Oak Publications.

Russell, Ian, ed. 1994. *A Festival of Village Carols.* Unstone, UK: Village Carols.

Sharp, Cecil J., ed. 1916. *One Hundred English Folksongs for Medium Voice.* Boston: Oliver Ditson Company.

Sharp, Cecil J., and Charles L. Marson. 1904–9. *Folk Songs from Somerset.* 5 vols. London: Simpkin, Marshall.

Seeger, Peggy, and Ewan MacColl. 1960. *The Singing Island: A Collection of English and Scots Folksongs.* London: Mills Music.

Steeleye Span. 1972. London: Libra Music/Sparta Florida Music.

Vaughan Williams, Ralph, and A. L. Lloyd, eds. 1959. *The Penguin Book of English Folk Songs.* Harmondsworth, UK: Penguin Books.

Villiers Stanford, Charles. 1906. *The National Songbook: A Complete Collection of the Folk Songs, Suggested by the Board of Education (1905).* London, New York, n.p.

Walton, Jake. 1983. Keltische Folksongs. Frankfurt am Main: Fischer.

BOOKS

Appadurai, Arjun. 1998. *Modernity at Large: Cultural Dimensions of Globalization.* Minneapolis: University of Minnesota Press.

Andersen, Flemming Gotthelf, Otto Holzapfel, and Thomas Pettitt. 1982. *The Ballad as Narrative: Studies in the Ballad Traditions of England, Scotland, Germany, and Denmark.* Odense, Denmark: Odense University Press.

Armstrong, Frankie, and Jenny Pearson. 1992. *As Far as the Eye Can Sing: An Autobiography.* London: The Women's Press.

Atkinson, David. 1996. *English Folk Song: An Introductory Bibliography.* Vaughan Williams Memorial Library Leaflet no. 23. London: English Folk Dance and Song Society.

Bird, Brian. 1958. *Skiffle: The Story of Folk Song with a Jazz Beat.* London: Robert Hale.

Bohlman, Philip V. 1988. *The Study of Folk Music in the Modern World.* Bloomington: Indiana University Press.

Boyes, Georgina. 1993. *The Imagined Village: Culture, Ideology, and the English Folk Revival.* Manchester: Manchester University Press.

Bratton, J. S. 1975. *The Victorian Popular Ballad.* London: Macmillan.

Bronson, Bertrand Harris. 1969. *The Ballad as Song.* Berkeley and Los Angeles: University of California Press.

Broughton, Simon, Mark Ellingham, David Muddyman, and Richard Trillo. 1994. *World Music: The Rough Guide.* London: Rough Guides.

Butler, David, and Anne Sloman. 1980. 1980. *British Political Facts: 1900-1979.* (5th ed.). London: Mcmillian.

Cantwell, Robert. 1996. *When We Were Good: The Folk Revival.* Cambridge, MA: Harvard University Press.

Carlin, Richard. 1987. *English and American Folk Music.* New York: Facts on File Publications.

Carolan, Nicholas. 1997. *A Harvest Saved: Francis O'Neill and Irish Music in Chicago.* Cork, Ireland: Ossian Publications.

Chappell, William. [1859] 1965. *The Ballad Literature and Popular Music of the Olden Time.* 2 vols. New York: Dover.

Cohen, Ronald D. 2003. *Alan Lomax: Selected Writings, 1934–1997.* New York: Routledge.

Collins, Shirley. 2004. *America Over the Water.* London: Saf Publishing.

Connolly, Ray, ed. 1995. *In the Sixties.* London: Pavilion Books.

Cunningham, Mark. 1996. *Good Vibrations: A History of Record Production.* Chessington, UK: Castle Communications.

Curran, James, and Jean Seaton. [1981] 1991. *Power without Responsibility: The Press and Broadcasting in Britain.* London: Routledge.

Dannen, Fredric. [1990] 1991. *Hit Men: Power Brokers and Fast Money inside the Music Business.* New York: Vintage Books.

Davis, John. 1990. *Youth and the Condition of Britain: Images of Adolescent Conflict.* London: Athlone Press.

DeCurtis, Anthony, and James Henke. 1992. *The Rolling Stone Illustrated History of Rock & Roll.* New York: Random House.

Filene, Benjamin Peter. 1995. *Romancing the Folk: Public Memory and American Vernacular Music in the Twentieth Century.* PhD diss., Yale University.

Flender, Reinhardt, and Hermann Rauhe. 1989. *Popmusik: Geschichte, Funktion, Wirkung und Ästhetik.* Darmstadt: Wissenschaftliche Buchgesellschaft.

Flick, Uwe. 1995. *Qualitative Forschung: Theorie, Methoden, Anwendung in Psychologie und Sozialwissenschaften.* Reinbek bei Hamburg: Rowohlt.

Forrest, John. 1984. *Morris and Matachin: A Study in Comparative Choreography.* London: EFDSS.

Frame, Pete. 1994. *The Complete Rock Family Trees.* Zürich: Edition Olms.

Frey, Jürgen, and Kaarel Siniveer. 1987. *Eine Geschichte der Folkmusik.* Reinbek bei Hamburg: Rowohlt.

Frith, Simon. [1983] 1984. *Sound Effects: Youth, Leisure, and the Politics of Rock 'n' Roll.* London: Constable and Company.

Geertz, Clifford. 1973. *The Interpretation of Cultures: Selected Essays.* New York: Basic Books.

Hamm, Charles. 1995. *Putting Popular Music in Its Place.* Cambridge: Cambridge University Press.

Händel, Heinrich, and Daniel A. Gossel. [1991] 1994. *Großbritannien.* Munich: Beck.

Harker, Dave. 1980. *One for the Money: Politics and Popular Song.* London: Hutchinson.

———. 1985. *Fakesong: The Manufacture of British 'Folksong,' 1700 to the Present Day.* Milton Keynes, UK: Open University Press.

Harper, Colin. 2000. *Dazzling Stranger: Bert Jansch and the British Folk and Blues Revival.* London: Bloomsbury.

Heylin, Clinton. 2000. *No More Sad Refrains: The Life and Times of Sandy Denny.* London: Helter Skelter.

———. [1987] 1988. *Richard Thompson: Twenty-One Years of Doom and Gloom.* Manchester: Marbohey Publications.

Hughes, Meirion, and Robert Stradling. [1993] 2001. *The English Musical Renaissance, 1860–1940: Construction and Deconstruction.* London: Routledge.

Humphries, Patrick. [1982] 1997. *Meet on the Ledge: Fairport Convention—The Classic Years.* London: Virgin Books.

———. 1996. *Richard Thompson: Strange Affair—The Biography.* London: Virgin Books.

Jerrentrup, Ansgar. 1981. *Entwicklung der Rockmusik von den Anfängen bis zum Beat.* Regensburg: Gustav Bosse.

Karpeles, Maud. [1973] 1987. *An Introduction to English Folk Song.* Rev. by Peter Kennedy. Oxford: Oxford University Press.

Laing, Dave, Karl Dallas, Robin Denselow, and Robert Shelton. 1975. *The Electric Muse: The Story of Folk into Rock.* London: Methuen.

Lieberman, Robbie. [1989] 1995. *"My Song Is My Weapon": People's Songs, American Communism, and the Politics of Culture, 1930–50.* Urbana: University of Illinois Press.

Ling, January 1997. *A History of European Folk Music.* Rochester, NY: University of Rochester Press.

Lloyd, Albert Lancaster. 1967. *Folk Song in England.* London: Lawrence & Wishart.

——— [1944]. *The Singing Englishman: An Introduction to Folk Song.* London: Workers' Music Association.

Lomax, Alan. [1968] 1994. *Folk Song Style and Culture.* New Brunswick, NJ: Transaction Publishers.

McAleer, Dave. 1993. *Hit Parade Heroes: British Beat before the Beatles.* London: Hamlyn.

MacColl, Ewan. 1990. *Journeyman: An Autobiography.* London: Sidgwick & Jackson.

MacKinnon, Niall. 1993. *The British Folk Scene: Musical Performance and Social Identity.* Buckingham, UK: Open University Press.

Macan, Edward. 1997. *Rocking the Classic: English Progressive Rock and the Counterculture.* New York: Oxford University Press.

Manuel, Peter. 1988. *Popular Musics of the Non-Western World: An Introductory Survey.* New York: Oxford University Press.

Melhuish, Martin. 1998. *Celtic Tides: Traditional Music in a New Age.* Kingston, ON: Quarry Press.

Merriam, Alan P. 1964. *The Anthropology of Music.* Evanston, IL: Northwestern University Press.

Middleton, Richard. [1990] 1995. *Studying Popular Music.* Milton Keynes, UK: Open University Press.

Moloney, Mick. 2002. *Far from the Shamrock Shore: The Story of Irish Immigration through Song.* West Link Park, Doughcloyne, Wilton, Cork, Ireland: The Collins Press.

Moore, Allan F. 1993. *Rock: The Primary Text—Developing a Musicology of Rock.* Buckingham, UK: Open University Press.

Munro, Ailie, ed. [1984] 1996. *The Democratic Muse: Folk Music Revival in Scotland.* Aberdeen: Scottish Cultural Press.

Myers, Helen, ed. 1992. *Ethnomusicology: An Introduction.* New York: Norton.

———, ed. 1993. *Ethnomusicology: Historical and Regional Studies.* New York: Norton.

Nettl, Bruno. 1976. *Folk Music in the United States: An Introduction.* 3rd ed. Rev. and exp. by Helen Myers. Detroit: Wayne State University Press.

———. 1990. *Folk and Traditional Music of the Western Continents.* 3rd ed. Rev. and ed. by Valerie Woodring Goertzen. Englewood Cliffs, NJ: Prentice Hall.

Nettl, Bruno, and Philip V. Bohlman. 1988. *Comparative Musicology and Anthropology of Music: Essays on the History of Ethnomusicology.* Chicago: University of Chicago Press.

Oliver, Paul. [1969] 1998. *The Story of the Blues.* Boston: Northeastern University Press.

Ó Riada, Seán. 1962. *Our Musical Heritage.* Ed. by Thomas Kinsalla. London: Dolmen Press.

Palmer, Roy. 1988. *The Sound of History: Songs and Social Comment.* London: Pimlico.

Pearsall, Ronald. 1973. *Victorian Popular Music.* London: David & Charles.

Peck, Abe. [1985] 1991. *Uncovering the Sixties: The Life and Times of the Underground Press.* New York: Citadel Press.

Pegg, Bob. 1976. *Folk: A Portrait of English Traditional Music, Musicians, and Customs.* London: Wildwood House.

Pickering, Michael, and Tony Green, eds. 1987. *Everyday Culture: Popular Song and the Vernacular Milieu.* Milton Keynes, UK: Open University Press.

Porter, James, ed. 1983. *The Ballad Image: Essays Presented to Bertrand Harris Bronson.* Los Angeles: Center for the Study of Comparative Folklore and Mythology, University of California, Los Angeles.

Porter, James, and Herschel Gower. 1995. *Jeannie Robertson: Emergent Singer, Transformative Voice.* Knoxville: University of Tennessee Press.

Porterfield, Nolan. 1996. *Last Cavalier: The Life and Times of John A. Lomax.* Urbana: University of Illinois Press.

Redwood, Fred, and Martin Woodward. 1996. *The Woodworm Era: The Story of Today's Fairport Convention.* Thatcham, UK: Jeneva Publishing.

Rosenberg, Neil V., ed. 1993. *Transforming Tradition: Folk Music Revivals Examined.* Urbana: University of Illinois Press.

Russell, Dave. 1987. *Popular Music in England, 1840–1914: A Social History.* Manchester: Manchester University Press.

Russell, Ian, ed. 1986. *Singer, Song, and Scholar.* Sheffield, UK: Sheffield Academic Press.

Schaffner, Nicholas. 1991. *Saucerful of Secrets: The Pink Floyd Odyssey.* New York: Harmony Books.

Schiffner, Wolfgang. 1991. Einflüsse der Technik auf die Entwicklung von Rock/Pop-Musik. PhD diss., Hamburg University.

Shaar Murray, Charles. [1987] 1991. *Crosstown Traffic: Jimi Hendrix and the Post-War Rock 'n' Roll Revolution.* New York: St. Martin's Press.

Sharp, Cecil. 1907. *English Folk-Song: Some Conclusions.* London: Simpkin and Novello.

Siniveer, Kaarel. 1981. *Folk Lexikon.* Reinbek bei Hamburg: Rowohlt.

Slobin, Mark. 1993. *Subcultural Sounds: Micromusics of the West.* Hanover, NH: Wesleyan University Press.

Spottswood, Richard. 1990. *Ethnic Music on Records: A Discography of Ethnic Recordings Produced in the United States, 1893 to 1942.* Vol. 5, *Mid-East, Far East, Scandinavian, English Language, American Indian, International.* Urbana: University of Illinois Press.

Stevenson, Douglas K. [1987] 1996. *American Life and Institutions.* Stuttgart: Ernst Klett.

Stevenson, John. [1984] 1990. *British Society, 1914–45.* London: Penguin.

Stewart, Bob. 1997. *Where Is Saint George? Pagan Imagery in English Folksong.* Bradford-on-Avon, UK: Moonraker Press.

Stump, Paul. 1997. *The Music's All That Matters: A History of Progressive Rock.* London: Quartet Books.

Toelken, Barre. 1995. *Morning Dew and Roses: Nuance, Metaphor, and Meaning in Folksongs.* Urbana: University of Illinois Press.

Van der Merwe, Peter. [1989] 1992. *Origins of the Popular Style.* Oxford: Clarendon Press.

Watson, Ian. 1983. *Song and Democratic Culture in Britain: An Approach to Popular Culture in Social Movements.* London: Croom Helm.

Woods, Fred. 1979. *Folk Revival: The Rediscovery of a National Music.* Poole, UK: Blandford Press.

Worth, Paul W., and Jim Cartwright. 1986. *John McCormack: A Comprehensive Discography.* Westport, CT): Greenwood Press.

ARTICLES AND PAPERS

Bartram, Chris. 1996. "The Fiddle in Southern England." *English Dance & Song* 58, no. 2 (Summer): 2–4.

Bayard, Samuel P. 1950. "Prolegomena to a Study of the Principal Melodic Families of British-American Folk Song." *Journal of American Folklore* 63: 1–44.

Berman, Chris. 1998. "Cecil Sharp in Somerset: Some Further Conclusions." Paper presented at the conference "Folksong: Tradition and Revival" (an international conference to celebrate the centenary of the founding of the Folk Song Society in 1898). Sheffield: University of Sheffield/National Centre for English Cultural Trandition/EFDSS.

Breandán, Breathnach. 1980. "Ireland, §II: Folk Music." In *The New Grove of Music and Musicians*): ed. Stanley Sadie, vol. 9, 316–25. London: Macmillan.

Cameron, Francis. 1992. "The Teaching of Ethnomusicology in United Kingdom Universities." In *European Studies in Ethnomusicology: Historical Developments and Recent Trends*, eds. Max-Peter Baumann, Artur Simon, and Ulrich Wegner, 26–41. Wilhelmshaven: Florian Noetzel.

Cohen, Norm, and Paul F. Wells. 1982. "Recorded Ethnic Music: A Guide to Resources." In *Ethnic Recordings in America: A Neglected Heritage*, 186–190. Washington, DC: Library of Congress.

Cohen, Sara. 1993. "Ethnography and Popular Music Studies." *Popular Music* 12, no. 2, 123–37.

Collinson, Francis. 1980. "Scotland, §2: Folk Music." In *The New Grove Dictionary of Music and Musicians*): ed. Stanley Sadie, vol. 17, 70–81. London: Macmillan.

Durant, Alan. 1985. "Rock Revolution or Time-No-Changes: Visions of Change and Continuity in Rock Music." *Popular Music* 5: 97–121.

Elbourne, Roger P. 1975a. "The Question of Definition." *Yearbook of the International Folk Music Council* 7: 9–29.

———. 1975b. "The Study of Change in Traditional Music." *Folklore* 86: 181–89.

Frith, Simon. 1981. "'The Magic That Can Set You Free': The Ideology of Folk and the Myth of the Rock Community." *Popular Music* 1: 159–68.

Grainger, Percy. 1908. "Collecting with the Phonograph." *Journal of the Folk Song Society* 3: 147–62.

Gregory, E. David. 2002. "Lomax in London: Alan Lomax, the BBC, and the Folk-Song Revival in England, 1950–1958." *Folk Music Journal* 8, no. 2: 136–69.

Guerdon, Gilbert. 1995. "Street Musicians." *English Dance & Song* 57, no. 1 (Spring): 6–8.

Hansson, Mats. 1994. "The Ex-Ritual Morris." *English Dance & Song* 56, no. 4 (Winter): 8.

International Folk Music Council. 1955. "Definition of Folk Music." *Journal of the International Folk Music Council* 7: 23.

Karpeles, Maud. 1955. "Definition of Folk Music." *Journal of the International Folk Music Council* 7: 6–7.

———. 1980. "England, §II: Folk Music." In *The New Grove Dictionary of Music and Musicians*): ed. Stanley Sadie, vol. 6, 182–91. London: Macmillan.

Livingston, Tamara. 1999. "Music Revivals: Towards a General Theory." *Ethnomusicology* 43, no. 1 (Winter): 66–85.

Lloyd, Albert Lancaster. 1954. "The Singing Style of the Copper Family." *Journal of the English Folk Dance and Song Society* 7: 145–49.

———. 1965. "Review: Cecil Sharp, English Folk-Song: Some Conclusions." *Sing Out!* 15, no. 5 (November): 96–101.

MacKenzie, Justin. 1979. "The Boring Question of Definition." *Folk Review* 8, no. 3 (January): 16–18.

Marriott, Beryl. 2003. "The gold badge awards 2002: Dave Swarbrick." EFDSS members' quarterly newsletter 65, no. 1 (spring): 10.

Merton, R. K., and P. L. Kendall. 1946. "The Focussed Interview." *American Journal of Sociology* 51: 541–57.

Moloney, Mick. 1982. "Irish Ethnic Recordings and the Irish-American Imagination." In *Ethnic Recordings in America: A Neglected Heritage*, 85–101. Washington, DC: Library of Congress.

Myers, Helen. 1993. "Great Britain." In *Ethnomusicology: Historical and Regional Studies*, ed. Helen Myers, 129–48. New York: Norton.

Olson, Ian. 1996. "Nationalism or Internationalism in Folk Dance and Song?" *English Dance & Song* 58, no. 3 (Autumn): 16–18.

Pegg, Carole A. 1986. "An Ethnomusicological Approach to Traditional Music in East Suffolk." In *Singer, Song, and Scholar*, ed. Ian Russell, 55–72. Sheffield, UK: Sheffield Academic Press.

Pickering, Michael. 1990. "Recent Folk Music Scholarship in England: A Critique." *Folk Music Journal* 6: 37–64.

Porter, James. 1993. "Convergence, Divergence, and Dialectic in Folksong Paradigms: Critical Directions for Transatlantic Scholarship." *Journal of American Folklore* 106: 61–98.

Richards, Sam. 1986/87. "'Folksong' and 'Song as Folklore.'" *Folk Song Research* 5: 14–16.

Schneider, Albrecht. 1991. "Traditional Music, Pop, and the Problem of Copyright Protection." In *Traditional Music and Cultural Policy*, ed. Max-Peter Baumann and Ulrich Wegner, 302–16. Wilhelmshaven: Florian Noetzel.

Seeger, Charles. 1948. "Reviews." *Journal of American Folklore* 61: 215–18.

———. 1949. "Reviews." *Journal of American Folklore* 62: 68–70.

———. 1977. "Versions and Variants of the Tunes of 'Barbara Allen.'" In *Studies in Musicology 1935–1975*. Berkeley: University of California Press.

Shepherd, John. 1982. "A Theoretical Model of the Sociomusicological Analysis of Popular Musics." *Popular Music* 2: 145–77.

Sykes, Richard. 1993. "The Evolution of Englishness in the English Folksong Revival, 1890–1914." *Folk Music Journal* 6: 446–90.

Tagg, Philip. 1982. "Analysing Popular Music: Theory, Method, and Practice." *Popular Music* 2: 37–67.

Winter, Eric. 1994. "Topic Records: A Bit of History." *English Dance & Song* 56, no. 3 (Winter): 24.

Yates, Michael. 1982. "Percy Grainger and the Impact of the Phonograph." *Folk Music Journal* 4: 265–75.

MAGAZINES AND PERIODICALS

Abbreviations: DL = *Dirty Linen*; FR = *Folk Roots/fRoots*; MM = *Melody Maker*; NME = *New Musical Express*

Abrahams, Roger D. 1966. "Folk Songs and the Top 40." *Sing Out!* 16, no. 1 (February/March): 12–21.

Anderson, Ian A. 1985. "Richard Thompson." FR 25 (July): 30–34.

———. 1986. "Oysterband: Pearls of Wisdom." FR 34 (April): 28–30, 47.

———. 1994. "Network Frenzy." FR 130 (April): 16.

———. 1996. "Doing the English." FR 155 (May): 42–47.

Anderson, Ian A., and Lawrence Heath. 1982. "Ashley Hutchings." *Southern Rag* no. 4: 10–13.

Anderson, Ian A., and Maggie Holland. 1985. "Carthy's Commitment." *Southern Rag* no. 24: 9–13.

Andrews, Harvey. 1973. "The State of Folk." *Folk Review* 2, no. 11 (September): 22–23.

Bellamy, Peter. 1973. "Steeleye Conversation." *Folk Review* 2, no. 7 (May): 8–10.

———. 1975. Review of Laing et al., *The Electric Muse*. *Folk Review* 4, no. 11 (September): 34.

Bond, Lahri. 1991. "Amoebas Are Very Small." *DL* 32 (February/March): 28–31.

———. 1993. "Clannad: An Interview with Lead Singer Máire Brennan." *DL* 47 (August/September): 51–55.

Bronson, Fred. 1998. "Chrysalis Charting Success." Billboard Advertising Supplement (October 31): 48-49.

Brown, David. 1977. "Swarb." *Folk Review* 6, no. 6 (April): 14–15.

Carter, Christine. 2000. "Pegging Out." *FR* 210 (December): 18.

Carthy, Martin. 1980. "'It Isn't Just Done to Sound Bizarre': 'Cross-Tuning' the Guitar." *Acoustic Music* (May): 45.

Coady, Tom. 1984. "Dave Mattacks." *Swing* 51, no. 8: 36–39.

Coleman, Ray. 1965. "Can There Ever Be a Boom on Folk?" *MM* (February 13): 10–11.

———. 1966. "Beatles Say—Dylan Shows the Way." *MM* (January 8): 3.

———. 1971. "Why Sandy Wants to Fly." *MM* (May 15): 13.

Cooney, Michael. 1972. "A 10¢ Description of the British Folk Scene and Some Ideas on Forming a British-Style Folk Club over Here." *Sing Out!* 22, no. 2 (April): 16–17.

Cooper, Mark. 1988. "A Passage to England." *The Guardian*, 29 December: 25.

Coxson, Sarah. 1990. "Oysters '89." *FR* 79/80 (January/February): 50–55.

———. 1992. "Deserters Songs." *FR* 106 (April): 17–19.

Dallas, Karl. 1965. "Are Folk Singers Overpaid?" *MM* (August 21): 4.

———. 1966a. "That Was the Folk Year." *MM* (January 1): 8.

———. 1966b. "Jansch Digs Back—To Tradition." *MM* (July 16): 15.

———. 1966c. "Hester—Not Ashamed to Do Some Folk Rock." *MM* (October 15): 13.

———. 1966d. "It's Hello Dolly, in Folk Again." *MM* (October 22): 12.

———. 1966e. "'Fine Feathered Folk.'" *MM* (December 17): 22.

———. 1967. "I Don't Want to Be Labelled, Says Sandy." *MM* (September 23): 12.

———. 1968a. "Once Again—Is It Folk?" *MM* (February 27): 19.

———. 1968b. "Shirley Is a Bit of a Good Fairy." *MM* (May 25): 18–19.

———. 1968c. "Jeannie: Undisputed Queen of Folksong." *MM* (December 14): 22.

———. 1969. "Hung Up on Sackbuts and Crumbhorns." *MM* (July 5): 21.

———. 1970a. "Suddenly Folk Rock Is Respectable Again." *MM* (February 7): 7.

———. 1970b. "Sandy and the New Band." *MM* (March 21): 13.

———. 1970c. "And Copyists Get All the Cheers . . ." *MM* (April 18): 21.

———. 1970d. "Fotheringay, the Sea, and Sandy Denny." *MM* (May 30): 15.

———. 1970e. "Steeleye, Spanning the Pop-Folk Gap." *MM* (July 25): 31.

———. 1970f. "'Pop Is So Male-Oriented. They Don't Think a Lady Can Tell Them Anything.'" *MM* (August 8): 27.

———. 1970g. "Electric Folk: An MM Survey of the Folk Who Plug In." *MM* (September 26): 37.

———. 1970h. "Fairport and After." *MM* (October 3): 24.

———. 1970i. "Is There a Future for Fotheringay?" *MM* (November 21): 15.

———. 1971a. "Electric Folk—The Second Generation." *MM* (January 9): 21.

———. 1971b. "Steeleye Span—Currently on Tour with Jethro Tull." *MM* (March 6): 30.

———. 1971c. "Steeleye: A Great Leap Forward." *MM* (March 13): 35.

———. 1971d. "The Folk Revival." *MM* (July 31): 28–29.

———. 1971e. "Folk on Radio One: What's Going On?" *MM* (September 11): 9.

———. 1971f. "A. L. Lloyd." *MM* (October 30): 28.

———. 1971g. "The State of Folk." *MM* (November 13): 20.

———. 1971h. "Electric Folk—Outlook Uncertain." *MM* (December 4): 21.

———. 1971i. "Shirley's Super Group." *MM* (December 11): 35.

———. 1972a. "Folk Is Reactionary." *Folk & Country* 3, no. 3 (January): 7–9.

———. 1972b. "The New St. George." *MM* (May 27): 37.

———. 1972c. "Davey Graham." *Folk Review*, 1, no. 9 (July): 4–5.

———. 1972d. "Sandy: Alone Again . . . Naturally." *MM* (September 2): 37.

———. 1972e. "Sandy's Finest!" *MM* (September 23): 15.

———. 1972f. "Pentangle: Five Years of Stability." *Folk Review* 2, no. 1 (November): 7–8.

———. 1973a. "Pentangle Dies . . . with a Whimper." *MM* (March 31): 21.

———. 1973b. "Steeleye Span—MM Band Breakdown." *MM* (April 14): 36–37.

———. 1973c. "Steeleye Needs a Drummer . . ." *MM* (July 14): 41.

———. 1973d. "Steeleye Go Glam-Folk." *MM* (September 8): 37.

———. 1974. "Full Steam Ahead! Solution to Energy Crisis: Etchingham Steam Band—Everything Is Acoustic!" *MM* (January 26): 41.

———. 1975a. "MacColl: A True Critic." *MM* (February 22): 40.

———. 1975b. "Acoustic Is Best." Interview with MacColl. *MM* (March 1): 50.

———. 1975c. "'I'm Just a Street Singer': Davey Graham Talks to Karl Dallas." *MM* (April 26): 67.

———. 1977. "The Carthy Tapes." *Folk News* (July): 8–10.

———. 1978a. "Folk Rock Is Dead!" *Folk News* (February): 1.

———. 1978b. "The First Lady of Folk Rock." *Folk News* (May): 3.

———. 1978c. "Conversation with the Misses Collins." *Folk News* (September): 12–14.

———. 1979. "The Last Rites." *Folk News/Acoustic Music* (June): 26–27.

———. 1980a. "Martin Carthy Pleads Guilty." *Acoustic Music* (May): 14–15.

———. 1980b. Interview with Dave Mattacks. *Acoustic Music* (July): 19, 21.

———. 1989. "MacColl: The Man, the Myth, the Music." *English Dance & Song* 51, no. 4 (Christmas): 10–14.

Dawbarn, Bob. 1965a. "Is the BBC Anti-Pop?" *MM* (May 22): 8.

———. 1965b. "How to Be a Folk Poet." *MM* (June 12): 10–11.

———. 1965c. "Thank Goodness—We Won't Get This Six-Minute Bob Dylan Single Britain." *MM* (August 7): 7.

———. 1969. "Pentangle: An English Music Band." *MM* (August 23): 9.

Dellar, Fred. 1975. "'Bert Jansch' Not Still Going, Is He?" *NME* (October 18): 25.

Denselow, Robin. 1970. "The Dangers of Success." *MM* (July 11): 22.

Donovan. 1965. "Donovan on Newport." *MM* (July 31): 3.

Dunson, Josh. 1966a. "Folk Rock: Thunder without Rain." *Sing Out!* 15, no. 6 (January): 12–17.

———. 1966b. "The British Revival." *Sing Out!* 16, no. 3 (July): 44.

Eldridge, Royston. 1969. "Pop Goes on the Fiddle." *MM* (September 6): 12.

Falstaff, John C. 1992. "Fairport Convention." *DL* 41 (August/September): 42–45; 90.

Fisher, T. L. 1972. "American Revival: How It All Started." *Folk Review* 1, no. 10 (August): 8–9.

Fuller, Chris. 1998. "Nothing Compares to Chrysalis." Billboard Advertising Supplement (October 31): 43.

Gammon, Vic. 1977. "Face the Tyger." *Folk News* 1/2 (July): 12–13, 15.

Gilbert, Jeremy. 1970a. "Pentangle Percussion." *MM* (March 21): 70.

———. 1970b. "The Heart behind Steeleye Span." *MM* (April 25): 30.

———. 1970c. "Carthy Joins Steeleye Span." *MM* (April 25): 31.

———. 1970d. "Fairport Take Their Own Ball to America." *MM* (May 16): 19.

Gleason, Ralph J. 1967. "Bob Dylan: The Rolling Stone Interview." *Rolling Stone* (December 14): 12–14.

Grossman, Stefan. 1968/69. "The British Folk Scene as Seen by an American." *Sing Out!* 18, no. 5 (December/January): 56–58.

———. 1977. "The Martin Carthy Story. Part I: Instrumental Technique: 'Carthy's Guitar.'" *Folk News* (June): 15.

Grosvenor Myer, Valerie and Michael. 1975. "Hyperstar?" *Folk Review* 4, no. 5 (March): 4–8.

Hanneken, Bernhard. 1991. "Die Oyster Band: Es ist eine fantastische Zeit für Musik." *Folk-Michel* (January/February): 8–12.

———. 1991/92. "Oyster Band." *Munzinger-Archiv/Pop-Archiv International* (B 0002955): 1–5.

Harper, Colin. "The Book of Bert." *FR* 129 (March): 42–45.

Hart, Tim. 1972. "Rape, Incest, Sadism, and Suspect." *NME* (November 18): 47.

———. 1973. "The Poor Relation of Rock." *NME* (January 13): 46.

Hemsley, Andy. 1994. "Ashley Hutchings on Morris and Dance." *English Dance & Song* 56, no. 1 (Spring): 21.

Henessey, Mike. 1965. "Baez: Not So Much a Folk Singer, More a Politician." *MM* (May 22): 3.

Herman, Janet. 1994. "British Folk-Rock; Celtic Rock." *Journal of American Folklore* 107, no. 425 (Summer): 419–23.

Holland, Maggie. 1988. "This Time, Roses." *FR* 65 (November): 34–41.

———. 1993. "Roots of Renbourn." *FR* 118 (April): 28–31.

Hollingworth, Roy. 1970. "Swarbrick: The Un-Conventional Fiddler." *MM* (October 24): 31.

———. 1971. "The Rocking Success Story of the Violin." *MM* (January 16): 20/21.

Hunt, Ken. 1979. "Shirley and Dolly Collins." *Swing* 51, no. 1: 4–19.

———. 1980a. [with David Suff]. "Shirley and Dolly Collins." *Swing* 51, no. 2: 6–29

———. 1980b. "Shirley and Dolly Collins." *Swing* 51, no. 3: 6–7.

———. 1982. "Richard and Linda Thompson." *Swing* 51, no. 6: 34–37, 54.

———. 1983. "Richard and Linda Thompson." *Swing* 51, no. 7: 34–37, 54.

———. 1984. "Richard and Linda Thompson." *Swing* 51, no. 8: 12–13, 40.

———. 1989. "Anne Briggs." *Swing* 51, no. 13: 8–16.

———. 1996a. "Baez Reporting." *FR* 157 (July): 26–31.

———. 1996b. "Dog Boy Days." *FR* 160 (October): 46–47.

———. 1997a. "Folk Routines." *FR* 167 (May): 37–41.

———. 1997b. "All Our Yesterdays." *FR* 173 (November): 17–19.

———. 1998. "Over the Water." *FR* 177 (March): 17–19.

———. 2000. "Wireless Tales." *FR* 206/7 (August/September): 62–65.

Irwin, Colin. 1973. "Steeleye: Back to the 16th Century." *MM* (December 22): 3.

———. 1975. "Has Folk Gone Underground?" *MM* (September 27): 41.

———. 1985a. "Unhung Heroes." *FR* 25 (July): 23–25.

———. 1985b. "Café Society." *FR* 27 (September): 28–30.

———. 1985c. "English Folk Revival: The Early Years, 1957–1961." *Southern Rag* 19: 23–25.

———. 1985d. "English Folk Revival: The Boom Years, 1962–1967." *Southern Rag* 20: 15–17.

———. 1989. "Folk's Willie Nelson." *FR* 69 (March): 32–37.

————. 1993a. "Accompanied Policy." *FR* 115/16 (January/February): 62–65.

————. 1993b. "The Thompson Directory." *FR* 119 (May): 42–45, 69.

————. 1993c. "Band without Portfolio." *FR* 124 (October): 34–37.

————. 1996. "Waterdaughters." *FR* 155 (May): 24–31.

————. 1997. "This Is England." *FR* 166 (April): 36–41.

————. 2000. "Chief Chieftain." *FR* 204 (June): 29–31.

————. 2002. "Still Shouting." *FR* 234 (December): 20–27.

————. 2003. "Anarchisms." *FR* 235/236 (January/February): 51–53.

Jackson, Bruce. 1966. "Newport." *Sing Out!* 16, no. 3 (August/September): 7–15.

Johnson, James. 1974. "'Rumours of My Retirement Were Rather Exaggerated.'" *NME* (August 24): 28.

Jones, Max. 1965. "Dylan—Fastest Sell-Out Yet." *MM* (March 27): 7.

————. 1966. "Will the Real BOB DYLAN Please Stand Up!" *MM* (May 14): 3.

Jones, Simon. 1988. "Prior Engagement." *FR* 61 (July): 34–37, 59.

————. 1991. "Exchange and Maart." *FR* 93 (March): 15–16.

————. 1995a. "Ashley Beats." *FR* 141 (March): 39–41.

————. 1995b. "To the Woods." *FR* 142 (April): 21–23.

————. 1997a. "Ric Shure." *FR* 169 (July): 23–24.

————. 1997b. "Dad Shaped." *FR* 170/71 (August/September): 65–67.

————. 1998. "Pudding Club." *FR* 178 (April): 14–15.

Lamb, Derek. 1965. "The British Music Hall." *Sing Out!* 15, no. 4 (September): 34–35.

Lee, Jim. 1995. "Ashley Hutchings: A Conversation with the Guv'nor." *DL* 57 (April/May): 19–21.

————. 1996. "Norma Waterson: Certainly Not What You'd Expect." *DL* 65 (August/September): 25.

Lloyd, A. L. 1968. "Folksong Is Doomed!" *MM* (January 20): 15.

Logan, Nick. 1969. "No Group Has Worked Harder for a Hit than Fairport." *NME* (August 16): 10.

————. 1970. "Introducing Fotheringay—and Why Sandy Left Fairport." *NME* (March 14): 12–13.

Lust, Joe. 2002. "The Anglican." *FR* 233 (November): 43–45.

MacDonald, Ian. 1973. "Incredibles Eight Years On." *NME* (March 10): 32.

McGrath, T. J. 1995. "Jackson C. Frank: Lost Singer Found." *DL* 57 (April/May): 27–33, 98.

McShane, Rod. 1975. "Richard Thompson: He's Unique, Classy, and Just About the Best We've Got." *NME* (May 3): 32.

Marshall, Austin John. 1980/81. "Bert's New Peak." *Acoustic Music* (December/January): 23.

Marshall, John. 1973. "Phoenix Phairport." *NME* (September 22): 14, 67.

Means, Andrew. 1970a. "Carthy Comes Home." *MM* (October 3): 29.

————. 1970b. "John Renbourn." *MM* (October 31): 15.

————. 1971a. "Fond Farewell to Fotheringay." *MM* (February 6): 20.

————. 1971b. "Guitars in Folk: Acoustic Is Still Where It's At." *MM* (March 20): 26.

————. 1971c. "Reflections of Jacqui." *MM* (October 16): 15.

————. 1971d. "No Roses for Shirley." *MM* (November 6): 44.

————. 1971e. "The Lloyd Lecture." *MM* (November 13): 54.

————. 1972a. "Conventional Changes." *MM* (March 11): 31.

————. 1972b. "The Folk Revival." *MM* (March 18): 31.

———. 1972c. "The Hart of Steeleye Span." *MM* (June 10): 33.

———. 1972d. "Liege on the Radio Waves." *MM* (October 7): 60.

———. 1972e. "The World of Ewan MacColl." *MM* (November 11): 69.

———. 1972f. "When Is a Folk Singer Not a Folk Singer?" *MM* (December 9): 17.

———. 1972g. "Steeleye Mania Hits States! (Would You Believe?)" *MM* (December 23): 23.

Miller, Sheila. 1977. "Is the Folk Scene Ready for This Amazing Work?" *Folk News* (November): 13.

Morman, James. 1998. "Tempest: Ten Electric Years." *DL* 78 (October/November): 20–24, 96.

Murray, Alan. 1993. "Carthy's Treasure." *FR* 120 (June): 19–21.

Murray Winters, Pamela. 1996. "The Merry Mighty Morris." *DL* 64 (June/July): 37–40, 106.

Nelligan, Tom. 1995. "Dancing to the New St. George." *DL* 57 (April/May): 22–25, 98.

———. 1996. "Joe Boyd—The Listener." *DL* 65 (August/September): 21–26.

———. 1999/2000. "Great Big Sea: Aggressive Folk." *DL* 85 (December/January): 44–46, 96.

Nelson, Paul. 1965. "What's Happening?" *Sing Out!* 15, no. 5 (November): 6–7.

———. 1966. "Bob Dylan: Another View." *Sing Out!* 16, no. 1 (February/March): 69–71.

Nickson, Chris, and Dave Thompson. 1996. "Electric Folk." *Discoveries* 102 (November): 24–32.

Norman, Tony. 1972. "Richard Thompson: The Session Great That Nobody Knows." *NME* (July 22): 39.

Owston, Chuck. 1992. "The Many Faces of Matty Groves." *DL* 38 (February/March): 13, 80.

Peters, Brian. 1994. "Club Death?" *FR* 136 (October): 28–31.

Poole, Chris. 1973. "Fiddling with Folk." *NME* (October 13): 60.

Reuss, Dirk. 1965. "So You Want to Be a Folklorist." *Sing Out!* 15, no. 5 (November): 40–42.

Ridgeway, John. 1994. "'Folk-Rock'—From Fairport Forward: A Personal Perspective." *The Living Tradition*, 6 (July/August): 16–17.

Roberts, Andy. 1994. "Stringtangle." *FR* 132 (June): 23.

Schofield, Derek. 1990. "Grand National." *FR* 93 (May): 16–19.

———. 1994a. "Seaside 'Shuffles.'" *FR* 133 (July): 28–31.

———. 1994b. "1903 and All That." *English Dance & Song* 56, no. 1 (Spring): 16–20.

Shaar Murray, Charles. 1972. "Front Row Reviews: Steeleye—Doing the Jacobite." *NME* (August 12): 16.

———. 1973a. "Steeleye Span versus the Time Warp." *NME* (March 10): 46.

———. 1973b. "Vibrant Steeleye." *NME* (April 14): 16.

———. 1974. "Imagine All These N.Y. Hooks Watchin' a Mummers' Play." *NME* (October 12): 53.

Silber, Irvin. 1965a. "What's Happening." *Sing Out!* 15, no. 4 (September): 4–5, 97.

———. 1965b. "What's Happening." *Sing Out!* 15, no. 5 (November): 5–6.

Smith, Jeff. 1965a. "Focus on Folk." *MM* (January 30): 5.

———. 1965b. Special "Living Music: Organizing Folk." *MM* (January 30): iii.

———. 1965c. "Like Trad., Like Folk?" Interview with Ewan MacColl. *MM* (May 8): 13.

Smith, Jim. 1972. "Steeleye Shine on Harum Tour." *NME* (November 25): 58.

Stewart, Tony. 1971a. "The Five Sides of Pentangle." *NME* (October 23): 18.

———. 1971b. "Fairport in the Future." *NME* (December 11): 27.

———. 1972a. "Sandy Denny Breaks Her Silence." *NME* (January 15): 16.

———. 1972b. "The Turning Point for Steeleye Span." *NME* (April 8): 6.

———. 1972c. "With No Original Members Remaining Fairport Back to Square One, Says Dave Pegg." *NME* (April 22): 15.

———. 1972d. "Pentangle Take a Stride ahead Solomon's Seal." *NME* (September 16): 12.

———. 1972e. "Sandy Solo: Changing, but You Can't Expect Me to Be a Janis Joplin Overnight." *NME* (October 7): 18.

———. 1972f. "Fairport: This Time It's for Keeps." *NME* (December 30): 11.

———. 1973. "Fairport and the Mysterious Lady." *NME* (July 7): 18.

———. 1974. "Sandy Denny Talks to Tony Stewart: A Curse on the House of Fairport?" *NME* (April 20): 29.

Thompson, Allan Currie. 1977. "Electric Undercurrents." *Folk Review* 6, no. 11 (September): 4–6.

Tobler, John. 1991. "Open Hart." *FR* 95 (May): 25–30.

———. 1995. "Thyme Honoured." *FR* 148 (October): 33–37.

Traum, Happy. 1969. "The Swan Song of Folk Music." *Rolling Stone* (May 17): 7–8.

Watts, Michael. 1970a. "Fairport's Wounds Have Healed." *MM* (July 18): 14.

———. 1970b. "Sandy's Success: A Victory for Music." *MM* (July 25): 16.

Weir, Rob. 1995. "Prior Commitment: The Staying Power of Maddy Prior." *Sing Out!* 39, no. 4 (February/March/April), 40–51.

Williams, Richard. 1970. "The X Certificate Songs of Mr. Fox." *MM* (October 10): 37.

Williamson, Nigel. 1997. "It's Incredible!" *FR* 172 (October): 37–42.

———. 2000. "Live: Paul Simon/Martin Carthy." *FR* 210 (December): 75.

Wilson, Tony. 1968a. "Two Sides of a Pentangle." *MM* (June 1): 19.

———. 1968b. "It's Easy to See the Change in Sandy." *MM* (July 27): 11.

———. 1968c. "A Day in the Life of John Peel." *MM* (November 23): 12.

———. 1969a. "The Missing Dimension in the Folk Revival." *MM* (February 15): 22.

———. 1969b. "Fairport Convention Present the New English Electric Sound." *MM* (July 26): 16.

———. 1969c. "Dave Turns On to Electric Fiddle." *MM* (August 9): 14.

Winick, Steve. 1996. "Ensemble Galilei: Musical Meeting Place." *DL* 65 (August/September): 11–12, 106.

———. 1998. "The Chieftains." *DL* 78 (October/November): 47–53.

Winter, Eric. 1965. "Is Folk a Dirty Word?" *MM* (July 3): 8.

———. 1966. "Seeger on the Problem of Folk on TV." *MM* (December 3): 10.

———. 1971a. "BBC Kills Club Singers." *NME* (September 11): 20.

———. 1971b. "Iron Core of Span." *NME* (October 9): 20.

———. 1971c. "Eric Winter on London Folks." *NME* (November 13): L6.

———. 1971d. "That Company in Incredible Integrity." *Folk & Country* 2, no. 2 (December): 121–23.

———. 1973a. "Albion's Driving Force." *NME* (January 6): 16.

———. 1973b. "On the Fall of Mr. Fox." *NME* (April 14): 40.

———. 1974a. "Past, Present, and Future." *NME* (February 2): 44.

———. 1974b. "Another Load of Old Crumhorn." *NME* (August 24): 29.

———. 1990. "The Big Ewan." *FR* 79/80 (January/February): 31–32.

Woffinden, Bob. 1975a. "Now Steeleye Got a Brand New Bag." *NME* (October 4): 22.

———. 1975b. "The Ballad of Steeleye Span." *NME* (December 20): 12–13.

Woods, Fred. 1972. "Love, Life, and the Lady." *Folk Review* 2, no. 13 (November): 4–6.

———. 1973a. "'And So We Sang': Ewan MacColl Talks to Fred Woods." Part 1. *Folk Review* 2, no. 7 (May): 4–7.

———. 1973b. "'And So We Sang': Ewan MacColl Talks to Fred Woods." Part 2. *Folk Review* 2, no. 8, (June): 4–7.

———. 1973c. "'And So We Sang': Ewan MacColl Talks to Fred Woods." Part 3. *Folk Review* 2, no. 9, (July): 4–8.

ARTICLES PUBLISHED ON THE INTERNET (AS OF APRIL 2003)

In those cases where the date of Internet publication could not be established, the date refers to the year in which I checked the source (2003).

Cutting, Jennifer. 1993. "From Fol de Rol to Sha Na Na: The Electrification of British Folk Music." A lecture delivered April 20, 1993. *Electric Folk: Jennifer's Lectures, Panels, and Resource Lists*. http://www.kinesiscd.com/jennifercutting/efolk.htm.

Jackson, Bruce. 2002. "The myth of Newport '65: It Wasn't Bob Dylan They Were Booing." *Buffalo Report*. http://buffaloreport.com/020826dylan.html. (August 26, 2002)

Miller, Scott. 2003. "Ian A. Anderson's 'Royal York Crescent': Masterpiece or Embarrassment? An Appreciation." http://www.kinesiscd.com/jennifercutting/nsghome.htm.

Trust, Brian. 2003. "Too Many Dragons: A Historical Essay." http://www.kinesiscd.com/jennifercutting/breakup.htm.

Murray Winters, Pamela. 2003. "The New St. George: An Appreciation." http://www.kinesiscd.com/jennifercutting/breakup.htm.

CD BOOKLETS

Many performers and groups—such as Martin Carthy, Shirley Collins, and Steeleye Span—have written extensive liner notes commenting on their sources and musical approaches. Their early recordings were often also accompanied by introductions by well-known names in the scene; A. L. Lloyd, for instance, wrote introductions for Anne Briggs and Shirley Collins, Martin Carthy's first recording was introduced by Ian Campbell, and Pentangle's first album contained a note by radio DJ John Peel. These original texts have been omitted from the following list, as they are often no longer available—in many cases having been abridged or completely omitted from the reissued CDs. In other cases, however, these comments have been revised or expanded by the performers, sometimes accompanied by additional carefully researched background information about the performer or the original recording. These booklet texts, which often more accurately represent the history of this genre than do magazine articles, are listed alphabetically under the authors of the secondary materials.

Arthur, David. 1994. "A. L. Lloyd: A Brief Biography." *Classic A. L. Lloyd*, Fellside.

Berman, Leslie. 1993. "Watching the Dark: A History of Richard Thompson." Richard Thompson, *Watching the Dark: The History of Richard Thompson*, Hannibal.

Boyd, Joe. 1987. Fairport Convention, *Heyday: BBC Radio Sessions, 1968–69*, Hannibal.

Carthy, Martin. 1974. Martin Carthy, *Sweet Wivelsfield*, Deram.

Copper, Bob. 1998. Alan Lomax, *The World Library of Folk and Primitive Music: England*, Rounder.

Dallas, Karl. 1996. *The Electric Muse: The Story of Folk into Rock*, Castle.

Fowler, Eric. 1992. "The Story of the Transports," Peter Bellamy, *The Transports*, Topic.

Gregory, Hugh. 1997. "Wasn't That a Time?" *The Best of the Weavers*, Half Moon.

Hall, Reg. 1994. Margaret Barry and Michael Gorman, *Her Mantle So Green*, Topic.

Harper, Colin. 1992. Pentangle, *Anniversary*, Hypertension.

———. 1993. Bert Jansch, *Nicola Plus Birthday Blues*, Demon.

Hunt, Ken. 1990. *Classic Anne Briggs*, Fellside.

———. 1991. Martin Carthy with Dave Swarbrick, *Byker Hill*, Topic.

Leigh, Spencer. 1990. Davy Graham, *Folk Blues and All Points in Between*, See for Miles.

Pegg, Bob and Carole. 1996. Mr. Fox, *Mr. Fox and the Gypsy*, Castle.

Pelletier, Paul. 1992. *Lonnie Donegan: Putting on the Styles*, Sequel.

Penhallow, John. 1995. Sandy Denny and Trevor Lucas, *The Attic Tracks*, Raven.

Rodd, Marcel. 1978. *The Original Sandy Denny*, B & C.

Suff, David. 1992. The Albion Band, *Rise Up Like the Sun*, EMI/Harvest.

———. 1993a. *The Complete Brass Monkey*, Topic.

———. 1993b. Shirley and Dolly Collins, *For As Many As Will*, Hokey Pokey.

———. 1994. Ashley Hutchings, *The Guv'nor*, vol. 1, HTD.

———. 1995. *Etchingham Steam Band*, Fledg'ling.

Suff, David, and John Tobler. 1993. Shirley and Dolly Collins, *Anthems in Eden*, Harvest.

Tobler, John. 1991 (LP). Steeleye Span, *Hark! The Village Wait*, Mooncrest.

———. 1991a. Steeleye Span, *Please to See the King*, Mooncrest.

———. 1991b. Tim Hart and Maddy Prior, *Folk Songs of Olde England*, vol. 1, Mooncrest.

———. 1992. Steeleye Span, *Now We Are Six*, BGO.

Murray Winters, Pamela. 1998. Sandy Denny, *"Gold Dust"—Live at the Royalty*, Island.

RADIO, TELEVISION SHOWS, AND VIDEOS

Revival and electric folk music has been well documented in numerous radio and television shows. A number of the BBC radio sessions have been reissued, and television documentaries include *Travelling for a Living: The Watersons*. The techniques of guitarists Martin Carthy, John Renbourn, and Richard Thompson have, thanks to the efforts of Stefan Grossman, been well documented in numerous video workshops.

[Carthy, Martin]. 1993. *British Fingerstyle Guitar*. Stefan Grossman's Guitar Workshop. Video. Music Sales.

Howkins, Alun. 1981. *The Other Music: The Folk Song Revival, 1945–81, and Its Roots in the British Folk Tradition*. Radio BBC 2 (October 27).

Kovit, Paul. n.d. *Fairport Convention: It All Comes 'Round Again*. Video. Island Visual Arts.

Knight, Derrick, and Partners. 1966. *Travelling for a Living: The Watersons in the Sixties—The Early Years*. BBC broadcast. PAL and VHS copies.

Sandy Denny—Who Knows Where the Time Goes? A Radio 2 Tribute. 1988. Radio BBC 2 (April 20).

INTERVIEWS

All quotations that appear without source attributions in the text have been taken from the following interviews with the author.

Frankie Armstrong. Cardiff, September 2, 1996.

Joe Boyd. Telephone, September 18, 1996.

Martin Carthy. Robin Hood's Bay, October 20, 1996.
Shirley Collins. Brighton, August 8, 1996.
Jennifer Cutting. Washington, DC, October 28, 1997.
Ashley Hutchings. Stockport, September 4, 1996.
Rick Kemp. Cardiff, September 6, 1996.
Jacqui McShee. Redhill, September 1, 1996.
Simon Nicol. Oxford, August 5, 1996.
Maddy Prior. Carlisle, September 5, 1996.
John Renbourn. Written correspondence, October 1996.
Ian Telfer. London, September 8, 1996.
John Tobler. London, June 21, 1996.

SOURCE CREDITS

The author and publisher have made every attempt to trace copyright holders but were unable to reach one or two. We would be grateful if the authors concerned could contact us.

Special thanks go to Ian Anderson (*fRoots*), Scott Atkinson (*Sing Out!*), Karl Dallas, Don Fleming (Alan Lomax Archive and Estate) Vic Gammon, Stefan Grossman, Paul Hartman (*Dirty Linen*), James Parker (Virgin Book Publications), Anthony Seeger (International Council for Traditional Music), Brian Shuel, and John Tobler for granting permission to use the material (the sources are indicated in the text).

Quotation from Alan Lomax in "The Other Muse: The Folk Song Revival, 1945–81, and Its Roots in the British Folk Tradition," Radio BBC 2 (October 27, 1981), reproduced by kind permission of the BBC and the Alan Lomax Estate.

Quotations from Patrick Humphries, *Meet on the Ledge: Fairport Convention—The Classic Years* (London, 1997), reproduced by kind permission of Virgin Books Ltd..

Quotations from Stefan Grossman, *British Fingerpicking Guitar* (Pacific, MO: Mel Bay, 1990), reproduced by kind permission of the author.

Quotations from Ian A. Anderson and Lawrence Heath, "Ashley Hutchings," *Southern Rag* 4 (1982), reproduced by kind permission of the publisher (Southern Rag Ltd.).

Quotations from Ian A. Anderson and Maggie Holland, "Carthy's Commitment," *Southern Rag* 24 (1985), reproduced by kind permission of the publisher (Southern Rag Ltd.).

Quotations from Sarah Coxson, "Oysters '89," *Folk Roots* 79/80 (January/February 1990), reproduced by kind permission of the publisher (Southern Rag Ltd.).

Quotation from Karl Dallas, "Interview with Dave Mattacks," *Acoustic Music* 21 (July 1980), reproduced by kind permission of the author.

Quotation from Karl Dallas, "The Carthy Tapes," *Folk News* (July 1977), reproduced by kind permission of the author.

Quotation from Vic Gammon, "Face the Tyger," *Folk News* 1/2 (July 1977), reproduced by kind permission of the author.

Quotations from Laing et al., *The Electric Muse: The Story of Folk into Rock* (Methuen, 1975), reproduced by kind permission of the authors.

Quotations from Tom Nelligan, "Dancing to the New St. George," *Dirty Linen* 57 (April/May 1995), and "Joe Boyd—The Listener," *Dirty Linen* 65 (August/September 1996), reproduced by kind permission of the publisher (*Dirty Linen*).

Quotations from Colin Irwin, "Accompanied Policy," *Folk Roots* 115/116 (January/ February 1993), reproduced by kind permission of the publisher (Southern Rag Ltd.).

Quotations from Irvin Silber, "What's Happening," *Sing Out!* (1965), reproduced by kind permission of the publisher (*Sing Out!*).

Quotations from John Tobler, "Open Hart," *Folk Roots* 95 (May 1991), reproduced by kind permission of the publisher (Southern Rag Ltd.).

Quotations from John Tobler, CD booklet, Steeleye Span, *Now We Are Six* (BGO Records 1992), reproduced by kind permission of the author.

Quotations from John Tobler, LP liner notes, Steeleye Span, *Hark! The Village Wait* (Mooncrest 1991), reproduced by kind permission of the author.

Quotations from John Tobler, CD booklet, Steeleye Span, *Please to See the King* (Mooncrest 1991), reproduced by kind permission of the author.

Quotations from John Tobler, CD booklet, Tim Hart and Maddy Prior, *Folk Songs of Olde England*, vol. 1 (Mooncrest 1991), reproduced by kind permission of the author.

Quotations from Rob Weir, "Prior Commitment: The Staying Power of Maddy Prior," *Sing Out!* 39/4 (1995), reproduced by kind permission of the publisher (*Sing Out!*).

Karl Dallas, "Pentangle Dies . . . with a Whimper" © *Melody Maker* (March 31, 1973)

Karl Dallas, "Steeleye Needs a Drummer" © *Melody Maker* (July 14, 1973)

Colin Harper, CD booklet, *Pentangle: Anniversary* © Hypertension (1992)

Ken Hunt, "Shirley and Dolly Collins I" © *Swing* 51, no. 1 (1979)

Ken Hunt, "Anne Briggs" © Swing 51, no. 13 (1989)

Ken Hunt, CD booklet, Martin Carthy with Dave Swarbrick, *Byker Hill* © Topic Records

A. L. Lloyd, "The Singing Style of the Copper Family" © *Journal of the English Folk Dance and Song Society 7*

A. L. Lloyd in CD booklet, The Watersons, *Frost and Fire* © Topic Records

A. L. Lloyd in CD booklet, *Classic A. L. Lloyd* © Fellside/Topic Records

Alan Currie Thompson, "Electric Undercurrents" © *Folk Review* 6, no. 11 (September 1977)

Tony Wilson, "It's Easy to See the Change in Sandy" © *Melody Maker* (July 27, 1968)

Tony Wilson, "A Day in the Life of John Peel" © *Melody Maker* (November 23, 1968)

Fred Woods, "'And So We Sang': Ewan MacColl Talks to Fred Woods" © *Folk Review* 2, no. 8 (June 1973)

n.a., "Jagger Swipes at Folk Fakers—after Dylan, What?" © *Melody Maker* (June 12, 1965)

n.a. "Folk Star Ian Slams Back at Mick Jagger" © *Melody Maker* (June 26, 1965)

LYRIC CREDIT

"New St. George" by Richard Thompson © Warlock Publishing Ltd.

INDEX

8960083